Momma's Secret Recipe for RETIREMENT SUCCESS

Published by CelebrityPress®, Orlando, FL.

CelebrityPress® is a registered trademark.

Printed in the United States of America.

ISBN: 978-0-9980369-3-9
LCCN: 2019937327

This publication is designed to provide accurate and authoritative information with regard to the subject matter covered. It is sold with the understanding that the publisher is not engaged in rendering legal, accounting, or other professional advice. If legal advice or other expert assistance is required, the services of a competent professional should be sought. The opinions expressed by the authors in this book are not endorsed by CelebrityPress® and are the sole responsibility of the author rendering the opinion.

Most CelebrityPress® titles are available at special quantity discounts for bulk purchases for sales promotions, premiums, fundraising, and educational use. Special versions or book excerpts can also be created to fit specific needs.

For more information, please write:
CelebrityPress®
520 N. Orlando Ave, #2
Winter Park, FL 32789
or call 1.877.261.4930

Visit us online at: www.CelebrityPressPublishing.com

Momma's Secret Recipe for RETIREMENT SUCCESS

CelebrityPress®
Winter Park, Florida

CONTENTS

SECTION 1

MOMMA'S SECRET RECIPE FOR RETIREMENT SUCCESS

The Truth About The Stock Market, Risk, Fees, & Annuities

By Dan Ahmad & Jim Files with Jack Canfield

SECTION 2

THE SECRET INGREDIENT FOR YOUR RETIREMENT RECIPE

*Everything You Wanted To Know About
Fixed Index Annuities With Income Riders
But Were Afraid To Ask
Is Revealed In The Chapters That Follow*

SECTION 1

MOMMA'S SECRET RECIPE
For Retirement Success

The Truth About The Stock Market,
Risk, Fees, & Annuities

FOREWORD

BY JACK CANFIELD

In 1926, just three years before the start of the Great Depression, several banks and insurance companies began distributing little pamphlets on financial success all across the United States. These short stories used fictional parables to make their points in an entertaining and informative way with the goal of helping people understand their money and teaching them to make successful financial decisions. The most famous of these pamphlets was a book titled, The Richest Man in Babylon, and its author, George Clason, became an instant inspiration to many.

The opening principle that Clason explains at the start of his story is the practice of paying yourself first. The rule states: "A part of all you earn must be yours to keep." This is one of the key ingredients to financial success. Clason asserts that the main character begins by setting aside at least 10% of his earnings in a type of rainy day fund—totally inaccessible for expenses. If he keeps adding to it, then in time, he could see that amount build up into a rather large nest egg. And, with the power of compound interest, that money could then be invested and actually start earning more money all on its own. Clason went on to espouse several other general financial strategies, which enabled many people to make millions, even in the heart of the Depression. If you are retired or nearing retirement, you may be familiar with this "savings first" mentality and could have used this method yourself while preparing for retirement.

But there is an even greater wealth-building principle at work here. Taking place behind the economic implications of saving and investing is an underlying philosophy of success. This philosophy has allowed people to go from rags to riches, and riches to fortunes, in every era of human history.

If you think back to that time, 1926, it may have been pretty hard for the average American to imagine that such financial devastation, unlike any ever experienced in the United States before (or after), would occur, or even could occur, in just three short years. In fact, on December 7, 1926, in his State of the Union Address to Congress, Calvin Coolidge, President of the United States of America, said, "I find it impossible to characterize it other than one of general peace and prosperity."

Well, all of us know what happened in 1929 and the years following: Financial Armageddon. Banks closed and people lost their savings. The stock market crashed and people lost their investments. Entire companies shut down, and jobs were nowhere to be found. People lost their homes, families, and their ability to provide themselves with basic necessities like food. Some even lost their sanity. Maybe just as painful, they lost all hope. The idea, notion, and meaning of "success" was basically stricken from their hearts and minds.

Even the best savers, who had taken Clason's advice of paying themselves first, were subjected to the same complete desperation, utter hopelessness and unrelenting despair as the rest of the American public, as their nest eggs vanished. The problem was, after they saved it, no one told them how they could protect it. While there was an option available for people in 1926 that would have safe-guarded their assets from the financial devastation that occurred just a few years later, very few Americans knew about it and even fewer took advantage of it. This is one of the secrets you will learn about in this book.

Momma's Secret Recipe For Retirement Success was written to help those people who have used the principles of "savings first" to protect their hard-earned nest egg from any future financial devastation or stock market crashes.

Believe You Are Worth It

It all starts with your belief. Before you can become wealthy, you must believe you are valuable and worthy of acquiring wealth. Like great achievements in all areas of life, financial success begins as an inside job.

You must take the first step by simply deciding to become wealthy. Most people never do this, and as a result, they never accumulate the type of wealth that they could have.

I call this belief a "positive consciousness" about money. And developing it allows you to start visualizing what is financially possible for your life. You can begin to analyze your spending and saving habits, in accordance with your financial goals, and make adjustments where needed. But even more importantly, your "visualization" must be accompanied by a written plan to sum up where you're currently at and detail where you want to go. Your money is not a good listener; it will not act in a certain way just because you want it to. Your money will only act in the way you make it act. And you can successfully make it act any way you want by creating a written plan, which documents all the details.

A good place to start with this new way of thinking about money is to determine your net worth. To do so, simply subtract all your liabilities from your total assets. Next, look at your savings on hand. Consider your income stream or streams. Do you know exactly how much your fixed expenses are for the month? What about your discretionary spending?

Then, reflect on the amount of debt you may have. Do you know the interest rate on the loans you are paying? What about taxes and insurance? Do you have a financial plan, an estate plan, or a will? When do you want to retire, and how much will you need to maintain your desired standard of living?

These are all good, basic questions to get you headed in the right direction. Don't let the answers, or lack thereof, overwhelm you. However, never ever include those answers as a part of your plan unless they are finalized in writing. A written plan is like a navigation system for your car. Questions like these are designed to help you determine exactly where you are on the map so that you can plan accordingly for arriving at your desired financial destination (and never get lost along the way).

The Ingredients for Holistic Wealth and Financial Success

The authors of this book have presented multiple strategies that are worth considering. Many of their chapters will address these topics and more in greater detail. However, while the information provided in this book comes from some leaders in the financial field, the data is not intended as a recommendation for you to follow, or to convince you to buy a financial product. It is meant to, finally, educate you on subjects that are crucial to the financial success of you and your family.

While the authors of this book have over 400 years of combined experience, and have dedicated their lives to teaching and helping people just like you to learn more about their money, please be responsible with the information you are about to read. It is important to remember to always vet the professionals you select to help you along in your financial journey. No matter whom you choose to work with, it is very wise to check into their experience, background, and credentials.

As I wrote in my book, The Success Principles, wealth has several aspects. There are "human assets" like love, spirituality, happiness, and well-being. Then there are "intellectual assets" such as learned skills, acquired education, and ideas. There are also what I call "civic assets," which are things like private foundations that are set up in someone's honor and charitable contributions. And finally, there are the "financial assets" that include most things that people typically associate with wealth. These are items like cash in the bank, real estate investments, a retirement plan, and stocks and bonds. Considering all of these aspects will give you a more holistic view of wealth and financial success.

As you grow in your own financial literacy and develop a positive money consciousness, be discerning in the advisors you select. Don't put all your eggs in one basket. Diversify when needed. Do not manage your money for investment sake itself. Manage your money in a way that allows you to improve your life and the lives of others. Give to others as you feel led—not just in money, but also with time and talents – these too are the treasures of life. Keep an abundance mindset. Finally, be sure to always maintain a feeling of appreciation and gratitude. Such ingredients are critical for achieving your winning recipe for financial success.

Remember, as George Clason wrote in The Richest Man in Babylon, it is very important to save first, but I also urge you to remember the lessons of history: it is even more important to protect what you have worked so hard to save! I hope you enjoy Momma's Secret Recipe For Retirement Success as much as I did. Learning new information is always the key toward taking a step forward to your ultimate destination. I wish you nothing but success!

PREFACE

BY DAN AHMAD & JIM FILES

Momma's Secret Recipe For Retirement Success was written in large part to help retirees and pre-retirees avoid large stock market losses, not run out of money during their lifetimes, and make them aware at the time this book was written that we were long overdue for the next bear stock market. The original draft of this book was finished at the end of September 2018, when we were riding a bull stock market for 9 ½ years. We believed investors were in a very precarious position because historically, since 1929, the stock market has had a bear stock market every seven (7) years on average and had lost an average of -39.5% each time. This means when this book was written, we were two-and-a-half (2½) years overdue for what has been a "normal occurrence" of a big -39.5% loss that has occurred historically every seven (7) years.

This majority of the draft of this book was completed before September 30, 2018. We had been planning on using December 31, 2017 as the day of the last calendar year (2017) we would use data for examples, illustrations, and content. Sounded like a great plan, as the stock market was up and down during the 2018 year, but things seemed fairly calm as the stock market had just hit all-time highs on September 20, 2018.

But as we started editing the book in early October 2018 , the stock market started to exhibit an extremely high level of volatility. And rather than subside, the volatility increased in both frequency and magnitude. Basically, the stock market decided to go on a roller-coaster ride that was literally historical.

On Christmas Eve, December 24th 2018, the S&P 500 Index had lost almost 20% from its high-point and closed at 2,351. This was -19.76% down from its high of 2,930 on September 20th 2018. Technically, this huge loss did not count as a bear market because the stock market didn't close down 20% or more from it's high-point.

We can all remember the 2008 Financial Crisis that lasted for 16 months decimated the financial markets. The S&P 500 Index lost more than 53% from October 2007 through March 2009. No one knew it back then, but on March 9, 2009, the stock market would enter into the longest bull stock market in history. After getting crushed during the 2008 Financial Crisis, it was bound to rebound, but no one imagined such a long, sustained recovery.

From October 2018 through December 2018, people across the United States lost a lot of money. Some people lost thousands, some lost tens of thousands, some lost hundreds of thousands of dollars, and some lost even more. This was exactly what we, the authors, were worried about, and exactly what we have been warning consumers about. And for retirees and pre-retirees, they really can't afford these types of losses. During this time period we met with new potential clients, all retired or planning to retire, who were so worried about their money they had no idea what to do. They did know they didn't want to go through so much volatility any longer, now that they were retired or soon to be retired.

Like you, we don't have a crystal ball telling us when the stock market is going to crash. And like you, we don't have anyone sending us a text message saying the stock market is going to crash and telling us to *"get out"* before it crashes. *IT JUST HAPPENS!* And when it does happen it seems shocking, but it shouldn't. It is a normal occurrence. What we do have is the ability to take emotions out of our view of the stock market. We take emotion out of our decision-making process to try and protect the assets of retirees and pre-retirees against big stock market losses, and to make sure they will not run out of money for as long as they live. We are never going to tell our clients:

- "Ride out the market!"
- "Hang in there."
- "Don't worry, you're in it for the long run."
- "The loss is just short-term and only on paper."

We are always going to tell you that you should always protect your money from big losses, because you don't have the time or circumstances to make back up a big loss.

We feel the only reason retirees and pre-retirees have taken so much risk with their money is that they have been told they will earn huge rates of return by doing so. But unfortunately, that may not be the case. If you go all the way back to the year 2000, on January 1, 2000 the S&P 500 Index was at 1,469. Then looking all the way forward to December 31, 2018 the S&P 500 Index closed at 2,506. The S&P 500 Index grew from 1,469 to 2,506 over 19 years which seems like a huge growth rate, but this calculates out to only a 2.85% average annual compounded increase.

We really don't think a 2.85% average annual increase over 19 years is worth the risk. Do you think it is? We also do not think a 2.85% average annual increase over 19 years was worth all the volatility, worry, and anxiety you went through from October 2018 through December 2018. Do you?

Momma's Secret Recipe For Retirement Success is even more important now that you have had to live through so much volatility and fear at the end of 2018. All the caution, warnings, and conservative planning methods, techniques, and financial products discussed in this book are even more important to learn about now that we have entered into what could end up being a very long period of tremendous, and continued, volatility. Why would we, and why would you, expect anything different? While the stock market may show signs of life and recover in the short-term in 2019, we believe there will remain a significant amount of danger for investors through 2020. We worry that the huge decline at the end of 2018 isn't the end of the losses.

As you will learn from reading this book, Rule #1 is to protect your principal from large stock market losses at all times, and never get sucked into the "ride-out-all stock-market-losses" mentality of your current broker or favorite website.

We have created an awesome website based on this book at: www.myezretire.com. We will continue to update and add more information to the website as time goes on. Please go to the site and bookmark it for future reference. You can sign up for additional information, seminars, downloads, videos, and a ton of other information.

We hope after reading Momma's Secret Recipe For Retirement Success you do everything you possibly can do to protect your assets and your retirement security, from all large stock market losses and from running out of money during retirement.

A few months from now, a year from now, or even a few years from now, we don't want to have to tell you:

WE TOLD YOU SO!

INTRODUCTION

BY DAN AHMAD & JIM FILES

The team of national financial experts who wrote this book collectively have over 425 years of experience helping people just like you plan for a successful retirement focusing their efforts on one single goal: **helping the clients they meet with have a safe, secure, worry-free, and very enjoyable retirement**. We spend every day working with retired people and those nearing retirement, collectively called "retirees", helping them make the best decisions about their money to have a successful retirement. Now retired, or soon to face retirement, you have a completely different financial picture and view of your money than you did 20 years ago.

What is a successful retirement?

Our definition for a successful retirement is, *"Guaranteeing you will never run out of income for as long as you live and you never suffer a devastating stock market loss like 2008 ever again."* It's that simple, if you accomplish these two (2) things, you will have an extremely high probability of retirement success, and you can stop worrying about your money.

We wrote this book because we believe in:
- What many think to be impossible.
- Challenging the status quo.
- Uncovering and exposing the truth.
- Leading, not blindly following.
- Coaching and guidance.
- Oversight of all things financial.
- Giving the power back to the people.
- That if you're the kind of person who wants to take control over your finances, we can help you restore order and change your life.

- Helping you attain your own version of *financial freedom.*

The concept of financial freedom seems so simple, yet many people can't define it. That's because it means so many different things to different people, it's personal to each and every one of us. Which of the following definitions of financial freedom speaks to your heart?

- ❖ Knowing, feeling, enjoying, regardless of markets, politics, or the economy, I'll be just fine.
- ❖ It's about redefining my own vision of retirement, my happiness, my safe harbor.
- ❖ It means I no longer feel embarrassed about my Financial IQ—I'm feeling in charge.
- ❖ It means never having to worry about running out of money, or feeling guilty about spending it.
- ❖ Accepting that we deserve to live the best retirement our dreams can imagine.
- ❖ Improving our lives by not having to worry about our money anymore.
- ❖ It's knowing with 100% certainty that someone has my back and my family's back, at all times.
- ❖ It's about having the confidence to keep taking trips of a lifetime, over and over again.
- ❖ Knowing that honesty, thoughtfulness, and my happiness designed the plan for my future.
- ❖ It is knowing our family's future is totally secure.
- ❖ Changing our lives, taking back control, restoring order, feeling better.
- ❖ Is like a crystal ball telling of a beautiful future, without fear or anxiety.

We guided others just like you to change their lives by helping to:

1. Expose the true risk you're taking, not the risk you've been told, and to know for certain what will happen if things go south. <u>NEVER</u> be in a position to experience another 2008-type stock market loss again.
2. Eliminate the need to watch the stock market every minute of every day, by reducing volatility. Use your time for better stuff.
3. Protect, not lose what you've worked so hard for. Try to make money

but don't take excessive risks. Protect and grow your assets.

4. Eliminate your fear of running out of money. Create dependable income that is guaranteed for life.
5. Uncover the total fees you pay—both direct and indirect (the hidden fees).
6. Understand and then learn to manage your income taxes.
7. Rely on yourself to remain financially independent for life.
8. Feel free to spend money—without guilt and worry.
9. Express needs and establish goals, if any, that you have for beneficiaries.
10. Require complete transparency. Don't accept not understanding your money any longer. Demand everything, all details, in writing.
11. Stop worrying about your money.

We've titled this book *Momma's Secret Recipe For Retirement Success* because creating a successful plan for retirement seems just as elusive, just as mysterious, just as secret, as that favorite recipe *Momma* used to make that one heavenly dish. *Momma* never gave up the recipe, so no one else was able to replicate her success. Many retirees and pre-retirees feel this same way about planning for retirement because they all think someone has the secret recipe for retirement success, but it is hidden. Over the years they have tried different ingredients (investments), they have tried different restaurants (brokerage firms), they have tried different cooks (advisors), and they have even tried searching endlessly for the recipe on their own (internet searches, seminars, listening to financial shows on talk radio), and still they come up empty.

We will lay the secret recipe out for you in a way that will let most of you understand your money for the first time in your life. We will educate you on the truth about the stock market, risk, fees, written plans, and the one secret ingredient you are not sure if you should add to your own retirement recipe: *fixed index annuities with income riders*. Many of the subjects discussed in *Momma's Secret Recipe For Retirement Success* will be completely new information to you. Much of the information will correct inaccurate data you have been given and heard for years. But all of this information is accurate and vital to your financial well-being for a safe and secure retirement.

By reading *Momma's Secret Recipe For Retirement Success* you will learn how important it is to:

- Know exactly how much risk you have in your portfolio right now, meaning how much you could lose if the stock market crashed. You need to have a risk test performed on your portfolio the same way you would have your heart checked out with a cardiac stress test.
- Minimize portfolio volatility and losses, pinpoint the amount of risk you really want to take, create your perfect allocation to match your desired risk level, ensuring you never go through another 2008 stock market crash again.
- Use multiple conservative asset strategies to help you meet your specific financial goals.
- Provide the opportunity to earn competitive rates of return without exposing your assets to excessive risks.
- Obtain full disclosure in writing detailing your plan advantages, disadvantages, costs/fees, how each asset works, and how you will use each asset as part of your overall comprehensive plan.
- Know how much income you will receive throughout your retirement, what income is guaranteed, and what income is "maybe income" (not guaranteed). Create a written retirement income plan to guarantee you won't run out of money for as long as you live by outlining a step-by-step process, a virtual roadmap for you to follow to maximize your retirement success.
- Audit your current fees and learn what are the true "direct costs" you are paying as well as expose the "indirect costs (hidden fees)" you didn't know you were paying. Manage and reduce your fees.
- Manage your income taxes by calculating the total annual income taxes you will pay, your effective tax rate, and the amount of net after-tax income you will have to spend every month.
- Design and implement a plan to achieve your goals for your beneficiaries.
- Understand if you are like 90% of the retirees and pre-retirees we have interviewed:
  - You will lose a large amount of your portfolio in the next stock market crash.
  - You don't have your assets positioned correctly for safety and income.
  - You are not guaranteed to recover quickly, or at all, after the next stock market crash.
  - You will not earn 10% in the stock market every year.
  - You are probably not paying 1% in total fees, you are likely paying 3% or more per year.

o You cannot take 5%-6% out of your portfolio every year without a high probability of running out of money.

o You are not paying 35% or more in federal taxes. The typical retired couple with $150,000 of annual gross income is only paying 12% in federal taxes.

o You have not been adequately rewarded for the risk you have taken in the stock market.

o The stock market has lost an average of -39.5% every seven (7) years since 1929.

o It's OK to spend your money now. It's not OK to wait to enjoy your retirement until some later date.

o A large portion of your losses were probably caused because you were taking far more risk than you thought.

o Your assets are incorrectly positioned in "asset accumulation mode" and they should have been transitioned into "asset preservation and income distribution mode."

If you learned all of these things, you would know what's necessary to have a successful retirement, you would know *"Momma's Secrets."* As a bonus, we have included a special section exclusively discussing a powerful secret ingredient for your own recipe for retirement success: *fixed index annuities with income riders.*

Should you spend a few hours of your day reading this book? Our biased opinion is of course you should. This book is a collaborative effort of 21 of some of the top retirement income planners and professionals in the United States today. The book discusses what retirees, just like yourself, want when planning for retirement. Usually, when you get any type of financial advice, you are just receiving one person's point of view. Whether that advice is good or bad, it still leaves you as a consumer in a vulnerable position. The data and opinions in this book should carry far more weight and be exponentially more beneficial for you, because you are receiving a financial education from 21 experts, not just one.

MEET THE ADVISORS

BY DAN AHMAD & JIM FILES

The 21 financial professionals who wrote this book are very proud of creating what we all believe to be the first-of-its-kind resource for retirees exposing: *"the truth about risk, the stock market, fees, and annuities."* We are honored to provide this information to you, in hopes that it changes your life.

The authors of *Momma's Secret Recipe For Retirement Success* collectively have spent more than an estimated 100,000 hours studying, discussing, and researching retirement income planning. This is the equivalent of someone working full-time for 16 straight years, doing nothing except studying, discussing, and researching retirement income planning. Bottom line – this group knows its stuff! To give you the scope and depth of the financial acumen of the 21 financial professionals who wrote this book, it is important to understand their experience and success. As a collective unit they have :

- ✓ Over 425 years of combined experience.
- ✓ Conducted workshops for over an estimated 105,000 people.
- ✓ Consulted with close to an estimated 45,000 people.
- ✓ Worked with an estimated 25,000 clients.
- ✓ Helped place an estimated $330,000,000 of new assets in 2017.
- ✓ Helped place an estimated $3 billion of assets in their careers.
- ✓ Taught an estimated 1,400 financial seminars at colleges.
- ✓ Hosted an estimated 1,300 financial talk radio shows.
- ✓ Current clients with total net worth estimated at close to $7 billion.
- ✓ Won an estimated 165 awards.
- ✓ Trained an estimated 1,600 people in the financial industry.
- ✓ Professional Designations include:

- Certified Financial Planner
- Certified Public Accountant
- IRS Enrolled Agent
- Accredited Tax Advisor
- Chartered Life Underwriter
- Chartered Financial Consultant
- Certified Management Accountant
- Retirement Income Certified Professional
- Financial Services Certified Professional
- Registered Investment Advisor & Investment Advisor Representative
- Certified Long-Term Care Consultant
- Life Insurance Licensed
- Chartered Retirement Planning Counselor
- Certified Identity Theft Risk Management Specialist
- National Social Security Advisor
- Life and Annuity Certified Professional
- Life Underwriter Training Council Fellow
- Mortgage Broker and Real Estate Licensed
- MBA
- Ph.D.

If you are like most retirees, you have gotten advice and followed recommendations of one advisor, one person, at a time. This advice may have been prudent, but it also could have been biased and not necessarily in your ultimate best interests. We think the vast amount of detailed information in this book will open your eyes to information you should have been provided many years ago and will help you view your money in an entirely new and different way.

As a *Special Bonus*, we have added a "Cliff Notes" version of the book that follows next.

"CLIFF NOTES"- THE BOTTOM LINE

BY DAN AHMAD & JIM FILES

If you are like most people, finances are a foreign language, and you may not like dealing with your money. One reason is that you have received so much conflicting information from so many sources, it can't help but being confusing. Do you remember Cliff Notes? Didn't you just love them? Up front, right now, we are going to give you all the answers buried in this book, "Cliff Note"-style. We're going to tell you all the secrets up front. You've never been told or learned most of the information we are going to give you right now. But this information is vitally important to your long-term financial security. We respect your time, so after reading this section, if you are not convinced to read the rest of the book, don't waste your time, just give it to someone else who is retired or nearing retirement.

Here are the key points, the Cliff Notes of Momma's Secret Recipe For Retirement Success:

1. Retirees want, but are not getting, seven (7) things from their money including:

   a. Guarantees they won't run out of money for as long as they live.

   b. Avoiding all large stock market losses and never experiencing another 2008 again.

   c. Maximizing their income during retirement without getting killed with taxes.

   d. Earning acceptable rates of return without taking excessive risks, not losing what they have.

e. Understanding and reducing the total fees they are paying both direct and indirect (hidden).

f. Knowing what they can potentially leave their beneficiaries after using their assets for income.

g. Having their entire plan in writing.

2. If you don't know how much money you can safely take out of your assets for income, how long your money will last, how to guarantee you won't run out of money, how to protect your assets against Stock Market volatility and losses, how much income tax you will pay on your income distributions, how much you will lose in the next stock market crash, if it's OK to start using some of your money, what your total fees are and how you can reduce them, and what's going to happen if you or your spouse pass away, *you are basing your entire plans for retirement on hope and luck.*

3. "Riding out the stock market" doesn't work. Between 2000 and 2018 the S&P 500 Index only increased by an average of 2.85% per year before fees. This is because the stock market lost approximately -50% from 2000-2002 during the Technology Bubble, made +100% just to recover, then lost approximately -50% again from 2007-2009 during the 2008 Financial Crisis, and then made +100% again by 2013 just to break even.

4. During the 2008 Financial Crisis between October 9, 2007 through March 5, 2013 which is a period of 5½ years, the Dow Jones Industrial Average Index increased by 0.10% per year before fees.

5. If you suffer a -35% or larger loss like what happened twice in the last 20 years, you only have a 61.1% probability of getting back to even over any 5-year time period, meaning you have a 39.9% chance not only that you won't make any money, but you won't even get back to even.

6. Starting in 1996, there are nine (9) 15-year time periods ending 2018. In all nine (9) 15-year time periods, the S&P 500 Index averaged an annual compounded increase of just 4.17% before fees.

7. From January 2000 through 2018, the S&P 500 Index increased by an average annual 2.85%, the Dow Jones Industrial Average increased by an average annual 4.06%, and the NASDAQ increased by an average annual 2.61%, with all these increases calculated before any fees.

8. A -50% loss requires a +100% recovery gain just to break even, a -40% loss requires a +67% recovery gain, a -30% loss requires a +43% recovery gain, a -20% loss requires a +25% recovery gain, while a -10% loss only requires a +11.1% recovery gain and a -5% loss only requires a +5.3% recovery gain.

9. If you're a moderate investor you must be willing to lose between -20% and -39% of your assets.

10. The current bull stock market is over nine (9) years old.

11. There have been 13 severe bear stock markets since 1929 that average a -39.5% loss.

12. This means on average every seven (7) years there is an average -39.5% loss in the stock market.

13. As of October 2018, we were historically more than two (2) years overdue for a large stock market loss.

14. If you are a 55-year old couple, based on history you will go through five (5) more -39.5% stock market losses in your lifetimes. If you are a 60-year old couple you will suffer through four (4) more -39.5% losses. If you are a 65-year old couple you will also suffer through four (4) more -39.5% losses. A 70-year old couple can plan on battling through three (3) more -39.5% losses during their lifetimes. A 75-year old couple can plan on limping through two (2) more -39.5% losses, and an 80-year old couple can also plan on struggling through two (2) more -39.5% losses during their lifetimes.

15. If you have $1,000,000 and earn +50% and then lose -50%, your portfolio value is only worth $750,000 as you have just lost -$250,000.

16. Riding out the stock market through big losses gets you nowhere. Riding out the stock market simply means riding the stock market down. From 2000 through 2018, if you rode out the stock market, as represented by the S&P 500 Index, and you received returns equal to the S&P 500 Index, your assets would have grown at an average annual compounded rate of just 2.85% before fees were deducted.

17. If you started with $1,000,000 in 2000 and rode out the stock market through 2018, received returns equal to the S&P 500 Index, and paid 3% per year in total fees – like the average American is paying without even knowing it – your $1,000,000 would have been reduced to $963,890 by the end of 2018 without you taking any income from your portfolio.

18. If you started with $1,000,000 in 2000 and rode out the stock market through 2018, received returns equal to the S&P 500 Index, paid 3% per year in total fees, and took out $50,000 of income per year, you would have run out of money, had $0 left, by March 2013.

19. If you have a $1,900,000 portfolio and suffer a -55.2% loss that was common during the 2008 Financial Crisis stock market meltdown, you would have lost -$1,048,800 leaving only $851,200 left in your portfolio. The $851,200 remaining in your portfolio would have to earn +123.2% just to recover back to the original $1,900,000 value, assuming you didn't take out any income and you didn't pay any fees.

20. The typical retiree believes they are paying only 1% in total fees per year, when they really could be paying 3%, 4%, or even 5% in fees every year without even knowing it. If you own a variable annuity you could be paying up to 6.5% per year in fees.

21. If you have $1,000,000 of assets, paying 3% in fees could cost you $551,415 over a 15-year time period.

22. The "Safe Income Withdrawal Rates," which is the percentage of income you can withdraw from your portfolio during retirement and have a high probability your income won't run out, has steadily decreased over the years. In the 1980s, the financial industry thought the "Safe Income Withdrawal Rate" was 6%, then in the 1990s it

dropped to 5%, then in the 2000s it dropped to 4%, and now in the 2010s it stands at 3%. There is some discussion in the financial industry that this 3% rate could drop to 2.5%.

23. *Momma's Secret Recipe For Retirement Success* has seven (7) steps in the recipe.
We created *The 7 Rules To Live By For Retirement Security* to include:

   a. Avoid large losses – use the "5% to 10% Rule."
   b. Minimize fees.
   c. Significantly reduce volatility.
   d. Earn a reasonable rate of return.
   e. Manage taxation.
   f. Generate "certain income" from your assets that is guaranteed to last for as long as you live, not "maybe income" that could end at any time.
   g. Have a written retirement income plan.

24. There are two (2) stages of money in retirement planning:
   a. Stage 1 – Asset Accumulation while you're working. Growth is very important and you don't worry as much about risk, needing income for life, or safety and liquidity.
   b. Stage 2 – Income Distribution and Asset Preservation when you're retired. You must shift your focus to first guarantee lifetime income, liquidity and safety, and growth is less important.

25. The "3-Bucket Safe Money Approach" will allow you to control your assets the way you want to by:

   a. Placing a portion of your assets into the *guaranteed lifetime income bucket* that will protect your assets against all stock market losses and provide you income for as long as you live.
   b. Placing a portion of your assets into the *liquid/safe bucket* that will protect your assets against all stock market losses and be completely liquid for access.
   c. Placing a portion of your assets into the *growth bucket* for the opportunity for a higher rate of return focusing on risk reduction.

26. Fixed index annuities with income riders will protect your assets against all stock market losses—if the stock market crashes -50% you will receive a 0% return that year. In addition, they:

    a. Provide you with income guaranteed to be paid to you for as long as you live.
    b. May allow you to start drawing income immediately.
    c. Continue to pay your income for as long as you live (even if you use up all of your principal).
    d. Guarantee you will not lose any of your past or current gains from future stock market losses.
    e. Provide the opportunity for competitive rates of return based on a low-risk asset.
    f. May provide the opportunity for future increased income that is guaranteed for your lifetime.
    g. Typically carry low total fees of approximately 1%.
    h. Pass 100% of remaining assets to your beneficiaries when you pass away.

    Some of the negatives are (a) you can't take 100% of your funds out for a specific time period without a surrender penalty, (b) you will not get stock market rates of return, (c) you will pay a fee, and (d) you can't place 100% of your money into this type of plan.

27. Liquid/Safe assets are placed in the bank and will be available for any purpose and will be protected against all stock market losses. You should continue to add money into the bank every month during retirement. The biggest negatives are that you will not earn a high rate of return and guarantees may be capped at certain FDIC limits.

28. Growth assets are typically needed as a crucial part of a proper asset allocation model for both retirees and pre-retirees. You can potentially reduce your risk of loss from large stock market losses by using risk mitigation models such as Stop Losses.

29. From 2000 through 2018, a period of 18 years, if you invested $1,000,000 in 2000 and received annual stock market rates of return equal to the S&P 500 Index, by December 31, 2018 your $1,000,000 would have grown to $1,705,632 and you would have gone through two (2) separate time periods that saw the stock market lose approximately -50%.

30. From 2000 through 2018, a period of 19 years, if you invested $1,000,000 in 2000 and received annual rates of return up to a maximum (CAP) of 6% based on stock market rates of return equal to the S&P 500 Index, but never had to suffer any losses, by December 31, 2018 your $1,000,000 would have grown to $1,909,687. The lesson here is that it may be far more important to protect your principal against large stock market losses than trying to earn the highest rates of return.

31. If you invested $1,000,000 in 2000 and received annual stock market rates of return equal to the S&P 500 Index, took out $50,000 of income per year, and paid 0% per year in fees, your entire portfolio would have been depleted to $0 by 2018.

32. If you invested $1,000,000 in 2000 and received annual stock market rates of return equal to the S&P 500 Index, took out $50,000 of income per year, and paid 1% per year in fees, your entire portfolio would have been depleted to $0 by 2016.

33. If you invested $1,000,000 in 2000 and received annual stock market rates of return equal to the S&P 500 Index, took out $50,000 of income per year, and paid 2% per year in fees, your entire portfolio would have been depleted to $0 by 2014.

34. If you invested $1,000,000 in 2000 and received annual stock market rates of return equal to the S&P 500 Index, took out $50,000 of income per year, and paid 3% per year in fees, your entire portfolio would have been depleted to $0 by 2012.

35. The +117% gain of the S&P 500 Index over 3½ years from May 22, 1996 until December 31, 1999 was completely erased by the -54% loss of the S&P 500 Index over 9+ years from December 31, 1999 until March 9, 2009.

36. Stop-Loss strategies on stock market assets can potentially reduce the severity of a large stock market loss. A Stop-Loss strategy does not eliminate losses.

37. No one is born with a "money gene." You really are not confused about your money, and it's not that you don't understand your plan, it's that you don't actually have a plan. You need everything about

your money and your plans for retirement in writing. You need a comprehensive written retirement income plan that includes a complete retirement income projection showing exactly how much income you will receive every year of your retirement, where your income sources will come from, the risk you are taking, the fees you are paying, an income tax analysis, a beneficiary analysis, and all the details about your plan in writing.

38. There are four (4) parts to a comprehensive written retirement income plan:

    a. Retirement income projection: *income analysis + risk analysis + fee analysis.*
    b. Income tax analysis.
    c. Beneficiary asset transfer analysis (legacy plan).
    d. Full plan details.

39. A hypothetical case study shows assets of $1,600,000 were allocated to increase annual income by $60,000. The case study included $56,000 of joint guaranteed lifetime income.

40. A hypothetical case study shows assets of $1,600,000 were allocated to reduce loss risk by 80%, and reduce recovery gain needed by 90%.

41. A hypothetical case study shows assets of $1,600,000 were allocated to reduce annual fees by $32,000, saving over $984,000 in fees from age 65 through age 85.

42. A hypothetical case study shows gross annual income increasing from $78,000 to $138,000 with an effective federal and California combined income tax rate of 15%. This means a total of 15% income tax was paid on their $138,000 of gross annual income.

43. If you are 65 and had $1,600,000 of retirement assets, took out approximately $60,000 of income per year from your assets, earned a 4% annual rate of return, had taken out over $1,370,000 of income by age 85 when you passed away, you would leave over $1,530,000 to your beneficiaries after you had taken out all that income. The lesson is that you may not have to earn a high rate of return to achieve your financial goals.

44. The "full plan details" of a comprehensive written retirement income plan should include all the plan advantages, disadvantages, costs/fees, what you are doing, why you are doing it, when/how each asset will be used, and the step-by-step process you will use to meet your goals.

45. A 2nd Opinion about your money will tell you either your current plan is on track to meet your goals or that there are steps you need to take to increase your probability of retirement success. You need to know this information now, not ten (10) years from now.

46. On the website of the Securities and Exchange Commission (SEC), the first paragraph of the SEC's definition of an annuity is:
   An annuity is a contract between you and an insurance company that is designed to meet retirement and other long-range goals, under which you make a lump-sum payment or series of payments. In return, the insurer agrees to make periodic payments to you beginning immediately or at some future date.

47. An annuity policy is a legally-binding enforceable written contract. Every single thing the annuity company promises you, all guarantees, fees, and everything about how your annuity works is given to you in writing. Mutual funds, portfolio managers, advisors, and brokerage accounts don't do this.

48. Annuities, and their ancestors, are some of the oldest financial instruments in history, believed to date back as far as 225 A.D. – then called *"annua"* which is translated as "annual stipends."

49. Annuities first came to the United States in 1759, even before the first "market for stocks" was started by 24 brokers in 1792.

50. In the 1700's, it is believed some of the most prominent annuity buyers included Benjamin Franklin, George Washington, and Beethoven.

51. In modern times, a few notable purchasers of annuities are believed to include Winston Churchill, Babe Ruth, Charles Schulz, Jane Austin, Ben Stein, Ben Bernanke, and Shaquille O'Neill.

52. We have found most people spend more time planning their vacations each year than on planning for their retirement.

53. To receive $100,000 per year of income throughout a 30-year retirement, you will need a lump sum of $2,040,108 based on a hypothetical 6% annual earnings rate and 3% inflation rate.

54. From 1971 to 1981 the average inflation rate per year was nearly 7.5%, meaning the cost of your goods and services would double in a decade. At age 60, an inflation rate of just 3.5% per year would require your income to double by age 80.

55. A single premium immediate annuity is one of the oldest types of annuities where you pay a lump sum to an insurance company, and they pay you income guaranteed for a single or joint life or for a specified time period. The guaranteed income payments are not affected by stock market volatility or losses. There is no opportunity for growth as this type of annuity is meant for one thing and one thing only: income. Once the insurer has your funds, you almost always lose control of your asset moving forward, except for the guaranteed payments you receive.

56. A fixed deferred annuity requires a lump sum or periodic payments to an insurance company with contributions guaranteed to grow at a stated rate, but may grow at an even higher current rate. The insurance company will pay you guaranteed income or your principal plus interest at some time in the future, meaning your income benefit is deferred. Your principal and income are not affected by stock market volatility or losses. There are special types of fixed deferred annuities called "multi-year guaranteed annuities", "MYGA" for short. MYGA's are very similar to a CD, but have additional benefits. MYGA's provide a fixed rate of return guaranteed for a set number of years, for example "4% guaranteed for 5 years." Most fixed deferred annuities do not have a front-end load and do not assess annual fees, but almost all of them will assess a surrender charge for a specific time period for premature withdrawals.

57. A variable annuity "VA" is considered a "security" in the same way stocks and mutual funds are, because the entire variable annuity value can decrease, meaning you can lose principal from market

volatility and losses. With a variable annuity, you pay the insurance company a lump sum of money, and the insurance company allows you to allocate your money into one or more subaccounts, which are kind of like higher fee mutual funds. Your subaccounts will increase or decrease each year providing you a gain or loss for the year. You have a potentially higher upside with potentially higher risk. Most variable annuities do not have a front-end load, but total annual fees can reach as high as 6.5% per year, every year. Variable annuities seem to be responsible for the majority of the controversy and bad press on annuities. Ken Fisher's infamous "I Hate Annuities" campaign originally targeted, and focused on, the negative aspects of variable annuities.

58. When an advisor makes a blanket statement like, "All annuities are bad and they are the worst things for you," it almost always means the advisor is uneducated about all the different types of annuities available in the marketplace, and/or can't legally sell annuities, and/or simply prefers to sell other things, and/or is not looking after the true best interests of his/her clients.

59. A $550,000 hypothetical CD that was earning 5% paid $27,500 per year, or $2,292 per month, income. A 1% CD rate, closer to current rates, would only produce $5,500 per year, or $458 per month, of income, an income loss of $22,000 per year, or $1,834 per month.

60. Some fixed index annuities with income riders can provide guaranteed lifetime income starting immediately, meaning you put money in today and your income starts next month, and will be paid to you every month for as long as you live, even past age 100, regardless of stock market losses and volatility.

61. The life insurance industry has provided financial protection to millions of American's unlike any other financial services sector. This protection includes periods of time during horrific wars, depressions, recessions, deadly worldwide epidemics, stock market crashes, inflation, and deflation. During the Great Depression, life insurance companies provided the financial bedrock for Americans when more than 10,000 banks failed. Many people are surprised to know that the insurances companies of the United States bailed out the banking industry during this time, not the federal government.

It's reported Babe Ruth used annuities in 1934 when he retired to create $17,500 of guaranteed annual income, which is $300,000 per year in today's dollars. When Babe died, his wife Claire was able to continue living a comfortable lifestyle on a guaranteed income provided by another annuity he had set up to protect her. No one has ever lost $1 of guaranteed principal, income, or death benefit in a fixed annuity or fixed index annuity with an income rider due to the stock market crashing, the economy collapsing, or insurance companies failing. Even if the annuity was purchased the day before the Great Depression, and before the stock market crashed -90%, no guaranteed annuity principal was lost, no guaranteed income payments were lost, and no guaranteed death benefits were lost.

62. Stockbrokers always like to state the stock market has earned +10% per year since 1900. Sounds great, but they forget to tell you that this is before fees, and more importantly, that since 2000 the S&P 500 Index has only increased by approximately +2.85% before fees. No one reading this was alive in 1900, but most of us have lived through the volatile stock market between 2000 through 2018.

63. There are four (4) basic but important questions you need to be able to answer about your portfolio: (1) how safe is the portfolio if the stock market crashes, (2) how much income can be generated and is it guaranteed for life, (3) what is the potential rate of return of the portfolio, and (4) how liquid is the portfolio?

64. From 1979 through 2008, a period of 30 years, the stock market averaged a 7.23% annual increase. If you had $1,000,000 and took annual income distributions of $50,000 (5%), you would have run out of money during the 30-year time period because of what is called "sequence of returns," simply meaning your financial success is predicated by the luck of when the different annual growth rates in the stock market actually happen and when you take distributions.

65. If you take $120,000 of income distributions from a hypothetical $3,000,000 portfolio for 10 years, and in the first year you lose -50% (like 2000-2002 and 2007-2009) and then earn +12% the next nine (9) years from years two (2) through ten (10), meaning you lost -50% and then made +108%, at the end of ten (10) years your $3,000,000 would have been reduced to $2,053,770 not accounting for fees or income taxes.

66. A "stretch IRA strategy" using a fixed guaranteed annuity with an income rider may allow your beneficiaries to take distributions of your inherited IRA over their entire lifetime, reducing the income-tax burden on your IRA.

67. The typical retired couple, who increases their gross annual income from $100,000 to $200,000 thinks they will get killed in income taxes, but in reality they usually won't. They will pay an estimated 14.69% effective federal income tax rate on their $200,000.

68. The income that is guaranteed to be paid to you for as long as you live from a fixed index annuity with an income rider cannot be reduced or terminated by the insurance company unless you take excess withdrawals from your plan. This means you can take the maximum income amount guaranteed by the insurance company for your life and it can't be changed because it is a legally-binding enforceable written contract. _Hypothetical example_: Let's assume you are married and buy a fixed index annuity for $3,000,000 that pays you a joint guaranteed lifetime income benefit of $150,000 per year. The insurance company has to continue to pay you and your spouse $150,000 per year for as long as at least one of you is living, even if past age 100. Your income cannot be reduced or terminated for any reason including stock market crashes, even if your account reaching a value of $0, and all remaining assets in the plan when you die are passed on to your beneficiaries.

69. The happiest and healthiest retirees are those with the highest level of fixed monthly income sources such as pensions, Social Security, and annuities. Many reports have highlighted this data including a recent study by Towers Watson.

70. Income tax planning is very important during retirement. Gross income is not important, net income after income taxes is important, it's what you really have to spend. With our national debt increasing from $5.7 trillion in 2000 to $21 trillion in 2018, and with the soaring expenses of Social Security, Medicare, Medicaid, interest on the national debt will eventually take up 92 cents of every tax dollar. This could push the need for higher income tax rates.

71. Four (4) of some of the biggest risks you will face during retirement

include (a) market volatility risk, (b) retirement income plan risk, (c) income tax risk, and (d) longevity risk. Wall Street-type traditional investments typically cannot reduce all of these risks. A fixed index annuity with an income rider can help you reduce, and in some cases potentially eliminate, these risks.

You have just been given the facts, the bottom-line answers, the secrets about your money from some of the top financial professionals specializing in retirement planning in the nation who have over 425 years of combined experience. How do you honestly feel after reading the "Cliff-Notes" of what's in this book?

1. You may feel shocked because no one has ever told you these things, in fact they have probably told you the opposite!

2. You may feel scared because you now know the truth and you may have based the fate of your financial success during retirement on misinformation, bad advice, or simply lies.

    OR

3. You may feel like some lucky people, you may feel exhilarated, you may feel very interested in learning about your money, you may feel that very warm ray of hope, because your eyes have been opened to what has really been happening to your money all these years. Many retirees and pre-retirees we meet with have told us they have always had feelings about their money that things just didn't seem right, what they were told by their advisors didn't feel comfortable and didn't answer their questions, and what was happening to their money year-after-year just didn't make sense.

Our job is to help you for the first time in your life understand your money so that you no longer have to worry about it. We have just given you the summary, now we will provide you all the supporting data to prove all of the above statements.

DISCLOSURE

BY DAN AHMAD & JIM FILES

The content within this book is for educational and information purposes only and does not constitute any solicitation, recommendation, promotion, endorsement or offer by others, of any particular security, other investment products, annuity product, transaction, investment, or service. In addition, it is not intended to give you specific retirement planning, annuity, life insurance, tax, investment, real estate, legal, estate, accounting, or financial advice. It is not intended to show you how the strategies presented can specifically apply to your own retirement planning, annuity, life insurance, tax, investment, estate, accounting, or financial position, but rather to offer an idea of how these principles generally may apply. There is no representation about the suitability of the information presented.

Any and all opinions, commentary, news, research, analyses, website content, or other information contained within is informational only and does not constitute advice. Any opinions, views or information regarding financial strategy expressed are those of each contributing author, and as such, are just his/her individual opinion, and have not been verified. Views and opinions are subject to change without notice.

Co-authors are not liable for any loss or damage, including without limitation, any loss of principal, any loss of income, which may arise directly or indirectly for individuals use of, or reliance on, such information. Do not implement any of the ideas or strategies discussed in this book without the help of qualified financial, tax, estate, and legal advisors.

Nothing is directly or indirectly guaranteed by anything in this book. Past performance is not a guarantee of future results. Your results will be different and could be higher or lower. Reasonable measures have been taken to review information. However, all such information is provided "as is" without warranty of any kind. The information contained herein is subject to change after print date. There is no representation about the suitability of the information presented. The text, charts, and graphs should not serve as the sole determining factor for making investment decisions.

S&P 500 Index data, Dow Jones Industrial Average (DJIA) Index data, and NASDAQ Index data used for educational purposes only. Past performance is not a guarantee of future results. The hypothetical analysis is based on assumptions, and nothing is directly or indirectly guaranteed. Your results will be different and could be higher or lower. You cannot invest directly into the S&P 500 Index, Dow Jones Industrial Average (DJIA) Index, and NASDAQ Index. Unless noted, illustrative numbers are shown without income taxes taken into consideration. S&P 500 Index data, Dow Jones Industrial Average (DJIA) Index data, and NASDAQ Index data from Yahoo Finance and/or www.1stock1. com, and are shown without dividends, and without any fees or costs. When someone says the stock market has always earned a specific rate of return, such as "10%", it does not mean you will earn this rate, it typically doesn't include any deductions for fees, and does not mean you would earn this every year because of annual return volatility. When we use the term "stock market" we will be referring to the S&P 500 Index unless stated differently.

Losses and recovery gains illustrated are hypothetical and for educational purposes only. Your results will be different and could be higher or lower. Based on the type of investor you think you are, you could lose more or less than the amounts discussed. The loss amounts discussed are baselines and are not maximum loss amounts. You could suffer through more or less large losses during your lifetime than what is discussed. Your losses could be more than -40% or less than -40%. The Golden Rule Of 5% To 10% does not guarantee against loss, nor does it guarantee you will never lose more than 5% to 10%, it serves as a planning methodology used to set potential loss parameters into your plan. In Chapter 12, the S&P 500 Index data is presented without any fees or cost, with 3% fees, and with 3% and 4% Income, your results could be higher or lower. Your income sources could be higher or lower. Your deductions could be higher or lower. Your taxable income could be higher or lower. Your income taxes could be higher or lower. Your net after-tax income could be higher or lower. Your monthly expenses could be higher or lower. Your net income available for savings per month could be higher or lower. Verify your tax position with your tax professional.

"Safe Income Withdrawal Rates" do not guarantee your assets will not run out during your lifetime and do not guarantee your income will last for as long as you live, they are just hypothetical baselines to use as starting points in creating your actual income plan. The Vanguard S&P 500 Index fund and Vanguard Total Bond Market Index fund are used for illustrative purposes only based on the study completed by Beacon Capital Management; your results will be different and could be better or worse, you could lose principal, not make any gains, and your income could run out. Assumptions behind the Monte Carlo simulations in this book may not be accurate or realistic. A Monte Carlo simulation is a risk analysis tool that uses random sampling to build possible outcomes and success probabilities, and should not be considered a fact, but may be considered as a viable tool in understanding your finances. Investment returns may not follow a normal distribution, which may impact the simulation outcome, especially with respect to extreme events. The Monte Carlo simulation does not consider taxation and other important factors that may affect the simulation outcome. Fees are not taken into consideration.

The *7 Rules To Live By For Retirement Security* do not guarantee specific investment results, specific risk reduction or specific income amounts, but rather serve as an educational platform on how you may decide to put your overall plans for retirement together. The Golden Rule Of 5% To 10% does not guarantee against loss, nor does it guarantee you will never lose more than 5% to 10%, it serves as a planning methodology used to set potential loss parameters into your plan. There is no guarantee you will reduce your fees. Your assets may continue to exhibit substantial volatility. You may not earn a rate of return, and you could lose principal value.

Your income sources, deductions, taxable income, income tax rates, income taxes, net after-tax income, and effective income tax rate could be higher or lower. You may be subject to state and/or local income taxes, phase-outs of itemized deductions, alternative minimum tax, business income/expense restrictions, real estate income/expenses restrictions, etc. Marginal income tax brackets and rates pertain to your highest level of taxation on the highest portion of your income. Your effective income tax rate is the single income tax rate you pay on all of your gross income, basically serving as the overall average income tax rate on your total gross income.

The hypothetical analysis is based on assumptions and is not guaranteed. Your return rate results, losses, income taxes, benefits, and/or fees will be different and could be higher or lower. Bank accounts and CD's are guaranteed up to FDIC limits. Your bank and/or CD rates can be higher or lower. Monte Carlo simulations do not guarantee results, returns, income, or success, they are mathematical simulations using historical data. Stock dividends are not guaranteed and could increase, decrease, or cease altogether.

You could lose more or less than -10% in a -10% stop-loss program. After a stop-loss is activated, you will not receive the full upside of the next stock market upside. An extremely volatile stock market could create multiple stop-losses in a short time period causing multiple losses. Your fees could be higher or lower than the hypothetical examples in this book. Your risk reduction could be more or less than the hypothetical examples discussed in this book. Your income could be higher or lower than the hypothetical examples discussed in this book. Risk analysis data is based on 3rd party information. Based on the type of investor you think you are, you could lose more or less than the amounts discussed. The loss amounts shown above are baselines and are not maximum loss amounts. Income tax analysis is based on current federal income tax rates which could change, and your income taxes could be higher or lower. Your written plan should be signed by your advisor.

Any comments regarding fixed index annuities with income riders as safe or secure investments or guarantee of insurance related income refer only to fixed insurance products and do not refer in any way to securities or investment advisory products.

Fixed index annuities with income riders are long-term investments and are not a direct or indirect investment in the stock market and while protecting principal against all stock market losses, will in almost all cases earn a lower rate of return than the stock market in positive stock market growth years, meaning you will not receive full stock market participation. Income riders in a fixed index annuity may provide a specified and guaranteed lifetime income amount and a specified and guaranteed "roll-up rate" that increases the guaranteed minimum withdrawal benefit which increases future guaranteed lifetime income, but is not available in a lump sum. Income riders will typically carry an annual fee of approximately 1%, and your fee could be higher or lower. Principal guarantees, lifetime income guarantees, and guaranteed death benefits discussed are backed by the financial strength and claims-paying ability of the issuing insurance company.

The guaranteed lifetime income amounts referenced in this book are hypothetical and do not pertain to a specific insurance carrier. Your income will be different and could be higher or lower. The hypothetical lifetime income referenced in this book discussing possible annual income increases are not guaranteed to occur, you may receive no raises if the indexes you choose never create index gains in your account.

There are benefits that retirees and soon-to-be retirees can potentially receive from a fixed indexed annuity with an income rider such as guaranteed lifetime income, guaranteed principal, guaranteed returns, and guaranteed growth for income purposes, but have surrender charges and/or penalties, market value adjustments, liquidity limitations, return limits, fees, loads, expenses, loss of bonus, loss of indexed interest, loss of fixed interest, and other disadvantages. The fixed index annuity index concept analysis uses hypothetical index calculations. One hypothetical example used is an annual point-to-point methodology with a 0% floor and 6% annual cap, but others could also be used. Another hypothetical example that discusses increasing guaranteed lifetime income uses a 3% annual cap on potential annual raises. The hypothetical returns for fixed index annuities are not guaranteed but used as a comparison to the stock market to show a lower return potential than the stock market.

There is no guarantee you will earn anything at all in a fixed index annuity. For educational purposes only, examples in this book include a hypothetical annual fixed index annuity income rider annual "roll-up rate", including a hypothetical 6% annual roll-up rate, yours could be higher or lower. We believe a fixed index annuity with an income rider is appropriate only if the buyer has a current or future need for guaranteed income, and/or wants principal protection, and/or wants protection for beneficiaries. Fixed index annuities with income riders are not appropriate for all individuals or situations. Fixed index annuities with income riders are not FDIC insured, check with your state for state guarantees.

Fixed index annuities with income riders provide an opportunity for tax-deferred growth on non-qualified (non-IRA) assets. Any gains that are distributed from non-qualified plans will be taxed as ordinary income, any principal distributed will be income tax-free. Distributions from IRAs holding fixed index annuities with income riders are fully taxed as all IRA distributions are. Distributions from IRAs and non-qualified plans before 59 ½ can cause an IRS penalty.

Bonus Annuities may include annuitization requirements, lower capped returns, higher fees, or other restrictions that are not included in similar annuities that don't offer a premium bonus feature.

Stage One (1) of Retirement Planning - Asset Accumulation and Stage Two (2) of Retirement Planning - Income Distribution and Asset Preservation are used to describe different time periods of planning for retirement and the "3 Bucket Safe Money Approach" is the name given to the allocation methodology discussed in this book and do not guarantee specific investment results, specific risk reduction, specific income amounts, but rather serve as an educational platform on how you may decide to view your assets when you are retired and when you are close to retirement; all three have risk, and you can still lose money. None of the information provided guarantees you will make any money, never lose money, or that you will lose less than you have previously. Your assets may continue to exhibit substantial volatility. You may not earn a rate of return, and you could lose principal value. Your return rate results, losses, income taxes, benefits, and/or fees will be different and could be higher or lower. The hypothetical returns discussed for Bucket #1 fixed index annuities and Bucket #3 growth are not guaranteed but used for educational purposes only. There is no guarantee you will earn anything at all in a fixed index annuity. There is no guarantee you will earn anything at all in the growth Bucket #3; growth is not guaranteed, and you could suffer a principal loss.

Any mention of "private pension" is referring to a stream of income that would be paid to you for life and is not part of a formal company-sponsored pension plan and is not covered under the Pension Benefit Guarantee Corporation.

The sale or liquidation of any stock, bond, IRA, certificate of deposit, mutual fund, annuity, or other asset to fund the purchase of an annuity may have tax consequences, early withdrawal penalties, or other costs and penalties as a result of the sale or liquidation. We are not recommending that you buy a fixed annuity of any type or invest your money in any way. The hypothetical returns for the growth bucket are not guaranteed, and you could suffer a principal loss and is used as a comparison to the stock market to show a lower return potential than what the stock market may provide. In Chapter 29, the annual income from assets, cumulative income from assets, portfolio assets remaining, portfolio 4% rate, bank assets remaining, bank 1% rate, real estate assets remaining, real estate 1.5% rate, and total assets remaining are not guaranteed and could all be higher or lower; yours will be different.

Not adhering to minimum mandatory distributions for IRAs and inherited IRAs can result in a 50% penalty as well as taxation. Contributory Roth IRA plans allow income tax-free distributions of funds any time after five (5) years from the date the initial Roth IRA contribution was made. Roth IRA conversions place the five (5) year waiting time period for income tax-free withdrawals on each separate Roth IRA conversion. Talk to your income tax professional before making any IRA or Roth IRA decisions.

The graph titled "Asset Client Owned" does not include all assets available for ownership, it only includes assets the author has encountered in the past. You could own, or could have owned, different assets and your results could be better or worse.

All case studies and examples are hypothetical, and your results could be different. You should seek the advice of a qualified professional advisor regarding your own financial situation.

The individual co-authors ("contributing authors") are not affiliated and may represent various firms as insurance agents, investment advisor representatives, and registered representatives. If available, please review the ADV 2B ("supplemental brochure") for further information about the representative and/or the ADV 2A ("Firm Brochure") for information on the Firms they may represent. This information may be found via the IAPD link: www.adviserinfo.sec.gov or brokercheck.com.

The individual co-authors may be insurance-licensed individuals who are appointed as insurance agents in various states where they conduct their business.

CHAPTER 1

RECENT STUDIES SHOW RETIREES WANT SEVEN (7) MAIN THINGS FROM THEIR MONEY

BY DAN AHMAD & JIM FILES

With 10,000+ Americans retiring every day, there have been countless studies completed detailing what retirees want from their money. There are many opinions and differing answers depending on the study and the participants. We have reviewed many of these studies, with some focusing on risk, some on investing, others on generating income, several on longevity, and many on the fears and concerns retirees have about their money in general. While all of the studies differed, we noticed a common core, basic similarities, in the results of the studies we reviewed. We found retirees want seven (7) main things from their money:

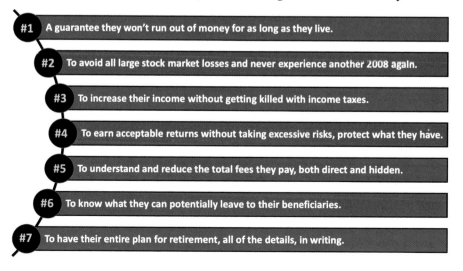

#1 A guarantee they won't run out of money for as long as they live.

#2 To avoid all large stock market losses and never experience another 2008 again.

#3 To increase their income without getting killed with income taxes.

#4 To earn acceptable returns without taking excessive risks, protect what they have.

#5 To understand and reduce the total fees they pay, both direct and hidden.

#6 To know what they can potentially leave to their beneficiaries.

#7 To have their entire plan for retirement, all of the details, in writing.

#1 – *Retirees want a guarantee they're not going to run out of money for as long as they live.* That sounds pretty simple, but it's very difficult for retirees to figure out how to do this. They get conflicting advice. Some advisors might tell them, "Well, it's okay if you take 6% out of your portfolio per year, and you'll never run out of money." Some might say 5%, 4%, or even 3%. Whatever the number is, you have to make sure whatever amount of income you are taking out, is guaranteed to last for as long as you live, and if you're married, for as long as your spouse lives. If your income ends before you die, your plan for a successful retirement goes up in smoke.

#2 – *Retirees want to avoid all large stock market losses and never suffer another 2008 again.* Small losses can potentially be acceptable, but large losses are very, very difficult to recover from. For example, in 2000 through 2002, and 2007 through 2009, the stock market in general went down by about 50% each time. If you lose 50%, you have to receive a 100% gain just to recover where you originally started from. For example, if you have a million dollars in your IRA and you lose 50%, you're down to $500,000. Well, the $500,000 must earn $500,000, which is a 100% rate of return, just to break even. This could take a long time, and it might not happen at all. The recovery can be even more difficult, maybe even impossible, if you are receiving income distributions during the downturn and through the recovery. You must avoid all large stock market losses.

#3 – *Increase their income without getting killed with taxes.* Many retirees feel very uncomfortable increasing their income significantly during retirement, because they're afraid of taxes, and it's simply because no one has explained how the income tax rates actually work. You could make $150,000 per year in retirement income, which is substantial for the average retiree, and the typical retiree will pay less than 14% in federal taxes on their $150,000 of gross income. Think about it, $150,000 of income equaling 14% of tax. You shouldn't be afraid of increasing your income during retirement. Check with your tax advisor and make sure the numbers fit for you.

#4 – *Earn acceptable rates of return without taking excessive risks, protect what they have.* You are retired, and it's no longer prudent to focus on earning the highest possible rates of return because if you try to get the highest rates of return, you have to take the highest level of risk. And when you have taken the highest level of risk in the past, what has happened? You probably either lost a lot of money or did not earn anything close to what you had hoped to earn based on the amount of risk you took. You need to make sure you know what the rate of return objective for your plan is, meaning, what rate of return do you need to make your plan work, which might only be a 3%, 4%, or 5% rate of return to make your plans for retirement successful.

#5 – *Understand and reduce the total fees they pay, both direct and hidden.* Many retirees think they are paying 1% in total fees on your portfolio because that's all they can see on their statements or that's what their broker has told them. But what if you found out that you, like most retirees we have seen, are actually paying 3%, 4%, or even 5% per year in fees? That would really hurt your plans for retirement and will probably make your money run out a lot sooner than you had planned. You must understand your direct and indirect (hidden) fees, then reduce them as much as possible, and get your fees in writing.

#6 – *Know what they can potentially leave to their beneficiaries.* Most of us want to leave money to our kids, grandkids, and/or charities, but we don't want to sacrifice our own retirement security and happiness in doing so. If you are like the majority of retirees we have interviewed, you want to make sure you have as much income as you need for as long as you live and never run out, then leave all remaining funds to your beneficiaries. We have found that knowing what you can leave to your beneficiaries will make it easier for you to be willing to spend some of your money.

#7 – *Have their entire plan for retirement, all of the details, in writing.* This is possibly the most important of all seven (7) of these items. Retirees want a plan, they no longer are willing to settle just for investments or asset statements, they want every detail about their plans for retirement written down, so they can read it, understand it, and make sure they're not going to forget what their entire financial plan, what their entire retirement success, is based on. If you are like the overwhelming majority of retirees, you probably feel you don't understand and are confused about your plan. This is not because you don't understand or are confused, it's because you don't have an actual written plan. If everything about your money was written down for you in plain English, there is a high probability you would understand your plan.

These seven (7) items are all part of the one (1) thing we found thousands and thousands of retirees want:

They all want to finally be able to stop worrying about their money.

The Bad News: Retirees have not been provided these things by their current broker/advisor.

The Good News: The right financial professional will happily give you all these things and more. The authors of this book strive to do this every day.

What does a typical new client that usually needs comprehensive retirement income planning look like? Someone who is between 55-80 who has accumulated between $250,000 and $20 million dollars of investible assets like IRA's, 401(k)'s, stocks, bonds, mutual funds, bank accounts, annuities, CD's, and other types of portfolio assets not including real estate, businesses, or other illiquid assets. The retirement income planning specialists who wrote this book will work with people with investible assets of $250,000 up to $100,000,000 or more.

The best part about reading this book is that you will finally learn the truth about your money!

CHAPTER 2

QUESTIONS YOU MUST BE ABLE TO ANSWER TO HAVE A SUCCESSFUL RETIREMENT

BY DAN AHMAD & JIM FILES

Most retirees have not gotten answers to their most pressing questions about retirement from their current brokers, advisors, employers, or own research. If you can't answer basic questions about your retirement, how can you expect to succeed, feel secure, and feel confident you are making the right decisions about your money? You can't feel good about it.

If you can't answer basic questions about your money, it means your plans for retirement are based on hope and luck. It means you are hoping you will be lucky and things will work out.

Your broker or advisor might seem to know a lot about your portfolio and managing the assets because that is what they mainly talk to you about. Your broker or advisor may say you are diversified, state they have great money managers, let you know you are positioned for good rates of return, tell you if you want less risk they can put a larger percentage of your assets in bonds, and will often confirm you can expect an 8%-10% average annual rate of return. However, when you ask the important questions about your money, they don't have any answers. Moreover, your broker or advisor has never put your plan in writing. This means your current broker or advisor is comfortable with you basing your plans for retirement on hope and luck. Are you?

In our 50+ years of experience, we have found there is certain data (see diagram on following page) you must have to build a secure plan and to be able to stop worrying about your money:

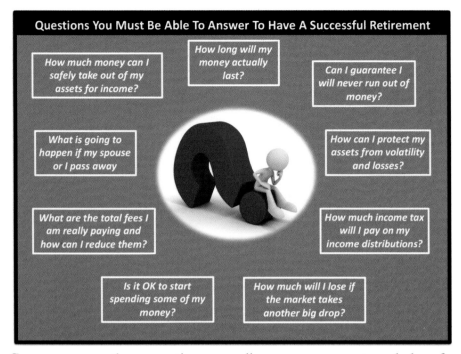

Questions You Must Be Able To Answer To Have A Successful Retirement

- How much money can I safely take out of my assets for income?
- How long will my money actually last?
- Can I guarantee I will never run out of money?
- What is going to happen if my spouse or I pass away
- How can I protect my assets from volatility and losses?
- What are the total fees I am really paying and how can I reduce them?
- How much income tax will I pay on my income distributions?
- Is it OK to start spending some of my money?
- How much will I lose if the market takes another big drop?

Can you answer these questions regarding your own assets and plans for retirement? If you can't answer these questions, it means your entire plan is based on hope and luck. Are you willing to bet your retirement security and your financial success on hope and luck? I bet you really aren't, but no one has given you the answers before. If your current advisor has not answered these questions and not put the answers in writing for you, it may be time to find a new advisor. Make sure you develop a plan that can answer every single one of these questions and make sure those answers are in writing.

1. ***How much income can you safely take out of your assets for income?***

   If you are not sure how much income you can take out of your assets, you may not be taking as much as you could because you are worried about running out, or you may be taking too much, and you will run out. Either way, you are not in a good position.

2. ***How long will your money actually last?***

   If you don't know how long your money will really last, you will either take less income than you could, or worse yet, take no income at all because you are worried about running out of money. This means you will do without, and you will continue to worry.

3. Can you guarantee you will never run out of money for as long as you live?

The biggest fear retirees and pre-retirees have is running out of money during their lifetimes, and if you can't guarantee your income won't run out, you will continue to feel anxious and fearful about using your money. The key is to learn how to create "Certain Income" from your assets that will never run out, for as long as you live.

4. How can you protect your assets from volatility and losses?

If you lived through 2000-2002 and 2007-2009, you probably are a little, or maybe a lot, worried about volatility and losses. If your assets have a high level of volatility, you can't take much income out. If you are taking income distributions from your assets and then suffer through volatility and losses, the negative impacts of the volatility and losses are magnified. Fees increase the severity of losses.

5. How much income tax will you pay on your income distributions from your assets?

Retirees and pre-retirees fear big losses and running out of money, but they also are afraid of income taxes. Many retirees believe they will pay a huge amount of income taxes if they use their assets for income, so they don't use their assets. The fact is that most retirees will not be in a high effective income tax bracket so they should take income from their assets to live the retirement of their dreams.

6. How much will you lose in the next big stock market crash?

With the stock market continuing on its path of all-time highs, most people worry about the next big stock market crash because it's not if it will happen, it's when will it happen and how big will it be? If you have no idea how much you could lose, this only increases your anxiety about your money.

7. Is it OK to start spending some of your money?

A large percentage of retirees decide not to use their assets for income when they retire because they are worried about losses, their money running out, income taxes, and not leaving enough for their beneficiaries. Also, think about it, the only reason you saved all your money while you were working was to be able to use it to create income during retirement. So, if you are afraid to use your money now that you are retired, this is a terrible way to feel about your money because you will not be able to do all the things you planned to do. If you can guarantee your income won't run out for as long as you live, you can eliminate your fear of running out of money.

8. *What are the total fees you are really paying and how can you reduce them?*

We believe close to 100% of retirees and pre-retirees are not aware of the true cost of having their assets managed. Most people believe they are paying "about 1%," but when we perform fee audits as part of a 2nd Opinion About Your Money, we find the average retiree is paying approximately 3.25% in direct and indirect (hidden) fees. This is a shame as the typical retiree with a proper plan may pay less than half of this amount.

9. *What's going to happen if you or your spouse pass away?*

It's a very difficult conversation to have discussing what happens if you or your spouse pass away. What will happen to the survivor? Will your finances continue to be secure? Will your lifestyle have to change? Because these are difficult and emotional topics, you may avoid them. But we promise, not knowing the answers to these questions are far worse than having the conversation.

The goal of prudent and proper retirement planning is to develop a plan that can answer all of these questions, because if you can answer all of these questions, you won't have to worry about your money any longer.

CHAPTER 3

HOW DO YOU WANT YOUR MONEY TO ACT?

BY DAN AHMAD & JIM FILES

Years ago, when you made your first investment, you were told "not to watch your money," …"it will go up and down but don't worry," …"you will need to ride out losses," …"over the long-run you should be OK and make good money," and …"you must take risk to get high returns to succeed." From the beginning, you have been told, "You cannot control your money." What if all these things you have been told are incorrect, and not in your best interest? What if you could control your money, actually make your money act any way you want it to? Don't let your broker or advisor control your money; it's not their money, it's yours. You must learn how to control your money the way you want it to act. If you are like most people, you have probably been given two (2) main "pillars of knowledge" that have guided your investment decisions:

1. It's best to "hang in there" and "ride it out" when there are big stock market losses.
2. If you "hang in there" and "ride out" stock market volatility and losses, you should get an annual rate of return of 10% or more.

You have invested based on these two (2) premises, both old-school and outdated, and the problem is that neither are in your best interests, and they simply aren't true. They are myths, and they are myths that, if believed, can ruin your retirement. We call these: ***The myth of "riding out the market" and the myth of "getting a 10%+ annual return."***

Here's the truth that no one has ever told you. The S&P 500 Index was at 1,469 in January 2000 and ended at 2,506 in 2018. This looks like a huge gain. However, to receive this growth, you had to "ride out the market." In fact, you had to ride out two (2) large approximately -50% stock market losses, the first during the Technology Bubble from 2000-2002 and the second during the 2008 Financial Crisis from 2007-2009. But if you were a "good investor" and "hung in there", you "stayed in the market" and you "rode it out", you were rewarded with this seemingly large gain from 2000 through 2018 with the S&P 500 Index growing from 1,469 to 2,506. The problem is, no one has told you the truth, because the average annual compounded increase to the S&P 500 Index from 2000 through 2018 was only 2.85%. And this is before fees. Many retirees pay 3% or more in total fees without even knowing it, so the potential growth net of fees could be non-existent.

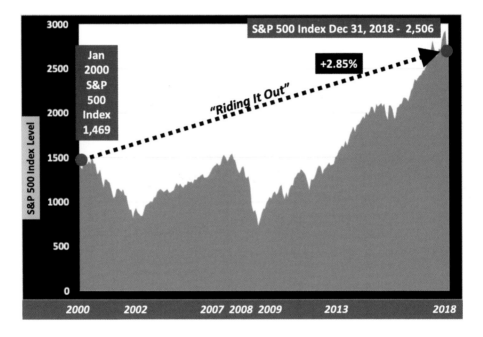

The 2.85% average annual increase to the S&P 500 Index between 2000 through 2018 is an accurate number because you "rode out" an approximate -50% stock market collapse during the Technology Bubble between 2000-2002, recovered by 2007, and then "rode out" another stock market collapse of approximately -50% during the 2008 Financial Crisis between 2007-2009. After the -50% loss from 2000-2002, you had to make +100% just to recover by 2007. Then after the second loss of -50% from 2007-2009, you had to make +100% again just to recover by 2013. Two (2) -50% losses required two (2) +100% recovery gains just to break even, not to make any gains, just to recover.

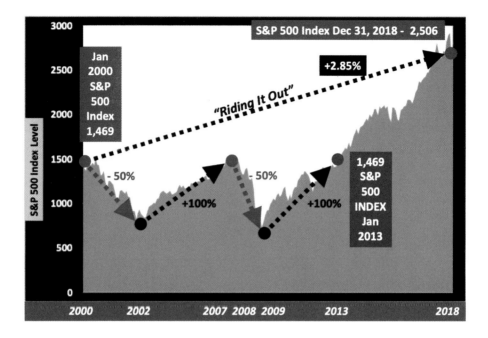

The S&P 500 Index was at 1,469 in January 2013, the exact same level as January 2000. These two (2) separate sets of approximately -50% stock market losses caused a 0% increase to the S&P 500 Index from 2000-2013, a period of 13 years, before fees.

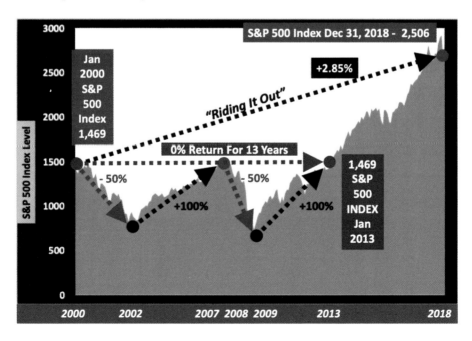

Think about what the previous chart is really showing. Between 2000 and 2013 the stock market, represented by the S&P 500 Index, had two (2) -50% losses and two (2) +100% gains. The two (2) -50% losses total -100% in losses and the two (2) +100% gains total +200% in gains. And yet, contradicting all the math you have ever been taught, -100% in losses plus +200% in gains equal a zero percent (0%) gain over 13 years. Maybe this is what the kids call "New Math?" The stock market lost -50% between 2000 through 2002 and then fully recovered by 2007. And then the stock market lost -50% from October 2007 through March 2009, and then fully recovered by January 2013. However, for 13 years, between 2000 through 2013, the stock market was completely flat, increasing 0% per year.

By "hanging in there" and "riding it out," the stock market recovered all of its' losses over 13 years. But here is the key, while you were saving money, did you base your plans for retirement, how much income you could take out of your assets, and how long your money would last on earning 0% for 13 years? Additionally, you must reduce the 0% annual increase for 13 years by any fees you paid. If you were taking income out during this time period it was even worse because if you study the previous graph closely, the market was under the 0% return line for almost the entire 13-year time period. This means you were almost always taking income distributions out while your account was in a loss position, simply meaning everything was worse, and you could run out of money faster.

After looking at the last chart on the preceding page, many retirees and pre-retirees have told us the graph and numbers simply can't be true because their accounts grew by more than 2.85% during the time period between 2000 through 2018 while they were working. We then tell them their account value could have increased by more than we are saying, probably not from stock market growth, but because they continued to add large deposits into their 401(k) and other plans. Most of their growth actually came from their own additional contributions.

During the Technology Bubble stock market collapse from 2000 through 2002, you were told to ride out the market volatility and losses because you are in it for the long-term and you would be rewarded with a big rate of return because the stock market always averages a 10%+ rate of return. So in 2000, after the market dropped -10%, you were told "don't worry about it," …"it's just a short-term loss," …"you will recover quickly," …"it won't go down that much," …"don't watch it all the time," and …"the return you get will be worth all the risk you are taking." You probably heard some of these same instructions from your advisor recently because of how volatile the stock market has been.

And then the market went down a second -10%, bringing your total losses to -20%, and you were told the same things. Then the market went down a third -10%, bringing your total losses to -30%, and you were fed the same information. Then the market went down a fourth -10%, bringing your total losses to -40%, and guess what, the same things were said. Then the stock market went down a fifth -10%, bringing your total losses to -50%, and they told you the same things: "don't worry about it," …"it's just a short-term loss," …"you will recover quickly," …"it won't go down that much," …"don't watch it all the time," and …"the return you get will be worth all the risk you are taking."

But guess what? None of them were true. It didn't work out that way at all. During the 19-year time period from 2000 through 2018, if you "rode out" the market you:

- Suffered two (2) different approximate -50% losses.
- Needed two (2) different +100% returns just to recover, not to make any money, just to recover.
- Were rewarded with a whopping +2.85% annual compounded increase from the S&P 500 Index. The 2.85% annual compounded increase was before fees.

You could have gotten a higher rate of return from CD's in the bank. If you had bought a 5-year CD in 2000, renewed it at a lower rate in 2005, renewed it at an even lower rate in 2010, and renewed it at an even lower miniscule rate in 2015, you would have beat the stock market returns. Based on data provided by www.gobankingates.com and www. jumbocdinvestments.com, the average annual compounded return from 5-year CD's from 2000 through 2018 would have been 4.15%. We aren't saying to put all your money into CD's as current rates are very low. We are just emphasizing the fact that the stock market did not provide you anywhere close to the rate of return you were told you'd earn and you should have received based on how much risk you were taking.

We believe you should never "ride out big losses in the market." We will never tell you to ride out big losses in the stock market. Every plan we create is to avoid big losses in the stock market because as a retiree, you can't afford to take a big loss at this time in your life. Here's the big question: can you plan, take a high level of consistent income, and feel secure if your assets are behaving like this? The answer is you can't. It's basically mathematically impossible, for you to plan, take a high level of consistent income, and feel financially secure you will never run out of money for as long as you live, especially net of fees, if your assets are subject to high volatility.

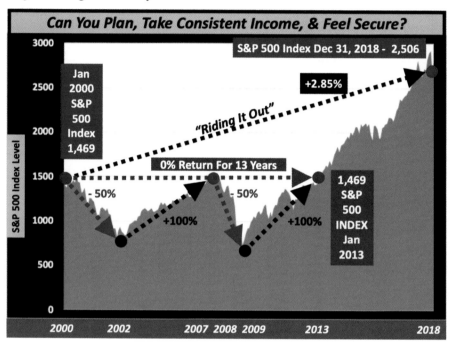

We have heard many advisors and retirees say we will never have another stock market decline like the Technology Bubble between 2000 through 2002 or the Financial Crisis from October 2007 through March 2009. When we hear these comments, we are dumbfounded, shocked, and concerned, because we believe you will most assuredly go through not just one more big stock market crash and loss in your life, but actually many of them between now and the time you pass away. Not a real warm and fuzzy thought, we know. Large stock market losses are just part of the normal cycle the stock market will always go through. It goes up, it goes down, it goes back up, it goes back down, and so on.

So here is the key: *Stock market losses aren't bad, they are normal, and they are supposed to happen*. What's bad is if you are a retiree and you don't protect your assets against the large stock market losses that will inevitably happen.

Do you think you will need to navigate any more -40% stock market losses in your lifetime? The truth is you probably will. Depending on how old you are, you may have to navigate many more -40% stock market losses. Isn't that a scary thought? What if you are using your assets for income and you lose 40% of your portfolio? We will show you in later chapters how many more -40% stock market losses you should be prepared to go through.

CHAPTER 4

WHY SHOULD RETIREES AVOID VOLATILITY?

BY DAN AHMAD & JIM FILES

We think 15-years is a long time. If you're 70, then 15-years could represent your life expectancy. Let's look at a 15-year graph of the S&P 500 Index starting in 1999 and ending in 2013, that's when we finished writing the text of one of our books titled *Don't Bet the Farm*. We did a significant amount of research on the S&P 500 Index to complete that book. Because we only work with retirees, we wanted to review what happened over the previous 15 years in the stock market to prepare for what types of pitfalls may lie ahead in the next 15 years based on normal average life expectancies. There was volatility, and there was growth. But what we ultimately found out was nothing short of astonishing.

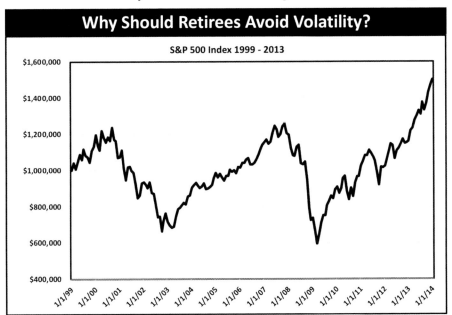

When you first started saving, you were told to "invest money," "don't watch it," "don't worry about it," "always leave it in" and "ride it out." And if you did all of these things, you were told the stock market would always go up and you'd earn a really good rate of return. If you don't believe the stock market will always go up over time, you'd better not have any money invested in the stock market! We believe the stock market will always go up over time. But that's not the complete answer, as we must look at three (3) variables to explain our complete opinion:

#1. The first variable is to determine how much volatility you have to go through during the time period your money's invested in the stock market? If you look at the graph above showing the stock market between 1999 through 2013, you can easily see there was a tremendous amount of volatility. The Tech Bubble between 2000 through 2002 caused a huge loss, and the Financial Crisis in 2008 did the same. But if you stayed in the stock market, "rode it out" and you "never got out," starting in 1999 you made money, you lost money in 2000 through 2002, you made back losses in 2003 through 2007, you lost money again in 2008, and then you potentially made your losses back from 2009 through 2013.

#2. The second variable is the time period money was invested to achieve the ultimate rate of return. In this case, the time period is 15 years, a very reasonable time period to use for analytical purposes for a retiree.

#3. The third variable is to then calculate out the actual rate of return achieved by "riding it out" over the specified time period. Your broker or advisor probably stated you made a great rate of return by "riding it out" because the S&P 500 Index started at around 1,200 in 1999 and ended at close to 1,800 in 2013. In this chapter, we will show you the annual average compounded increase to the S&P 500 Index during the 15-year time period from 1999 through 2013.

From 1999 to 2000, the stock market, measured by the S&P 500 Index, went up by 19.53%, so people made a lot of money. They were happy. You probably thought the stock market wasn't going to go down for a long time.

Then came the Tech Bubble when the S&P 500 Index lost -46% between 2000 and 2002. You were probably told to "ride it out," and by doing so you lost a lot of money. You may have been fed the famous line of

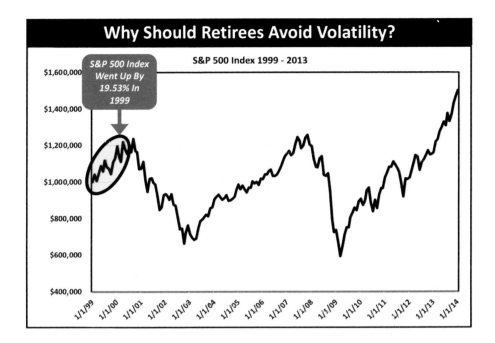

malarkey saying "your loss is only on paper." Here's a secret: If it's on paper, it means you lost money. It took until 2007 just to recover, and you hadn't made any money. Fees you paid and income you withdrew would elongate the recovery process.

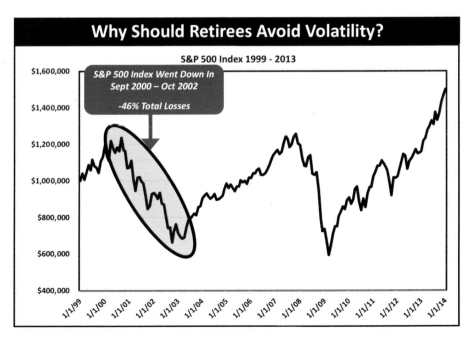

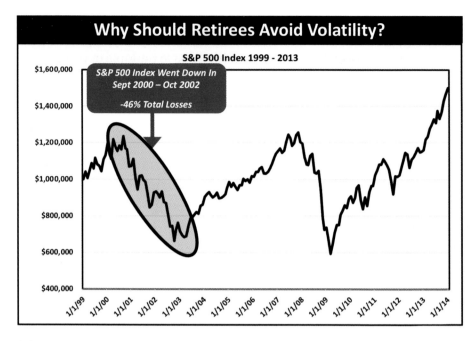

After recovering by 2007, the S&P 500 Index then lost -53% from November 2007 through March 2009. It took until 2013 to break even again, not making any gains. Fees and income distributions would increase the problem. This means for 13 years the stock market didn't increase at all. …0%! …Zilch! …Nada!

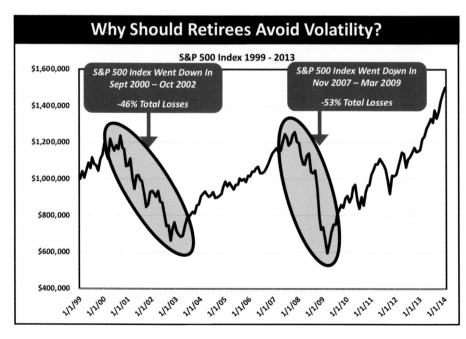

As we asked before, do you think you'll have to live through any more of these types of losses in your lifetime? If you say yes, you get an "A+" because you are correct. You will most likely have multiple of these types of losses during the rest of your lifetime. Why is this important? Because losses are very hard to make up and the recovery is not guaranteed.

It is paramount to understand the impact of these types of large stock losses to your portfolio and your retirement security. Let's look at data published by Craig Israelsen. He is a professor at Brigham Young University, and he wrote *The Math of Gains and Losses*. He stated with his research that if you suffer a 35% portfolio loss, you only have a 61.1% chance of getting back to even over any five (5) year time period. This means that if you suffer a 35% portfolio loss, it's projected that almost 40% of the time you will not recover over the next five (5) years. That's a scary thought, isn't it? During retirement, you have to ask yourself one main question, do you really have five years to hope you get back up to even, not to make money, but hope that you just get back up to even? The answer is "NO!" You don't have five years during retirement to hope to get back up to even.

> **"If you suffer a 35% portfolio loss, you will only have a 61.1% probability of getting back to even over the next five years."**
>
> *According to "The Math of Gains and Losses," Craig L. Israelsen Ph.D. from Brigham Young University*

You have heard of the phrase "risk equals reward." So, based on the amount of potential risk you took from 1999 through 2013 in the stock market, the graph shows you should have been rewarded with a good rate of return, after all, you suffered a -46% loss followed by a -53% loss. But you weren't rewarded at all.

For all the risk you took, you would have been rewarded with a whopping 2.75% annual compounded increase to the S&P 500 Index before fees further reduced your returns. Is a 2.75% annual compounded increase, minus fees, worth all of the risk you took during this time period? Of course it wasn't, but 2.75% is a mathematical fact.

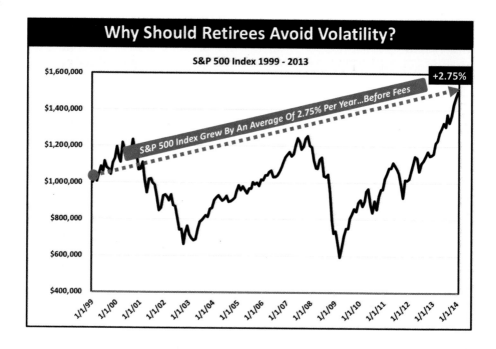

That's right, just 2.75% average compounded annual increase before fees. What if you were paying 3% or more in fees like we find the average retiree is paying? What did you really earn? Nothing.

Think back to when you were working, and the stock market was volatile, and you saw losses happening, but even so, over time you saw your account grow. Where do you think most of the growth of your accounts when you were working came from? The majority of your growth probably came from the additional contributions you made every year to your accounts while you were working.

If all these results weren't amazing, in our research we found something even more astounding. There was a time period between 2000 and 2013, that was a period of 13 years, where the S&P 500 Index started at 1,469 points in January 2000 and ended at 1,469 points in January 2013.

This means for 13 years the S&P 500 Index increased by an average of 0%, basically a 0% annual increase before fees. If you paid 3% fees, that means for 13 years you lost 3% per year compounded for 13 years. These are facts, black and white, there's no gray area. Someone should have provided you this data before you invested the first time. But it's not too late to learn about your money. By truly learning about, and understanding your money, you can make better decisions with how much risk you're willing to take and hopefully obtain that type of rate of return you're shooting for.

If you had earned a 0% rate of return for 13 years before you retired while you were working, you could make changes to try and still succeed during retirement:

- You could have decided to save more.
- You could have decided to retire later.
- You could have decided you could live on significantly less income during retirement.
- You could have decided to retire anyway and then work at a different job either full-time or part-time.

But what if this had happened after you had already retired? You can't really decide to save more during retirement. You could try and get your old job back, or find a new job, but neither option may be viable or attainable. You can live on less income but you would sacrifice the retirement lifestyle you planned for and dreamed about. But you could probably find a part-time job to replace the lost income, but you'd have to work at the part-time job for as long as you live.

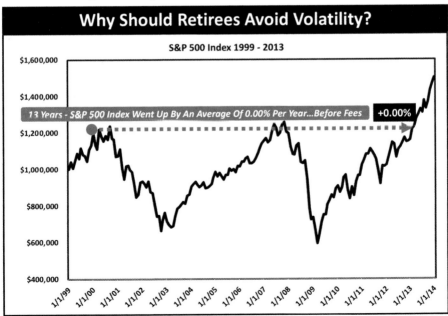

As a retiree, the most important thing to understand about stock market volatility and large losses is that they will significantly reduce or completely eliminate the amount of income you can take out of your accounts and that your money may very well run out during your lifetime. As a retiree, you must always remember the number one (1) reason you saved money while you were working; so that you could use the assets for income to protect and improve your lifestyle when you were retired. You didn't work hard and save your money to watch it go up and down and not use it, or worse, lose it during retirement; you saved it to provide you income that would not run out for as long as you lived. And above all, you didn't save it to have to worry about it, you saved it so you'd have less worries during retirement.

If your assets are acting volatile, just described with a -46% loss between 2000 through 2002 and then followed by a -53% loss over 16-months between November 2007 through March 2009, it is mathematically impossible for you to take out a high level of income out of your assets that is guaranteed to last for as long as you live. The higher the portfolio volatility, the less income you can take out of your accounts.

Industry Standard Safe Income Withdrawal Rates

If an asset exhibits volatile behavior like the S&P 500 Index graph above, you can't take a high level of income and be assured it will last for as long as you live. Volatile asset behavior equals volatile income behavior. Retirees want to know how much income they can safely take out of their assets? This question is loaded with potholes. What does "safely" mean to you? Does it mean that no matter what, under all stock market conditions with 100% certainty, your income will continue to be paid to you for as long as you live? Are you OK with a 90% probability that your money won't run out? An 80% probability that your money won't run out? A 70% probability that your money won't run out? If your income isn't guaranteed to last for as long as you live, if there is any chance whatsoever you could run out of income, you will continue to worry.

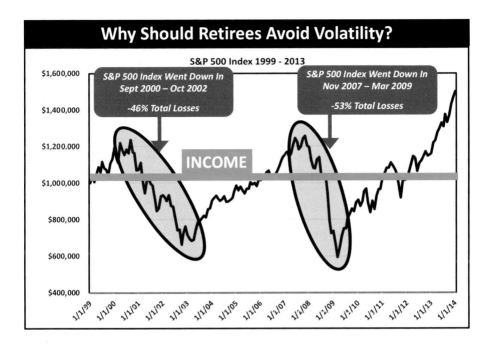

For years, the financial industry has set what ended up being standards in "safe income withdrawal rates." You can probably remember way back when, maybe 30+ years ago, it was thought the "safe income withdrawal rate" was "6%" – meaning you could take out 6% income from your assets every year with a high probability of not running out of money. Then around 20 years ago, as the stock market got more volatile and interest rates declined, the "safe income withdrawal rate" dropped to 5%. About ten years ago, the thought was that 4% might be the new industry standard "safe income withdrawal rate." Then amazingly, with the second longest bull stock market in history running strong, 2-3 years ago the "safe income withdrawal rate" was reduced again to 3%. It is currently being debated whether the 3% should be reduced to 2.5%.

One of the most important aspects in understanding the significance of "safe income withdrawal rates" is that this is not a rate that guarantees your income will last for as long as you live, it is the rate the financial industry believes provides you a "high probability" your income will not stop. To us, rather than calm your fears of running out of money during your lifetime, "safe income withdrawal rates" actually continue to fuel your anxiety that you could run out of money. Because of this, it is our opinion that "safe income withdrawal rates" should be based on written

85

contractual guarantees that the income will be paid to you for as long as you live and will not be affected by stock market volatility or losses. Now that is what we think should be the definition of "safe income."

CHAPTER 5

IS THE STOCK MARKET BEHAVIOR BETWEEN 1999 THROUGH 2013 TYPICAL OR ABNORMAL?

BY DAN AHMAD & JIM FILES

After seeing the S&P 500 Index data for the time period between 1999 through 2013, many people asked us if this time period was unique or if it was the norm? To answer this question, a more comprehensive analysis was performed. We went back to 1996 and reviewed every 15-year time period starting with 1996 through 2010 and ending with 2003 through 2018. The results from the analysis are eye-opening:

Abnormal Behavior Or Par For The Course?
9 MOST RECENT 15 YEAR PERIODS OF THE S&P 500 INDEX – BEFORE FEES
Three (3) 15-Year Time Periods Starting 1996
• 1996 through 2010 – <u>5.12%</u> annual compounded increase
• 1997 through 2011 – <u>3.82%</u> annual compounded increase
• 1998 through 2012 – <u>2.83%</u> annual compounded increase
15-Year Time Period Between 1999 Through 2013
• 1999 through 2013 – <u>2.75%</u> annual compounded increase
Five (5) 15-Year Time Periods Starting 2000
• 2000 through 2014 – <u>2.27%</u> annual compounded increase
• 2001 through 2015 – <u>2.96%</u> annual compounded increase
• 2002 through 2016 – <u>4.55%</u> annual compounded increase
• 2003 through 2017 – <u>7.69%</u> annual compounded increase
• 2004 through 2018 – <u>5.57%</u> annual compounded increase
4.17% Average Compounded Annual Increase Before Fees

There are nine (9) separate 15-year time periods from 1996 through 2018. The average annual compounded increase to the S&P 500 Index during all time periods was 4.17% before fees.

- If you paid 1% in fees, and earned returns equal to the S&P 500 Index, maybe you only netted 3.17%.
- If you paid 2% in fees, and earned returns equal to the S&P 500 Index, maybe you only netted 2.17%.
- If you paid 3% in fees, which includes direct and hidden fees, like the typical retiree is paying, and earned returns equal to the S&P 500 Index , maybe you netted 1.17% per year.

What was really surprising was that there was only one (1) 15-year time period that yielded an average annual compounded increase of 6% or higher, that would be considered only minimally acceptable based on the amount of risk you had to take, and that was the time period from 2003 through 2017 – which included one of the strongest bull markets throughout US stock market history. During this time period the S&P 500 Index increased an average of 7.69% per year before fees. After fees, you were back down into the unacceptable level. The time periods we studied include a total of 23 years. For most of our clients, this is a good number to use based on their life expectancies. Anything else did not make sense to use. It's important to understand the annual average increases to the S&P 500 Index were so low because of the very significant losses that were incurred in every one of the nine (9) 15-year time periods. The market did make a lot of money, but the large losses reduced the actual net after loss returns to these unacceptable levels.

The key is to remember that the stock market has always been volatile and always will be volatile.

The truths about the stock market include:

1. The stock market will probably always have some periods of significant gains.
2. The stock market will probably always have some periods of significant losses.
3. The stock market will probably always have some periods of 0% growth.

4. The stock market will probably not provide a consistent annual return that you can rely on for a consistent amount of income guaranteed for as long as you live.

5. During retirement, you must protect yourself against stock market volatility.

CHAPTER 6

DO MARKET HIGHS MEAN GOOD THINGS FOR INVESTORS?

BY DAN AHMAD & JIM FILES

The stock market has hit all-time highs. That should be great for investors. Over the last few years, how many times have you heard the stock market has hit all-time highs? Probably a thousand times, sometimes you hear it 20 times in a day. Well, that should be great for investors. What we found is most retirees and soon-to-be retirees don't feel like their portfolios have hit all-time highs. Do you? To understand the true effect of stock market high points, let's examine the Standard & Poor's 500 Index, the Dow Jones Industrial Average, and the NASDAQ, starting on January 1, 2000 and ending on December 31, 2018:

Index	S&P 500		DJIA		NASDAQ	
Starting Index Value	1/1/00	1,469	1/1/00	10,940	1/1/00	4,069
Ending Index Value	12/31/18	2,506	12/31/18	23,327	12/31/18	6,635

Based on this data, it looks like all three (3) major stock market indices did extremely well; and that is what the financial industry and your broker/advisor want you to think. It looks like a home run and makes you feel like all the risk you took was worth it because you made a ton of money. The problem is that these numbers are very deceiving. The following graph shows the actual compounded annual increases to all three (3) indices before any reduction for fees you would have to pay.

Index	S&P 500		DJIA		NASDAQ	
Starting Index Value	1/1/00	1,469	1/1/00	10,940	1/1/00	4,069
Ending Index Value	12/31/18	2,506	12/31/18	23,327	12/31/18	6,635
Annual Compounded Increase Before Fees	2.85%		4.06%		2.61%	

In January 2000, the Standard & Poor's 500 Index was at 1,498. Then 19 years later on December 31, 2018, the Index was at 2,506, an increase of 1,008 points, which sounds like a huge gain. The problem is, that's only a 2.85% average compounded increase per year for 19 years. And it's important to note this 2.85% average annual compounded increase includes the huge gains the stock market produced since 2009 in the longest bull stock market in history. If you think about all the volatility you went through during these 19 years, all for a 2.85% average increase, ask yourself, if it was worth it? Did the risk equal the return? Was it worth going through two (2) separate approximately -50% market crashes for this type of growth? And maybe even more importantly, the 2.85% average annual compounded increase is without any reduction for fees. If you earned 2.85%, but paid 3% in fees like you may very well be, what was your real return? Right about -0.15%.

Then we can look at the Dow Jones Industrial Average. The Dow looked like it really made a lot of money. In January 2000, the Dow was at 10,940. Then 19 years later on December 31, 2018, the Index was at 23,327, an increase of an astonishing 12,387 points! Your brain right now is shouting "HUGE GAIN! HUGE GAIN! HUGE GAIN!" But alas, this isn't the case. This is another example of financial illusion. The Dow had an average annual compounded increase of 4.06% per year for 19 years before any reduction for fees. How about the NASDAQ? The NASDAQ started in 2000 at 4,069 and ended on December 31, 2018 at 6,635. Looks like a big gain, but the NASDAQ had an average annual compounded increase of 2.61% per year for 19 years before any reduction for fees.

When retirees think about their assets, and what has happened to them since 2000, most people think they have done exceptionally well. Many thinking they have earned between 8%-12% on average every year. But to date, we have never seen one (1) person who has earned these types of returns during the time period we are examining.

Retirees think they have earned huge rates of return because:

- The stock markets as outlined previously have hit all new record highs.
- The index numbers look like they've made huge gains.
- You have made some very big gains in individual years.
- If you were working during this time period, your main growth was from your ongoing contributions.
- You have recovered from large losses.
- Your broker or advisor has told you that you have made huge gains.

Here is why you probably didn't come close to getting an 8%-12% annual compounded rate of return:

- The data shows the S&P 500 Index averaged an annual increase of 2.85% during the 19-year time period between 2000 through 2018, the Dow averaged 4.06%, and the NASDAQ average 2.61% per year, all before fees.
- It's very difficult to earn stock market rates of return, as we believe based on our research that less than 5% of all money managers can beat the stock market over any five (5) year-time period. DALBAR reported the average equity mutual fund investor earned 3.98% per year in stock mutual funds over the last 30 years ending December 31, 2016.
- You had to pay fees, in many cases 3% or higher per year.
- You lost close to -50% in 2000 through 2002 and then had to make a +100% gain just to recover, before you made any gain.
- You lost approximately -50% again in 2007 through 2009 and then had to make another +100% gain just to recover, before you made any gain.

The majority of retirees we have met with to provide them a 2nd Opinion About Their Money stated that just recently they have finally gotten ahead from where they were before the stock market crashed in 2000 and again in 2008. This assumes they did not make any more contributions to increase their portfolio values.

Sit back and think about these questions: *Have you ever wondered why your account didn't grow as much as you thought it should? Did you ever lose far more than you ever imagined? Did it ever seem like the only growth you realized was from the additional deposits you were making to your accounts? Did it seem like a long time from when you lost money to when you finally recovered? Did you worry about your money? Did you feel confused about your money?* For most retirees, if they are honest, they have to answer "yes" to all these questions.

We recently performed a rate-of-return audit for a new potential client:

- In 2000, Bob had $1,500,000 in his portfolio.
- By 2002, his portfolio was worth $810,000 after the 2000-2002 stock market crash.
- By 2007, his portfolio was back up to $1,425,000.
- By March 2009, his portfolio was back down to $785,000.
- By December 2017, his portfolio was back up to $2,250,000.
- Bob feels like he has made a huge rate of return, his portfolio value is now $2,250,000! He started with $1,500,000 and now he had $2,250,000!
- Bob made a net 2.27% annual compounded rate of return.
- Bob was sad to hear he would have made more money if he would have bought 5-year CD's.

CHAPTER 7

LOSSES ARE VERY HARD TO RECOVER

BY DAN AHMAD & JIM FILES

Brokers and advisors love to talk about the huge gains you have made in the past, are currently making, or will make in the future, in the market. Hey, we get it, talking about huge gains and making a lot of money is a lot more fun than talking about big losses. We have previously discussed that huge gains may happen for the moment, but they can just as quickly and easily disappear if your assets are left "naked in the market." You may get a good gain in one (1) year or two (2) years only to have the gains and part of your original principal wiped out with a big loss in year three (3). We have found that the vast majority of brokers and advisors love to talk about big gains but they don't like to talk about big losses. This book was written for retirees, so your focus should be on risk mitigation first, and return second. Why? Because our clients, retired people just like you, do not want, and literally can't afford, to lose any of the assets they worked so hard to accumulate. They want to make competitive rates of return, but they do not want to take excessive risks in doing so.

Right now, without even knowing it, because you have never been told by your broker or advisor, there is a high probability your current portfolio could lose -30%, -40%, or -50% if we have another stock market crash like the Financial Crisis of 2008. We believe there will be more stock market crashes during your lifetime; it's not <u>if</u> there will be any more crashes, it's <u>when</u> will the crashes happen and how severe will they be. So here are two (2) extremely important questions for you:

Question #1: *"As a retiree would you be helped more by a +50% gain or hurt more by a -50% loss?"*
Every single retiree client we ask this question replies they would be

far more hurt by a -50% loss than they would be helped by a +50% gain.

Question #2: *"As a retiree do you want to try and be rich or do you want to guarantee you will never be poor?"*
Every single retiree client we ask this question replies they never want to run out of money, they never want to be poor.

So, based on the responses to these two (2) questions, if the overwhelming number of retirees don't want to incur a large loss and want to guarantee they will not run out of money for as long as they live, why are their assets almost always positioned not to meet their goals? It's simply because their current broker or advisor, or the internet or a friend, tells them it's OK to take risk. In fact, they tell you that you must take risk to get a high rate of return so you will succeed. They may not be telling you the truth. We have found during retirement, the more risk you take; the more you will lose in a stock market crash, the less income you can safely take out of your assets, and the higher the probability that you will run out of money during your life.

What would you do right now if you found out your current portfolio could lose -30%, -40%, -50%, or even more in the next stock market crash? You'd better not say you would just ride it out, because as a retiree, you no longer have the time to make up large losses. So, why are we harping on all of this? It's simply because losses are very hard to recover from. Losses are much harder to recover than you would think. Losses are much harder to recover than what seems fair. Losses are far more painful than gains are pleasurable. And for retirees, losses are much harder to recover if you are taking income off of the assets and if you are paying fees.

Using common sense, it just seems if you lose 10% you should only have to make 10% to be back up to even, to recover fully. If you lose 20%, you should only have to make 20% to be back up to even, to recover, sound right? If you lose 50%, it seems like you should only have to earn 50% to recover, to get back up to even. You lost 50%, you made 50%, BINGO – you're even! Unfortunately, the math does not work that way. The bottom line is that every loss requires a bigger recovery gain than the original loss that was incurred just to break even. Many of you right now are thinking or commenting out-loud, "Say What?" But it's true.

The chart below shows what we call the "No Loss Limit" range of potential portfolio losses. Here is the bottom line:

- **If you lose -50% you must make +100% just to recover, if you lose -40% you must make +66.7% just to recover, if you lose -30% you must make +42.9% just to recover, and if you lose -20% you must make +25% just to recover.** *Does this seem fair? NO! But is it mathematically accurate? YES!*

Losses Are Very Hard To Recover From						
	Percent Loss	Portfolio Value Before Loss	Loss	Portfolio Value After Loss		Recovery Gain Needed To Break-Even
	-50% Loss	$1,000,000	($500,000)	$500,000		100%
No Loss	-40% Loss	$1,000,000	($400,000)	$600,000		66.7%
Limit	-30% Loss	$1,000,000	($300,000)	$700,000		42.9%
	-20% Loss	$1,000,000	($200,000)	$800,000		25.0%

How easy is it to make +100%, +66.7%, +42.9%, or even +25.0%? And how long will it take to make it up? Are you guaranteed to recover your losses in a certain amount of time? What if you are taking income out and you suffer a big loss, is it even more difficult to recover and make the loss back up? What if you are paying fees and you suffer a big loss, doesn't this make it even harder to recover? This is why all retirees must protect their assets against all potential large losses. Let's say a hypothetical retiree has a $1,000,000 IRA and then loses -50% in a Stock market crash. That $1,000,000 IRA is now down to $500,000. If the retiree makes a +50% gain on the $500,000, which is a big gain, has the IRA fully recovered? No, because +50% of $500,000 is only a $250,000 gain, so now the $500,000 IRA has only grown to $750,000. The retiree is still down $250,000 from the original starting $1,000,000 IRA value. The retiree needs to make a +100% rate of return on the $500,000, to make a $500,000 gain, to fully recover and just be back to the $1,000,000 starting IRA value before the whole nightmare started. And you cannot put yourself in this position during retirement.

The diagram below illustrates the comparison:

Imagine what it would feel like to suffer a -50% loss on your $1,000,000 portfolio, reducing your portfolio down to $500,000. Then you were able to earn +50% on the $500,000, and your portfolio only grew back to $750,000. Can you imagine what a disaster that would feel like? You must avoid all large losses.

CHAPTER 8

AN ACCURATE MEASUREMENT OF YOUR TRUE RISK

BY DAN AHMAD & JIM FILES

How much money did you lose in 2008? 20%? 30%? 40%? Many retirees reply -50%. Remember back to 2008, did you think you could lose as much money as you lost? Did you actually know how much risk you were taking before the loss? Did your broker or advisor make you keenly aware of how much you could lose if the stock market had a significant loss?

If you were made aware you were taking so much risk before the loss, meaning you were actually told you could lose -30%, -40%, -50% or even more of your portfolio, would you have gone ahead and taken that amount of risk? Probably not, but the sad thing is that you were never given the opportunity because your broker or advisor never discussed this aspect of portfolio risk management with you. Or if they did, they stated incorrectly that you were invested conservatively, or moderately, you were very diversified, and you didn't really have that much risk. If you had discussed this with your broker or advisor, and they had provided you accurate data, you wouldn't have lost as much money as you did in 2008 because you would have immediately reduced your risk level. In recent reports, consumers state only 43% of their advisors discuss bear stock markets, meaning only about 4 out of every 10 advisors discusses the potential for losses with their clients.

Why is it that most retirees are taking far more risk with their assets than they really want to take? How many 65-year-old people really want to have a -40% risk factor, meaning if we have another 2008-type stock market crash they would lose -40% of their assets? They think they're taking 10% risk, but many are actually taking 40% risk. This means in

99

a big stock market drop they could potentially lose up to 40% of their assets, and that's just not acceptable during retirement. So why do so many retirees, maybe including you, have this much risk currently in their portfolio? It's because they have not been accurately measured for how much risk they want to take.

It's like buying a pair of shoes. If you guess at your size, or worse, if your shoe salesman guesses your size without measuring your foot, you buy the shoes, they don't fit, and now you have a problem. You have wasted money and you are not going to feel comfortable if the shoes are too tight or if they are too loose. If they are too tight, they may cause pain and long-term physical damage to your feet. If they are too loose, they may cause blisters and cause you to trip and fall, potentially causing permanent injury. And all of this could have been avoided if your feet had been measured before you bought the shoes.

The same goes with investing your money. You should not invest your money until the true risk you want to take is measured, until you know how much risk you are really willing to take (your shoe size), and until your portfolio allocation matches your risk (the shoes you buy are the right size). This seems like common sense. This seems like exactly what you should do. But it likely has never been done for you … yet. So how do you actually and accurately measure your true risk tolerance? It's not by filling out a 10-20 question risk tolerance questionnaire your broker or advisor has had you complete in the past. We have found these standardized forms will almost always advise you to take more risk than you really want to. We've seen retirees that filled out these types of questionnaires before 2008 and stated they wanted to be conservative, end up losing -30%, -40%, -50%, and even more. How could this happen when they filled out the questionnaire? It's because the questionnaire doesn't work.

First of all, let's discuss how risk should be defined for a retiree. For a retiree, risk should be defined as "how much money you are really willing to lose at this time of your life." There is a two (2) step process in establishing your true risk tolerance:

Step 1 – Help you decide how much risk you are really willing to take by having you state specifically, and putting it down in writing, how much you are really willing to lose.

Step 2 – Create a portfolio that matches the exact amount of risk you are really willing to take in Step 1.

In this chapter we will discuss Step 1, and in a later chapter we will discuss Step 2. During retirement you have to rearrange the priorities for your portfolio. When you were younger, it was OK that your top portfolio priority was getting the higher rate of return possible with risk reduction being pushed far down the list. But now retired, your number one (1) investment priority must be to preserve your portfolio by eliminating all large losses.

One of the biggest mistakes a retiree can make is trying to link how much risk they are willing to take with the rate of return they are trying to achieve (basically trying to chase high returns). During retirement, this is a big NO-NO! You have to decide on how much you are willing to lose regardless of the rate of return desired. If you don't separate these, it is guaranteed you will take too much risk and lose more than you ever thought possible in the next market downturn.

We have created a system to first teach you about risk and then measure your risk tolerance accurately based on how much money you are really willing to lose. We start the process with our Risk Tolerance Tachometer. Our tachometer starts at zero (0) and goes all the way up to ten (10), with zero (0) signifying low risk and the ten (10) signifying high risk starting in the "yellow zone" and moving into the "red zone."

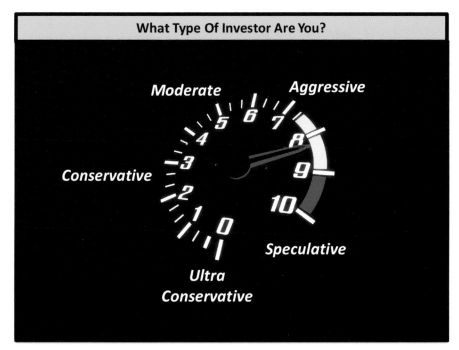

101

We strive to make numbers and finance fun and interesting so you can grasp important concepts without the stress and guilt many people have about not understanding their money. We want you to take this test and really be able to comprehend it.

So, the first question we ask is, "What type of investor are you?" We've created five (5) categories: ultra-conservative, conservative, moderate, aggressive, or speculative. We want you to define yourself as the type of investor you see yourself as or what type of investor your broker or advisor defines you as. You might say, "Well, I'm moderate." We'll say, "Okay, write that down." A married couple will each need to write down their answers separately, because each spouse may answer differently. You may be moderate and your spouse may be aggressive, or you may be conservative and your spouse may be moderate. Whatever the outcome, make sure to write it down.

The second question we ask is, "If the market goes down by 40% in a 12-month time period like it did in 2008, now that you're retired or close to retirement, how much are you willing to lose as a percentage of your total portfolio?" You may say something like "Well, I think I would be OK with a -30% loss". We ask you to write this percentage down and also have your spouse state his/her percentage and write that number down also.

> **If The Market Drops -40% Like It Did In Calendar Year 2008, What Percentage Of Your Assets Are You Willing To Lose?**

Typically, people will initially say something like "10%, 20%, 30%, and in rare occasions 40%." We ask them to write it down. Married couples will each need to write down their answers separately.

Some people say they are moderate and only want to lose a maximum of 10%. Some people say they are aggressive and only want to lose a maximum of 20%. Some people say they are conservative and don't want to lose anything at all – 0%. We now need to match up how they define themselves and the true amount of risk they want to take.

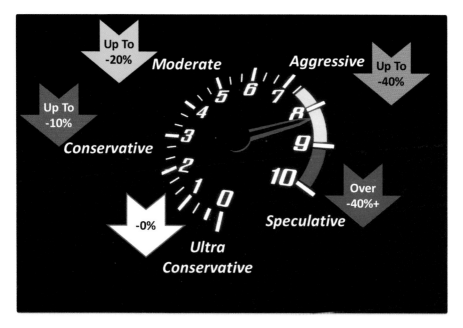

This chart shows if the stock market drops -40% like it did in 2008:

- If you're ultra conservative, you don't want to lose anything.
- If you're conservative, you must be willing to lose up to -10%.
- If you're moderate, you must be willing to lose up to -20%.
- If you are aggressive, you must be willing to lose up to -40%.
- If you're speculative, you must be willing to lose more than -40%; meaning you're willing to lose more than the stock market.

Let's say a retiree says they are aggressive and then says they don't want to lose more than -10%. Do you see the discrepancy? The description and the potential for loss don't match. They are really conservative and their portfolio allocation must be adjusted to match their true risk tolerance.

Once in a while, a retiree will say they are aggressive and willing to lose up to -40%. When we inform them a -40% loss on a $1,000,000 portfolio means they would have to be willing to lose -$400,000, almost every single retiree tells us they are not willing to lose -$400,000 of their $1,000,000 portfolio. Many retirees initially state a large loss such as -40% is acceptable because we find a high percentage of retirees really don't understand how loss percentages relate to their actual portfolio dollar losses.

Based on how much risk you are willing to take, meaning how much you are willing to lose, we now quantify your true risk tolerance with the following chart.

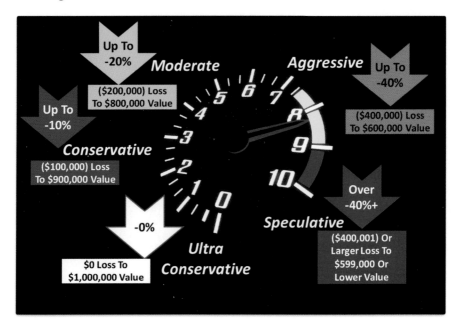

- If you're ultra-conservative it means you don't want to lose even $1 of your $1,000,000.
- If you're conservative it means you have to be willing to lose -10%, or -$100,000 of your $1,000,000, reducing your portfolio value to $900,000.
- If you're moderate it means you have to be willing to lose -20%, or -$200,000 of your $1,000,000, reducing your portfolio value to $800,000.
- If you're aggressive it means you have to be willing to lose -40%, or -$400,000 of your $1,000,000, reducing your portfolio value to $600,000.
- If you're speculative it means you have to be willing to lose more than -40%, or more than -$400,001 of your $1,000,000, reducing your portfolio value to $599,999 or less.

What we find at the end of this exercise is that most retirees say something different than what they originally said. Initially, most say they can handle more risk because the risk was not attached to a specific amount of dollar loss. But when specific dollars are pinpointed as potential losses, everyone wants to take less risk. The reason: *percentages are not personal – but dollars are personal.*

In our combined 425+ years of experience, we asked thousands of retirees how much risk they want to take, meaning how much are they really willing to lose. Once they understand risk, and how much a large loss can significantly decrease their financial security, over 99% of retirees we have interviewed gravitate to feeling comfortable with a risk tolerance profile of between -5% and -10%, meaning they never want to be in a position to ever lose more than -5% up to a maximum of -10% of their assets.

This maximum risk tolerance of -5% to -10% fits perfectly with what we call our *Golden Rule Of 5% to 10%*. We will discuss this Rule in-depth in the next chapter.

CHAPTER 9

THE GOLDEN RULE OF 5% TO 10%

BY DAN AHMAD & JIM FILES

Because of how painful losses can be to retirees, we created *The Golden Rule Of 5% To 10%*. The Golden Rule Of 5% To 10% states you should never have your assets positioned to lose more than -5% to a maximum -10% of your total portfolio, even if the stock market crashes and loses -50% or more.

If you are like most retirees, right now you may be very nervous, anxious, and worried about your money simply because you are afraid of suffering through the next big stock market crash. You are not sure how much you could lose, but you know at this time in your life, a big loss could be devastating. If your money is currently unprotected in the stock market, you should be nervous because none of us like uncertainty. Following *The Golden Rule Of 5% To 10%* will help decrease your worries.

The Golden Rule Of 5%-10%					
	Percent Loss	Portfolio Value Before Loss	Loss	Portfolio Value After Loss	Recovery Gain Needed To Break-Even
No Loss	-50% Loss	$1,000,000	($500,000)	$500,000	100%
	-40% Loss	$1,000,000	($400,000)	$600,000	66.7%
Limit	-30% Loss	$1,000,000	($300,000)	$700,000	42.9%
	-20% Loss	$1,000,000	($200,000)	$800,000	25.0%
	-10% Loss	$1,000,000	($100,000)	$900,000	11.1%
Golden	-9% Loss	$1,000,000	($90,000)	$910,000	9.9%
Rule	-8% Loss	$1,000,000	($80,000)	$920,000	8.7%
Of	-7% Loss	$1,000,000	($70,000)	$930,000	7.5%
5%-10%	-6% Loss	$1,000,000	($60,000)	$940,000	6.4%
	-5% Loss	$1,000,000	($50,000)	$950,000	5.3%

The first section of the chart above is called "No Loss Limit" which shows the tremendously negative impact of large stock market losses on your portfolio including -50% losses, -40% losses, -30% losses, and -20% losses coupled with the "Recovery Gain Needed To Break Even."

What we are discussing right now is called the "recovery factor," simply meaning how much do you need to earn after a loss just to break even. We created this "recovery factor" concept to make retirees aware of the true total risk they are taking. Think about it, is the true risk the -50% you could lose or is it the +100% you must earn to get back to even? *The answer: true risk is the combination of the initial loss followed by the recovery gain required to make up that loss.*

It's very important to remember that there are actually two (2) components to risk: the loss itself and the recovery gain needed before you just break even. From the chart above consider the -50% loss – step one (1) – of the risk and consider the +100% recovery gain – step two (2).

We call the "No Loss Limit" being "Naked In The Market," meaning you have no protection against the elements. The "No Loss Limit" section shows the following:

If you suffer a -50% portfolio loss, your $1,000,000 portfolio would lose -$500,000, dropping your portfolio value to $500,000 after the loss. You need a +100% recovery gain on your $500,000 decreased portfolio value just to get back to even at $1,000,000. How long would it take you to make a 100% gain just to get back up to even, not get ahead, just to recover? Do you have that amount of time to wait during retirement for it to recover before you use it for income? Probably not, because you're in retirement and you're not adding to those savings any longer. Are you guaranteed it will recover for sure? Are you guaranteed it will recover in a certain amount of time? Are you guaranteed it will recover if you are taking income distributions? You are not guaranteed any of these things.

This -50% type of stock market loss happened from 2000 through 2002 and then again from October 2007 through March 2009. If you lost -50% from 2000 through 2002, you needed to make +100% just to get back to even by 2007. Then you lost -50% again from October 2007 through March 2009, then had to make +100% from April 2009 through January 2013 just to break even again. And this doesn't account for the fees you paid and lost over that entire 13-year time period.

What if you suffer a -50% portfolio loss and you are taking income distributions out of the account? You have a big problem that may prove to be catastrophic to your long-term financial security as your money might run out.

If you suffer a -40% portfolio loss, your $1,000,000 portfolio would lose -$400,000, dropping your portfolio value to $600,000 after the loss. You need a +66.7% recovery gain on your $600,000 decreased portfolio value just to get back to even at $1,000,000. You need to understand what this is really saying. In this example, you have first lost -40%, and then you made 66.7% just to fight to get back to even. You haven't made any gain at all.

What if you lose 30% and your $1,000,000 dollars goes down to $700,000 during retirement? How would that feel? How much does $700,000 have to earn to get back up to even? You have to earn a 42.9% rate of return on the $700,000 just to get back up to even, not to make any money, just to get back to even.

If you suffer a -20% portfolio loss, your $1,000,000 portfolio would lose -$200,000, dropping your portfolio value to $800,000 after the loss. You need a +25% recovery gain on your $500,000 decreased portfolio value just to get back to even at $1,000,000.

How easy is it to make +25%, +42.9%, +66.7%, or +100% gains? Not very easy. Are you guaranteed to make these types of large gains immediately after a loss? Are you guaranteed you will make these types of large gains up over a certain time period after a loss? All these types of gains required for recovery are huge, and it could take a long time before you fully recover. That's why we've created *The Golden Rule Of 5% To 10%.*

The second section of the chart, directly below the "No Loss Limit" section highlighted in red is, *"The Golden Rule Of 5% To 10%"* – which is highlighted in gold. The concept is simple but is the most important thing for you to adhere to throughout your retirement: never be in a position to lose more than -5% up to a maximum of -10% of your portfolio. Why? Because -5% to -10% losses are easier to make up than -20% to -50% losses. Why? Because of the math!

If you suffer a 10% loss of your $1,000,000, your portfolio would drop to $900,000, and you would need to earn a +11.1% recovery gain to break even. The mathematical fact is that +11.1% is easier to make up than +25%, +42.9%, +66.7%, and +100%. Making up +11.1% is doable over a shorter time period.

What if you have a -9% loss and your portfolio drops to $910,000? A 9% loss requires a +9.9% recovery gain.

What if you have an 8% loss and your portfolio drops to $920,000? You need an 8.7% recovery.

A 7% loss dropping your portfolio to $930,000 requires a 7.5% recovery gain.

A 6% loss dropping your portfolio to $940,000 requires a 6.4% recovery gain.

And a 5% loss, meaning your $1,000,000 million goes down to $950,000 would only require a 5.3% recovery gain to get back up to even.

If you limit your losses to between -5% to -10%, that means your required recovery gains only are between +5.3% up to a maximum of +11.1%.

The mathematical fact is that it is easier to make recovery gains between +5.3% to +11.1% than it is to make recovery gains of between +25% to +100%.

Let's dive deep into what happens psychologically when you suffer a big loss during retirement. If you lose -20%, -30%, -40%, or -50%, you will be scared and won't want to invest aggressively and risk your money any longer. But to recover from a big loss, and if you need to make up gains of +25%, +42.9%, +66.7%, or +100%, how must you invest your money? Can you invest your money conservatively and hope to get these returns? The only chance, the only possibility you will have to potentially recover from a large loss is to invest aggressively. And think about it, this will be exactly opposite of what you will want to do. But if you limit your portfolio losses to between 5% to 10%, the recovery gains needed are significantly lower and you won't have to invest as aggressively after the loss to try and recover.

We have found that most retirees are comfortable with a risk tolerance between -5% to -10%, which fits perfectly with *The Golden Rule Of 5% To 10%*.

CHAPTER 10

BULLS, BEARS, AND THE ELEPHANT IN THE ROOM

BY DAN AHMAD & JIM FILES

When you think about it, the stock market is really like a wild animal. Beautiful, dangerous, unpredictable, and untamable. When you really think about the terms that are used in the stock market, it proves our point. The two (2) most notable terms are "bulls" and "bears." Does a bull seem like a nice friendly safe animal? Heck no. Does a bear seem like a warm, cuddly, huggable animal? Heck no again. They are wild, not to be messed with or taken lightly, never to turn your back on, never to take your eyes off, basically unpredictable, just like the stock market.

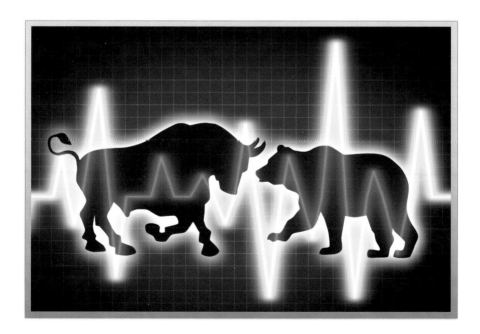

A bull is a large muscular animal that has horns and can be very dangerous. But on the other hand, the bull can provide some tasty steaks! A bull stock market means the stock market is going up, many times like a crazy ride, reminiscent of the bulls that run the streets in Pamplona, Spain that run over a lot of people who shouldn't have been trying to run with them in the first place. It is exciting, exhilarating and spiritual. Some people believe it requires courage to participate, while others believe it requires a lower IQ. Another example is trying to "ride a bull" in a rodeo. You are deemed a "winner" if you can ride the bull for seven (7) seconds, and everybody knows no matter what, you will get bucked off at some point. Bull riding is exciting, exhilarating, spiritual, and again some believe requiring courage while others believe requiring lower IQ's.

A bear is a large extremely powerful animal that has big claws and teeth and can be very dangerous. A bear stock market means the stock market is going down. Think of the stock market going down like a bear attacking you. You probably aren't going to win because in most cases you do not have any power or control over the bear.

Let's talk about the elephant in the room; let's talk about your money and that the stock market has been on a "bull run" since March 2009, recording the longest bull stock market in history. For almost ten (10) years the stock market has basically gone straight up, never suffering a 20% or larger loss. Why is this statistic so important? Simply because what goes up must come back down, the stock market has cycles, and now that you're retired, you can't afford a large loss.

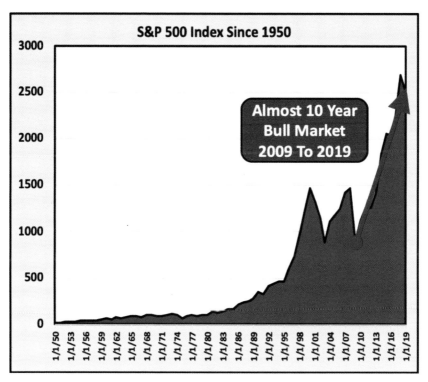

While it's important to understand the current bull stock market is almost ten (10) years old and counting, it's just as important to understand there have been 13 bear stock markets with average losses of -39.5% since 1929.

Bear Markets Since 1929 – The Market Drops An Average of -39.5%

There Have Been 13 Bear Markets Since 1929

Date	Percent Decline
October 9, 2007 - February 23, 2009	-52.50%
March 24, 2000 - October 9, 2002	-49.10%
July 16, 1990 - October 11, 1990	-19.90%
August 25, 1987 - December 4, 1987	-33.50%
November 28, 1980 - August 12, 1982	-27.10%
January 11, 1973 - October 3, 1974	-48.20%
November 29, 1968 - May 26, 1970	-36.10%
February 9, 1966 - October 7, 1966	-22.20%
December 12, 1961 - June 26, 1962	-28.00%
August 2, 1956 - October 22, 1957	-21.50%
May 29, 1946 - June 13, 1949	-29.60%
March 6, 1937 - April 28, 1942	-60.00%
September 7, 1929 - June 1, 1932	-86.20%
Average	-39.50%

This Means It Happens On Average Every 7 Years

To most people, learning that we've had 13 bear stock markets that average -39.5% losses since 1929 doesn't seem that bad, just doesn't seem that it happens very often. But this does mean -39.5% losses happen an average of every seven (7) years, and remember, we have been in a bull stock market that has lasted almost ten (10) years. So, what does all of this mean? The elephant in the room is that we are two (2) years overdue for one of the average -39.5% bear stock market declines that has happened every seven (7) years historically since 1929. Remember, it's not if the market will go down, it's when it will happen.

The easy thing to do is to pretend that there isn't an elephant in the room with you. Why would you want to dwell on losing money? Why would you want to worry about a big stock market loss? Because if you don't worry about it, and protect yourself against it, your retirement could be in jeopardy.

Every day we ask new potential clients, who are all retirees, if they believe there will be another -40% loss in the stock market? We are amazed that some people actually think we will never, ever, have another -40% stock market loss in their lifetimes. These are some ferociously optimistic people. You talk about those people who think the glass is one-half full, these people think the glass somehow refills itself!

When people tell us they don't think the stock market will ever have another big crash like 2008, we ask them this simple question: "Do you think you are smarter than Bill Gates?" They always laugh and say, "Of course I don't think I am smarter than Bill Gates." We tell them they must think they are way smarter than Bill Gates, because on February 28, 2018, Melia Robison reported in *Business Insider* that on February 27, 2018 Bill Gates stated, "That it is a certainty we will have another financial crisis and big stock market loss like 2008." Then we ask the same people if they think they are smarter than Warren Buffett. Now they laugh even harder and say, "Of course I'm not smarter than Warren Buffett." We then tell them in the same article Bill Gates said he and Warren Buffett talk about this subject and Warren Buffett agrees.

But whether you think there will be another big stock market loss in your lifetime or not, you have to study the past to make sure you don't make a big mistake now or in the future. The majority of people think big stock market losses are bad, terrible, maybe even a little bit evil by stealing a retiree's wealth. But as we have stated before, big stock market losses aren't bad, terrible, or evil, they are natural. They happen with regularity.

If you think the stock market will always go up and never go down, you probably shouldn't have money you need for your financial security invested in the stock market.

Big stock market losses are part of a normal long-term market and economic cycle. Think about it, if every seven (7) years on average since 1929 the stock market suffers a -39.5% loss, shouldn't you consider this normal? Shouldn't you plan that it will probably happen again? More importantly, shouldn't you plan that it will probably happen multiple times again during your lifetime? Isn't that a scary thought?

We have analyzed, based on historical data, and current life-expectancy tables, how many more -39.5% stock market losses retirees of different ages will potentially go through. One good piece of news is that the older you are, the lower the number of -39.5% losses you will probably go through. The bad news is that unless you are well into your 80's, you will probably experience one (1) or more -39.5% losses during your lifetime.

The chart below shows how many more -40% losses (actually a -39.5% loss rounded up) retired couples age 55, age 60, age 65, age 70, age 75, and age 80 should plan to live through. The chart below assumes the next -40% loss happens 24 months from now, and then each subsequent -40% loss happens every seven (7) years thereafter.

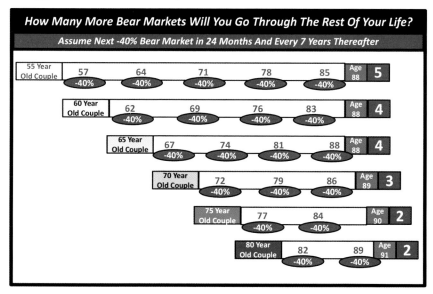

A 55-year old couple have a life expectancy to age 88, meaning at least one of them will live to age 88. The previous chart shows our current nine (9) year bull stock market continuing to grow for two (2) more years and then we have a -40% bear stock market loss when the couple is at age 57. Then seven (7) years later, they suffer a second -40% loss when they are at age 64. They suffer their third -40% loss when they are at age 71. They suffer their fourth -40% loss when they are at age 78. And they should plan on suffering their fifth -40% loss when they are at age 85. *This means a 55-year old couple should plan on going through five (5) more -40% losses during their lifetime.*

A 60-year old couple have a life expectancy to age 88, meaning on average, at least one of them will live to age 88. The previous chart shows our current nine (9) year bull stock market continuing to grow for two (2) more years and then we have a -40% bear stock market loss when the couple is at age 62. Then seven (7) years later, they suffer a second -40% loss when they are at age 69. They suffer their third -40% loss when they are at age 76. And they should plan on suffering their fourth -40% loss when they are at age 83. *This means a 60-year old couple should plan on going through four (4) more -40% losses during their lifetime.*

A 65-year old couple have a life expectancy to age 88, meaning on average, at least one of them will live to age 88. The previous chart shows our current nine (9) year bull stock market continuing to grow for two (2) more years and then we have a -40% bear stock market loss when the couple is at age 67. Then seven (7) years later, they suffer a second -40% loss when they are at age 74. They suffer their third -40% loss when they are at age 81. And they should plan on suffering their fourth -40% loss when they are at age 88. *This means a 65-year old couple should plan on going through four (4) more -40% losses during their lifetime.*

A 70-year old couple has a life expectancy to age 89, meaning on average, at least one of them will live to age 89. The previous chart shows our current nine (9) year bull stock market continuing to grow for two (2) more years and then we have a -40% bear stock market loss when the couple is at age 72. Then seven (7) years later, they suffer a second -40% loss when they are at age 79. And they should plan on suffering their third -40% loss when they are at age 86. *This means a 70-year old couple should plan on going through three (3) more -40% losses during their lifetime.*

A 75-year old couple have a life expectancy to age 90, meaning on average, at least one of them will live to age 90. The previous chart shows our current nine (9) year bull stock market continuing to grow for two (2) more years and then we have a -40% bear stock market loss when the couple is at age 77. And they should plan on suffering their second -40% loss when they are at age 84. *This means a 75-year old couple should plan on going through two (2) more -40% losses during their lifetime.*

An 80-year old couple have a life expectancy to age 91, meaning on average, at least one of them will live to age 91. The previous chart shows our current nine (9) year bull stock market continuing to grow for two (2) more years and then we have a -40% bear stock market loss when the couple is at age 82. And they should plan on suffering their second -40% loss when they are at age 89. *This means an 80-year old couple should plan on going through two (2) more -40% losses during their lifetime.*

What does this really mean for a 65-year old couple? Charles and Diane, a hypothetical 65-year old couple, have a $1,000,000 portfolio. If they suffer a -40% loss at age 67, their assets drop to $600,000, assuming no fees and no income distributions. Their $600,000 has to earn a +67% rate of return by age 74 just to recover their losses and be back at $1,000,000, assuming no fees and no income distributions.

Then at age 74, their $1,000,000 loses -40% again, and they are back down to $600,000. They have to earn a +67% rate of return a second time now by age 81 just to recover their losses and be back at $1,000,000, assuming no fees and no income distributions.

Then at age 81, their $1,000,000 loses -40% a third time, and they are back down to $600,000. They have to earn a +67% rate of return again (3rd time) by age 88 just to recover their losses and be back at $1,000,000, assuming no fees and no income distributions.

And at age 88, their life expectancy, they lose -40% again for the fourth time, decreasing their assets to $600,000 again. At this point, with only $600,000 left, what if they need long-term care? How will they feel leaving so much less to their beneficiaries? What does this type of movement remind you of? It should make you think of a hamster wheel. The poor little hamster is running as fast as he can, making a lot of noise, but not getting anywhere, just like your portfolio.

119

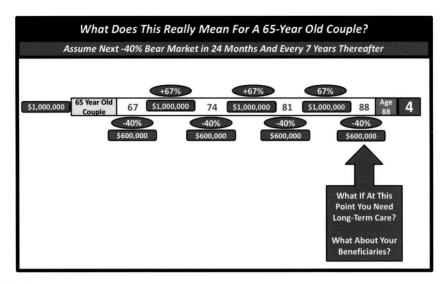

While this data may be quite shocking, it is very important in helping retirees look at what they must prioritize as their number one financial goal: *protect their assets against big stock market losses for their entire lifetimes.*

CHAPTER 11

THE BIG QUESTION?

BY DAN AHMAD & JIM FILES

We have discussed that many retirees don't know, and have never been told, how much risk they are taking. These people worry about losing money but don't realize the potential financial jeopardy they are in.

On the other hand, some retirees do realize they are taking significant risk, and do so willingly. Why have some retirees taken so much risk with their money even when they are retired? It's because they have been told they:

- Have to take risk to get high rates of return.
- Have to get high rates of return so they can receive high amounts of income.
- Need high rates of return to succeed during retirement.
- Don't have to worry about the risk because over the long-haul everything should be OK.
- Should "ride out" all market downturns.
- Will get 10% or higher annual returns if they stay invested.
- Are diversified with many different funds in a beautiful colored pie chart.

But as we examined in previous data, the stock market has not necessarily provided high rates of return. Let's remember the 2.85% annual increase, before fees, to the S&P 500 Index from 2000 through 2018. And let's remember the 4.17% average annual compounded increase, before fees, to the S&P 500 Index during the nine (9) separate 15-year time periods from 1996 through 2018.

But let's say regardless of the data we have provided, you are very optimistic about the stock market, and you think the market is going to go up by another +50% gain before we have the next crash, and you want to participate in the gain. But you are also a realist and know the market will have a -50% loss sometime in the future. You are also a realist and believe the higher the stock market goes up the higher the probability for a big stock market loss. So, the big question is "do you believe the stock market will keep climbing at its' current pace?"

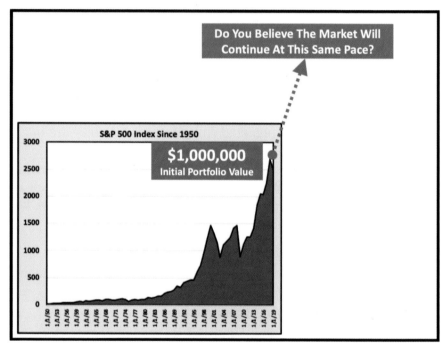

So, you think long and hard about this question and decide you have hit the "jackpot" because you are in a "no-lose" situation. You believe this because you think if the stock market goes up by +50% like you think it will, and then has a -50% loss like it inevitably will, you are convinced you haven't lost anything at all. You think if you make a +50% gain and then suffer through a -50% loss, you are back to even. You think you have no risk by leaving your money in the market, even after a nine (9) year bull stock market run.

Pretend right now you have a hypothetical portfolio with a value of $1,000,000. Remember you are very bullish on the stock market and believe there is still plenty of room for the stock market to grow another +50% before any major downturn. If your $1,000,000 grew by +50%, your new increased portfolio value would be $1,500,000. That would be a nice tidy little gain!

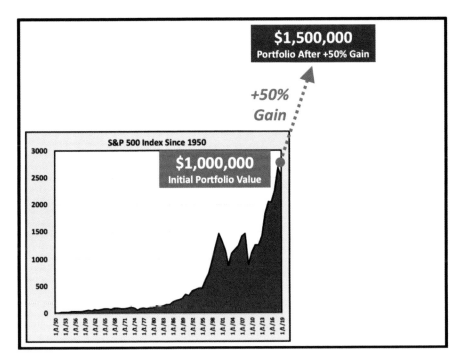

It's important to understand that this could happen. No one knows where the stock market will go from here.

    -- Up?
    -- Down?
    -- Sideways?

The important thing to realize at this point is that to make a large gain such as +50%, you have to be willing to take a significant amount of current and ongoing risk. It's even more important to remember as we previously discussed that losses cause significantly more financial pain than gains provide benefits. If your $1,000,000 grew to $1,500,000 you would probably be happy.

But math is not fair when it comes to your investments. If after your $1,000,000 grows to $1,500,000, you then suffer a -50% loss, you haven't just lost your +$500,000 gain, your $1,500,000 portfolio has decreased to $750,000 ($1,500,000 X -50%).

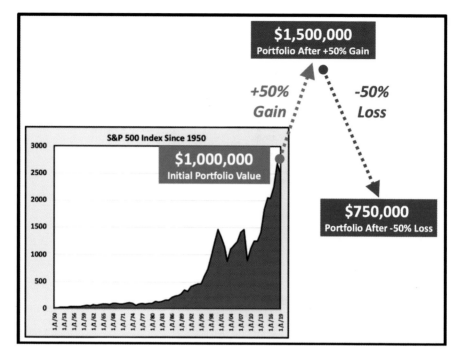

What if this all took place over the next five (5) years? Let's pretend that you made +50% over the next two (2) years and then lost -50% over the following three (3) years like what happened during the 2000 through 2002 Tech Bubble stock market crash. How would you feel if five (5) years from now your $1,000,000 that grew to $1,500,000 was only worth $750,000?

Moreover, the $750,000 value would need to be reduced by any income you took out during the time period and reduced by all fees you paid during the time period.

So even if the market does go up another +50% from here, all that does is bring us closer to the next -50% loss.

As a retiree, you don't benefit from this type of risk, no matter what your broker says.

CHAPTER 12

HAVE YOU BEEN TOLD TO "RIDE OUT THE MARKET" BEFORE?

BY DAN AHMAD & JIM FILES

Almost all investors have been told to "ride out the market," "hang in there," "you're in it for the long-run," and/or "don't worry the market will always come back up." When you think about it, did this advice really benefit you, or did it benefit your broker and his/her financial firm? When someone tells you to "ride out the market" what does this mean? Does it mean "riding the market up" or does it mean "riding the market down"? It means down. Has anyone ever made any money by "riding an investment down"? Nope.

Why do so many people give you this advice? It's because your broker doesn't want you to ever take your money out of the market, even when it's going down. Your broker has been trained to tell you, regardless of market conditions, to stay in the market no matter what. Here's why; if you take your money out of the market there are only three (3) things you can do after that:

1. You can put it back in the market with your broker.
2. You can keep it out of the market.
3. You can invest with a new broker.

Your broker only benefits from one (1) out of three (3) of these options. This means your broker has a 67% chance he/she will lose your business if he/she advises you to take your money out of the market. And let's face it, your broker is no dummy!

If you are retired, we never think you should ride out large market losses. You don't have the time to make back the losses; the more volatile your portfolio is, the less income you can take out, and if you take out income during and after a big loss, there is a higher probability you will run out of money. Let's pretend it is the year 2000, you just retired, and you have $1,000,000 in your portfolio. Let's also assume you kept your money in the stock market as advised by your broker from 2000 through 2002 and 2007 through 2009. The chart below shows what would have happened between 2000 through 2018 if you could have earned returns equal to the S&P 500 Index, didn't pay any fees, didn't take any income out, and "rode out the market." The solid green line in the following chart shows your assets would have grown to $1,705,632 assuming you didn't take out any income and didn't pay any fees. At first glance, this seems pretty good, $1,000,000 grows all the way to $1,705,632, but wait, there's way more to it than meets the eye.

Assume you invested $1,000,000 in the stock market in January 2000. There are two (2) motivating emotions when it comes to investing: greed and fear. When you first invest your money, you are typically motivated by greed – you want to make a lot of money from your investment. But if you invested $1,000,000 on January 1, 2000, and went through the 2000-

2002 Technology Bubble and the 2008 Financial Crisis, the S&P 500 Index would have increased just 2.85% per year compounded through December 31, 2018. The 2.85% annual increase is denoted by the dotted black line in the following chart. The 2.85% annual increase is before any fees you would have paid. Was all the risk you took worth a 2.85% return before fees?

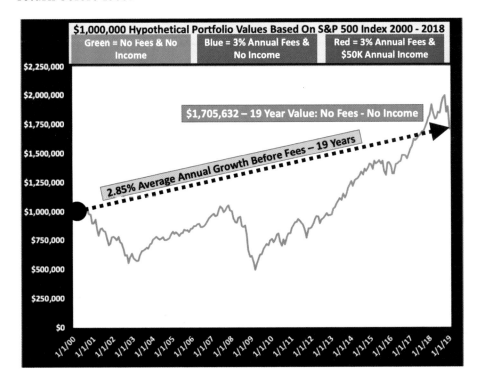

You may be thinking that during this time period you were still working and your accounts did much better than the chart we are showing. But think back and try to guess where the majority of your account increases came from? Can you guess? The majority of your account increases probably didn't come from market growth, <u>it came from your ongoing payroll contributions!</u> What if you were contributing $20,000 per year to your 401(k)/403(b)/457/SEP plan for five (5) years during a time your account increased by $100,000? The $100,000 was all from your contributions ($20,000 per year X five years = $100,000). You would have made more money during this time period if you used five (5) year CD's and kept rolling them over.

If you invested $1,000,000 on January 1, 2000 your portfolio would have lost significant value between 2000 through 2002. In 2002 when your portfolio had been decimated, you now experience the second emotion of investing: fear. Once you lose a significant amount of money, you no longer dream of those huge gains and how much money you are going to make, you only think about one (1) thing: getting back to even, getting your money back. The dotted purple line on the next chart shows your "break-even" or "recovery level" assuming you paid no fees at all and did not take out any income distributions.

So, if you rode the stock market down from 2000 through 2002, you finally got back to even by 2007. If you took all your money out right then, you would have been even. But because you now had recovered, you no longer were under the spell of fear, you now were captivated again by greed in the normal cycle of stock market ups and downs. Because the market had recovered and had "gone up" for five (5) straight years between 2003 through 2007, you expected the market to continue to go up and make you a lot of money just like you had hoped for in 2000 when you originally invested. Then the 2007 through 2009 Financial Crisis hit and your portfolio crashed again, not to fully recover until 2013. Then if you "rode it out" and stayed in the stock market the entire time, the reward was the previously mentioned 2.85% annual compounded growth rate before fees.

Now let's look at how fees would have affected the portfolio. Let's assume you paid 3% in total annual fees, including direct (visible) and indirect (invisible) fees. We have found the typical retiree is paying at least 3% in total fees without even knowing it. Without taking out any income distributions, your original $1,000,000 invested in 2000 would be worth $963,890 at the end of 2018 as shown by the solid blue line on the following chart. If you paid 3% in total fees from 2000 through 2018, and earned S&P 500 Index equivalent returns, your $1,000,000 would have decreased in value by -$36,110 from 2000 through 2018, all because of fees.

If this happened to you, all you could probably think about would have been getting back to even. Let's assume you are retired and 65 years old in 2000. The market crashes and you decide you will start using your assets for income as soon as you recover. When did you recover and start using your money? When did the solid blue line intersect with the dotted purple line? Not until almost 2018! That means in 2018, you would finally have the $1,000,000 you originally invested in 2000 back in your account!

You can also see on the chart below the true cost of 3% in fees being $741,742 from 2000 through 2018. This is because there is a negative compounding effect from having less in your portfolio after paying the fees and then having to try and make up for the big losses. You basically fall farther, and farther, and farther behind. It's important to note that the blue line shows no income distributions coming out, it only shows fees being assessed.

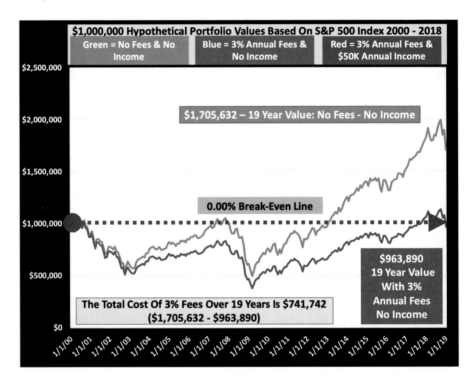

Now let's assume you are the same 65-year old who is retired. But now let's further assume you need to take out 5% of your $1,000,000, or $50,000 per year starting in 2000 to maintain your lifestyle. The chart on the following page shows what happened if you took out $50,000 of income per year starting in 2000, and paid your 3% in total annual fees, you'd be completely out of money by March 1, 2013, as shown by the solid red line in the following chart.

$1,000,000 Hypothetical Portfolio Values Based On S&P 500 Index 2000 - 2017

Green = No Fees & No Income | Blue = 3% Annual Fees & No Income | Red = 3% Annual Fees & $50K Annual Income

$1,705,632 – 19 Year Value: No Fees - No Income

$963,890 - 3% Annual Fees – No Income

$0 Portfolio Value On 3/1/2013 After 3% Annual Fees & $50,000 Annual Income

You probably wonder how it could work this way? It would happen this way because:

1. You were taking income distributions from a very volatile asset.
2. The asset, the stock market, had two (2) large losses.
3. You paid fees of 3%.
4. The stock market only increased by 2.85% per year before fees.

Here's the summary:

1. You took $50,000 of income for 13 years, totaling $650,000 of distributions.
2. At the end of 13 years you had $0 left in your portfolio.
3. Your broker got paid for all 13 years between 2000 through March 1, 2013.
4. Wall Street got paid for all 13 years between 2000 through March 1, 2013.

Based on this information, who won? You? Your broker? Wall Street? You can cross "You" out!

CHAPTER 13

BUT THE BIGGER QUESTION IS ...

BY DAN AHMAD & JIM FILES

"Whether the stock market crashes or not...
do you really want to have any of your retirement assets...
those assets you need to provide you income for as long as you live...
in anything that could crash and ruin your retirement?"

Retirement Nest Eggs

Most retirees will answer this question with a resounding "No, I do not want my retirement assets in anything that could crash!" If this is true, why do so many retirees have a large portion of their retirement assets, the assets they saved to provide them income for as long as they live, in a portfolio that has a high probability of *crashing multiple times during their lives*? Why are they risking their retirement security? It's simply because of the advice they are currently being given. Either their broker is having them take too much risk, or an outside service is having them take too much risk. Let's look at examples of each:

1. *Their broker is having them take too much risk.*
   We met with a new client we will call Larry, who was referred to our firm by his brother. Larry is age 68, married to Sheila, who is 62 years old, and they've had a broker for 30 years who has become one of Larry's friends. We asked Larry how much risk he thought he had and how much he thought he would lose, if we had another 2008 Financial Crisis when the stock market crashed -53.8%. Larry said he had recently met with his broker friend and had requested that the risk in his portfolio be reduced significantly because he was going to retire soon. Larry's broker told him not to worry, and he would modify the portfolio into a "conservative allocation" model.

   We completed a risk analysis of Larry's portfolio, and discovered if we had another 2008 Financial Crisis when the stock market crashed -53.8%, Larry's portfolio would be projected to lose -55.2%. Larry had $1,900,000 of assets, meaning his current portfolio would lose -$1,048,800 with a -55.2% loss, leaving him $851,200 of remaining assets, requiring a +123.2% recovery gain just to break even as follows:

Starting Portfolio Value	$1,900,000
-55.2% Loss	-($1,048,800)
=Portfolio Value After -55.2% Loss	= $851,200

=Portfolio Value After -55.2% Loss	$851,200
+123.2% Recovery Gain	+$1,048,800
=Ending Portfolio Value After +123.2% Recovery Gain	=$1,900,000

This portfolio was judged by his current broker to be "conservative." You probably are thinking "no way, this can't be true," Larry's current broker couldn't or wouldn't think the portfolio on the previous page, which had a calculated risk profile of -55.2%, was actually "conservative." But unfortunately, the truth is, we analyze supposed "conservative portfolios" almost daily that have risk profiles of -30%, -40%, -50%, and even – 60%.

Brokers are trained to always tell you, "they will get you high rates of return," that you need to "ride out the market" and "hang in there," that "you're in it for the long-run" and "don't worry, the market will always come back up." Brokers are trained to say you aren't taking too much risk, but invariably, most people are. Brokers are trained in this way because they are far more afraid that you'll leave them because you won't get a high enough rate of return versus leaving them because you lost money.

Why is this? If the market goes up everyone should make money; you are not worried about losing money, so the only way to measure success is to see how much you made. If you "don't make enough," brokers are afraid you will go around sniffing for higher returns from someone else. But if the market goes down, the broker assumes everyone lost money, so other brokers won't look any better. In addition, if you've lost money, you didn't want to leave your broker who says he/she can make up the losses for you rather quickly. But a quick recovery from a large loss during retirement is far easier said than done. How long will it take to make back a +123.2% recovery gain? The correct answer: a very long time. If Larry is taking income distributions from the account and paying fees on the account, he might never make the losses back up during his lifetime.

2. *An outside service is having them take too much risk.*
Over 99% of the retirees we work with saved money in a 401(k)/457/403(b) plan at their employer. To decide how to invest their money, most of these retirees had access to either an allocation recommendation to diversify their assets or to what is called a "target date" fund.

(i). <u>Asset allocation model recommendation by her 401(k)</u>
Let's assume Betty had an allocation recommendation program

at her company. She filled out some kind of generic questionnaire that gave her guidelines on how to allocate her assets. She felt she answered the questions in a very conservative way. She was told she was best suited for a "moderate portfolio" with an allocation that was 30% bond funds and 70% stock funds.

This sounded fine because:

1. She filled out the questionnaire.
2. Her employer approved the questionnaire and the recommendations.
3. The investment company making the recommendations was a huge well-respected company that advertised a great deal on TV.
4. She didn't have all her money in the stock market, so she assumed she couldn't lose too much.
5. She was invested in what she was told was a diversified portfolio of mutual funds, which reduced her risk.
6. She was told the individual mutual funds were less risky than individual stocks.
7. She really didn't know what all this meant, and most importantly, she didn't know, and was not told, how much she would lose if we had another stock market crash like we did during the 2008 Financial Crisis.

We asked Betty how much of her $1,000,000 account was she willing to lose? She said no more than a -10% loss, and she would prefer her risk being closer to -5%. A risk analysis revealed that Betty's portfolio, based on her recommended allocation, actually had a risk factor of -32.3%. This means if we have another 2008 type market crash, Betty should be prepared to suffer a -32.3% loss, meaning she better be prepared emotionally and financially to lose -$323,000 of her $1,000,000. She had better be comfortable with a reduced portfolio value of $677,000. And she had better be comfortable with having to obtain a 47.7% recovery gain just to get back to even. This made Betty very uncomfortable!

(ii). Target date fund

Let's assume Ron has a target date fund program available. Target date funds were created to provide an investor with what is supposed to be a time-sensitive risk-reduction method to invest their assets based on when they would need to use their assets for income when they retire. Basically, target date funds are meant to invest more aggressively the longer you have until you retire and reduce the risk the closer you get to your "target."

The theory is great, but like many theories, the outcome may be far different than was predicted and expected. One of the unexpected outcomes from the target date fund creation is that many employees are thought to believe that target date funds are designed "not to lose money", meaning they don't have the risk of principal loss. And this is not a good thing to believe because it's not true. Ron believed he had some risk investing in the target date fund, but believed his risk was limited to "about -10%." Ron was comfortable with a maximum -10% risk tolerance.

Using a Morningstar research tool, we were able to complete a risk analysis of Ron's target date fund, and it showed that this fund had lost -42.04% over a 12-month period between March 2008 and February 2009. This was four (4) times the risk Ron wanted, and believed, he was taking.

Another potential issue with a target date fund is that if you are unlucky enough to suffer a big loss, it is going to be even harder to make up the loss because the target date fund will invest for less growth as time goes on. So how would you like to suffer a big loss and then have an even lower probability you will recover? Doesn't sound too good, does it?

There is a potentially even bigger problem with target date funds. To take advantage of the bull stock market, some target date funds are thought to have increased their risk even more, to try and capture higher rates of return. A target date fund is designed so you will have less risk as you approach retirement, and because of this, provide a lower rate of return that is a result of the lower risk. But as we discussed before, when the stock market is going straight up, everybody measures success by outright performance. We have always been amazed at the high level of risk so many people have in their target date fund when we complete a risk analysis for them.

When we tell people how much risk they are carrying, at first, they don't believe us. They think there is no way they have that much risk. Then we show them data from 3rd party sources and they are literally shocked by the truth. They finally realize they just haven't had much risk and volatility in the last almost ten (10) years because the market has gone straight up, there have been no big losses.

Recently there was an eye-opening, hair-on-the-back-of-your-neck-raising article that was published that makes this discussion even more important and timely. On March 5, 2018, Yahoo Finance published a Reuters article written by Tim McLaughlin and Renee Dudley titled – *Special Report: Fidelity Puts 6 Million Savers On Risky Path To Retirement*. The authors stated Fidelity target date funds had not been performing well until 2014, at which time Fidelity made major changes, including increasing exposure to stocks, including emerging markets, no longer adhering to strict allocation models, and allowing managers to now try and time the market, with all these changes increasing the risk for investors, and without investors realizing they had significantly more risk. The article quotes Ron Surz, President of research firm Target Date Solutions as saying: "These funds with high concentrations in stocks are a ticking time bomb." Mr. Surz added, "The sector is even riskier today than 2008 when some funds lost more than -40%."

The authors wrote that a spokesperson for Fidelity, Vincent Loporchio, replied: "Today's American savers can handle more risk because they retire later and live longer, allowing more time to recover losses." In our minds and opinion, there are just so many things so violently wrong with what Mr. Loporchio said, it would take a whole different book to give our responses to Mr. Loporchio's comments justice. But there are three (3) main glaring points we see with Mr. Loporchio's comments:

1. The article makes it almost sound like Mr. Loporchio is saying Fidelity is deciding how much risk you want to take, and that you can handle it.

2. The article makes it almost sound like Mr. Loporchio is saying Fidelity is basically saying it's OK if you have losses because you are going to have more time to recover because you are working longer.

3. The article makes it almost sound like Mr. Loporchio is saying you may not be able to retire early because of big losses, and this is OK, because you can just work longer.

We of course can't tell you what Fidelity, or its' spokesman, is or isn't thinking, we can only provide our thoughts and opinions based on what was printed in the article.

The article adds that Jeff Holt, an analyst from Morningstar, said, "In the long run, the biggest risk in target date funds is that they won't meet investor expectations for avoiding losses."

CHAPTER 14

WHAT IS THE ONLY THING WORSE THAN A STOCK MARKET LOSS?

BY DAN AHMAD & JIM FILES

Stock market losses can devastate a portfolio and your chance for long-term success, but now we're going to talk about something that could be even more devastating than a stock market loss. You probably think, "What could that be?" because stock market losses can ruin your retirement. The answer is ... high fees!

High fees are the thing that can be worse than the stock market loss, because, think about it: if the stock market goes down, you lose money, if the stock market goes back up, you can potentially recover. When you pay high fees, can you ever recover those high fees that you've paid? Of course not, the answer is no because they won't pay you back your fees. You have to understand what high fees mean.

We are unique in our planning process, in that all we work with are retirees and people nearing retirement. Because our clients are older, most of the new clients we meet with have had an advisor for many years. When we meet with a prospective new client, many times they will say something like, "we really like our current advisor," "our current advisor is very nice," "the staff always treats us so well," "we've gone to dinner," "we go to the same church," "we've been friends for a long time," and maybe even "our kids hang out together."

The bottom line is that they really like their advisor as a person, they feel like their advisor is their friend.

At this point we will then say, "Well, that's great. You probably wouldn't have had them as an advisor for the last 20 years unless you really liked them. I am sure they are a nice person, and the staff is probably fantastic."

And then we say, "But now, let's talk about your money." When we say this, the clients usually cross their arms and look a little confused and perturbed, because they know everything about how nice the advisor is, but they really don't know anything about their own money.

We then ask the client "What are you paying in fees?" The clients will typically answer in one of two ways:

1. They'll either say emphatically, "We're paying 1% in fees."

-OR-

2. The husband will look at the wife and ask, "Honey, what do you think we're paying?" The wife will usually respond, "I'm not sure, honey, what do you think we're paying?" The husband will typically respond with "I'm not sure, maybe 1%"?

What do you think both answers mean? It means they really have no idea what they are paying in fees!

We ask them, "Why do you think you are only paying 1% in fees?" and they will almost always respond, "This is what our advisor told us, we are only paying 1% in total fees." And the truth is they probably are paying their advisor about 1%, that would be normal, but in almost all cases, that is nowhere close to the actual total fees they are paying. We have found fees of 1% are a fraction of what the typical retiree pays in total fees, both direct (visible) and indirect (hidden).

1.00%	Typical Advisor Fee (The Only Fee Client Thought They Were Paying)

But then when we look at their statements, most people have a ton of mutual funds and we see there are a lot of trades being made. There could be two (2) trades a week, ten (10) a week, or even twenty (20) trades a week. But either way, there are a lot of trades being made. We will ask the client, "Why are these trades being made?" Almost every client responds that they don't know why the trades are being made. We tell the client they need to understand why the trades are being made because there are typically extra fees associated with a lot of trades.

We then ask the client if their advisor is making all these trades and they will usually say their advisor is not making the trades. We then say to the client "Well, someone's making these trades and if it's not your advisor, who's doing that? It's probably a money manager and do you think the money manager's going to do all that work for free?" The client thinks about it, and they will usually say, "Of course not, the money manager will want to get paid too." The typical money manager fee would be about 1%, so the client thought they were paying 1%, but now they see they could be paying 2%.

1.00%	Typical Advisor Fee (The Only Fee Client Thought They Were Paying)
1.00%	+Typical Money Manager Fee

Many retirees we meet with have 20 or more mutual funds, some having 40 or more mutual funds in their portfolio. We ask retirees, *"Why do you have so many mutual funds?"* They will usually respond, *"For diversification and to reduce my risk because they all won't go down together."* Most retirees have been taught by their previous advisors that spreading their assets over many funds provides them diversification, the

143

best opportunity for growth, and dramatically less risk. Unfortunately, we have found these things might not all be true.

We believe, based on our research, once you own a good selection of a maximum of 12 equity mutual funds, you have sufficient diversification for risk reduction. If you own more than 12 mutual funds, you receive no measurably beneficial additional risk reduction through diversification. If you own more than 12 mutual funds, you also hamper your opportunity for growth and dilute your potential rate of return because many of the mutual funds will own the same stocks, and you then have what is called "overlap" which causes an overconcentration of certain stocks in the portfolio. If those stocks don't perform well, your portfolio performance will suffer, be diluted. Even worse, if the stocks you are over-concentrated in suffer big losses, the whole portfolio will be severely affected. There also can be more fees associated with owning more funds.

Since we are talking about mutual funds, let's talk about mutual fund expenses. We ask retirees *"What is the average mutual fund cost you're paying on your funds?"* Most of the retirees reply, *"We're not paying any mutual fund costs,"* and we ask them, *"Why do you think you're not paying any mutual fund costs?"* The retirees typically say, *"Well, because our advisor says the only fee we pay is the 1% fee to them, and the fees for the mutual funds don't show up on our statements."*

Well, it's true that the fees for the mutual funds don't show up on your statements, but you are paying them nonetheless. Every single mutual fund, whether it's a loaded mutual fund or a no-load mutual fund, has a mutual fund expense. These mutual fund expenses are deducted at the mutual fund level before you get your portfolio statement, so you don't "see" the mutual fund expenses, but it's still there, reducing your potential rate of return. If you own mutual funds, it's simply not true if your advisor states you are not paying any mutual fund expenses.

The good news is that mutual fund expenses have to be disclosed to you, but if this is the case, why don't most retirees know what their mutual fund expenses are? It's because of the bad news: the problem is that a mutual fund expense is buried somewhere deep in a book you hate to read that is called a prospectus. A prospectus might be 200 pages, printed on thin paper, in very small print, and the mutual fund expense might be on page 178. What if you have 30 funds, will you read through 6,000 pages just to find out what all your fund expenses are? The overwhelming vast majority of retirees will not. So even though you can find out what your mutual fund expenses are, you probably won't.

The average annual mutual fund expense is 1.23%, as reported by www.NewYorkTimes.com on 10/6/2012.

So now if you add the 1.23% of mutual fund expenses on to the 1% for the advisor and the 1% for the money manager, you are now at 3.23% in potential total fees.

1.00%	Typical Advisor Fee (The Only Fee Client Thought They Were Paying)	
1.00%	+Typical Money Manager Fee	
1.23%	+Average Mutual Fund Expense	www.NewYorkTimes.com 10/6/2012

At this point, the color usually drains from most retirees faces. They sit back and they start wondering, because they finally have been provided with the truth, they start thinking "I wonder how much I have actually paid in fees over the years?"

If this wasn't bad enough already, there's another cost that doesn't have to be disclosed to you. Every mutual fund, whether it's a stock or bond fund, will buy and sell assets that are in the mutual fund each year. Let's say we're talking about a stock mutual fund, and the mutual fund manager will sell a certain number of stocks currently held in the mutual fund and will purchase a certain number of new stocks.

This selling of current stocks and buying new stocks is called "turnover." In this example of a stock mutual fund, the percent of the mutual fund's stocks that are sold each year and then replaced by new stocks is called the "turnover ratio." The cost associated with buying and selling stocks at the mutual fund level is called the "trading costs." Retirees usually think that when their mutual funds are bought and sold by their broker or money manager, the cost of buying and selling the mutual funds are the "trading costs," but this is incorrect, as the cost of buying and selling the mutual funds are called "transaction costs."

You will see the transactions of your individual mutual funds being bought or sold by your broker or money manager, and you will see the costs for these transactions on your statements. But you will not see the sales and purchases of the different stocks in each mutual fund, and you will not see the costs associated with these "trading costs" at the mutual fund level.

It seems normal that a mutual fund manager would sell a few stocks each year that are "out of favor" and buy a few new stocks that "fit the mutual fund better." So, you would expect there to be a "turnover ratio," but you would probably expect it to be quite low.

Recently it's been reported that the average "turnover ratio" for stock mutual funds is approximately 80%. This means that the typical stock mutual fund is selling and then re-purchasing 80% of the value of total value of the mutual fund each year. This probably seems so counter-intuitive because you have always been told to be a long-term investor, but then the mutual funds themselves are selling stocks potentially at an 80% rate each year, which is more of a short-term investment strategy.

With an 80% turnover ratio, a $1,000,000,000 mutual fund is selling 80% of stocks each year, which is $800,000,000. The same mutual fund is repurchasing $800,000,000 of new stocks. This means the mutual fund is buying and selling a total of $1,600,000,000 of stocks each year. Will these $1,600,000,000 in buys and sells create a small amount of cost in the form of commissions and buy/sell fees, or will this create a large amount of costs? Bingo! A large amount of costs. The bad news is that the mutual funds do not have to tell you what that cost is! So, this is truly a "hidden cost." Unlike the transaction cost of replacing one mutual fund for another mutual fund which does show up on your statement, this trading cost at the mutual fund level does not show up on your statement.

The good news is that we know that the approximate average annual "trading cost" for a mutual fund is 1.44% as reported by www.Forbes.com on 4/4/2011. So now if you add the 1.44% of mutual fund "trading cost" on to the average 1.23% mutual fund expenses on to the 1% for the advisor and on to the 1% for the money manager, you are now at 4.67% in total potential fees.

1.00%	Typical Advisor Fee (The Only Fee Client Thought They Were Paying)	
1.00%	+Typical Money Manager Fee	
1.23%	+Average Mutual Fund Expense	www.NewYorkTimes.com 10/6/2012
1.44%	+Average Trading (Hidden) Costs	www.Forbes.com 4/4/2011

There is one last cost we must address. It is another "hidden cost" and it is what is called an "opportunity cost." An "opportunity cost" simply means what you could lose, or give up, because of "something you are doing." In this case, the "something you are doing" is investing in a mutual fund that holds cash as an asset in the mutual fund. The mutual fund may be holding cash to buy more stocks or bonds, or it may hold cash to be able to make distributions to you and other mutual fund owners. The cash that is being held in the mutual fund will be liquid and will earn a very low rate of return, such as a money market rate of return.

Now here is the problem, you will be paying fees on the total assets in the mutual fund, even the assets that are being held in cash. If you are paying a high level of fees on the assets that are being held in cash, and you are only earning a small rate of return on the assets that are being held in cash, are you getting ahead or falling further behind? You are falling further behind. This "hidden cost" is called "cash drag" because the cash is dragging your returns down. Just like the "trading costs," the mutual fund doesn't have to tell you how much you are losing in "cash drag" because the mutual fund is holding cash.

For example, let's say your mutual fund has to keep 5% of the mutual fund in cash. That mutual fund now can't earn a very high rate of return on that cash. They might earn a bank type return, but the mutual fund gets to charge you fees on all the assets in the portfolio, including the cash. What if you're only earning a low bank-type return on those assets that are in cash, but they're charging you 3% in fees, are you getting ahead or falling behind? It simply means you're falling behind.

The approximate average annual "cash drag cost" for a mutual fund is 0.83% as reported by www.Forbes.com on 4/4/2011. If you add the 0.83% mutual fund "cash drag," to the 1.44% of mutual fund "trading cost," to the average 1.23% mutual fund expenses, to the 1% for the advisor, and to the 1% for the money manager, the total potential fees are at 5.50%. Your actual fees could be higher or lower.

1.00%	Typical Advisor Fee (The Only Fee Client Thought They Were Paying)	
1.00%	+Typical Money Manager Fee	
1.23%	+Average Mutual Fund Expense	www.NewYorkTimes.com 10/6/2012
1.44%	+Average Trading (Hidden) Costs	www.Forbes.com 4/4/2011
0.83%	+Average Cash Drag	www.Forbes.com 4/4/2011
5.50%	=Total Potential Annual Fees For Managed Portfolio	

The majority of retirees think they are paying 1% in total fees, but in reality they are paying 2%, 3%, 4%, even up to 5.5% per year in fees, and they didn't even know it, and they were never told this before.

Even worse, if they own a variable annuity, which is one of the highest cost assets you can own, the total annual fees they are paying could be as high as 6.5%, and this fee is paid every year.

6.50%	=Total Potential Annual Fees For A Variable Annuity

Think about it, if you're potentially paying up to 5.5% or 6.5% per year in fees, how can you ever get ahead? You really can't get ahead; it's very difficult. You also might be thinking this is just so hard to believe, especially if your broker/advisor told you that you were "only paying 1% in fees." Unfortunately, you need to believe it because it's true. Excessive fees can devastate a portfolio; it's the hidden asset killer.

A recent Harris Poll reported only 39% of Americans thought they knew the fees they are paying. We think it's closer to 0%. Most retirees believe they're paying 1% in total fees annually, but they're really paying closer to 3.5%. Tony Robbins has recently been on a crusade, through lectures, television and radio appearances, even writing a new book to help consumers realize they're getting killed with hidden fees.

Thomas Coyle wrote in *Financial Advisor IQ* published on October 26, 2017, that cited Ameriprise, UBS, Morgan Stanley, Wells Fargo, and Merrill Lynch as the "Most Expensive Advice Firms" with advisory and fund fees as high as 3.5%. The 3.5% did not include "trading costs" or "cash drag" and only estimated an average 0.50% mutual fund expense! This is just shocking news!

Did you ever wonder why your return rate was nowhere near what the markets achieved? Well, hopefully, this will shine the light on how your money is being spent.

A $1,000,000 portfolio, assessed 3.5% fees versus 1.0% fees, levies an additional $500,000 in fees over 20 years. Unfortunately, this is typical and very well could be happening to you right now.

CHAPTER 15

HOW FEES AFFECT YOUR PORTFOLIO VALUES AND GROWTH RATES

BY DAN AHMAD & JIM FILES

We are spending a lot of time talking about fees because #1, you probably don't understand them, and #2, fees affect your portfolio values and your growth rates. You know this intuitively, but you have never been provided with easy-to-understand data to make sure you fully comprehend what is really happening to your money.

Let's review the performance of the S&P 500 Index during the 15-year time period from 1999 to 2013. We will use the S&P 500 Index to represent the stock market returns, and we will assume you earned the same annual return for these 15 years. Let's also assume you invest $1,000,000 in 1999, and you found a place where you could invest without paying any fees at all – that's right, 0% in fees. There are two (2) issues with our assumptions:

1. It is very difficult for an investor to get stock market return rates.
2. It is impossible to invest in the stock market without any fees at all.

But since this is a hypothetical example, we will go with the S&P 500 Index return rates and 0% fees!

If you invested $1,000,000 in 1999, earned S&P 500 Index annual returns, and paid no fees at all, your $1,000,000 would have grown to $1,503,523 assuming no taxes on the growth. Most people look at the following chart and they think they have made a good rate of return, especially looking at the annual rates of return of the S&P 500 Index received

151

during this time period. In 1999 you would have earned 19.53%, in 2003 you would have earned 26.38%, in 2009 you would have earned 23.45%, and in 2012 and 2013 you would have earned 13.41% and 29.60%. It looks like you killed it! The problem is that the four (4) loss years in 2000, 2001, 2002, and 2008 caused the S&P 500 Index during this 15-year time period to grow at a whopping 2.75% annual compounded rate! What this means is if you invested $1,000,000 in 1999, and earned 2.75% every year for 15 years, your account would be worth $1,503,523. Was a 2.75% rate of return, before fees, worth all the risk you took during this time period?

Year	S&P 500 Index Annual Change	Value With 0% Fees $1,000,000
1999	19.53%	$1,195,300
2000	-10.14%	$1,074,097
2001	-13.04%	$934,034
2002	-23.37%	$715,751
2003	26.38%	$904,566
2004	8.99%	$985,886
2005	3.00%	$1,015,463
2006	13.62%	$1,153,769
2007	3.53%	$1,194,497
2008	-38.49%	$734,735
2009	23.45%	$907,030
2010	12.78%	$1,022,949
2011	0.00%	$1,022,949
2012	13.41%	$1,160,126
2013	29.60%	$1,503,523

Most retirees would probably think the performance of their assets was excellent if their $1,000,000 grew to $1,505,523 in a 15-year time period. They would feel this way because their assets increased by +50%! But the +50% growth occurred over a 15-year time period, which is only a 2.75% annual compounded increase. It is important to note that the abysmal 2.75% annual compounded increase was caused initially by the losses, and subsequently by the recovery gains required. The S&P 500 Index had some great returns during many of the years that were significantly diminished by the losses.

Now, what would happen if you earned stock market rates of return and were now paying 1% in fees. Instead of your $1,000,000 growing to $1,503,523, you'd only have $1,293,118.

Year	S&P 500 Index Annual Change	Value With 0% Fees $1,000,000	Value With 1% Fees $1,000,000
1999	19.53%	$1,195,300	$1,183,347
2000	-10.14%	$1,074,097	$1,052,722
2001	-13.04%	$934,034	$906,293
2002	-23.37%	$715,751	$687,547
2003	26.38%	$904,566	$860,233
2004	8.99%	$985,886	$928,192
2005	3.00%	$1,015,463	$946,477
2006	13.62%	$1,153,769	$1,064,634
2007	3.53%	$1,194,497	$1,091,193
2008	-38.49%	$734,735	$664,481
2009	23.45%	$907,030	$812,099
2010	12.78%	$1,022,949	$906,726
2011	0.00%	$1,022,949	$897,659
2012	13.41%	$1,160,126	$1,007,855
2013	29.60%	$1,503,523	$1,293,118

If you earned stock market rates of return and paid 2% in fees your $1,503,523 would only be worth $1,110,456.

Year	S&P 500 Index Annual Change	Value With 0% Fees $1,000,000	Value With 1% Fees $1,000,000	Value With 2% Fees $1,000,000
1999	19.53%	$1,195,300	$1,183,347	$1,171,394
2000	-10.14%	$1,074,097	$1,052,722	$1,031,562
2001	-13.04%	$934,034	$906,293	$879,106
2002	-23.37%	$715,751	$687,547	$660,186
2003	26.38%	$904,566	$860,233	$817,656
2004	8.99%	$985,886	$928,192	$873,340
2005	3.00%	$1,015,463	$946,477	$881,549
2006	13.62%	$1,153,769	$1,064,634	$981,584
2007	3.53%	$1,194,497	$1,091,193	$995,909
2008	-38.49%	$734,735	$664,481	$600,332
2009	23.45%	$907,030	$812,099	$726,288
2010	12.78%	$1,022,949	$906,726	$802,725
2011	0.00%	$1,022,949	$897,659	$786,670
2012	13.41%	$1,160,126	$1,007,855	$874,320
2013	29.60%	$1,503,523	$1,293,118	$1,110,456

If you earned stock market rates of return and paid 3% in fees your $1,503,523 would only be worth $952,108 which is less than the original $1,000,000 you invested 15 years ago.

Year	S&P 500 Index Annual Change	Value With 0% Fees $1,000,000	Value With 1% Fees $1,000,000	Value With 2% Fees $1,000,000	Value With 3% Fees $1,000,000
1999	19.53%	$1,195,300	$1,183,347	$1,171,394	$1,159,441
2000	-10.14%	$1,074,097	$1,052,722	$1,031,562	$1,010,617
2001	-13.04%	$934,034	$906,293	$879,106	$852,468
2002	-23.37%	$715,751	$687,547	$660,186	$633,649
2003	26.38%	$904,566	$860,233	$817,656	$776,781
2004	8.99%	$985,886	$928,192	$873,340	$821,215
2005	3.00%	$1,015,463	$946,477	$881,549	$820,476
2006	13.62%	$1,153,769	$1,064,634	$981,584	$904,258
2007	3.53%	$1,194,497	$1,091,193	$995,909	$908,093
2008	-38.49%	$734,735	$664,481	$600,332	$541,811
2009	23.45%	$907,030	$812,099	$726,288	$648,800
2010	12.78%	$1,022,949	$906,726	$802,725	$709,765
2011	0.00%	$1,022,949	$897,659	$786,670	$688,472
2012	13.41%	$1,160,126	$1,007,855	$874,320	$757,372
2013	29.60%	$1,503,523	$1,293,118	$1,110,456	$952,108

If you earned stock market rates of return and paid 4% in fees your $1,503,523 would only be worth $815,040. In our experience, this is what we see as the typical scenario for an average fee variable annuity.

Year	S&P 500 Index Annual Change	Value With 0% Fees $1,000,000	Value With 1% Fees $1,000,000	Value With 2% Fees $1,000,000	Value With 3% Fees $1,000,000	Value With 4% Fees $1,000,000
1999	19.53%	$1,195,300	$1,183,347	$1,171,394	$1,159,441	$1,147,488
2000	-10.14%	$1,074,097	$1,052,722	$1,031,562	$1,010,617	$989,887
2001	-13.04%	$934,034	$906,293	$879,106	$852,468	$826,374
2002	-23.37%	$715,751	$687,547	$660,186	$633,649	$607,920
2003	26.38%	$904,566	$860,233	$817,656	$776,781	$737,558
2004	8.99%	$985,886	$928,192	$873,340	$821,215	$771,710
2005	3.00%	$1,015,463	$946,477	$881,549	$820,476	$763,067
2006	13.62%	$1,153,769	$1,064,634	$981,584	$904,258	$832,317
2007	3.53%	$1,194,497	$1,091,193	$995,909	$908,093	$827,230
2008	-38.49%	$734,735	$664,481	$600,332	$541,811	$488,476
2009	23.45%	$907,030	$812,099	$726,288	$648,800	$578,902
2010	12.78%	$1,022,949	$906,726	$802,725	$709,765	$626,771
2011	0.00%	$1,022,949	$897,659	$786,670	$688,472	$601,700
2012	13.41%	$1,160,126	$1,007,855	$874,320	$757,372	$655,092
2013	29.60%	$1,503,523	$1,293,118	$1,110,456	$952,108	$815,040

If you earned stock market rates of return and paid 5% in fees your $1,503,523 would only be worth $696,569. We have seen this as the typical scenario for a high fee variable annuity.

Year	S&P 500 Index Annual Change	Value With 0% Fees $1,000,000	Value With 1% Fees $1,000,000	Value With 2% Fees $1,000,000	Value With 3% Fees $1,000,000	Value With 4% Fees $1,000,000	Value With 5% Fees $1,000,000
1999	19.53%	$1,195,300	$1,183,347	$1,171,394	$1,159,441	$1,147,488	$1,135,535
2000	-10.14%	$1,074,097	$1,052,722	$1,031,562	$1,010,617	$989,887	$969,372
2001	-13.04%	$934,034	$906,293	$879,106	$852,468	$826,374	$800,818
2002	-23.37%	$715,751	$687,547	$660,186	$633,649	$607,920	$582,983
2003	26.38%	$904,566	$860,233	$817,656	$776,781	$737,558	$699,936
2004	8.99%	$985,886	$928,192	$873,340	$821,215	$771,710	$724,717
2005	3.00%	$1,015,463	$946,477	$881,549	$820,476	$763,067	$709,135
2006	13.62%	$1,153,769	$1,064,634	$981,584	$904,258	$832,317	$765,434
2007	3.53%	$1,194,497	$1,091,193	$995,909	$908,093	$827,230	$752,831
2008	-38.49%	$734,735	$664,481	$600,332	$541,811	$488,476	$439,913
2009	23.45%	$907,030	$812,099	$726,288	$648,800	$578,902	$515,919
2010	12.78%	$1,022,949	$906,726	$802,725	$709,765	$626,771	$552,761
2011	0.00%	$1,022,949	$897,659	$786,670	$688,472	$601,700	$525,123
2012	13.41%	$1,160,126	$1,007,855	$874,320	$757,372	$655,092	$565,764
2013	29.60%	$1,503,523	$1,293,118	$1,110,456	$952,108	$815,040	$696,569

This next chart shows the total cost of the fees in dollars that you would have paid in annual fees ranging from 1% to 5%. On a $1,000,000 investment, if you paid 3% in fees and earned stock market rates of return, after 15 years your ending value would be $952,108 and your total cost of fees were $551,415. The last line of the chart shows the percent of your original investment you paid in fees over 15 years, so if you paid 3% in fees with costs totaling $551,415, you paid 55% of your original $1,000,000 investment in total fees.

Year	S&P 500 Index Annual Change	Value With 0% Fees	Value With 1% Fees	Value With 2% Fees	Value With 3% Fees	Value With 4% Fees	Value With 5% Fees
		$1,000,000	$1,000,000	$1,000,000	$1,000,000	$1,000,000	$1,000,000
1999	19.53%	$1,195,300	$1,183,347	$1,171,394	$1,159,441	$1,147,488	$1,135,535
2000	-10.14%	$1,074,097	$1,052,722	$1,031,562	$1,010,617	$989,887	$969,372
2001	-13.04%	$934,034	$906,293	$879,106	$852,468	$826,374	$800,818
2002	-23.37%	$715,751	$687,547	$660,186	$633,649	$607,920	$582,983
2003	26.38%	$904,566	$860,233	$817,656	$776,781	$737,558	$699,936
2004	8.99%	$985,886	$928,192	$873,340	$821,215	$771,710	$724,717
2005	3.00%	$1,015,463	$946,477	$881,549	$820,476	$763,067	$709,135
2006	13.62%	$1,153,769	$1,064,634	$981,584	$904,258	$832,317	$765,434
2007	3.53%	$1,194,497	$1,091,193	$995,909	$908,093	$827,230	$752,831
2008	-38.49%	$734,735	$664,481	$600,332	$541,811	$488,476	$439,913
2009	23.45%	$907,030	$812,099	$726,288	$648,800	$578,902	$515,919
2010	12.78%	$1,022,949	$906,726	$802,725	$709,765	$626,771	$552,761
2011	0.00%	$1,022,949	$897,659	$786,670	$688,472	$601,700	$525,123
2012	13.41%	$1,160,126	$1,007,855	$874,320	$757,372	$655,092	$565,764
2013	29.60%	$1,503,523	$1,293,118	$1,110,456	$952,108	$815,040	$696,569
Total Cost Of Fees			($210,406)	($393,067)	($551,415)	($688,484)	($806,954)
Fees As A % Of $1,000,000			-21%	-39%	-55%	-69%	-81%

We have found that advisors don't like it when we show this specific data about how fees affect your portfolio values and growth rates, but CPA's and attorneys love it when we show you this data! Advisors don't want you to see this data because fees can significantly affect your portfolio values and growth rates.

The bad news is you may have paid far too much in fees during the last 15 years. The good news is that you no longer have to pay more than you should in fees because you are now educated on the subject.

CHAPTER 16

SAFE INCOME WITHDRAWAL RATE

BY DAN AHMAD & JIM FILES

What does the phrase "safe income withdrawal rate" mean to you? Most people would answer "the amount of income you can withdraw from your assets without the fear of running out of income during your lifetime." This seems cut and dried. But you have to look at what the word "safe" means to different people. "Safe" to some people might actually mean "safer than something else," such as you stating that you are "driving safe" because you are going 80 miles per hour while everyone else on the road is driving 90 miles per hour, but the posted speed limit is 65 miles per hour. And then, "safe" to other people might mean the chance of anything negative happening is 0%. In planning for retirement, safe better mean safe, something you can count on for sure. Safe better not mean "kind of safe."

When you were working and saving for retirement, you were probably taught, or simply thought, that you could:

- Save up a pile of money by the time you retired.
- Live off the earnings of your pile of assets.
- See your assets continue to grow, or at least stay level, while you were taking income distributions.
- Leave the exact same pile of your money to your kids and grandkids when you passed away.

Doesn't this sound just perfect? This is exactly what you want to happen with your assets. Save your money, use your assets for income throughout your retirement, and then pass all remaining assets to your kids and grandkids.

157

Unfortunately, it doesn't work this way. Do you remember *"The Gong Show"* from the late 1970's? Remember when someone failed or was wrong the "Gong" was hit and made a loud dismal sound signaling failure. I just hit the "Gong" about what you were taught or thought about how your money would act, because what you learned about how you could use your assets to create income is no longer accurate and is no longer a viable planning strategy.

For decades the financial industry has used resources such as Morningstar, Ibbotson, and other firms to provide a "safe income withdrawal rate" for retirees. The "safe income withdrawal rate" is typically based on some type of a success probability. In the 1980's the industry standard for a "safe income withdrawal rate" was 6%. This meant you had a high probability, typically a 95% chance [for you math eggheads out there this means within two (2) standard deviations], that you could take out 6% of your assets for income each year and not run out. This also meant you had a 5% chance you would run out of money during your lifetime because your income wasn't guaranteed. And during retirement, we feel 95% success probability is 5% too low.

If you remember back to the 1980's you could have earned 8% in the bank, so 6% was not a stretch. But over time, the stock market has changed, interest rates have changed, the economy has changed, and the world has changed, all helping to shape the historical progression of safe income withdrawal rates:

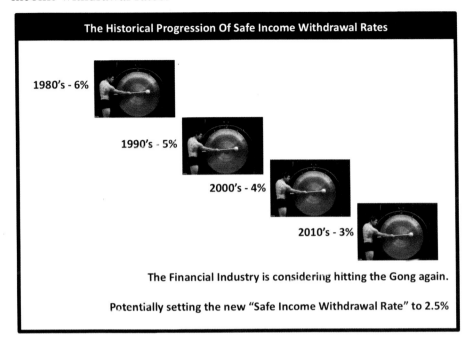

- In the 1980's it was thought 6% was the "safe income withdrawal rate," then the Gong was hit signifying that 6% was too high.
- In the 1990's it was thought 5% was the "safe income withdrawal rate," then the Gong was hit signifying that 5% was too high.
- In the 2000's it was thought 4% was the "safe income withdrawal rate," then the Gong was hit signifying that 4% was too high.
- In the 2010's it was thought 3% was the "safe income withdrawal rate."
- Now in 2018 the Gong may be hit again, as the financial industry is weighing the possibility that the "safe income withdrawal rate" should be reduced to 2.5%, meaning that on $1,000,000 of portfolio assets you shouldn't take out more than $25,000 per year. In many cases this may not be enough for you to live on.

In planning your retirement income, you must have a high probability for success that your income will never run out, or you will worry every day throughout your retirement. Right now, you may have a high probability your money will run out and just not know it. Or, you may be working with an advisor, or doing the planning by yourself, and you incorrectly have been told, or think, that you can't be hurt by having a low probability of retirement income success. You cannot let yourself stay in this position.

Here's an example: If you watched the comedy *Dumb and Dumber*, you will recall Lloyd played by Jim Carey was interested in Mary, played by Lauren Holly. One of the most memorable scenes has been nicknamed "1 in a million." In this extremely memorable scene, Lloyd and Mary have the following dialogue:

Lloyd: "What do you think the chances of a guy like you (he was nervous so he called Mary a guy), and a girl like me (again nervous so he calls himself a girl), ending up together?"

Mary replied, "Well Lloyd, that's difficult to say, and we really don't…"

Lloyd interrupted: "Hit me with it, just give it to me straight. I came a long way just to see you Mary. Just, the least you can do is level with me. What are my chances?"

Mary replied tentatively: "Not good."

Lloyd replied after a long pause: "You mean not good like 1 in 100?"

Mary replied "I'd say more like 1 in a 1,000,000."

Lloyd replied optimistically: "So you're telling me there's a chance, Yeah!"

In matters of the heart, it's OK to take a chance and not have a high level of probability of success. But in planning income for your retirement years, you must design a plan that has the highest level of potential success rate, with 100% as the goal. A guaranteed 100% is even better.

There are several main reasons the "safe income withdrawal rate" has decreased by 50%, and possibly more, since the 1980's:

1. The stock market's increased volatility.
2. Interest rates declined to historic lows.
3. Life expectancy has increased.

These changes create necessary modifications to your plans for retirement, as the traditional asset allocation models you have been using may not work any longer to be able to provide you lifelong retirement income success.

CHAPTER 17

ACCOMPLISH YOUR GOALS USING:
THE 7 RULES TO LIVE BY FOR RETIREMENT SECURITY

BY DAN AHMAD & JIM FILES

Up to this point we have talked about all of the things you must be aware of that could cause you tremendous financial pain and could put your retirement in jeopardy. We've had many retirees tell us they feel sick to their stomach after learning all of these "truths about their money". You may feel the same way. But now is the time for answers, solutions, and developing a plan to make you feel financially secure throughout your retirement. We have found the only way retirees can really feel secure is if they have a plan. We have also found that the best way to create a plan that is understandable by all retirees is to have rules for the plan.

Now it's time to learn the secrets of how to succeed in retirement. This entire book was written for retirees and pre-retirees just like you, to help you learn the truth, to help you learn the secrets you haven't been told, to help you succeed. Now it's time to learn Momma's Secret Recipe For Retirement Success. It's time to let Momma's Secret Recipe For Retirement Success out of the bag. There are seven (7) steps in the recipe. We view the seven (7) steps of the recipe as rules to follow in order to successfully navigate through the complexities of retirement.

To make it easy to follow Momma's Secret Recipe, we have created *The 7 Rules To Live By For Retirement Security*, a seven (7) step process to help our clients accomplish their goals:

7 Rules To Live By For Retirement Security:

1. Avoid large losses – use the "5%-10% Rule".

2. Minimize fees.

3. Significantly reduce volatility.

4. Earn a reasonable return rate.

5. Manage taxation.

6. Generate "Certain Income" from your assets that will last for as long as you live, not "Maybe Income" that could end at any time.

7. Have a Written Retirement Income Plan.

Think about how confusing planning your finances has always seemed. Everything might have felt up in the air, no direction, no answers, a great deal of risk, anxiety, no real plan at all, and nothing ever in writing. Has anyone ever given you rules to live by to maximize your financial success? Probably not. This means you have not really had a road map to follow to get from point a (while you are working) to point b (when you retire) to point c (through your entire retirement).

Would you follow seven (7) simple rules if you were guaranteed to increase your probability of retirement success by following them? It is guaranteed you will increase your probability of having a successful retirement if you follow: *The 7 Rules To Live By For Retirement Security.* By following these rules some of you will increase your success probability significantly and some will increase your success probability to a lesser degree, but you are all guaranteed to be in a better financial position for retirement.

Let's Look At Each Of The 7 Rules And Why Each Rule Is Important To Your Success:

Rule #1: Avoid Large Losses – Use The "Golden Rule Of 5% To 10%"

Almost all retirees and pre-retirees tell us they do not want to ever lose more than -10% in their portfolios. But the majority of these people do not know, or haven't been told, their current portfolio could lose -20%, -30%, -40%, -50%, and even up to -60% in a stock market crash like the 2008 Financial Crisis.

Retirees must avoid large losses at all costs. You know this is true, but why haven't you done anything about it? It's because no one has helped you to do it. If you are like the typical retiree we meet with, there is a high probability your current broker is doing just the opposite, he/she is actually placing your assets at risk of a large loss. When you were young and working, you could afford to take risks because you had a long time until retirement, you were continuing to save money every month, and you didn't need to use your assets for income. If the stock market crashed you had enough time to make up losses, you would continue to invest every month allowing you to buy shares at lower prices, and you didn't need income from your assets for 10, 20, or even 30 years.

Remember our discussion previously that losses are very hard to recover? If you suffer a -50% loss like the 2000 through 2002 Technology Bubble stock market crash or the 2007 through 2009 Mortgage and Housing Crisis stock market crash, you need a +100% recovery gain just to break even. If you lose -40% you need a +67% recovery gain just to recover. A -30% loss requires a +43% recovery gain to break even. A -20% loss requires a +25% recovery gain to break even. And while a -10% loss only requires an +11.0% recovery gain to break even, an even smaller -5% loss only requires a +5.3% recovery gain to break even.

The *"Golden Rule of 5%-10%"* was created to construct portfolios mathematically projected, based on historical market and asset data, not to lose more than -5% up to a maximum of -10%, even when the stock market drops -50% like it did in 2000-2002 and 2007-2009. *And remember that on average since 1929 the stock market is going to suffer a -40% loss every seven (7) years. If you are 65 years old right now you should plan on going through four (4) more -40% stock market crashes!*

How much less you would worry if your portfolio was allocated to reduce your risk from a potential -50% loss all the way down to a potential projected -5% loss? Would you worry as much? You'd probably feel great and worry a whole heck of a lot less! And during retirement you must plan for the worst-case scenario. You have to plan for the biggest potential loss, because it's not if a big loss will happen, it's when it will happen and how many more times it will happen after that. It's also because no one is going to give you a do-over. If you didn't know you could lose -40% in the next stock market crash, but you do lose the -40% anyway, and your $1,000,000 drops to $600,000, do you think your broker is going to pay you back the -$400,000 you lost? No way!

What that means is, you must position your portfolio and allocate it properly for principal safety. So even in the worst stock market conditions where the stock market loses -50%, as it did in 2000 through 2002 and 2007 through 2009, you must position your assets so you are projected to lose no more than -5% to up to a maximum -10%. You can recover from a -5% to -10% loss. It is very difficult to recover from a -20% to -50% loss.

One of the psychological benefits to living a successful retirement is to feel secure, to feel safe. So, imagine if you had $2,000,000 of retirement assets and you have pretty much invested the money the same way now as you did when you were working. Let's assume in 2008 you lost -50%. This means if we have another 2008 you should plan on losing another -50%, or to be more specific, you should plan that your $2,000,000 portfolio will lose -$1,000,000, and will only be worth $1,000,000 after the loss. How would you feel? What would you do? Can you imagine now that you're retired or nearing retirement, having to make a +100% gain just to recover, not to make any gains, but just to recover?

Now let's imagine you had a portfolio that had a projected -5% risk factor if the stock market crashed -50%. In this scenario your $2,000,000 portfolio would be projected to lose -$100,000 and you would still have $1,900,000 left in your portfolio after the loss. Now think how you would feel. How do you view only having to make up a recovery gain of +5.3% on the $1,900,000 to be back at the original $2,000,000? Making up +5.3% during retirement is reasonable but making up a +100% recovery gain isn't.

Here is a simple recipe on how you can develop a Golden Rule of 5%-10% portfolio by:

1. Implementing a stop-loss strategy on your stock market investments. Don't ride the stock market down to the bottom. Imagine how a 10% stop-loss would have felt back in 2008!

2. Buying contractual principal and lifetime income guarantees from highly-rated insurance companies that have been operating successfully for a long time, preferably for at least 90 years. These companies have fulfilled their guarantees and promises to their customers even through the Great Depression.

3. Keeping money in the bank. Liquidity and safety are so-underrated, and rarely recommended by most brokers, because it doesn't make the broker any money. But if you're retired, bank money will make you feel safer, will not lose value in a stock market crash, typically doesn't have any fees, and is available for spending.

4. Diversifying your investments. The perfect allocation has a portion of the portfolio in the stop-loss bucket, a portion of the portfolio in the guaranteed lifetime income bucket, and a portion in the bank bucket.

We've seen this methodology help retirees create a portfolio to reduce their risk by up to 90%!

Rule #2: Minimize Fees

Excessive fees can devastate a portfolio; it's the hidden asset killer. Most retirees believe they're paying 1% in total fees annually, but when we do an analysis, a fee audit, we find out they're typically paying over 3% in fees which can severely affect their portfolio values, amount of income they can take out of their assets throughout their retirement, and the amount of money they can leave their beneficiaries.

A $1,000,000 portfolio, assessed 3.5% in annual fees versus 1.0% in annual fees, costs an additional $500,000 in fees over 20 years. Unfortunately, this is typical and probably happening to you right now. How could this happen? One reason is your broker told you your total fees are only 1%, but this 1% is the amount being paid to the broker, and you have already learned there are a significant amount of potential additional fees.

A second reason you're in the dark is that the information is very difficult for you to obtain. The 1% paid to your broker doesn't include other hidden costs that significantly erode your nest-egg such as additional asset management fees, typically 1%, to have your funds watched and moved around in your portfolio, mutual fund fees paid on every single mutual fund that average 1.23%, trading costs at the mutual fund level that average 1.44%, and cash drag that averages 0.83%.

None of these individual costs are very high, but when added together the typical retiree could easily be paying 3.0% or more in fees every single year without even knowing it. If you have a $3,000,000 portfolio and reduce your fees by 1% per year, you have just decreased your total annual fees by $30,000. A proper fee analysis in writing can potentially provide you significant fee reductions. To minimize fees, you have to understand all the potential fees you could be paying, and then you have to have all fees disclosed to you in writing, both the direct (visible) fees and the indirect (hidden) fees.

Rule #3: Significantly Reduce Volatility

Retirees want consistent income throughout retirement. Retirees don't want to worry about suffering large losses during retirement. Retirees don't want to have to worry about running out of money during retirement. Portfolios with high volatility cannot provide consistent income, do not protect the assets against large losses, and do not guarantee you will not run out of money for as long as you live. Retirees must avoid volatility. Between January 1, 2015 and December 31, 2016, a period of two (2) years, the S&P 500 Index fluctuated 26.15% from top to bottom. Between September 20, 2018 and December 24, 2018, a period of roughly three (3) months, the S&P 500 Index fluctuated by 19.76%.

During the "Tech Bubble Crisis" between 2000 and 2002, the stock market dropped by almost 50%, requiring a 100% recovery gain just to get even by 2007. The market then lost approximately 54% during the 2008 Financial Crisis, requiring a 113% recovery gain by mid-2013. During this period of 13 years, the market provided a 0% annual compounded increase: huge volatility for no reward. If you're taking out income during this time period, your portfolio value decreased significantly. Any fees you paid would have decreased your assets further and provided you with a "negative" rate of return during this time period.

Note: It is imperative to avoid this type of volatile asset behavior during retirement.

You could be thinking that you didn't lose money from 2000 through 2013, your accounts didn't go down, they went up, and they went up a lot. And this could be true if this was when you were working and were making additional contributions into your 401(k)/403(b)/457/SEP account. A large portion, possibly the majority, of your growth most likely came from your additional contributions, not stock market growth. You cannot plan, take consistent income, or feel secure if your assets are fluctuating wildly in values. Wide volatility is acceptable while you are working during Stage 1 of Retirement Planning – which is called the Asset Accumulation Phase of Retirement Planning, but volatility is unacceptable when you are retired during Stage 2 of Retirement Planning – which is called the Asset Preservation and Income Distribution Phase of Retirement Planning.

Many retirees have been led to believe the more risk they take:

1. The better off they will be.
2. The higher the rate of return they will receive.
3. The more income they can safely take out of their accounts.
4. The better the chance their money will last for as long as they live.
5. The higher their probability of success during retirement.
6. The more money they will leave their beneficiaries.

But reality may end up being just the opposite because:

A. Most retirees have not earned high rates of return by taking a lot of risk during the last 20+ years as evidenced by the data we previously provided. The risk they have taken has not even been close to the rates of return they have received.

B. The higher the volatility in your portfolio, the lower the amount of income you can safely withdraw. If you look back 30 years ago, the rule of thumb in the financial industry was that you could take out 6% of your portfolio safely every year and your money had a high probability of lasting. Then with increased stock market volatility, the "safe income withdrawal rate" dropped the "6% Rule" to the "5% Rule," to the "4% Rule", and then currently to the "3% Rule." This means you shouldn't take more than 3% income distributions from a volatile portfolio if you want your money to have a high probability of lasting.

Rule #4: Earn A Reasonable Return Rate

While you were working and younger, you probably tried to earn as high a rate of return as possible to grow your assets. You didn't worry as much about losses back then because you could rely on a salary, you didn't need income from the assets yet, you would continue to make contributions, and you had time on your side. So, trying to earn the highest rate of return was acceptable. You might have earned +20% or more in some years. Then you probably ran straight into the twin buzz saws called the 2000 through 2002 Technology Bubble and the 2007 through 2009 Mortgage and Real Estate Crisis when you probably lost a lot of money, possibly somewhere between -30% and -60% each time.

If you want the highest return you have to take the highest risk, and this goes directly against Rule #1! And if you are going to try and follow the rules, you can't start the process by breaking the first one! Thousands of retirees told us their brokers said they would always earn annual returns of 8%, 9%, 10%, 11%, or even 12%, because it's what the stock market has always earned. This is the definition of an "unrealistic expectation."

It will be difficult, if not impossible, to earn 8%, 9%, 10%, 11%, or even 12% returns year-after-year based on the fact that during the last nine (9) 15-year time periods beginning in 1996 and ending on December 31, 2018, the S&P 500 Index has averaged a 4.17% annual compounded increase for every period. Not 8%, 9%, 10%, 11%, or 12% returns, a 4.17% annual average compounded increase, before fees. The 4.17% annual compounded increase is so low because most of the big gains between 1996 through 2018 had to make up for an approximate loss of -50% between 2000 through 2002 and an approximate loss of -54% between 2007 through 2009.

Here's a hypothetical example: Dave and Barb had $1,500,000 of assets in 2000. Their portfolio grew to $2,250,000 by 2018 without any additional investments and without income distributions. This means their assets increased by 50%. Their broker always has talked about 10%-12% stock market returns, so Dave and Barb naturally thought they must have earned close to the 10-12% annual returns. But they didn't. From 2000 through 2018, their portfolio grew by an annual 2.16% compounded rate of return. That's right, for their assets to grow from $1,500,000 to $2,250,000, their assets only grew by 2.16% per year, seriously. If they'd earned 10% every year, they'd have $9,173,000 right now.

Note: We have found retirees typically need to average 4%-5% returns for a successful retirement plan. If Dave and Barb earned 4% on their money, they would have accumulated $3,160,000 by 2018.

Here's another example: In 2017, the S&P 500 Index increased by +19% without considering fees or income taxes. Everyone will agree that this was a great year for the stock market. But it's important to understand what you must be willing to do for a +19% return in 2017. The same S&P 500 Index lost -53.8% between October 2007 through March 2009. This means to be able to earn a +19% rate of return you have to be willing to suffer a loss of the magnitude of -53.8%. Does this seem reasonable? No!

How about a hypothetical alternative using realistic potential return goals while minimizing risk? What if you could reduce the risk of the stock market as measured by the -53.8% loss by up to 90%? What if you could actually own a portfolio that was mathematically tested, using historical data, to have a -5.0% risk of loss during the same time period the stock market lost -53.8%? If you have $1,000,000, how would you have liked to create a portfolio that has a projected loss of -$50,000 versus a projected loss of -$538,000? But here's the key, what rate of return would you think was fair for you to earn in 2017 if your risk was reduced to a projected -5% versus -53.8%? What if you could have invested in a portfolio that had a return goal between +8% to +12% in 2017 when the stock market earned +19%, while reducing your risk by up to 90%? The 19% stock market return is a lot higher, but we have found most retirees feel it is far better to take a lower potential rate of return if risk can be reduced significantly. This is the type of portfolio we have found most retirees feel comfortable with.

Rule #5: Control And Manage Taxation

Let's face it, the vast majority of retirees don't understand how income tax rates actually work and most are deathly afraid of taxes. Many retirees won't increase their income because they are afraid of paying significantly higher income taxes, so they defer taking IRA distributions until age 70 ½ as they are advised by their broker. This strategy might save taxes for a few years, but then it will increase the amount of your IRA required minimum distributions (RMDs) at 70½, increase your taxes for the rest of your life, increase the income taxes your beneficiaries will pay, and give you less money to spend when you're young!

The first thing to know about income taxes is that you don't pay income taxes on all of your gross income, you pay tax only on your taxable income after deductions. Secondly, your taxable income is not taxed at one (1) rate, it's spread out over up to seven (7) graduated rates.

The second thing you need to know is the average income tax rate you pay on every dollar of your income. This is called your effective income tax rate. Your effective income tax rate is not going to be as high as you are afraid it will be, for example, the typical retired couple would pay the following effective tax rates based on these gross annual incomes:

Gross Annual Income	Federal Income Taxes	Federal Effective Tax Rate
$125.000	$11,750	9%
$175,000	$23,100	13%
$250,000	$40,600	16%

This means a hypothetical retired couple could make $125,000 of gross income, assuming $60,000 of joint Social Security benefits and $65,000 of combined pension and IRA income, and they would actually only pay an effective federal tax rate of 9% on the $125,000! If you made $125,000 of gross income in retirement, would you be afraid of a 9% effective tax rate? Probably not, it just has never been explained to you before.

Note: During retirement you will most likely pay a significantly lower tax rate than you originally believed and you should not be afraid of taxes. Consult and verify with your income tax advisor.

This hypothetical retired couple could make $175,000 of gross income, assuming $60,000 of joint Social Security benefits and $115,000 of combined pension and IRA income, and they would actually only pay an effective federal tax rate of 13% on the $175,000! If you made $175,000 of gross income in retirement, would you be afraid of a 13% effective tax rate? Probably not, it just has never been explained to you before.

And it also means a hypothetical retired couple could make $250,000 of gross income, assuming $60,000 of joint Social Security benefits and $190,000 of combined pension and IRA income, and they would actually only pay an effective federal tax rate of 16% on the $250,000! If you made $250,000 of gross income in retirement, would you be afraid of a 16% effective tax rate? Probably not, it just has never been explained to you before.

While you were working, you saved your money so you could use it during retirement. You didn't save it not to use it because you were worried about how much income taxes you would pay. And if you are 60 years old and planning not to touch your assets until you are age 70½, do you really think this is the wisest decision? Can you spend the money better at age 60 or age 70½? What if you ultimately end up paying more income taxes over your lifetime because you deferred your IRA until age 70½?

Rule #6: Generate "Certain Income" From Your Assets That Will Last For As Long As You Live, Not "Maybe Income" That Could End At Any Time

The #1 fear retirees have is that they'll run out of money during their lifetimes. To eliminate this fear, you need to create income that is guaranteed to be paid to you for as long as you live. First you will need to decide how much income you want to be "certain income" – income that is guaranteed to be paid to you for as long as you live, such as pension income, social security, and lifetime income from annuities. Secondly, you will need to decide how much income you're comfortable with being "maybe income" – income that is not guaranteed and can decrease or stop at any time such as portfolio income, interest income, dividend income, real estate and REIT income, and income based on the potential growth or earnings of an asset.

What is the only single thing you can do as a retiree to totally eliminate the fear of running out of money? You have to create as much "certain income" from your assets as possible, income that is called "guaranteed lifetime income," that will be paid to you, and your spouse if married, for as long as you live, even if you live past 100 years old, even if the stock market crashes, and even if you use up all your asset values!

Why do many retirees not use their assets for income or not take as much income out of their assets as they could? It's simply because they are afraid if they use it now, it will run out later, that it won't last for as long as they live. You saved money while you were working for the sole purpose to use it for income when you retired, not to look at it and worry about it for the next 30 years during retirement without using it.

How would you feel if your monthly income from your assets was guaranteed to be paid to you for as long as you and your spouse lived? Imagine if you could increase your income right now, and regardless of stock market volatility or losses, knew you would receive the exact same amount of income this month, next month, every month for the rest of this year, every month next year, and every month for as long as you lived; how would you feel? Would you worry as much? What if the stock market crashed -53.8% like it did in 2007 through 2009, and your income was not disturbed and you kept receiving the same amount every month? If you knew your income was contractually guaranteed to be paid to you for as long as you lived, would you feel more financially independent? Would you be willing to spend more, take more trips, do the remodel, buy the car, help your kids and grandkids? Wouldn't this make you happier? Isn't it how you planned to live your retirement? Couldn't this potentially give you financial freedom?

Although it's said, "money can't make you happy," we have found retirees who don't have enough income are definitely not happy, and if they are married it can cause a lot of stress between the spouses. Most retirees want as much "certain income" as possible during retirement, they just don't know how to create it. It's very wise to create the maximum amount of "certain income" because studies show the happiest retirees, and those that are healthiest and live the longest, are retirees with the highest levels of "certain income", income that is guaranteed to last for their entire lives. And right here, right now, we are going to create a new saying: *Income that is guaranteed to be paid to you for as long as you live will make you happy.*

Most retirees have never been told and don't understand that they can buy contractually guaranteed lifetime income and contractual principal guarantees from A+ insurance companies that have been operating for at least 90 years. These companies have fulfilled their guaranteed lifetime income and guaranteed principal promises to their customers even through the Great Depression.

Rule #7: Have a Written Retirement Income Plan

Would you buy a $500,000, $1,000,000 or $3,000,000+ house without getting everything in writing? Of course you wouldn't. So why would you give your advisor, or invest yourself, $500,000, $1,000,000 or $3,000,000+ without having a written plan, meaning everything about your money in writing? It's because you didn't know you could get a written plan, you've always wanted one, you just never got one. Your broker may seem smart, may seem like he/she knows what they are doing, but they have never put anything down about your money in writing. This is a "red flag warning sign!"

The single most important aspect of planning a secure retirement is not trying to invest in the best assets, or getting the highest rates of return, it's making sure you have a written plan to guide you through retirement, to be used as a map and navigation tool, act as a measuring stick for proper progress, and explain every detail of your plan for retirement success so you won't forget anything. If you have an advisor, or you do it yourself, and if you don't have an actual plan in writing, you actually don't have a plan at all. Having a written plan will help you avoid confusion, misunderstandings, mistakes, and will significantly improve the probability of a successful plan throughout your retirement. It also holds your advisor responsible and accountable for all the promises he/she is making to you about your money.

When new clients come into our offices, many times they tell us how much they really love their current advisor. We tell them that it's very important to have a strong relationship with an advisor, and we are happy they have had the opportunity to work with someone they cared about. We state their current advisor must also care about them a great deal, and based on how much their advisor cares about them, their current advisor must have provided them a comprehensive written retirement income plan. This plan should detail exactly how they will use their assets for retirement income for as long as they live, how much risk they're taking, how much income tax they'll pay, the total fees they pay (both direct and hidden), how much they'll leave their beneficiaries, the advantages, disadvantages, and all details about their plan spelled out.

We then ask the new clients to provide us a full copy of their comprehensive written retirement income plan that their current advisor has created for them for our review. And at this point the room goes deathly quiet…

it is the best example of the proverbial "pin-drop", because their current advisor has not given them anything in writing except quarterly statements that they don't even understand.

Sound familiar? It should, because in our over 425 years of combined experience we have found over 99% of retirees and people planning for retirement have never been given a comprehensive written retirement income plan from their current advisor. Most retirees and pre-retirees we meet with have worked with their current advisor for 5, 10, 15, 20, 25, and even 30 years or longer. They have discussed their investments on countless occasions, they receive statements (which they really don't understand), they are told to "ride out the market" and "everything will be fine over the long run" and they will receive "high rates of return between 8% to 12% like the market has always provided." You might have even broached the subject of a written plan with your current advisor but to-date nothing has even been completed. This is the sad truth retirees across America face every day.

But all this means is that you don't have a plan at all, you just have a portfolio that you probably don't really understand, other than it goes up and down on a monthly basis. Most retirees don't have a written plan because their broker doesn't have the expertise to put it together and won't spend the large amount of time required to complete the whole plan. In addition, the broker doesn't want the responsibility, accountability, and liability that comes with creating a written plan.

Recent studies report one of the main things retirees and pre-retirees want from their financial advisor is to have an actual plan created for them, and to have that plan put in writing. That's what retirees and pre-retirees want. You probably love the idea of a comprehensive written retirement income plan, but what's in it? There are four (4) main components to a properly prepared comprehensive written retirement income plan:

(i). Retirement Income Projection – This section of your plan will show how much income you will receive every year throughout your retirement. For each year it will show when each income source starts, stops, increases, decreases, what income is guaranteed ("certain income"), and what income is not guaranteed ("maybe income"). You will be able to "see" how your different sources of income will flow to you throughout your retirement. This section of your plan will also calculate

the current risk you have in your portfolio and your new reduced risk level in your new recommended portfolio allocation. You will know how much risk you are taking before you invest your money; wouldn't that be a breath of fresh air? This section of your plan will also calculate the total fees, even the hidden fees, you are paying on your current portfolio and then will calculate the total fees, even the hidden fees, you will be paying on your new recommended portfolio allocation. Again, you will know what fees you will be paying before you invest!

(ii). Income Tax Analysis – This second section of your plan will show your total gross annual income and how much of the gross income you receive is considered taxable. After deducting the higher of your projected itemized deductions or your standard deduction, your total federal and state income taxes will be calculated using the latest income tax rates. Then one of the most important calculations is performed to determine your effective income tax rate, meaning the percentage of tax you will pay on every dollar of gross income you receive. This section of your plan will then show you what your gross monthly income will be, how much income tax you should have withheld every month, and the most important number of all; what your monthly net income after taxes will be. This section will also show how much money you have available to save each month after you pay for all your normal monthly expenses.

(iii). Beneficiary Asset Transfer Analysis – This section illustrates how much income you are projected to take out of your portfolio for every year throughout your retirement, the cumulative amount of income you are projected to receive, and how much you can reasonably expect to pass on to your beneficiaries after you have taken income from your assets every year and earned a moderate rate of return.

(iv). Full Plan Details – This section of your plan will cover every detail of your final plan and will typically be between 12 to 24 pages in length and will tie all aspects of your plan together. This section of your plan will include:

- What you are trying to achieve with planning.
- What you want your money to do for you.
- Your goals, wants, and needs.
- What you want to make sure happens no matter what.
- What you want to make sure doesn't happen no matter what.

- Your current portfolio allocation including a listing of all your current investments.
- Your new portfolio allocation including all of your modified portfolio investments.
- How much risk you are currently taking.
- How much risk you really want to take.
- The risk of your new plan.
- How much you are projected to lose in your current portfolio in the next market crash.
- How much you are projected to lose in your new portfolio in the next market crash.
- How much in total fees you are currently paying.
- How much in total fees you will pay in your new plan.
- Where you currently stand financially.
- One (1) to two (2) pages of advantages of your new plan.
- One (1) to two (2) pages of disadvantages of your new plan.
- Step-By-Step process you will follow to complete your plan.
- How and when you will use each asset.
- Liquidity needs and access to funds.
- How each asset is passed on to beneficiaries.

The entire document should be read out loud to you and give you the opportunity to ask questions about your final plan. This process provides the highest probability that you will understand more about your money than you ever have, and that you will be able to remember your plan because the whole thing is in writing. Your plan should be finalized by you signing your plan stating you understand your plan and your advisor should sign your plan as your advisor. Your advisor should back up every single thing they say, every promise they make, putting every part of your plan, in writing. Has anyone ever done that for you before?

SUMMARY

THE 7 RULES TO LIVE BY FOR RETIREMENT SECURITY

Until you read this book, you never heard about the (7) rules you could follow that would virtually guarantee you'd increase your chances for a successful retirement. If you'd heard about them before, you'd already be following them, because *The 7 Rules To Live By For Retirement Security* serve as your roadmap to your financial security during retirement. If you had such a roadmap you'd probably use it, it's just that no one has given you the roadmap until now.

So, think about it, if you followed all seven (7) of *The 7 Rules To Live By For Retirement Security*, do you think you'd increase your probability of success during retirement? Of course you would. If you are reading this book the one thing you want to make sure happens is that you have a successful retirement. By following these seven (7) rules, you might only increase your probability of success a little bit, or you might be one of those clients that increases their probability of success a tremendous amount. But every single person, if they follow these seven (7) rules, will increase their chances for a successful retirement. The seven (7) rules are not about a specific investment, they are about an actual plan. Based on how our clients have told us they have felt after going through the process, establishing a plan to follow *The 7 Rules To Live By For Retirement Security*, which includes getting every part of their plan in writing, we can tell you that you will most likely feel:

- Secure, happy, maybe even overjoyed.
- Less burdened, anxious, and worried.
- Relieved, less confused, and younger.
- Confident things will work out and you can spend your money without guilt or worry.
- Empowered and in control of your money.
- Safer, no longer fearful of being poor in your old age.
- Proud that you have an actual plan.
- Comforted that you, your spouse (if married), and your family have been taken care of.
- Extremely grateful that you finally found a firm to provide you with true financial peace of mind.

Once retirees learn about *The 7 Rules To Live By For Retirement Security*, they understand the guidelines and see the process as a "roadmap" for them to follow for their retirement success. They typically want to know what they actually have to do to create a plan to follow the rules. They like the ideas, but they wonder how can they implement the ideas? We will discuss the two (2) lessons we have created to teach you how to follow the seven rules in the next two (2) chapters.

CHAPTER 18

FOLLOW THE 7 RULES
LESSON #1
THE TWO STAGES OF MONEY IN RETIREMENT

BY DAN AHMAD & JIM FILES

The first lesson in following *The 7 Rules To Live By For Retirement Security* to create retirement success is understanding there are two (2) distinct stages in retirement planning when you're talking about money.

The first stage you know very well, it's called Stage One of Retirement Planning - Asset Accumulation. Stage One is when you're working, making a salary, investing monthly, and have many years until retirement. During Stage One you want the maximum growth you can get from your assets, are tolerant of high volatility, will accept large losses, will continue to make contributions, have plenty of time on your side, and don't need income from your assets for many years. Basically, in Stage One, you can handle a high level of risk.

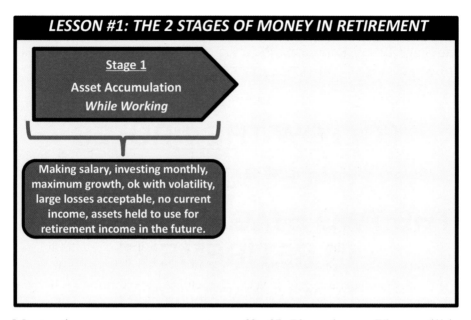

LESSON #1: THE 2 STAGES OF MONEY IN RETIREMENT

Stage 1

Asset Accumulation
While Working

Making salary, investing monthly, maximum growth, ok with volatility, large losses acceptable, no current income, assets held to use for retirement income in the future.

Most retirees we meet, many at age 60, 65, 70, and even 75, are still in Stage One mode. You, or your current broker, might have done a great job accumulating assets up until this point in time, and you might have gotten a little bit lucky with this current Bull Market still thriving after almost ten (10) years. We say you might have gotten lucky because we are almost three (3) years over-due for the next -40% stock market correction that has happened every seven (7) years on average since 1929. You are probably continuing to do most of the same things with your money that you did when you were young and working, in many cases taking a lot of risk and not creating an income plan.

For Stage One to be the proper planning methodology for you now that you are retired, you have to be able to say you are perfectly comfortable not making your previous salary, it doesn't bother you that you are not investing money every month like you used to, you have no issue with high volatility, you are not afraid of large losses, you feel you have enough time to make up any large loss, and you don't want or need income from your assets for a long time. Very few retirees can say all these things are true. Can you? Can your spouse?

Here is the issue – if you are retired, or within five (5) to ten (10) years of retirement, you should have already transitioned out of Stage One and into Stage Two of Retirement Planning - Income Distribution and Asset Preservation. Here's why:

1. If you are retired, ask yourself if you suffer through another market crash like 2008, will your retirement be unaffected by the loss? Will you feel safe taking the same amount of income out of your assets and feel confident your income won't run out? Will you feel secure things will still work out if the stock market crashed -50% again? If you are retired, how will your spouse feel?

2. If you are within five (5) to ten (10) years of retirement, ask yourself if you suffer through another stock market crash like 2008, will you be able to retire on-time as planned or will you have to work longer, a lot longer? Will your projected future retirement income be unaffected by the loss? How will you feel if you have to work ten (10) more years instead of five (5) more years? Will you feel safe taking the same amount of income out of your assets and feel confident your income won't run out? Will you feel secure things will still work out if the stock market crashed -50% again? If you are within five (5) to ten (10) years of retirement, how will your spouse feel?

Stage Two is when you are retired or are within five (5) to ten (10) years of retirement:

1. You are no longer making your big salary.
2. You are no longer making any monthly investments into your 401(k)/403(b)/457/SEP.
3. You want and need the maximum security.
4. You do not want much volatility at all.
5. You cannot tolerate any large stock market losses.
6. You need to create the maximum amount of income and make sure the income is guaranteed to be paid to you and your spouse, if married, for as long as you both live, and the income must be available immediately or at a specific time in the future.

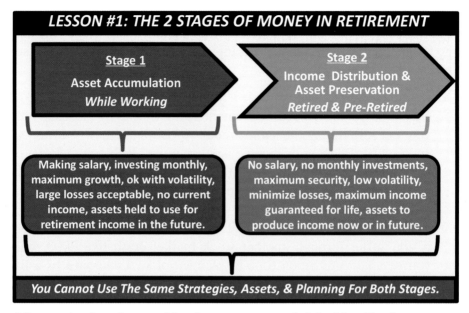

LESSON #1: THE 2 STAGES OF MONEY IN RETIREMENT

Stage 1
Asset Accumulation
While Working

Stage 2
Income Distribution &
Asset Preservation
Retired & Pre-Retired

Making salary, investing monthly, maximum growth, ok with volatility, large losses acceptable, no current income, assets held to use for retirement income in the future.

No salary, no monthly investments, maximum security, low volatility, minimize losses, maximum income guaranteed for life, assets to produce income now or in future.

You Cannot Use The Same Strategies, Assets, & Planning For Both Stages.

After reviewing the graphic above, you can plainly identify there are no similarities between Stage One and Stage Two. You can't use the same strategies, you can't use the same assets or allocations, you can't use the same planning techniques, and you can't use the same advisor for both strategies. Over 99% of the retirees and pre-retirees we meet with are still in Stage One of Retirement Planning - Asset Accumulation mode. As we said, you or your current broker might have done a great job accumulating assets up until this point in time, and you might have gotten a little bit lucky with this current bull stock market still thriving after nine (9) years. But remember, -40% market corrections happen every seven (7) years on average since 1929, so you'd better protect your assets against large losses.

If you are retired, or within five (5) to ten (10) years of retirement, and you haven't already transitioned from Stage One into Stage Two, this simply means your assets are not positioned properly. If you have an advisor, it means he/she is not looking after your best interests. Most advisors specialize in helping you to accumulate assets for retirement (Stage One). They are experts in asset accumulation, it is how they were trained, it's what they are good at, it's what they like to do, but the majority are not experts in Stage Two of Retirement Planning - Income Distribution and Asset Preservation. If you're still stuck in Stage One, you need immediate help from an expert in Stage Two. The history of the financial industry is that it was built based on the concept of asset accumulation.

We believe the traditional financial industry, and traditional brokers, don't want you to use your money. They want you to keep all your money in your accounts, so that they can maximize their own income- not yours!

CHAPTER 19

FOLLOW THE 7 RULES
LESSON #2
USE THE CORRECT PROCESS FOR FINANCIAL SUCCESS

BY DAN AHMAD & JIM FILES

The vast majority of retirees do not have their assets allocated properly to give themselves the highest probability that they can receive a high level of consistent income, will never run out of money for as long as they live, and will never suffer a big stock market loss like 2008 again.

In the previous chapter we just described in detail the differences between Stage One of Retirement Planning - Asset Accumulation and Stage Two of Retirement Planning - Income Distribution and Asset Preservation. When you meet with your current advisor, even now when retired, the conversation will almost always be focused on your portfolio. Your advisor will talk about:

- The growth of your portfolio (even though it actually hasn't probably grown much).
- How the market is doing "so well" and you need to ride the wave.
- How you are diversified by having your 20-30 mutual funds.
- Adding bonds to the portfolio, if you are worried about risk.
- How you are in it for the long-term and no matter what, you should "ride out all market volatility."
- How they have the best money managers.
- How they will get you high rates of return.
- Maybe they will throw in some technical terms like alpha, beta, Sharpe ratio, and standard deviation.

- How it's best to defer IRA distributions as long as possible, until age 70 ½, to minimize income taxes.

The advisor might say you are now invested moderately, or conservatively, but they don't define what this means in potential losses. So, your advisor says "moderate" or "conservative," and you are thinking "low risk," even though your current portfolio could lose -30%, -40%, or even -50% or more. The risk is caused by the portfolio's primary focus on growth.

As depicted by the following graph, during Stage One the most important aspect is growth. This is because you should only be in Stage One if you have a minimum of six (6) more years, and preferably ten (10) more years until retirement, so you have time on your side to recover from losses, you are continuing to earn a salary, will make additional monthly investments into your accounts, and you don't need income yet. In Stage One you aren't concerned with creating guaranteed lifetime income nor are you worried as much about liquidity and safety.

When you are retired or close to retirement, allocating your portfolio with growth as the #1 most important goal literally puts your entire retirement security at risk. During retirement, the focus of your advisor must be on helping you to create income that is guaranteed not to run out for as long as you live, and reduce your risk to eliminate the possibility of going through another catastrophic 2008 stock market type loss again.

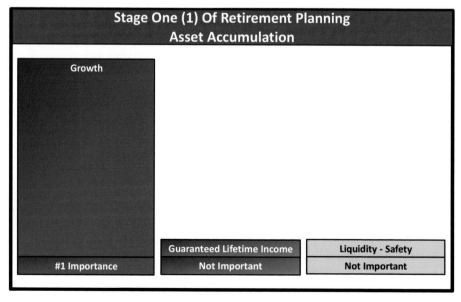

What is the single worst thing that can happen to your money in retirement? What's your biggest fear? Most retirees will say "running out of money before I die," and they think this means "running out of assets." But what they are really trying to say is "they are really afraid they won't have enough income every month for as long as they live." Asset values and monthly income are two (2) separate and distinct aspects of your money.

So, the number one most important thing you protect yourself against is "running out of income." Because if you run out of income, you can't pay for the things you need and want every month. If you run out of income, your lifestyle changes. If you run out of income, you can't save any more money in the bank every month. If you run out of income, you lose your financial independence and then have to rely on the government or your family members to support you. If you run out of income, your worst financial fear comes true.

During retirement, what do you have to make sure happens? You have to make sure your #1 fear, which is running out of money, doesn't happen. Running out of money means running out of the income you need. So, the #1 most important goal you have in retirement is creating the maximum amount of income that is guaranteed to be paid to you for as long as you live.

We don't think you have actually done the wrong things with your money. We do believe if you are like 99% of retirees we have met, you are stuck in Stage One by taking too much risk and not using your assets to create the highest level of income guaranteed to last for as long as you live. So, we don't think you are doing the wrong things with your money, we just think you are probably going about planning for retirement by using the "wrong process," by not transitioning into Stage Two.

To explain the concept of using the wrong process we like using the example of baking a cake. Pretend you are going to bake a birthday cake. You take the pan out, and you spray the non-stick stuff in it. You put the cake mix in. You put two eggs in there, but you don't crack them, you put the eggs in whole, shell and all, and then you mix everything together. You bake those ingredients for half an hour. You take the pan out of the oven and mix in the frosting, the oil, the water and the vanilla. You stir it all around. You put in every single ingredient you were supposed to. It should have all worked out, right? So, you serve that cake. Is it a good cake or a nasty cake? That's a very nasty cake. You had the right ingredients, but you did not use the correct order, you did not use the right process. For 99% of retirees, the same thing is happening right now with your money. If you don't use the right process, you're not going to get a good end result.

If you are retired or within five (5) to ten (10) years of retirement, and you are focusing on growth first and not paying too much attention, if any, to creating guaranteed lifetime income and safety/liquidity, your retirement security is potentially in jeopardy.

Transitioning from Stage One (1) of Retirement Planning—Asset Accumulation—to Stage Two of Retirement Planning—Income Distribution and Asset Preservation—can be psychologically tough. First of all, to switch from Stage One to Stage Two you have to admit one painful thing, and that is that somehow, against all of your best efforts, you have gotten older. In our experience, this seems to be tougher on males than females. Stage One allowed you to be aggressive with your investments and take risks, some of the key characteristics of "youth." Now we are saying, "Hey, you need to slow your aggressive behavior down," you need to "act your age," and we understand how you might at first want to rebel. But to ensure your retirement financial security, you must make this transition.

The second psychological hurdle, and possibly the most difficult thing to do for both males and females is switching from being a "saver" to a "spender." Think about it, for years and years while you were working, you saved and saved, you did without and sacrificed, you tried to be frugal, allowing you to be a "master saver," a "master asset accumulator." It's not easy to turn off the "accumulation switch," it's very difficult to visualize "spending" the money you "saved." But you have to remember why you saved all the money in the first place – it was to actually use the money you saved to create income when you retired that would last for as long as you lived. It was to improve your life during retirement. You "saved it" so you could "spend it."

So, how do you actually transition from Stage One to Stage Two? You simply re-prioritize how your assets are allocated to give you the best chance you will never run out of money for as long as you live, and will never suffer a big stock market loss like 2008 again. To bake your perfect retirement cake, to create your perfect portfolio, the correct process of allocation of your assets during Stage Two of Retirement Planning – Income Distribution and Asset Preservation, the opposite of Stage One, – is prioritized:

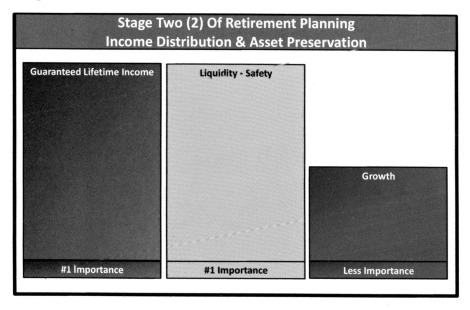

During retirement, Stage Two, you have to shift how you view and handle your money. At this time of your life, you are hurt far more by losses than you are helped by big gains. Remember back to when we discussed what would happen to your $1,000,000 portfolio if you first earned a +50% rate of return and then you suffered a -50% loss. A +50% gain would propel your portfolio up to $1,500,000 and then a -50% loss would drive the $1,500,000 back down to $750,000. You probably have not transitioned into Stage Two because no one has advised you to do so, and no one has helped you do it. No one has given you the answers.

The secret to successfully transition from Stage One to Stage Two is to use the concept we call the "3 Bucket Safe Money Approach":

> ➤ Bucket #1: *Guaranteed lifetime income* – Step 1 is to decide how much income you need from your assets for the rest of your life. Invest the amount needed into Bucket #1 to create a stream of income that is guaranteed to be paid to you for as long as you live.

➤ Bucket #2: _Liquidity/Safety_ – Step 2 is to decide how much money you should keep liquid in the bank.

➤ Bucket #3: _Growth_ – Step 3 is to invest the remaining assets for growth. But don't accept full stock market risk and do not follow the "old school" advice you have been given in the past to "Ride Out All Market Losses."

If you allocated your assets for guaranteed lifetime income first, liquidity/safety second, and growth third, would you understand your money better in retirement? Would you worry about it as much? Would you have a higher probability to achieve your goal of retirement success? Has anyone ever discussed this exact process and order with you before: guaranteed lifetime income first, liquidity/safety second, and growth third? We know they haven't, but why not? What do stockbrokers tell you to do? They tell you to put all your money in the stock market. What do bankers tell you to do? They tell you to put all your money in the bank. What do life insurance and annuity salespeople tell you to do? They tell you to put all your money in annuities and life insurance.

Does it make any sense to put all your money in just one of the three (3) categories? Of course it doesn't. So why do they tell you to do it anyway? It's because that's how they get paid. To design the proper retirement plan, an advisor has to have access to all three (3) categories. If your advisor does not work with and advise you to use all three (3) categories, they are not looking after your best interests, they are looking after themselves.

It is important to have access to all three (3) asset categories to ensure the best plan to help you meet your goals. If you don't have access to all three (3) categories, you might not be able to design the best plan for you. You need the ability to have guaranteed lifetime income assets, assets in the bank, and growth assets in the stock market.

CHAPTER 20

UNDERSTANDING AND CONTROLLING THE THREE BUCKETS

BY DAN AHMAD & JIM FILES

Now imagine if you, not your broker, get to decide how much money you want to put into the guaranteed lifetime income bucket, how much money you want to put into the safe and liquid bucket, and how much money you want to put into the growth bucket. Do you think you would start to understand your money better? Now you would get to control your assets, make them act the way you want them to act. You would learn the behavior of each bucket:

1. If you put money into the liquid and safe bucket, would you expect these assets to earn high rates of return or provide a high level of income? Of course not, you would expect these assets to be secure against stock market losses and available for you to access at any time.

2. If you put money into the guaranteed lifetime income bucket, would you expect these assets to earn stock market rates of return and be completely liquid or would you expect these assets to provide you the highest level of income guaranteed for as long as you live and be protected against all stock market losses? You'd expect lifetime guaranteed income and no stock market losses.

3. If you put money into the growth bucket would you expect these assets to be free of volatility and free of losses? No, you would expect a higher level of risk for the opportunity for a potentially higher rate of return.

To properly allocate your assets as a retiree you will use what we call the *"3 Bucket Safe Money Approach"*:

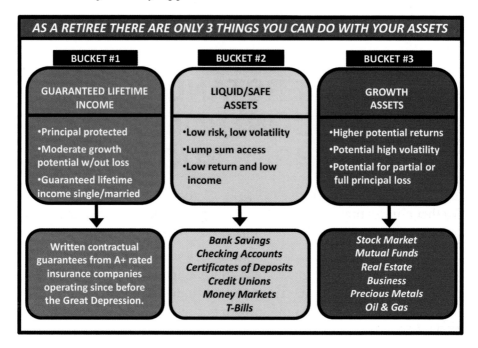

AS A RETIREE THERE ARE ONLY 3 THINGS YOU CAN DO WITH YOUR ASSETS

BUCKET #1	BUCKET #2	BUCKET #3
GUARANTEED LIFETIME INCOME	**LIQUID/SAFE ASSETS**	**GROWTH ASSETS**
•Principal protected •Moderate growth potential w/out loss •Guaranteed lifetime income single/married	•Low risk, low volatility •Lump sum access •Low return and low income	•Higher potential returns •Potential high volatility •Potential for partial or full principal loss
Written contractual guarantees from A+ rated insurance companies operating since before the Great Depression.	*Bank Savings* *Checking Accounts* *Certificates of Deposits* *Credit Unions* *Money Markets* *T-Bills*	*Stock Market* *Mutual Funds* *Real Estate* *Business* *Precious Metals* *Oil & Gas*

If you had these three (3) buckets of different types of assets that you could use to allocate your assets, would you feel for the first time that you could actually "control" how your money was going to act? Could you eliminate the unwelcome surprises from big losses or decreased income? You could do both.

One of the main reasons retirees don't understand their money is because they have not allocated their assets into these three (3) buckets that provide separate and distinct benefits. Instead, most retirees have allocated their assets into one (1) portfolio managed by their broker that is supposedly diversified between many mutual funds or stocks that they really don't understand. Then you have to ask your overall portfolio to try and do all of the things the three (3) buckets can do, and you have undoubtedly found over time your traditional portfolio has been unable to do this. Your traditional portfolio recommended by your broker fails at delivering the total combined benefits the three (3) buckets can provide.

You can look at the three (3) buckets as "deconstructing your portfolio" to make each asset a separate "bucket" of your money, with each "bucket" assigned specific and attainable tasks based on the actual capabilities of each "bucket." This way you will only ask each "bucket" to do what is possible and what you want it to do, significantly increasing your understanding of your assets and the probability that your financial goals will be met. This way you will not be asking any of your assets to do "too much."

There are many reasons why your current broker/advisor has not provided you with a comprehensive written retirement income plan. Your broker/ advisor may not have the ability to create a plan, may not want to spend the considerable amount of time necessary to create a plan, or may not want the responsibility, accountability, and liability to create a plan. But one of the main reasons he/she hasn't provided you a plan is because he/she has invested your assets into a portfolio that mixes everything together eliminating the possibility of assigning specific, attainable tasks to each asset that the *"3 Bucket Safe Money Approach"* provides.

How can you make your assets act the way you want them to act? How do you implement the *"3 Bucket Safe Money Approach"?*

Step #1

Bucket #1: First decide how much guaranteed income you need from your assets for the rest of your life.

Bucket #1 focuses on providing:

(1) Income guaranteed for as long as you live, whether you are single or married – even if to age 100+.
(2) Principal protection so you will never suffer a stock market loss even if the stock market loses -53.8% like it did in the 2008 Financial Crisis, you will lose 0%.
(3) The opportunity to earn a competitive rate of return based on a low-risk asset.
(4) The Protection of current and future gains against stock market losses, so you can never lose what you earn.
(5) The facility to pass on all remaining assets to beneficiaries.
(6) Low total fees of approximately 1%.
(7) Income starting immediately or when needed.
(8) The opportunity for future income increases.
(9) Income for as long as you live even if you use up all of your principal.

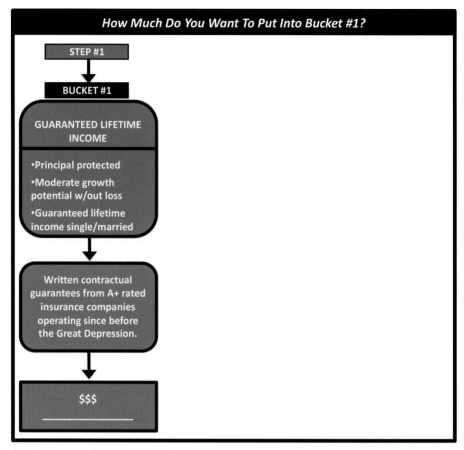

At the same time, you can't take out all your money from Bucket #1 in a lump sum without a penalty for a certain time period, but typically you can take out 10% of your account per year starting after 12 months, you do not get all the stock market gains, you will get less. For a hypothetical example, when the market was up 19% in 2017, the return goal for Bucket #1 was between 8% and 12%. These returns are not guaranteed but if you had no stock market risk, would you be willing to accept a lower potential return? And you do have to pay a fee that averages 1%, but this is probably much lower than you are paying on your current investments.

Bucket #1 uses contractual guarantees from A+ rated insurance companies that have been operating since before the Great Depression, with these companies fulfilling all their promises and guarantees even through the worst financial crisis the United States has ever seen. ***Bucket #1 is called a fixed index annuity with an income rider.***

Step #2

<u>Bucket #2:</u> Second, you must review how much money you need in the bank for liquidity and safety.

You may have been told before to keep money in the bank for potential emergencies, but the main reasons we advise you to keep money in the bank is so you can spend it and keep it safe. Ask yourself if you are more willing to spend the money you have in the bank or the money you have in the stock market? Most people say the bank. Keeping money in the bank helps to reduce the overall risk of the portfolio because even if the stock market crashes by -53.8% as it did in the 2008 Financial Crisis, you will lose 0%, you will not lose any money in the bank. Keeping money in the bank also helps to reduce the overall fees you are paying on your assets because you don't pay fees on money you have in the bank.

We also want you to be able to add money to your bank every month. Most advisors won't tell you to put money in the bank because they don't get paid when you do. Our clients love to have more and more money in the bank. The goal of a properly-designed comprehensive retirement income plan is to create enough income to pay for all of your monthly expenses including travel, save enough for future large expenses like cars, remodels, and kids/grandkids education, and save for future costs that you are not currently aware of, so each month you should add money to your bank account.

You are not putting the money into Bucket #2 to get a high rate of return, you are putting it there to be safe and accessible. You can use your bank or credit union for holding the funds. If you can find a higher rate of return at a different bank, by all means go ahead and use the higher paying bank.

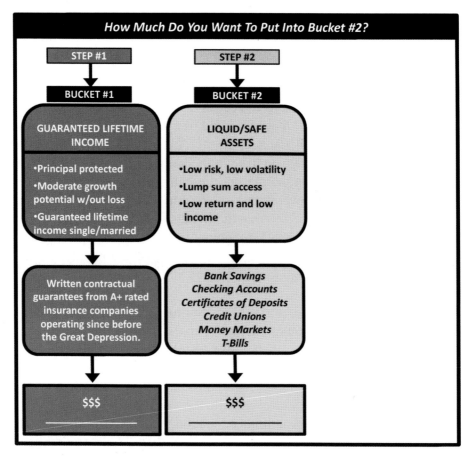

Step #3

Bucket #3: After deciding how much money to put into Bucket #1 for guaranteed lifetime income, and Bucket #2 for liquidity and safety, the remainder of the funds can be placed in Bucket #3 for growth.

Bucket #3 provides you the opportunity to potentially earn higher rates of return than Bucket #1 and Bucket #2. The assets placed in Bucket #3 will have considerably more risk of loss than Bucket #1 and Bucket #2. You can suffer a partial or full principal loss in Bucket #3. But think about it, if you have all the guaranteed income you want and need covered by the funds you place in Bucket #1 along with principal safety, and you have all the liquidity and principal safety covered with the funds you place into Bucket #2, wouldn't you feel more comfortable, wouldn't you feel less risky, placing assets in Bucket #3? Basically, if you didn't have to worry about your income or having funds accessible for large purchases or emergencies, you probably would feel more inclined to take some risk with some of your money for growth in Bucket #3.

If Bucket #1 can't lose any money in a stock market crash, and Bucket #2 can't lose any money in a stock market crash, even if you have money in Bucket #3 haven't you just significantly reduced your overall risk? Of course you have! We also will set up income distributions coming out of Bucket #3, if needed, for your comprehensive written retirement income plan to be successful. The income coming from Bucket #3 is not guaranteed, it is considered "maybe income," but risk management techniques can be used to give you a high probability this income stream will not run out for as long as you live.

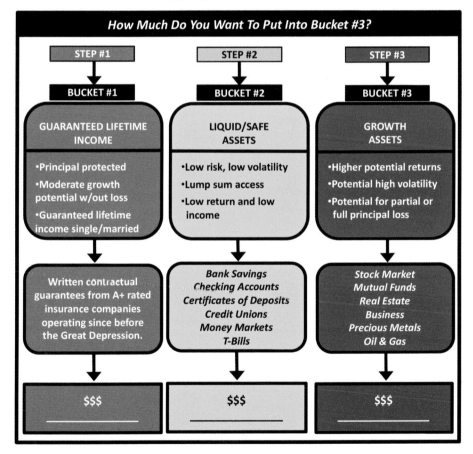

If you get to decide how much money you want to put into Bucket #1, Bucket #2, and Bucket #3, you have just learned how to control your potential income, access to large lump sum distributions, risk, fees, and potential growth.

CHAPTER 21

DESIGNING A RETIREMENT ASSET ALLOCATION FOR SAFETY, GROWTH, AND INCOME FOR LIFE

BY DAN AHMAD & JIM FILES

We have discussed the *7 Rules To Live By For Retirement Security*, and if you are like most retirees, you probably love the idea of having a "Retirement Planning Roadmap":

7 Rules To Live By For Retirement Security:

1. Avoid large losses – use the "5%-10% Rule".

2. Minimize fees.

3. Significantly reduce volatility.

4. Earn a reasonable return rate.

5. Manage taxation.

6. Generate "Certain Income" from your assets that will last for as long as you live, not "Maybe Income" that could end at any time.

7. Have a Written Retirement Income Plan.

The reality is, one (1) investment alone will not allow you to follow *The 7 Rules To Live By For Retirement Security.* You can only receive the benefits of following all seven (7) rules if you have an actual plan that ties everything about your money together and if you use the *"3 Bucket Safe Money Approach."* If you are serious about your financial security, your next question is probably "OK, I really like the idea, but how do I implement it?" Do you remember the chapter discussing the *"3 Bucket Safe Money Approach?"* We are now going to look at the 3 Buckets as a pie chart, an allocation of assets chart. The most important thing to notice about our pie chart is it is not just a bunch of mutual funds crammed into one (1) pie, with a lot of the mutual funds behaving similarly. Our pie chart has three (3) separate and distinct sections (buckets) that all act differently, but in concert with one another to help you meet your goals.

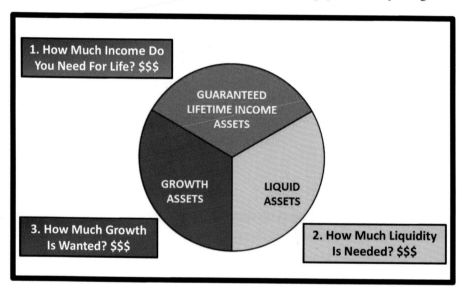

First, we determine the amount of income you need for the rest of your life and allocate the assets to Bucket #1 required to produce this amount of income. Second, we determine how much liquidity you need and allocate the assets required to Bucket #2. And third, we determine how much growth you want and allocate the assets required to Bucket #3.

For Bucket #1 we have to create a high level of income that is guaranteed to be paid to you for as long as you live. We use contractually guaranteed insurance products that are called fixed index annuities with income riders. We use A+ rated insurance companies that have been operating since before the Great Depression, with these companies keeping all of their financial guarantees and promises to their contract owners even through the worst economic time period the United States has ever been through.

And we know, we used the bad "A-word" called *annuities*, which is a dirty word to a lot of people because you've heard bad things about annuities. A lot of the bad things you have heard about annuities are actually accurate when you are talking about variable annuities. Variable annuities do not provide principal protection against stock market losses, and they can carry annual fees as high as 6.5%. So, we agree, variable annuities are not for you, and our firm does not work with variable annuities. When you hear bad things about annuities, in the majority of cases, someone is probably talking about a variable annuity. But let's look at how a fixed index annuity with an income rider works.

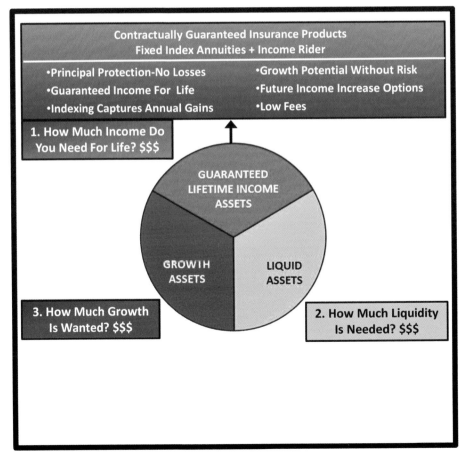

Fixed index annuities with income riders are specifically designed to:

- Guarantee you won't lose any principal from stock market losses. If the stock market crashes -53.8% like it did in the 2008 Financial Crisis, you would lose 0%.

- Provide you income guaranteed for as long as you live, and if married, for as long as your spouse lives. Some plans allow for immediate income (within 30 days) while many plans allow income after 12 months. While income can start immediately, you can't take all of your principal out for a certain time period without paying a premature withdrawal penalty (like a CD).

- Even if you live past life expectancy and use up all the assets in your fixed index annuity with an income rider, and your account value goes to $0, you will still continue to receive the same income for as long as you live. You can't outlive your income!

- Guarantee you won't lose any of your current or future gains from stock market losses. For example, if you earn a hypothetical 6% rate of return for five (5) straight years and then the market crashes -50%, 100% of your original principal is protected from losses and 100% of all the gain you made during the five (5) years is protected. What you earn can't be lost.

- Potential competitive growth rates from a low-risk asset. What does "competitive" mean? It does not mean stock market rates of return. If you want to earn stock market rates of return, you must be willing to take stock market risks. The stock market, as measured by the S&P 500 Index, grew by +19% in 2017, which was a great year. But if you wanted the opportunity to earn +19% in 2017, you have to be willing to take the -53.8% risk the stock market lost in the 2008 Financial Crisis. In 2017 when the stock market grew by +19%, the return goals for fixed index annuities with income riders would have been between +8% to +12%, without principal risk. So, the +8% to +12% return goals were competitive, but they were short of the +19% the market earned, and there is no guarantee the funds will grow at all.

- Allows the assets to grow income tax-deferred until you take distributions. Unlike a portfolio of mutual funds, stocks, and bonds, all annual gains are not reported on your tax return if you are not taking distributions.

- Provide the opportunity for future income increases either through guaranteed increases by deferring income or with potential annual increases based on index performance.
- Carry low fees. The typical total annual fee for a fixed index annuity with an income rider is between 0% to 2%, with the average being right about 1%.
- Passes 100% of assets remaining in your account when you die to your beneficiaries, the insurance company does not keep your money.

So, if fixed index annuities with income riders actually did all of these things, would it be a good place to put some of your retirement assets? In many cases it would. Would the word "annuity" be a bad word or a very good word? Seems like a pretty good word now. Should you put all of your money in a fixed index annuity with an income rider? Definitely not, because you will have a surrender penalty for a certain time period. You put the portion of your assets into a fixed index annuity with an income rider that you want immediate or future guaranteed income from and that you want 100% principal protection from all stock market losses. It's important to understand fixed index annuities with income riders _are not designed to_:

- Give you 100% liquid access to all your funds starting immediately.
- Give you 100% of the stock market upside and gains.
- Be used as a short-term asset alternative.

For Bucket #2 we have to determine how much liquidity is needed for your plan. This money you will typically put into the bank, credit union, money markets, CD's, and T-Bills. We have previously discussed the reasons you need money in Bucket #2:

- Liquidity – you can access funds immediately.
- Safety – you will not lose any money if the stock market crashes.
- Fees – you typically don't pay any fees to put your money in the bank.
- Freedom – you will feel more financially independent the more money you have in the bank because you will feel more comfortable spending it.
- Emergencies.
- Decreases need to borrow money in the future – pay for large purchases with cash.

Right now, if you are thinking that the banks all pay such low rates of return... you are correct. But we do not advise you to put money in the bank for you to get a high rate of return from those assets, we use the bank for liquidity, safety, and no fees. Let's say you're going to buy a car two years from now and it's going to cost you $50,000. What if you don't put the money in the bank, what if you keep the money in the stock market and then the stock market goes down by -50%. What if you still have to buy that same car that's going to cost $50,000? How much does that new car now cost you? It costs you $100,000.

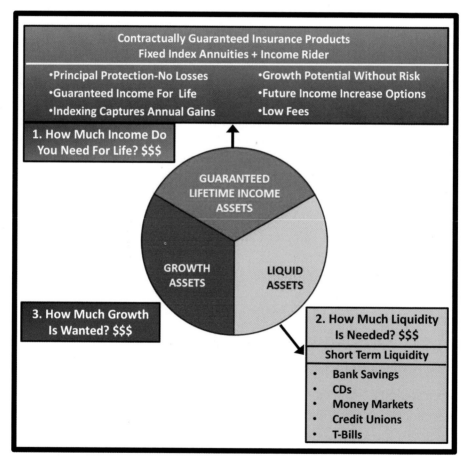

What if you're going to do a $100,000 home remodel two years from now, you keep the money in the stock market, and the stock market goes down by -50%. How much does that $100,000 remodel cost you? If you are good at math you will say $200,000, while mathematically accurate, it's not realistic. The remodel doesn't cost you anything because you don't do it. You've lost so much money, so you're afraid to use the money to do the home remodel at that point. We want to make sure you keep money liquid and you continue to add money in the bank every single month so you have money available to spend in the future. What if you saved money in the bank every month throughout your retirement, and every month your bank account balance got bigger and bigger, would you be terribly unhappy, or would you be blissfully peaceful and anxiety free?

Advisors don't advise you to put money in the bank because they don't get paid to do that. We advise you to put money in the bank because it's in your best interests. After filling Bucket #1 and Bucket #2 with the appropriate amount of assets to provide you the guaranteed lifetime income, liquidity, and safety you want, it is time to work on Bucket #3.

For Bucket #3 we want to create the opportunity for potential growth, but we do not want to take excessive risks. We want to invest in the stock market for the opportunity for good returns, but we don't want to subject assets to -50% or higher losses like what happened during the Technology Bubble between 2000 through 2002 and the Financial Crisis between 2007 through 2009. Bucket #3 must be able to provide an income stream that has a high probability of lasting for as long as you live. Bucket #1 provides "certain income" that is guaranteed for as long as you live while Bucket #3 provides "maybe income" that is not guaranteed. This means that Bucket #3 must be managed for volatility and loss reduction. Bucket #3 is liquid and available in a lump sum.

First of all, the assets you place in Bucket #3 cannot, and will not, be "naked in the stock market," you will not "ride out all losses," and you will not "subject these assets to unlimited risks." Bucket #3 will invest in low cost exchange traded funds (ETF's) or index funds, be managed professionally at a low total fully-disclosed cost, focus on stopping large stock market losses, employ a "stop-loss" and/or other risk mitigation strategy, and is system driven and is not affected by your emotions, the whim of your advisor, or the money manager's ego. There will be various fees associated with this type of asset management strategy. Make sure to get all fees disclosed to you in writing.

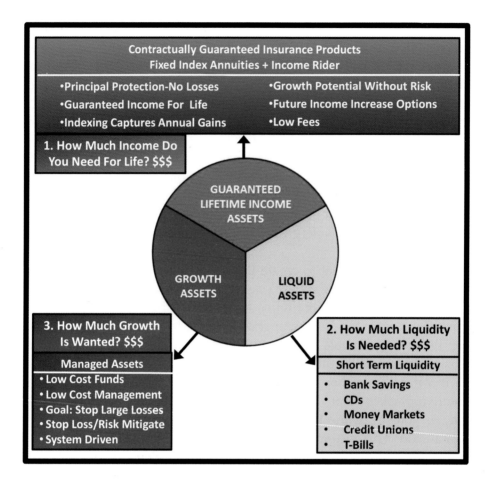

Many people ask why we would use a "stop-loss" strategy because they heard you can't time the market. It's 100% correct that you can't time the market. A stop-loss strategy does not time the market, it simply removes those assets from the stock market after the stock market shows a downward trend and suffers a specific loss. There is no market timing whatsoever, just a pre-determined, preset, level of loss acceptance, to avoid "riding the market down to the bottom." As you've read many times in this book, now that you are retired, do you really want to continue to do the same things you've been doing, continue to follow your brokers advice and "stay the course," "ride out all market losses," and "focus on the long term?" If you do this, all you will be doing is continuing to risk your retirement security by subjecting your assets to potentially large losses.

As an example, after suffering a -10% stock market loss, most retirees believe there is less risk in the stock market after the loss because they think there isn't as much the stock market can go down by after the loss. Think of this like a metal spring. If you push a spring down it goes down far easier at the top than after it has been compressed a certain amount. While this "compression phenomenon" is true with a metal spring, it is not accurate or applicable pertaining to the stock market, it is just the opposite. Analysis has shown that once the stock market drops -10%, there is a 56% probability the stock market will continue to go down at that point. If you have a greater than 50% chance you are going to lose money at any point in time, what should you do, leave your money in that investment? Heck no, you get it out of that investment at that time. This type of platform has the goal of reducing the risk, the potential for loss, of the stock market by 75%. This means you can still suffer a loss, but the goal is for the loss to be smaller.

Bucket #3 has goals of providing the opportunity for competitive growth rates from an asset that has less risk than the stock market. For Bucket #3 what does "competitive" mean? It means you will earn less than the stock market because you are taking less risk. As we have discussed previously, the stock market, as measured by the S&P 500 Index, grew by +19% in 2017. And we also stated if you wanted the opportunity to earn +19% in 2017, you had to be willing to take -53.8% risk which is the amount the stock market went down by in the 2008 Financial Crisis. In 2017 when the stock market earned +19%, the type of strategy used in Bucket #3 would typically have a return goal of between +12% to +14%. These potential return goals are far short of the +19% the stock market earned, and there is no guarantee you will earn anything at all in this type of strategy. We believe, in retirement, the most prudent strategy is to accept a lower potential rate of return with a significantly lower projected risk.

Bucket #1, Bucket #2, and Bucket #3 make up the conservative portion of your plan allowing you to follow *The 7 Rules To Live By For Retirement Security*:

- Bucket #1, the guaranteed lifetime income bucket, gives you complete principal protection against all stock market losses, provides you income guaranteed for life, offers the potential for competitive rates of return, and eliminates your fear of running out of money. Also knowing you will pay an average 1% in fees and you can't take your lump sum out for a specific number of years without penalty.

- Bucket #2, the liquidity and safety bucket, gives you complete principal protection against all stock market losses, full liquidity to your funds for any purpose, and the freedom to spend your money.
- Bucket #3, the growth bucket, provides you liquidity of all funds, the potential opportunity for growth, and potential risk reduction as compared to the stock market. Also knowing Bucket #3 carries risk of principal loss and carries fees.

The three (3) buckets can be used to create a powerful plan for you; we specialize in working with these conservative asset strategies. Many of our clients manage their riskier assets themselves such as real estate and individual stocks outside of the three (3) buckets.

You might own one (1) or more rental properties and you will continue to own and manage these real estate assets the way you always have. If you want to buy and sell individual stocks on your own, it is perfectly acceptable for you to have a self-managed account. The assets you allocate to a self-managed account will typically have a significantly higher risk level than the assets held in Bucket #1, Bucket #2, and Bucket #3. To keep the risk level of your total portfolio in the *Golden Rule of 5% to 10%* range, the amount of funds you allocate to your self-managed account must be manageable. You will typically not pay an advisory fee on these assets you are managing yourself.

If you know Bucket #1, Bucket #2, and Bucket #3 provides you risk mitigation, will you feel as worried about funds you have invested directly in real estate or your self-managed stock portfolio? Most retirees don't worry as much.

The "complete retirement asset allocation for safety, growth, and income for life" looks like this:

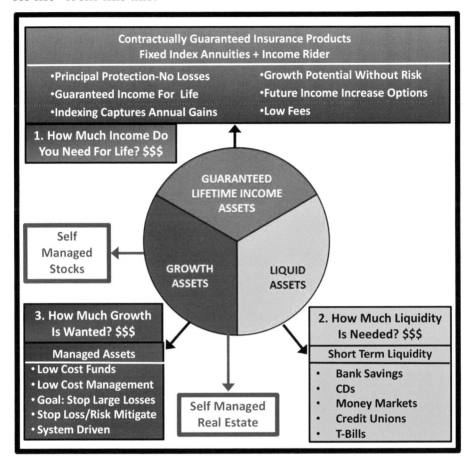

When retirees review the schematic above, almost every retiree we meet with agrees they should allocate their assets this way. The goal is to determine how much money you want to be put into each category to create the "customized allocation" that provides you with the highest probability of success to attain your goals.

Now, if you had your monies arranged this way using Bucket #1 for guaranteed lifetime income and principal safety, Bucket #2 for liquidity and principal safety, Bucket #3 for growth potential without excessive risks, and if you choose additional growth potential in your self-managed real estate, and additional growth potential in your self-managed stock account, you would have what we consider to be the "perfect customized allocation" for a retiree. You get to decide how much you want to put in each bucket, it's your decision, and because of this, you will finally feel in control of your money. We educate and coach you to help you arrive at the best decision for you and your family. Think about how that would feel.

Most retirees are very familiar with Bucket #2 – liquidity and safety, as they have always had money in the bank. in the next two (2) chapters we will examine the details of Bucket #1 – guaranteed lifetime income and Bucket #3 – growth.

CHAPTER 22

HOW BUCKET #1 – THE GUARANTEED LIFETIME INCOME BUCKET – ACTUALLY WORKS

BY DAN AHMAD & JIM FILES

A review of Bucket #1 – <u>Guaranteed Lifetime Income</u> (A fixed index annuity with an income rider.)

A fixed index annuity with an income rider provides:

- Guarantees you will never run out of income for as long as you live whether you are single or married.
- Guarantees your income for life even if your account value goes to $0.
- Guarantees you will never suffer a principal loss due to stock market losses, because even if the stock market loses -53.8% like it did in the 2008 Financial Crisis, you would lose 0%.
- The opportunity to earn a competitive rate of return based on a low-risk asset.
- Protection of current and future gains against stock market losses; you can't lose what you earned.
- Income tax-deferred growth of assets until distributions.
- The passing of all remaining asset to beneficiaries at your death.
- Extremely low total fees, typically averaging 1%.
- Income starting immediately or when needed.
- The opportunity for future income increases that are then guaranteed for life.

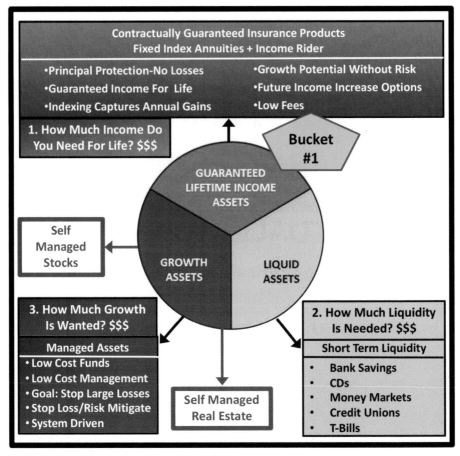

Some of the negatives about Bucket #1:

Guaranteed Lifetime Income – Fixed index annuities with an income rider include, but are not limited to:

- You can't take 100% of your funds out in a lump sum for a certain time period without a penalty like a CD (certificate of deposit) and many other financial instruments. In some plans, you can have immediate access to income (within 30 days), and in most plans every year after the first year you can have access up to 10% of your account without any penalty.
- You will not earn stock market rates of return. You will earn less. In 2017 the stock market earned +19% while the return goals for Bucket #2 was between 8% to 12%. This means you will almost certainly earn less than stock market rates of return in positive years.

- You will pay total annual fees of approximately 1%. This fee is typically 50% to 67% lower than a traditionally managed portfolio and typically 67% to 80% lower than a standard variable annuity. Almost all plans are no-load, meaning no commissions are deducted out of your investment. The insurance company pays the advisor commissions, you don't.
- Your account value could drop to $0 during your lifetime like any other asset, but your income rider would continue to pay you income for as long as you live, even if your account drops to $0.

Three (3) potential significant benefits you may receive from a fixed index annuity with an income rider include:

- Eliminating stock market losses.
- Opportunity to earn a competitive rate of return without taking excessive risk.
- Income that is guaranteed to be paid to you for as long as you live, regardless of stock market loses, and regardless of how long you live.

Benefit #1 – Eliminating potential stock market losses in a portion of your portfolio.

Let's look at an example of the stock market, the S&P 500 Index, from 2000 through 2018, a period of 19 years. There were some great annual rates of return:

Year	S&P 500 Index
2000	
2001	
2002	
2003	26.38%
2004	8.99%
2005	3.00%
2006	13.62%
2007	3.53%
2008	
2009	23.45%
2010	12.78%
2011	0.00%
2012	13.41%
2013	29.60%
2014	11.39%
2015	
2016	9.54%
2017	19.42%
2018	

When you look at the numbers in the chart above, it looks like you earned a huge rate of return from the stock market. In 2003, the S&P 500 Index increased by +26.38%; in 2006, it increased by +13.62%; in 2009, it increased by +23.45%; in 2010, it increased by +12.78%; in 2012, it increased by +13.41%; in 2013, it increased by +29.60%; in 2014, it increased by +11.39%; in 2016, it increased by +9.54% and in 2017, it increased by +19.42%. These were very good rates of return. There were only six (6) loss years:

Year	S&P 500 Index
2000	-10.14%
2001	-13.04%
2002	-23.37%
2003	26.38%
2004	8.99%
2005	3.00%
2006	13.62%
2007	3.53%
2008	-38.49%
2009	23.45%
2010	12.78%
2011	0.00%
2012	13.41%
2013	29.60%
2014	11.39%
2015	-0.73%
2016	9.54%
2017	19.42%
2018	-6.24%

But even when you look at the chart above, with the losses, it still looks like the stock market would have earned a great rate of return during the entire time period. The thirteen (13) gain years total +175.11% in gains while the six (6) loss years only total -92.01% in losses. With so much green and a little bit of red it looks like Christmas, and you received the biggest present, a big gain! The numbers above, at first glance, seem to support what everyone has always told you, "you will always earn a high rate of return in the stock market."

Unfortunately, the big gain, your nice Christmas present, didn't get delivered, it was more like a desert mirage, a sleight-of-hand. It looks like a big gain, but it really isn't. When you calculate the average annual compounded increase for the S&P 500 Index from 2000 through 2018, based on the numbers in the previous chart, you get a result of 2.85% before any deduction for potential fees. This means with all the gains and losses, when added together and averaged, they create a 2.85% increase per year. That's it, 2.85% per year. Has anyone ever told you this? Probably not, even though it is a fact.

If you had $1,000,000 in 2000 and earned the exact same rates of return as the S&P 500 Index from 2000 through 2018, your $1,000,000 would have grown to $1,705,632 before any fees. This seems like big growth, but it is only a 2.85% annual growth.

How could this happen with all those high rates of returns in all the good years? It's because, as we have discussed before, the losses are very painful to your financial progress.

The key point to think about right now is whether a 2.85% annual compounded return, before paying fees, is worth all the risk of the stock market during these 19 years? If you are like every retiree we have interviewed, you will say a 2.85% return, *minus fees*, is definitely not worth the risk.

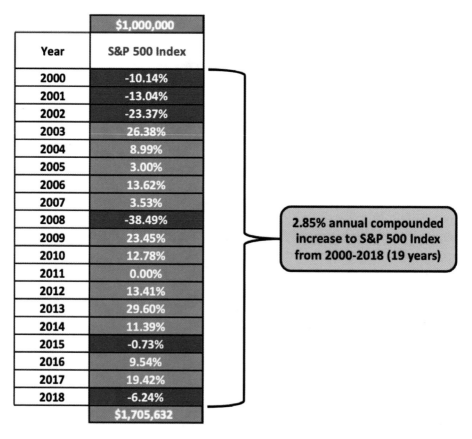

Year	$1,000,000 S&P 500 Index
2000	-10.14%
2001	-13.04%
2002	-23.37%
2003	26.38%
2004	8.99%
2005	3.00%
2006	13.62%
2007	3.53%
2008	-38.49%
2009	23.45%
2010	12.78%
2011	0.00%
2012	13.41%
2013	29.60%
2014	11.39%
2015	-0.73%
2016	9.54%
2017	19.42%
2018	-6.24%
	$1,705,632

2.85% annual compounded increase to S&P 500 Index from 2000-2018 (19 years)

So, what if someone would have come to you in 2000 and said, "Hey, we have this fantastic plan, it's called a fixed index annuity with an income rider and it has a 0% floor (no loss guarantee) and a 6% cap (maximum return in a single year). It uses an indexing concept. This means you can never lose money when the stock market goes down, meaning your worst annual return will be 0%, even if the stock market drops -50%. But it also means the maximum (cap) you can earn in any year is 6%." In 1999, would this have sounded good based on your knowledge about money back then before you read this book? It might not have sounded too good because the 6% cap might have seemed way too low to be able to do you any good. Here is an example of how the annual positive returns would have looked:

Year	S&P 500 Index	Indexing Concept 0% Floor & 6% CAP
2000	-10.14%	
2001	-13.04%	
2002	-23.37%	
2003	26.38%	6.00%
2004	8.99%	6.00%
2005	3.00%	3.00%
2006	13.62%	6.00%
2007	3.53%	3.53%
2008	-38.49%	
2009	23.45%	6.00%
2010	12.78%	6.00%
2011	0.00%	0.00%
2012	13.41%	6.00%
2013	29.60%	6.00%
2014	11.39%	6.00%
2015	-0.73%	
2016	9.54%	6.00%
2017	19.42%	6.00%
2018	-6.24%	

In 2003, the S&P 500 Index increased by +26.38%, but you would have only earned 6.00% in your plan. In 2009, the S&P 500 Index increased by 23.45% and you again would have only earned 6.00%. In 2013, the S&P 500 Index increased by +29.60% and you would have only earned 6.00%. And in 2017, the S&P 500 Index would have increased by +19.42% and yet again you would have only earned 6.00%. So, the cap makes it seem that you lost a whole lot of money by "not making the highest rate of returns."

But the key is not trying to earn the highest rates of returns, it is in doing everything you can to preserve your principal, to protect your money against large losses. The indexing concept protects you against all stock market losses:

- In 2000, when the S&P 500 Index lost -10.14%, you would have lost 0%.
- In 2001, when the S&P 500 Index lost -13.04%, you would have lost 0%.
- In 2002, when the S&P 500 Index lost -23.37%, you would have lost 0%.
- In 2008, when the S&P 500 Index lost -38.49%, you would have lost 0%.
- In 2015, when the S&P 500 Index lost -0.73%, you would have lost 0%.
- In 2018, when the S&P 500 Index lost -6.42%, you would have lost 0%.

Year	S&P 500 Index	Indexing Concept 0% Floor & 6% CAP
2000	-10.14%	0.00%
2001	-13.04%	0.00%
2002	-23.37%	0.00%
2003	26.38%	6.00%
2004	8.99%	6.00%
2005	3.00%	3.00%
2006	13.62%	6.00%
2007	3.53%	3.53%
2008	-38.49%	0.00%
2009	23.45%	6.00%
2010	12.78%	6.00%
2011	0.00%	0.00%
2012	13.41%	6.00%
2013	29.60%	6.00%
2014	11.39%	6.00%
2015	-0.73%	0.00%
2016	9.54%	6.00%
2017	19.42%	6.00%
2018	-6.24%	0.00%

And because of all this, if you had placed $1,000,000 in an indexing concept plan that provided you the annual returns listed in the previous chart, your $1,000,000 would have grown to $1,909,687 by 2018:

Year	$1,000,000 S&P 500 Index	$1,000,000 Indexing Concept 0% Floor & 6% CAP
2000	-10.14%	0.00%
2001	-13.04%	0.00%
2002	-23.37%	0.00%
2003	26.38%	6.00%
2004	8.99%	6.00%
2005	3.00%	3.00%
2006	13.62%	6.00%
2007	3.53%	3.53%
2008	-38.49%	0.00%
2009	23.45%	6.00%
2010	12.78%	6.00%
2011	0.00%	0.00%
2012	13.41%	6.00%
2013	29.60%	6.00%
2014	11.39%	6.00%
2015	-0.73%	0.00%
2016	9.54%	6.00%
2017	19.42%	6.00%
2018	-6.24%	0.00%
	$1,705,632	$1,909,687

After reviewing the previous chart, do you think it is more important to get the highest rates of return every year, or is it more important to protect your assets against losses? During retirement, your number one goal is to protect your assets against large stock market losses. Your focus has to be in protecting what you have worked so hard to accumulate. A fixed index annuity with an income rider provides you complete principal protection against all stock market losses.

Benefit #2 – The opportunity to earn competitive rates of return without taking excessive risks.

Most retirees really don't want to take too much risk with their money, but their assets are usually allocated with far more potential for loss than they know. Whether a broker places them at too much risk, or they do it themselves, or they just haven't made any changes for many years, when the next stock market crash comes along, they will lose far too much money.

Here are four (4) rules to be in a position to earn acceptable returns without gambling away your retirement:

1. Have the opportunity to earn a reasonable rate of return when the market goes up, an opportunity to earn a portion, not all, of the stock market upside. Translation: Don't be greedy.
2. Never suffer a loss of your principal regardless of how much the stock market loses.
3. Never lose any of your previous gains regardless of how much the stock market loses.
4. Never be in a position to have to recover from a large loss before you start making gains again.

Let's look at a graph of the numerical data from the previous chart comparing the S&P 500 Index and fixed index annuity with an income rider with a 0% floor and 6% cap from 2000 through 2018:

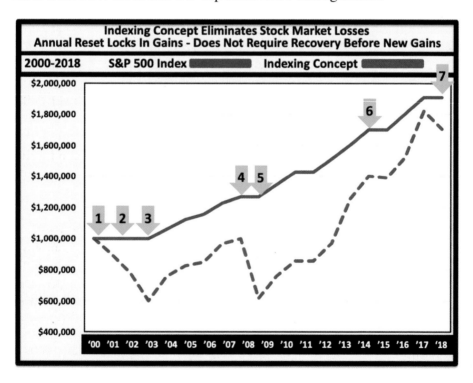

The "indexing concept" is what provides you the potential for competitive returns without taking losses. Let's review a hypothetical example of how the "indexing concept" works based on a $1,000,000 initial value:

Red Dotted Line: Represents what would happen to $1,000,000 from 2000 through 2018 based on the performance of the S&P 500 Index. Between 2000 through 2002, the red dotted line angles sharply downward with annual S&P 500 Index losses of -10.14%, -13.04%, and -23.37%. You would have been told by your broker to "ride it out," and you would have lost a lot of money, finally to recover by 2007, only to suffer a -38.49% loss for the 2008 year, again being advised to "ride it out," finally to recover again by 2013.

Blue Solid Line: Represents what would have happened to $1,000,000 from 2000 through 2018 based on the fixed index annuity with an income rider plan we previously discussed using the indexing concept with a 0% floor and a 6% cap:

Arrow #1 – shows the initial $1,000,000 as the "guaranteed principal balance" that cannot be affected by stock market losses.

Arrows #1, #2, & #3 – These arrows show there were no losses at all in 2000, 2001, or 2002. In 2000, when the S&P 500 Index lost -10.14%, the fixed index annuity with the income rider did not lose anything, it received a 0% rate of return for the year. In 2001, when the S&P 500 Index lost -13.04%, the fixed index annuity with the income rider did not lose anything, it received a 0% rate of return for the year. The S&P 500 Index lost -23.37% in 2002, and the fixed index annuity with the income rider did not lose anything, it received a 0% rate of return for the year. How would you feel if the stock market crashed, but you didn't lose anything at all? I bet you'd feel pretty smart!

Arrow #4 – By 2007, the S&P 500 Index finally recovered its losses, it didn't make any gains, it just got back to even. The fixed index annuity with the income rider started making new gains in 2003 because it didn't have to recover from losses before it started earning again. In 2003, the S&P 500 Index increased by +26.38% but really wasn't a gain, it was just part of the process of recovering from your losses. By 2007, the original $1,000,000 in the S&P 500 Index would be at $999,328 and the fixed index annuity with the income rider would be at $1,270,051.

Arrow #5 – In 2008, the fixed index annuity with the income rider didn't suffer a loss even though the S&P 500 Index lost -38.49%. The fixed index annuity with the income rider would have received a 0% return that year.

Arrow #6 – From 2009 to 2014, the S&P 500 Index increased significantly while the fixed index annuity with the income rider earned returns of 6.00% in 2009, 6.00% in 2010, 0.00% in 2011, 6.00% in 2012, 6.00% in 2013, and 6.00% in 2014. The fixed index annuity with the income rider didn't make as much as the stock market did, but the fixed index annuity with the income rider didn't have to make as much, because it didn't have to recover from any of the previous large losses.

Arrow #7 – In 2018 the S&P 500 Index decreased -6.42% with the fixed index annuity with the income rider earning a 0.00% return. At the end of 2018, the fixed index annuity with the income rider would be worth $1,909,687 while the S&P 500 Index value would be $1,705,632.

Benefit #3 – Creating income that is guaranteed to be paid to you, and spouse if married, for as long as you live.

You've just read how a fixed index annuity can protect your principal against stock market losses. By adding an income rider to your fixed index annuity, you have now just created a plan that guarantees your income will not stop for your entire lifetime, you receive a contractual guarantee you can't run out of money, no matter how long you live, regardless of stock market volatility and losses, and regardless of your account value. If you knew you didn't have to worry about how much income you would get every month for the rest of your life, where that income would come from, and it would never stop, how would you feel? Probably really, really, good.

So how does it work? Let's assume Bob, a hypothetical 65-year-old, has $2,000,000 of retirement assets. Bob wants to allocate $1,000,000 of his $2,000,000 portfolio into Bucket #1 to create guaranteed lifetime income. The analysis provides the following guaranteed lifetime income options:

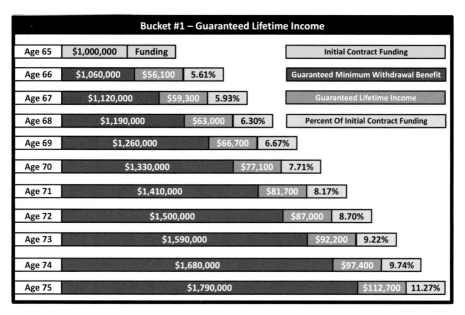

Bucket #1 – Guaranteed Lifetime Income			
Age 65	$1,000,000	Funding	Initial Contract Funding
Age 66	$1,060,000	$56,100	5.61%	Guaranteed Minimum Withdrawal Benefit
Age 67	$1,120,000	$59,300	5.93%	Guaranteed Lifetime Income
Age 68	$1,190,000	$63,000	6.30%	Percent Of Initial Contract Funding
Age 69	$1,260,000	$66,700	6.67%	
Age 70	$1,330,000	$77,100	7.71%	
Age 71	$1,410,000	$81,700	8.17%	
Age 72	$1,500,000	$87,000	8.70%	
Age 73	$1,590,000	$92,200	9.22%	
Age 74	$1,680,000	$97,400	9.74%	
Age 75	$1,790,000	$112,700	11.27%	

In this example, Bob could start taking income in as quickly as 12 months. There are fixed index annuities with income riders that actually allow income to start within 30 days – providing a zero-wait time period to access guaranteed lifetime income. In this example, after 12-months, Bob is contractually guaranteed to have a minimum of $1,060,000 in what is called his "guaranteed minimum withdrawal benefit" to provide him guaranteed lifetime income of $56,100. The "guaranteed minimum withdrawal benefit" is not available for Bob to take out in a lump sum, it is used to provide him income for as long as he lives. This means if Bob buys a fixed index annuity with an income rider today for $1,000,000, he is guaranteed that in 12-months he will receive $56,100 every year for as long as he lives, even if he lives past 100 years of age, even if the stock market crashes, and even if he uses up all the principal in his account. His income payments of $56,100 cannot end during his lifetime, thus eliminating his "fear of running out of money."

If Bob does turn on his guaranteed lifetime income at age 66, and he starts taking his $56,100 of annual income, when he passes away, any funds remaining in his account will be paid to his named beneficiaries; the insurance company does not keep the remaining assets. Think about it, isn't this what we always wanted: the maximum income we can get guaranteed to be paid to us for as long as we live that's not affected by stock market losses, and when we die, if anything is left in our account it's paid to our beneficiaries? If the stock market crashes before he starts taking income, or if the stock market crashed after he starts taking income, Bob's income will be unaffected, and he will receive the $56,100 every year for as long as he lives.

If Bob received $56,100 per year of additional income, that was guaranteed to be paid to him for as long as he lives, how would he feel? How would you feel? Would Bob have to worry about his income running out during his lifetime? Would you? It's pretty incredible that the $56,100 is equal to 5.61% of Bob's original funding of the plan, and it's guaranteed for life.

The reason Bob saved money while he was working was specifically to be able to use it to create income during retirement that would last for as long as he lived. Isn't that why you saved your money? Just like Bob, it's time you started using your assets for income the way you had planned to, without the fear of running out of money for as long as you live.

The diagram on the preceding page shows that every year Bob defers his income during the 10-year time period analyzed, his guaranteed lifetime income is guaranteed to increase until he starts taking his income. If Bob decides to defer his income for 24 months, his "guaranteed minimum withdrawal benefit" is contractually guaranteed to increase to $1,120,000 in 24 months regardless of stock market volatility or losses and guarantees to pay Bob $59,300 of income every year for as long as he lives. What if Bob can defer his payments for five (5) years? Bob's "guaranteed minimum withdrawal benefit" is contractually guaranteed to increase to $1,330,000 in 5 years regardless of stock market volatility or losses and guarantees to pay Bob $77,100 of income every year for as long as he lives. It's even more incredible that the $77,100 is equal to 7.71% of Bob's original funding of the plan, with the $77,100 of annual income guaranteed for as long as Bob lives.

Right about now, many of you, maybe all of you, will be thinking that you really love this strategy, but it sounds too good to be true. You love the idea of no losses, guaranteed lifetime income, and remaining assets passing to beneficiaries, but you wonder how the insurance company can do this? It's not too good to be true, because you are going to pay for these benefits, with the total annual fee for the typical fixed index annuity with an income rider at 1% per year, with no added or hidden costs. But to put this cost in perspective, right now you may be paying 3.0% or more per year for your current assets to be managed and you probably don't have much, if any, principal guarantee or guaranteed lifetime income.

Like Bob, you may benefit by allocating a portion of your assets into Bucket #1 funded with a fixed index annuity with an income rider. This example for Bob explains solving an income need starting as soon as 12 months. There are other options to start income immediately or to defer longer.

CHAPTER 23

HOW BUCKET #3 – THE GROWTH BUCKET ACTUALLY WORKS

BY DAN AHMAD & JIM FILES

Reading this book, you might get the impression that we don't really like the stock market, but that is simply not true. We believe in the stock market and we believe the stock market will always trend up in the long-term. However, there are five (5) specific things we don't like about and will not tolerate from the stock market:

I. *Potential Large Losses* – Large losses can devastate a retirement portfolio and you may not recover. In the Technology Bubble from 2000 through 2002, the stock market lost approximately -50% and then in the 2008 Financial Crisis, it lost -50% again. If you lose -50%, you have to make a +100% recovery gain just to break even, no profit. Large stock market losses are not unique and historically happen in short intervals. Since 1929 there have been 13 major bear stock markets that have averaged close to -40% losses. That means historically large -40% losses happen an average of every seven (7) years. If you lose -40% you need to make a recovery gain of +67% just to break even. So, this means every seven (7) years on average you could lose -40% and then after the loss you have to use the first +67% in gains you receive just to replenish all the funds that were lost.

Moreover, many retirees think it's easy to make up big losses, and this is also incorrect. A -50% loss requires a +100% recovery gain, and how easy is it to make +100%? Does all of this really seem like the stock market is working for you or does it seem more like you are a slave to the stock market? The concept of the stock market being "totally and completely liquid" is touted as a huge advantage over more conservative assets.

II. *Diminishing Or Evaporating Liquidity* – Stock market assets are typically considered liquid and available at any time for withdrawal. Liquidity is not the problem, the problem is how much is really available, actually liquid, on any given day, week, month, or year. Let's say it's October 2007 and you have $1,000,000 in the stock market, investing similarly to the S&P 500 Index. At that time, you have $1,000,000 of liquidity because that is the current value of your portfolio. Now let's fast forward 16-months into the future to March 2009, after the stock market has lost -53.8%. Now your portfolio is only worth $462,000, which means your liquidity has decreased to $462,000. Your liquidity has diminished, or evaporated by, $538,000! Based on this data, how "totally and completely liquid" was your $1,000,000?

III. *High Volatility Causing Low Income* – You may have been persuaded to believe the highest returns will translate into the highest success, highest income, and highest probability your income won't run out during your lifetime. This is pretty much the mantra on Wall Street. But, to put yourself in a position to earn the highest returns, you must then be willing to take the highest risk. For example, to be in a position to earn +19% as the stock market did in 2017, you must be willing to accept the -53.8% that the stock market lost during the 2008 Financial Crisis. A portfolio with high volatility does not provide the opportunity for high income, just the opposite in fact. Think about it, do you really believe you can take out a high level of income from a portfolio that has values that can significantly vary on an annual, monthly, weekly, even daily basis? No, you can't. It's why the "safe income distribution rate" industry accepted norm has dropped from 6% to 3% in a very short time period, and could potentially be dropping again to 2.5%.

IV. *Paying High Fees You Are Not Aware Of And Were Never Informed Of* – In the chapter that covered fees, we discussed how most retirees believe they are only paying 1.00% in total fees but the typical retiree is actually paying 3.00% or more every year in fees to have their assets managed. If the stock market, represented by the S&P 500 Index, has only increased 2.85% per year on average between 2000 through 2018, how can you get ahead?

V. *Does Not Provide "A High Probability" That Income Will Be Paid To You For As Long As You Live* – The stock market does not offer the security, the safety, the certainty, of providing you a secure and consistent income stream you can count on month-after-month, year-after-year, for as long as you live. Depending on how much income you are withdrawing, the rate of returns you receive, losses you suffer from, and total fees you pay, your income from stock market assets could reduce or terminate at any time in the future. And the one thing you want to guarantee never happens is that you run out of income during your lifetime. Based on tremendous volatility in the stock market during the last 20 years including losses in the year 2000 of -10.14%, year 2001 -13.04%, year 2002 -23.37%, and year 2008 -38.49%, it would have been almost impossible to take out a high level of income without putting yourself in jeopardy of running out of money.

Let's look at an example of you taking out $50,000 per year of income distributions from a $1,000,000 portfolio that earned the same rates of return as the S&P 500 Index between 2000 through 2018. The following chart shows how long your money would have lasted if you paid total annual fees of 0%, 1%, 2%, or 3%:

Starting Portfolio Value	Year Income Starts	Annual Income Withdrawals	Total Annual Fees	Year Income Ends - Account Values Go To $0
$1,000,000	2000	$50,000	0.00%	2018
$1,000,000	2000	$50,000	1.00%	2016
$1,000,000	2000	$50,000	2.00%	2014
$1,000,000	2000	$50,000	3.00%	2012

How would you like to have retired in 2000 with $1,000,000 and started annual income distributions of $50,000, thinking your money would last for as long as you lived, only to find out when it was too late, that you ran out of money. The first row under the headers shows the $1,000,000 portfolio, the $50,000 of annual income, 0.00% in annual fees, and your money running out in 2018, nothing left in the account for you to use for continued income and nothing left for your beneficiaries past 2018. The second row shows the same data except your total annual fees are now 1.00% and your money runs out in 2016. The third row shows 2.00% in total fees and your money running out in 2014. The fourth row shows a typical 3.00% in total fees with your money running out in 2012.

We are pretty sure you don't like these five (5) characteristics of the stock market either. So, let's make sure you "don't kill the messenger." We are providing you data you have never been given. If you had been given this information before, what would you have done? You wouldn't have invested your money the way you have up until this point, which means your current broker would not be your current broker, no matter how nice he or she is. That could be the main reason your current broker has not told you all of these things. We are going to say it again, we love the stock market, we just don't like our clients being "naked in the stock market," meaning we don't want you to have unlimited risk you are not aware of. We will never put our clients in the position of being "naked in the stock market" because we don't want you to first suffer a -50% loss and then be forced to earn +100% just to recover from the loss.

So, let's look at how Bucket #3, (the growth bucket in the diagram on the following page), can provide some solutions to the problems outlined above caused by traditional, "old school," outdated, stock market investment strategies you are probably still using.

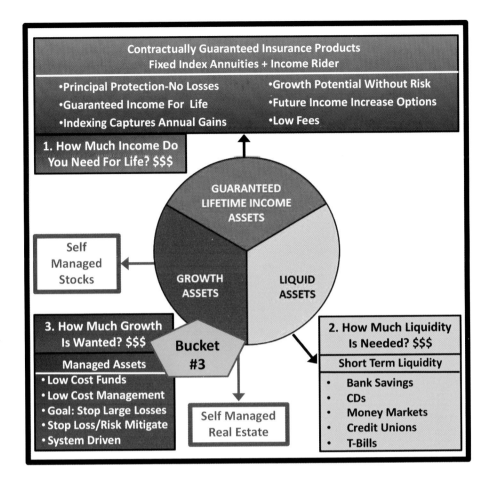

Using Bucket #3 for growth potentially provides the opportunity for gains without taking excessive risks. Bucket #3 is focused on attaining the following goals:

- Maintaining a high level of liquidity by focusing on risk reduction.
- Minimizing volatility, providing an opportunity for a higher level of consistent income.
- Provide an acceptable level of income with a high probability it will last for as long as you live.
- Minimize fees in writing, use exchange traded funds (ETF's) and/or index funds that carry low direct fund expenses, low turnover, and low trading costs at the fund level. Provide a fully disclosed total cost of portfolio management.
- Offer a stop-loss platform or other formal, structured risk mitigation strategy.

- Remove emotions from the decision-making process.
- Not use old-school ineffective strategies that advise you to "stay the course," "ride out all market losses," and "not to worry because everything will work out over the long-term." These outdated strategies have not worked out for many retirees.

On May 22, 1996, the S&P 500 Index was at 678 points. On December 31, 1999, less than four (4) years later, the S&P 500 Index climbed to 1,469 points, an increase of +117%! If you had a broker, you probably thought he/she was a genius, maybe even related to Warren Buffet!

Then, almost ten (10) years later, the S&P 500 Index closed at 676 on March 9, 2009, a decrease of -54%. In 2009, when you met with your broker, he/she told you everything was fine, because you'd only lost -54% since 1999, and you'd made a +117% gain before the loss, so you are still "far ahead." But are you really ahead? Nope! You started on March 9, 2009 with the S&P 500 Index at 678 and then ended with it at 676 on March 9, 2009. You would have made nothing.

How could this happen this way? Assume you have $1,000,000 invested on May 22, 1996, and you earn the same +117% rate of return as the S&P 500 index, your $1,000,000 would have grown to $2,170,000 by December 31, 1999. Then you lose the -54% the S&P 500 Index lost from December 31, 1999 through March 9, 2009, and your $2,170,000 decreases to $998,200, calculated as follows:

$1,000,000	portfolio value on May 22, 1996
+$1,170,000	portfolio gain of +117% between May 22, 1996 and December 31, 1999
=$2,170,000	new increased portfolio value on December 31, 1999
-$1,171,800	portfolio loss of -54% between December 31, 1999 and March 9, 2009
=$ 998,200	ending portfolio value after -54% loss on March 9, 2009

Let's review the following chart that highlights the pain of large stock market losses, when a +117% gain was completely wiped out by a -54% loss:

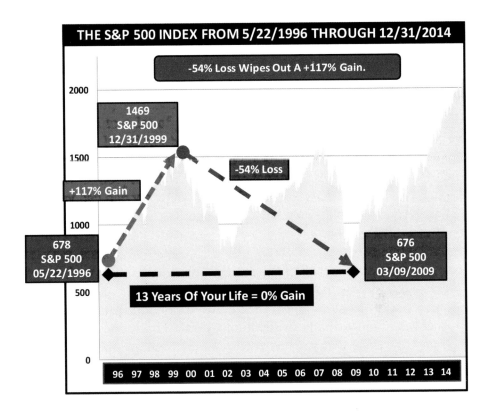

THE S&P 500 INDEX FROM 5/22/1996 THROUGH 12/31/2014

-54% Loss Wipes Out A +117% Gain.

1469
S&P 500
12/31/1999

-54% Loss

+117% Gain

678
S&P 500
05/22/1996

676
S&P 500
03/09/2009

13 Years Of Your Life = 0% Gain

While you are working it would be financially painful to lose all of your +117% gain because you suffered the-54% loss in the stock market between December 31, 1999 through March 9, 2009. What if this happened while you are retired? It would be most certainly financially devastating.

We have used the term "naked in the market" multiple times in this book, and this is the perfect example of what the term means. In this example, you simply had no "protection" against the harsh financial storms the United States stock market weathered from 2000 through 2002 and 2007 through 2009. These two (2) stock market collapses were the equivalent of you "standing naked in a hurricane." You went through a lot of pain yet you survived, but there was a tremendous amount of work, hope, and luck just to recover, rebuild, and get back to where you were before the storms.

While you are retired, you cannot subject your assets to unlimited and immeasurable risk and losses. If you do not limit your potential losses, you do not have a plan, you cannot have a plan, and you will not have a high probability that your money will last for as long as you live.

It's pretty simple, look at the previous chart and assume your assets act the same way the stock market did in the chart. Then ask yourself if there is any way possible you could take out a high level of income from an asset that acted that way, and still have a high degree of confidence your asset would last for as long as you live? As they say, "a picture is worth a thousand words." Your money would not last. Let's fix that. How about instead of listening to the "Wall Street chant" of "riding out all market losses," you stop riding the stock market up and down, you stop watching your asset values rise and sink without protection, you stop just watching your portfolio vary wildly in value as a powerless spectator; you do something about it.

For example, how about after the market goes down -10%, you get out of the stock market and invest your money in cash or bonds. You will then stay out of the stock market the entire time until the stock market has recovered and exhibits momentum by going back up, then you get back in. How does that sound? You will miss some of the upside, but you should not be worried about getting all of the upside, you should concentrate on making sure you don't suffer through all of the downside as you did from 2000 through 2002 and 2007 through 2009.

We don't know when the stock market will bottom out and we will never try to time the stock market, it just can't be done no matter what anybody says, so we'll get back in after the stock market starts going back up. In this example you will stay fully invested until the stock market goes down -10% again in the future, and it will go down; and when it goes down, we will get back out.

You have to talk yourself into "not being greedy" and the fact that you will not get all the upside gains, but instead focus your goals to be out of the majority of the downside. We think you'll be farther ahead, and worry far less, by protecting your assets with a stop-loss.

The following chart shows an example of making +117% and then when the market went down -10% you get out of the market, you do not "ride it out."

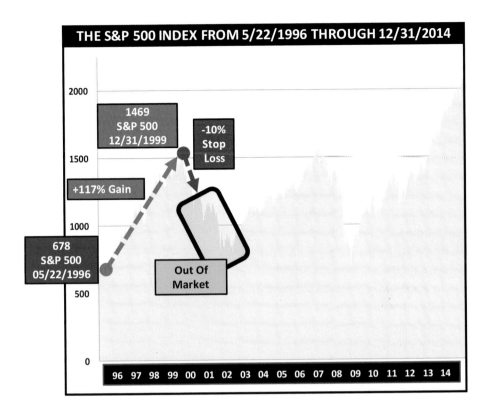

As an example, how would you have felt during the 2000 through 2002 stock market crash caused by the Technology Bubble if you would have gotten out of the market after a -10% loss? You would have felt great! How would you feel if after you got out of the market after the -10% loss in 2000, you stayed out of the stock market the rest of the time through 2002?

Then, you got back into the stock market sometime in 2003 after the stock market showed "positive momentum" as depicted in the chart on the following page:

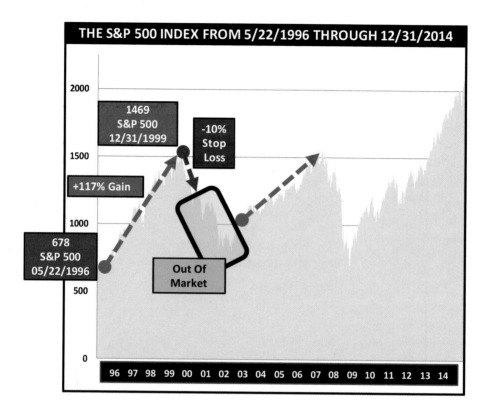

THE S&P 500 INDEX FROM 5/22/1996 THROUGH 12/31/2014

The point that has to be disclosed, and is very easy to see in the above chart, is that you will not ever get all of the stock market upside with this strategy. This is because if you want all of the upside of the stock market, you have to be willing to accept all of the downside of the stock market. And if you are still reading this book, you are not willing to accept all of the downside of the stock market. The goal is to be out of the stock market during the majority of the stock market crash and get back in on the way up. From 2003 through 2007, you, like every other American, thought the stock market would not stop going up and up and up. But then starting in October 2007 and lasting through March 2009, the entire world was hit with the devastating economic event that was called the 2008 Financial Crisis, which doesn't even come close to the proper description of what happened to the average retiree and people planning for retirement.

More accurate potential names for this time period include:

➤ *The 2008 Financial Catastrophe*
➤ *The 2008 Financial Devastation*

➤ *The 2008 Financial Time Machine*

We believe the best name is *"The 2008 Financial Time Machine"* because the stock market crash between 2007 through 2009 sent the value of your portfolio back in time to the same value on May 22, 1996. Your portfolio value went 13-years "back-in-time." Think about it.

How about instead of going back in time all the way to 1996, what if after the stock market dropped -10% starting in October 2007, you got out of the stock market, and stayed out of the stock market, until sometime in 2009 when the stock market showed significant signs of upward momentum? How would you have felt if you could have used these risk

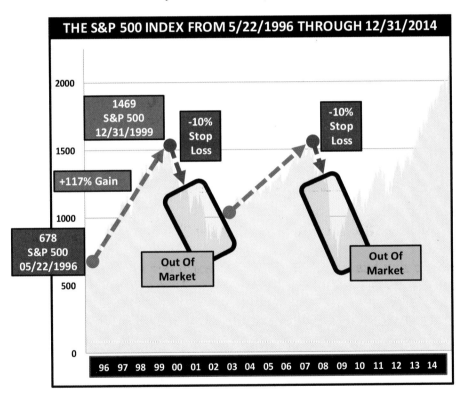

management techniques to have protected your portfolio back then? When you study the above graph, and you think about how many times you were told to "ride out the stock market," "hang in there," "you are in it for the long-term," did it really make any sense at all to leave your money in the stock market through this much volatility?

Again, it is important to note you would still have suffered a loss; the goal is to make it a great deal smaller. It is also important to note you did not get all of the upside once the stock market hit bottom and started climbing back up, you got back into the market on the way up, giving up some of the potential gains.

When you are told it's best to "ride out the stock market," what are they really advising you to do, what does it really mean? "Riding out the stock market" means riding the stock market down, accepting the loss, only to need to make an even bigger gain than the original loss just to recover. Why on earth would you ever want to do this?

The following chart highlights the key goals of the stop-loss strategy:

- Get out of the stock market after a -10% (or other pre-determined) decline.
- Do not "ride out large stock market losses."
- Do not try and time the stock market.
- Stay out of the stock market until there is a clear sign of potential recovery, have patience.

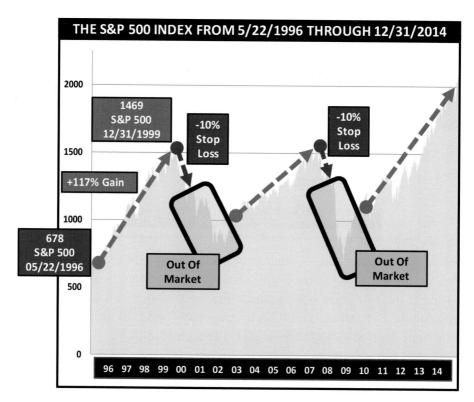

- Accept a portion of the stock market upside, don't be greedy.
- Give yourself the highest probability you can use your assets for income that won't run out.

Look at the previous graph and think about how someone who had $100,000,000 would invest their money. Would this person take their $100,000,000 to their broker and say, "Invest my money the best you can and I will see you in a year and I will hope everything will work out and there won't be any big stock market losses," or would the person take their $100,000,000 to their broker and say, "Invest my money the best you can but if the stock market goes down -10% you get all of my money out of the stock market." They'd probably say to get them out of the stock market after the -10% loss, because this person, just like you, needs to focus on protecting principal and limiting large losses.

You just haven't done this because no one told you that you should do this, and no one told you that you could do this. But now you do know this is a potential powerful strategy that may help reduce your risk throughout your retirement years, reducing your fear of suffering large stock market losses.

CHAPTER 24

MONEY IS SCARY, CREATES POWERFUL EMOTIONS, AND CAUSES A TREMENDOUS AMOUNT OF ANXIETY

BY DAN AHMAD & JIM FILES

Do you feel like this:

I Am Confused And Don't Understand My Plan

You think you are confused and don't understand your plan, because you worry about your money, and if you are like most people you blame yourself for your "lack of financial intelligence." But the fact is for 99% of you, your confusion and lack of understanding have nothing to do with any of your own shortcomings. You feel confused and don't understand your money because *you don't have an actual plan – you have nothing in writing.*

If you are the typical retiree or pre-retiree, you probably do not really understand your money. Think about it right now, do you really understand:

- The investments you own and why you own them?
- The statements you receive other than to check if the value went up or down?
- Why you didn't make as much money as you thought you should have?
- Why you lose so much money?
- Why it seems like your account values finally get back to even and then you lose more money?
- How income taxes work?
- How you will generate the income you need throughout retirement from your assets?
- When you should start using your assets for income?
- How much you pay in direct and indirect (hidden) fees?
- How much income you can safely take out of your assets?
- How to guarantee your income won't run out for as long as you live?
- How much income tax you will pay on your IRA distributions?
- How to protect all of your past and current gains from future stock market losses?
- How much risk you are taking and how much you could lose in the next stock market crash?
- That bonds will lose value when interest rates go up?
- The probability your money will last for as long as you live?
- The difference between asset accumulation and income distribution/ asset preservation?
- How much you can potentially leave to your beneficiaries?

Very few retirees can honestly state they understand the majority of the previous bullet points. We have found one of the hardest things for people to admit is that they really do not understand their money. Think about this; people don't understand their money, and because they don't understand their money they feel ashamed, and because they feel ashamed they find it very hard to ask for help to simply understand their money. So many of them keep doing the exact same things they have done with their money for many years even though now retired they know they need to make changes.

A high percentage of retirees and pre-retirees we meet with for the first time feel embarrassed, ashamed, guilty, even stupid because they don't understand their money. You may feel the same way. It doesn't matter who they are, how much money they have, their college education, or their career, they all feel this way. Bankers, lawyers, accountants, engineers, teachers, administrators, CFO's, CEO's, executives, salespeople, contractors, realtors, and people from almost every profession don't understand their money, and they feel like it is their fault. They feel like they are in the minority because they think everyone else does understand their money. Even people who have an advisor really don't understand their money, and because of this, they feel even more embarrassed because they have been working with an advisor for 5, 10, 15, even 20+ years and they still don't understand their money, and they still worry about their money.

Do you feel like you don't understand your money, are confused, and don't understand your plan? You may think everyone else understands their money. You may think everyone else is making the right decisions about their money. You may think everyone else is making a lot of money. You may think everyone else isn't losing a lot of money. You may think everyone else isn't worrying about running out of money. You may think everyone else is in better financial shape than you. And you are probably dead wrong. The majority of the people we meet with, people who have saved $1,000,000 to $7,000,000 or more of assets are in far better shape than their friends, neighbors, co-workers, and relatives. These types of people have succeeded, it's just that no one has told them so, and no one has ever built them a comprehensive written retirement income plan to prove it to them.

There are so many emotions associated with our money, it is overwhelming.

Society, friends, relatives, the media, even our own parents judge our success, status, and power by our money. And because of this, for some reason, everyone believes they should just somehow know "what they are supposed to do with their money." They believe they were supposed to be born with the ability to understand their money and with the capabilities of making the right decisions with their money straight out of the womb, like we are all supposed to have some kind of "money gene." And then if we don't understand our money and realize we don't have that "money gene," we think everyone else has, we will feel inferior, insecure, and not normal.

To help you start the process of understanding your money and your plan, we are going to tell you three (3) big secrets about your money:

1. No one has a "money gene" because it doesn't exist. You will either fail by not planning properly or succeed by planning properly. Genetics has nothing to do with your financial security during retirement, having the right plan does.

2. The reason you think you don't understand your plan or you are confused about your plan isn't because you don't understand your money. You don't understand your money and you are confused because you don't actually have a plan. You don't have anything in writing except for statements, and those are just report cards for how your assets have performed in the past. So how could you understand your money?

3. The only way you will eliminate your confusion and fully understand your money for the first time in your life is by creating a comprehensive written retirement income plan.

We feel some of the biggest benefits you will receive from demanding that any actions you take to plan for your retirement are part of a written plan include:

- It requires a very high level of responsibility and accountability from your advisor and his/her entire staff. You are owed responsibility and accountability from your advisor from day one of your relationship and every day thereafter!

- Eliminates the mystery of what exactly is supposed to happen – you can remember, your spouse can remember, and the advisor can remember your plan details. If any of you forget details about the plan – just open it and read it again!

- Communication between you and your spouse about finances increases dramatically, improving your overall relationship. For once you both will be talking the same language about money!
- Creates the building blocks for the strongest possible long-term relationship with your advisor. You are not "buying" a financial product from your advisor, you are implementing a comprehensive written retirement income plan!
- Makes you "the best type of client" for your advisor – you become an "educated client." Nowadays a retiree who understands a plan will move forward with plan implementation recommendations, those that don't understand won't *and shouldn't* move forward!
- Puts you, your spouse, and your advisor on the same "team." All of you will be playing by the same rules, the same "playbook" – your written comprehensive retirement income plan!
- Your advisor becomes your "consultant" not your "salesperson." You finally get what most retirees have been looking for and wanting for many years!
- Creates responsibility on you and your spouse always to notify your advisor of any changes in your finances so your plan can be updated and modified to keep you "on track." This creates an open communication line between you and your advisor, helping to minimize negatives and accentuate the positives!

If every aspect of your plan is put in writing you will have a lot higher probability that your plan will be successful and your goals will be met. The assets you have now are supposed to last you for the rest of your life.

Proper planning is necessary for your success. The first step to proper planning is *demanding* you have a comprehensive written retirement income plan. If you work with an advisor, *demand* the advisor provides you with one. If your spouse does the planning for you, *demand* that your spouse provides you with a plan in writing. Either way, just make sure you get it!

CHAPTER 25

YOUR ROADMAP TO SUCCESS – A COMPREHENSIVE WRITTEN RETIREMENT INCOME PLAN

BY DAN AHMAD & JIM FILES

We previously discussed the *7 Rules To Live By For Retirement Security* and the importance of a plan:

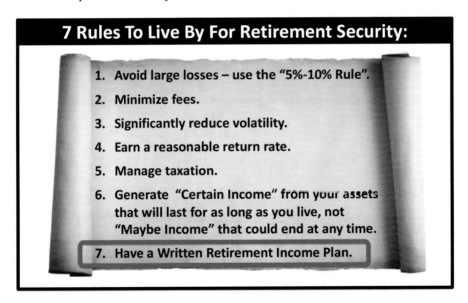

7 Rules To Live By For Retirement Security:

1. Avoid large losses – use the "5%-10% Rule".
2. Minimize fees.
3. Significantly reduce volatility.
4. Earn a reasonable return rate.
5. Manage taxation.
6. Generate "Certain Income" from your assets that will last for as long as you live, not "Maybe Income" that could end at any time.
7. Have a Written Retirement Income Plan.

A comprehensive written retirement income plan should include:

- ✓ Retirement income projection: income analysis + risk analysis + fee analysis
- ✓ Income tax analysis
- ✓ Beneficiary asset transfer analysis
- ✓ Full plan details

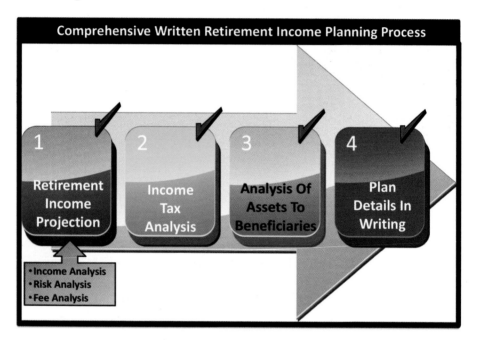

If your plans for retirement were based on the previous diagram, how would you feel? Probably a lot more secure. In our experience, working with retirees and pre-retirees, less than five (5) out of every 1,000 people have an actual written document that lays out their entire retirement income plan as highlighted above. Chances are extremely high that you don't have a plan. At the same time, studies show the number one (1) thing retirees want in planning for their retirement years is to have an actual written plan. And still they don't get one.

Let's examine a hypothetical case study to see how the comprehensive planning process works:

Bob & Carol Both Age 65

Retired 2 Years Ago

Current Income Sources:
- $24,000 Carol Pension
- $26,000 Carol Social Security
- $28,000 Bob Social Security

$1,600,000 Assets – Haven't Used For Income

Want To Travel – A Lot!

Worried About:
- Market Being So High
- Suffering Big Losses
- Money Running Out
- Paying High Income Taxes
- Not Leaving Money To Beneficiaries
- Not Having A Plan

Had A Broker For 22 Years Who Told Them:
- He'd Give Them A Written Plan – Never Did
- They Were Paying 1% In Fees
- Their Portfolio Was Moderate/Conservative
- Not To Take Distributions Until 70 ½
- In '00-'02 and '07-'09 To Ride Out The Market

Bob and Carol worked hard and saved their money for over 40 years. They'd done a great job accumulating retirement assets of $1,600,000 not including their home. They were great savers, didn't overspend, and had $0 in consumer debt. They've been retired for two (2) years already and receive $78,000 in total pension and Social Security income. The $78,000 of annual income is enough to pay for all of their monthly costs and bills but didn't leave them extra money for travelling. They had a broker for 22 years and he always told them the best planning strategy was to defer their income distributions until age 70½ so they wouldn't get killed with income taxes.

So how can they travel more if they don't have more income? They want to travel a lot, and they want to do it now. They are only 65 and in great health, so they feel there is no time like the present, and they shouldn't waste another moment. Bob has recently had a best friend his same age pass away from a massive heart attack and Carol's best friend has been battling cancer for several years. Bob and Carol fully understand they can't take their good health and their ability to travel for granted because they feel if they don't do it now they might not get the chance to do it in the future.

They are very worried about how high the stock market is and how the next stock market crash could be around the corner, because they lost -50% between 2000 through 2002 and lost another -50% between 2007 through 2009 and don't want to go through those recurring nightmares again. They are very afraid of running out of money because their broker has told them they need to grow their assets as much as possible to make sure they will have enough money. Then, on the other hand, the broker says if the market drops they will need to "ride the market out" again, and they really don't like the sound of that, because if they have to "ride the market out again" they will need to decrease or terminate their income distributions and their money will most likely run out sooner rather than later. And they won't be able to travel. Their broker and CPA have both told them taking additional income distributions will significantly increase their income taxes.

They became such great savers while they were working, that they have been afraid to use their assets for income now that they are retired. Now retired, they have not taken out any income, and this is a common trait we see in retirees who have been good at saving money. They simply have not learned how to spend it, in most cases because they are afraid of suffering big losses, their money running out during their lifetime, and that they will pay too much in income taxes for using their money.

The other common trait we see all the time with people like Bob and Carol is that they do not realize they have achieved success. Not just a little success, but they have achieved success at the highest possible level that will allow them to have the retirement of their dreams, without having to worry about big stock market losses and without ever having to worry about their money running out for as long as they live. They have no idea they have succeeded because no one has:

1. Told them they have already accumulated enough assets to actually attain their financial goals.
2. Told them they must transition from asset accumulation to asset preservation and income distribution.
3. Built a plan for them to reduce their risk and maximize their income.
4. Put their entire plan in writing.
5. Created a customized income plan stating they won't run out of money for as long as they live.

The clients we meet with every day are just like Bob and Carol in one major way: if they just had a plan, a detailed written plan, they could live out their retirement dreams starting today! And just like you, they don't have that plan.

We asked Bob and Carol why they saved the money in the first place while they were working? They replied they saved the money so they could use their assets during retirement to create income that would last for as long as they lived, so they could enjoy their retirement as much as possible. Carol answered, "So they could travel the globe." To do this, Bob and Carol have to convert or transition from a "saver" while they were working with a "money-hoarders" mentality to being a "spender" now retired with an "I-deserve-the-best-retirement" mentality.

Going from a saver to a spender is far harder to do than you would think. It is very, very difficult for many retirees to spend their money they have saved for so many years. They have always focused on save, save, save, save! Do without, do without, do without! Sacrifice, sacrifice, sacrifice! Hoard the money, hoard the money, hoard the money! Now it seems so strange, it almost seems like they're bad, doing something wrong, to even think about actually spending their money. We know the hesitation to use their assets comes from their fears. But what if Bob and Carol could have a retirement income plan that reduced their risk of large stock market losses and guaranteed they would never run out of income for as long as they both lived, and kept them in a low income tax rate on all their income? Do you think they would be willing to use their assets for income? You bet! This is the type of plan we will discuss.

Here is their current plan scenario analysis:

CURRENT PLAN SCENARIO			
Current Assets	Current Values	Annual Fees	Loss If Market Drops 53% Like 2008
Stocks - Broker Managed	$200,000	1.25%	($100,000)
Managed Mutual Funds	$1,000,000	2.92%	($500,000)
Variable Annuity	$380,000	4.61%	($190,000)
Bank	$20,000	0.00%	$0
Totals	$1,600,000	3.08%	($790,000)
		$49,218	-49.4%
			Current Plan Recovery Gain Needed
Current Plan Annual Income From Assets	$24,000		97.5%

Their $1,600,000 portfolio was allocated to $200,000 of stocks being managed by their broker, $1,000,000 of mutual funds being managed by their broker, a $380,000 variable annuity, and $20,000 of liquid cash in the bank. We asked them, "Why do you only have $20,000 in the bank? With $1,600,000 of total assets, that's not enough liquidity, and we'd recommend you have more." The wife was mad as she replied, "We wanted more money in the bank too, but our broker told us to take $380,000 out of the bank and put in the variable annuity so we can make a higher rate of return, but now we've lost some of our principal already."

We reviewed their assets and completed a fee analysis, analyzing direct (visible) fees and indirect (invisible) fees. They were paying 1.25% to have their stocks managed, 2.92% in total costs to have their mutual funds managed, 4.61% in total costs for their variable annuity, and paying 0.00% to keep their money in the bank. The average fees they were paying on their $1,600,000 of assets was 3.08%, amounting to $49,218 in fees per year. They were shocked, they had no idea they were paying so much. You, too, may be paying more than you think.

A risk analysis was completed to determine their "true risk level" by measuring how much they could potentially lose in the next market crash and how much gain was needed to recover the loss fully. The data (in the diagram on the preceding page) shows if the stock market lost -53% like it did during the Financial Crisis between October 2007 through March 2009, their $200,000 stock portfolio would lose -50% creating a -$100,000 loss, their $1,000,000 mutual fund portfolio would lose -50% creating a -$500,000 loss, their $380,000 variable annuity would lose -50% creating a -$190,000 loss, and their $20,000 in the bank would not lose anything at all.

Their $1,600,000 portfolio was projected to have -$790,000 of total potential losses, which is a -49.4% risk factor. Bob and Carol have to be able to look across the table from us and say, "We're 65 and we're okay with a -$790,000 loss on our $1,600,000 portfolio, we're okay with a -49.49% risk factor." Can Bob and Carol really say this and mean it? Of course not. Could you say that and mean it? Of course not. You could be in the same high-risk position as Bob and Carol and not even know it.

The previous chart also shows if they lose -49.4%, which is a -$790,000 loss, they will need a recovery gain of +97.5% just to get back to even, no gain at all, just recover. And the +97.5% gain needed doesn't account for fees Bob and Carol would pay or income they planned to take out. Their current assets were positioned in a classic portfolio example of Stage One of Retirement Planning – Asset Accumulation – focusing on growth and not worrying about possible large losses and not built for income. Their current plan was to take out $24,000 of income every year from their assets.

We met with Bob and Carol five (5) times to build their plan. We asked them about how much risk they really wanted to take and they replied they would like to keep their risk level between -5% to a maximum of -10%, meaning they don't want to lose more than -5% up to a maximum -10% of their assets. We asked them how much income they would like to be able to take out of their assets and they replied, "as much as possible as long as it will never run out for as long as they lived, and as long as they won't be in too high of an income tax bracket." We asked them if it was important for them to leave money to their beneficiaries and they replied, "Our number one goal is to make sure we have enough money for as long as we live and then we'd like everything left to be passed on to our children."

Here is the summary of what their new plan looked like:

NEW PLAN SCENARIO			
Planned Assets	Current Values	Annual Fees	Loss If Market Drops - 53% Like 2008
Stocks - Self Managed	$200,000	0.00%	($100,000)
Bucket #1 - Guaranteed Income Bucket	$800,000	0.95%	$0
Bucket #2 - Liquid/Safe Bucket	$100,000	0.00%	$0
Bucket #3 - Growth With 10% Stop Loss	$500,000	1.91%	($50,000)
Totals	$1,600,000	1.07%	($150,000)
		$17,150	-9.4%
			New Plan Recovery Gain Needed
New Plan Annual Income From Assets	$60,000		10.3%

We re-allocated their $1,600,000 portfolio by placing:

> $200,000 of their stocks in an account they will manage themselves (self-manage). We asked if they would do a lot of trading or primarily "buy-and-hold"? They said they would buy and hold three (3) main

stocks of companies they really like, including Apple, Google, and Home Depot. Their current broker buys and sells different stocks all the time and they are charged for additional trading costs and they don't like it. In the self-managed account, they don't pay any fees at all unless they buy and sell stocks, then they pay whatever the commission rate per trade is, which we see typically around $6. They no longer have to pay the broker 1.25% every year for doing nothing!

➤ $800,000 into Bucket #1, the guaranteed lifetime income bucket, because they only have one small $2,000 per month pension and we need to create a significant amount of income for them that is guaranteed for as long as they both live.

➤ $100,000 into Bucket #2, the liquidity safety bucket (the bank), and we will plan to add to this bucket every month throughout their retirement.

➤ $500,000 into Bucket #3, the growth bucket with the stop loss.

They have the same $1,600,000 with the funds just allocated to better meet their needs in retirement.

The new asset allocation was able to reduce their total fees from 3.08% down to 1.07%, creating an annual fee savings of $32,068. Many new clients ask us why we would create a plan that would focus on fee reduction when they know we get paid from the fees? First of all, it's the right thing to do. Secondly, if we can provide an opportunity for an individual to reduce the fees they pay to have their assets managed, it is a tremendous financial benefit to them. By helping reduce their fees, people see we really do have their best interest in mind and they end up doing business with us. Our clients are very happy with this transparency, and they refer other clients to our firm. We view this as an awesome win-win situation!

We are able to reduce the projected overall risk of their portfolio significantly. If the stock market drops -53% like it did during the Financial Crisis between October 2007 through March 2009, their $200,000 self-managed stock portfolio would be projected to lose -50% creating a -$100,000 loss, their $800,000 guaranteed lifetime income Bucket #1 funded with a fixed index annuity and income rider would not lose anything (-0%), their $100,000 in Bucket #2 bank funds would not lose anything (-0%), and the $500,000 invested into Bucket #3 for growth was projected to lose an estimated -10% creating a -$50,000 loss. Their total projected losses have now been reduced from -$790,000 all the way down to -$150,000, reducing their risk factor down from -49.4% to -9.4% and reducing their gain needed for recovery from +97.5% all the way down to +10.3%.

This means we reduced their loss risk by more than 80% and their recovery gain needed by almost 90%!

And the most exciting part of the plan was that we were able to increase the annual income from their assets from $24,000 up to $60,000!

What you have just reviewed is the summary for a hypothetical case study of a typical type of plan we implement on a daily basis for our clients. This type of planning is focused on transitioning your portfolio from Stage One of Retirement Planning - *Asset Accumulation* to Stage Two of Retirement Planning - *Income Distribution and Asset Preservation*. And while Bob and Carol's plan wasn't overly complicated or difficult, they received an opportunity to receive tremendous potential benefits:

1. More control of their assets.
2. Greater understanding of their money.
3. Fees reduced by over $32,000 per year, a savings of over 65%. Over 20 years fees estimated to be reduced by $640,000.
4. Risk of loss reduced by more than 80%, decreasing potential losses from $790,000 to $150,000.
5. Risk of recovery gain reduced by almost 90%.
6. Annual income from their assets increased to $60,000, with a majority guaranteed for as long as they both live.
7. No longer worried about their money.

CHAPTER 26

COMPREHENSIVE WRITTEN RETIREMENT INCOME PLAN
SECTION #1A
RETIREMENT INCOME PROJECTION

BY DAN AHMAD & JIM FILES

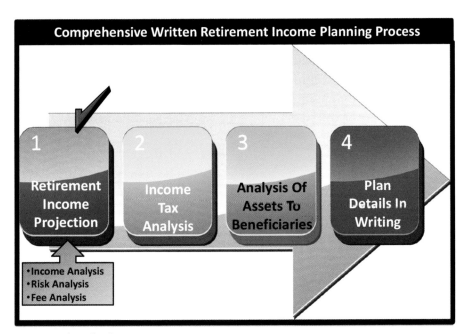

Comprehensive Written Retirement Income Planning Process

1	2	3	4
Retirement Income Projection	Income Tax Analysis	Analysis Of Assets To Beneficiaries	Plan Details In Writing

- Income Analysis
- Risk Analysis
- Fee Analysis

Income Analysis

When you retire, there are a lot of things to be anxious about. You'll be staying home and no longer be doing something every day you have been doing for 20, 30, 40, even 50 years. If you're like most retirees, the part about retirement you are most worried about is how will you create income every month for as long as you live that will allow you to pay for everything you need and want. You want to know and be able to see where your income is going to come from for the rest of your life. If you can't actually see where your income is going to come from, and if you can't be sure you will receive it for as long as you live, the worries, pressure, tension, anxiety, and fear will always be there haunting you.

When you were working, it was easy. Monday through Friday (and maybe some weekends) you woke up, took your shower, had your coffee, drove to work, had some more coffee, put in your hours, drove home, did it again, and like magic your accounting department sent you a paycheck every week, 2 weeks, or month. Now you are retired, and the accounting department no longer knows who you are, they definitely are not going to be sending you any more paychecks. Now you have to be your own accounting department and create your own paychecks from your assets for the rest of your life. This is what Bob and Carol needed to do.

As we have discussed previously, Bob and Carol are both 65, have been retired for two (2) years, receive $24,000 of pension income and $54,000 of joint Social Security Income, totaling $78,000 per year, which is $6,500 of gross income per month. Their current net after-tax monthly income was $5,800. Their monthly expenses not including travel were $5,700. They had just enough each month to pay for all of their needs, but no extra income for travel, emergencies, extra costs, or the future.

Bob and Carol had $1,600,000 in assets, and like many other retirees they weren't using their assets for income. The assets were just sitting there, assets they had saved for the single reason of using for income in the future when they retired. Bob and Carol stated their broker told them it was better for them to defer income distributions into the future—until they were age 70 ½. We told Bob and Carol their future is right now, it's not a year from now, it's not a couple years from now, and it's definitely not at age 70 ½ when they will be forced to take required minimum distributions from their accounts. Their future is right now because they want and need more income, and they are young enough and healthy enough to travel all over the place! On the following page, here is what their current income plan looked like:

							$200,000	$1,000,000	$380,000	$20,000	$0	$1,600,000
Annual Income Bob & Carol Current Income Plan							Broker Managed Stock Account	Broker Managed Mutual Funds	Broker Managed Variable Anuity	Liquid Safe Bank Funds	Bucket #1 Bucket #2 Bucket #3 Self. Man. Stocks	Total Annual Income Flow
Year	Bob	Carol	Carol PERS Income	Carol Social Security	Bob Social Security							
2018	65	65	$24,000	$26,000	$28,000		$0	$0	$0	$0	$0	$78,000
2019	66	66	$24,480	$26,390	$28,420		$0	$0	$0	$0	$0	$79,290
2020	67	67	$24,970	$26,786	$28,846		$0	$0	$0	$0	$0	$80,602
2021	68	68	$25,469	$27,188	$29,279		$0	$0	$0	$0	$0	$81,936
2022	69	69	$25,978	$27,595	$29,718		$0	$0	$0	$0	$0	$83,292
2023	70	70	$26,498	$28,009	$30,164		$0	$0	$0	$0	$0	$84,671
2024	71	71	$27,028	$28,430	$30,616		$0	$0	$0	$0	$0	$86,074
2025	72	72	$27,568	$28,856	$31,076		$0	$0	$0	$0	$0	$87,500
2026	73	73	$28,120	$29,289	$31,542		$0	$0	$0	$0	$0	$88,950
2027	74	74	$28,682	$29,728	$32,015		$0	$0	$0	$0	$0	$90,425
2028	75	75	$29,256	$30,174	$32,495		$0	$0	$0	$0	$0	$91,925
2029	76	76	$29,841	$30,627	$32,983		$0	$0	$0	$0	$0	$93,450
2030	77	77	$30,438	$31,086	$33,477		$0	$0	$0	$0	$0	$95,001
2031	78	78	$31,047	$31,552	$33,979		$0	$0	$0	$0	$0	$96,578
2032	79	79	$31,667	$32,026	$34,489		$0	$0	$0	$0	$0	$98,182
2033	80	80	$32,301	$32,506	$35,006		$0	$0	$0	$0	$0	$99,813
2034	81	81	$32,947	$32,994	$35,532		$0	$0	$0	$0	$0	$101,472
2035	82	82	$33,606	$33,489	$36,065		$0	$0	$0	$0	$0	$103,159
2036	83	83	$34,278	$33,991	$36,606		$0	$0	$0	$0	$0	$104,874
2037	84	84	$34,963	$34,501	$37,155		$0	$0	$0	$0	$0	$106,619
2038	85	85	$35,663	$35,018	$37,712		$0	$0	$0	$0	$0	$108,393
2039	86	86	$36,376	$35,544	$38,278		$0	$0	$0	$0	$0	$110,197
2040	87	87	$37,104	$36,077	$38,852		$0	$0	$0	$0	$0	$112,032
2041	88	88	$37,846	$36,618	$39,435		$0	$0	$0	$0	$0	$113,898
2042	89	89	$38,602	$37,167	$40,026		$0	$0	$0	$0	$0	$115,796
2043	90	90	$39,375	$37,725	$40,626		$0	$0	$0	$0	$0	$117,726
2044	91	91	$40,162	$38,290	$41,236		$0	$0	$0	$0	$0	$119,688
2045	92	92	$40,965	$38,865	$41,854		$0	$0	$0	$0	$0	$121,684
2046	93	93	$41,785	$39,448	$42,482		$0	$0	$0	$0	$0	$123,715
2047	94	94	$42,620	$40,039	$43,119		$0	$0	$0	$0	$0	$125,779

The above chart highlights in red for 2018 Carol's $24,000 pension, her $26,000 Social Security, and Bob's $28,000 Social Security, totaling $78,000 per year of gross annual income. The black highlighted area at the top shows the $1,600,000 of assets producing no income. After meeting with Bob and Carol several times and determining what they wanted their money to do for them, we created the following plan:

261

						($500,000)	($400,000)	($400,000)	($100,000)	($200,000)	($1,600,000)
Annual Income Bob & Carol New Income Plan			Carol PERS Income	Carol Social Security	Bob Social Security	Carol IRA Bucket #3 Growth With 10% Stop Loss	Carol IRA Bucket #1 Guaranteed Lifetime Income	Bob IRA Bucket #1 Guaranteed Lifetime Income	Bucket #2 Liquid Safe Bank Funds	Self Managed Stock Assets	Total Annual Income Flow
Year	Bob	Carol									
2018	65	65	$24,000	$26,000	$28,000	$60,000	$0	$0	$0	$0	$138,000
2019	66	66	$24,480	$26,390	$28,420	$60,000	$0	$0	$0	$0	$139,290
2020	67	67	$24,970	$26,786	$28,846	$60,000	$0	$0	$0	$0	$140,602
2021	68	68	$25,469	$27,188	$29,279	$60,000	$0	$0	$0	$0	$141,936
2022	69	69	$25,978	$27,595	$29,718	$60,000	$0	$0	$0	$0	$143,292
2023	70	70	$26,498	$28,009	$30,164	$9,198	$28,119	$28,119	$0	$0	$150,107
2024	71	71	$27,028	$28,430	$30,616	$9,382	$28,119	$28,119	$0	$0	$151,694
2025	72	72	$27,568	$28,856	$31,076	$9,570	$28,119	$28,119	$0	$0	$153,308
2026	73	73	$28,120	$29,289	$31,542	$9,761	$28,119	$28,119	$0	$0	$154,950
2027	74	74	$28,682	$29,728	$32,015	$9,956	$28,119	$28,119	$0	$0	$156,620
2028	75	75	$29,256	$30,174	$32,495	$10,155	$28,119	$28,119	$0	$0	$158,319
2029	76	76	$29,841	$30,627	$32,983	$10,359	$28,119	$28,119	$0	$0	$160,047
2030	77	77	$30,438	$31,086	$33,477	$10,566	$28,119	$28,119	$0	$0	$161,805
2031	78	78	$31,047	$31,552	$33,979	$10,777	$28,119	$28,119	$0	$0	$163,593
2032	79	79	$31,667	$32,026	$34,489	$10,993	$28,119	$28,119	$0	$0	$165,413
2033	80	80	$32,301	$32,506	$35,006	$11,212	$28,119	$28,119	$0	$0	$167,264
2034	81	81	$32,947	$32,994	$35,532	$11,437	$28,119	$28,119	$0	$0	$169,147
2035	82	82	$33,606	$33,489	$36,065	$11,665	$28,119	$28,119	$0	$0	$171,062
2036	83	83	$34,278	$33,991	$36,606	$11,899	$28,119	$28,119	$0	$0	$173,011
2037	84	84	$34,963	$34,501	$37,155	$12,137	$28,119	$28,119	$0	$0	$174,993
2038	85	85	$35,663	$35,018	$37,712	$12,379	$28,119	$28,119	$0	$0	$177,010
2039	86	86	$36,376	$35,544	$38,278	$12,627	$28,119	$28,119	$0	$0	$179,062
2040	87	87	$37,104	$36,077	$38,852	$12,880	$28,119	$28,119	$0	$0	$181,149
2041	88	88	$37,846	$36,618	$39,435	$13,137	$28,119	$28,119	$0	$0	$183,273
2042	89	89	$38,602	$37,167	$40,026	$13,400	$28,119	$28,119	$0	$0	$185,434
2043	90	90	$39,375	$37,725	$40,626	$13,668	$28,119	$28,119	$0	$0	$187,631
2044	91	91	$40,162	$38,290	$41,236	$13,941	$28,119	$28,119	$0	$0	$189,868
2045	92	92	$40,965	$38,865	$41,854	$14,220	$28,119	$28,119	$0	$0	$192,143
2046	93	93	$41,785	$39,448	$42,482	$14,504	$28,119	$28,119	$0	$0	$194,457
2047	94	94	$42,620	$40,039	$43,119	$14,795	$28,119	$28,119	$0	$0	$196,812

The above chart illustrates their new income plan for 2018, highlighted in red, showing Carol's $24,000 pension, her $26,000 Social Security, and Bob's $28,000 Social Security, and adds in $60,000 of additional annual income, increasing their total annual gross income to $138,000. We took $500,000 of their $1,600,000 and placed these funds into the red box titled, **"Carol IRA Bucket #3 Growth With 10% Stop-Loss"** and will use this bucket to provide Bob and Carol $60,000 of income distributions for five (5) years. After five (5) years income distributions from Bucket #3 will be reduced as shown.

Bob and Carol loved the idea of increasing their annual income from $78,000 to $138,000, but as they thought about it, they became apprehensive about how much income tax they would have to pay by increasing their income so much, because this meant they would be taking out $60,000 of taxable IRA distributions. Their broker had always warned them they would get hit hard with income taxes if they tapped into their IRA assets before age 70½. But like many things, their broker was wrong. Their broker wanted them to defer their assets for as long as possible because the more income they take out of their assets for income, the lower the amounts they will have in their accounts, and the less commissions and fees the broker will be paid. When Bob and Carol's broker, or your broker, says it's better to defer your IRA assets until age 70½, it is better for the broker, not for Bob and Carol, and not for you! We told Bob and Carol we would complete an income tax analysis to show them their taxes will not be a problem.

We then placed $400,000 of their $1,600,000 assets into the green box titled **"Carol IRA Bucket #1 Guaranteed Lifetime Income."** Carol deferred taking income from this account for five (5) years. By deferring, after five (5) years Carol is contractually guaranteed to receive $28,119 of income for life, for as long as she lives, even if she lives to 120! If Carol passes away, her $28,119 of annual income will be paid to Bob for as long as he lives, even if he lives to 120. If Carol and Bob both pass away, 100% of the remaining funds in this account are paid to their named beneficiaries. Carol's $28,119 of income will never be affected by stock market volatility or losses.

We then placed $400,000 of their $1,600,000 assets into the green box titled **"Bob IRA Bucket #1 Guaranteed Lifetime Income."** Bob was also planning to defer taking income from this account for five (5) years. By deferring, after five (5) years Bob also is contractually guaranteed to receive $28,119 of income for life, for as long as he lives. If Bob passes away, his $28,119 of annual income will be paid to Carol for as long as she lives. If Bob and Carol pass away, 100% of the remaining funds in this account are paid to their named beneficiaries. Bob's $28,119 of income will never be affected by stock market volatility or losses.

By allocating $800,000 of their $1,600,000 of retirement assets into Bucket #1, Bob and Carol are guaranteed to receive annual joint lifetime income of $56,238 for as long as they live, and all funds remaining in their account when they both have passed away will be paid to their beneficiaries. Their joint $56,238 of income will never be affected by stock market volatility or losses. Isn't that what most retirees really want? Have the highest amount of income paid for as long as they live, the income not affected by stock market losses, and anything they don't use is paid to their beneficiaries? That's precisely what most retirees want.

We then placed $100,000 of their $1,600,000 assets into the gold box titled **"Bucket #2 Liquid Safe Bank Funds."** As you can see in the previous chart, we are not using this bucket for income. These funds can be used for any purpose in the future such as to buy a new car, complete a home remodel, help grandkids with college, or anything else they need a large lump sum of money for. They also might never spend this money at all, and just use it to feel safer throughout retirement.

We then placed $200,000 of their $1,600,000 assets into the white box with red lettering titled, **"Self-Managed Stock Assets."** As you can also see in the previous chart, we are not using this bucket for income. These stock funds are planned to be held long-term and just like the money in the bank can be used for any purpose in the future. Bob and Carol loved their income plan because they could "see" how their income was going to be paid to them every year for as long as they lived. They were going to have $60,000 more in gross income starting immediately, and they were going to receive $56,238 of joint guaranteed annual income after five (5) years that would be paid to them for as long as they live. But they were still worried about their income taxes. We told Bob and Carol after we performed their risk analysis and fee analysis, we would complete their income tax analysis.

CHAPTER 27

COMPREHENSIVE WRITTEN RETIREMENT INCOME PLAN
SECTION #1B
RISK ANALYSIS

BY DAN AHMAD & JIM FILES

We have found the vast majority of retirees are taking far more risk with their assets than they thought they were. This is because most retirees have never had a risk analysis completed for their current portfolio showing how much money they could lose in the next significant stock market downturn. This is also because their current advisor doesn't want to complete a risk analysis because then the advisor would have to tell the retiree how much risk they were really taking, which is almost always much more than they want to take. Bob and Carol thought they couldn't lose more than -10% in their portfolio if the market crashed again like in 2008.

We completed the following risk analysis for Bob and Carol's current portfolio. First of all, they said their current advisor had never summarized their assets like this before so that they could "see" what they actually owned. We then used a sophisticated software program that allowed us to enter in every individual stock, bond, exchange-traded fund (ETF) and mutual fund they own. The software calculated how much Bob and Carol would lose if we have a stock market crash similar to the 2008 Financial Crisis, when the stock market lost -53.8%.

The $20,000 in the bank wouldn't lose anything. The program concluded Bob and Carol would lose -50% of the $1,580,000 in their stocks, bonds, mutual funds, and ETF's if we have another 2008 stock market crash.

This means their $1,580,000 would lose -$790,000. If you look at the far right column, it shows Bob and Carol had $1,600,000 of assets and if they lost -$790,000 their risk was -49.4%. Look at the area of the chart titled **"Golden Rule Of 5% To 10%"** and it is easy to see they are taking way too much risk, as they should be between -5% to -10% of risk, but they have -49.4% risk. If their $1,600,000 loses -49.4% they will have $810,000 left. The $810,000 will have to earn +97.5% just to break even assuming they don't take out any income and they don't pay any fees. This is not acceptable.

CURRENT ASSET ALLOCATION			Bob & Carol				
Account Name, Type, & Ownership	Company	Account Managed By	Current Value	Cash	Stocks, Bonds, Mutual Funds, ETFs	Totals
Bob's IRA	Big Brokerage House	Advisor	$225,000		$225,000	$225,000
Bob's IRA	Big Brokerage House	Advisor	$175,000		$175,000	$175,000
Bob's IRA	Discount Brokerage	Self	$80,000		$80,000	$80,000
Carol's IRA	Big Brokerage House	Advisor	$100,000		$100,000	$100,000
Carol's IRA	Big Brokerage House	Advisor	$300,000		$300,000	$300,000
Bob's Roth IRA	Discount Brokerage	Self	$100,000		$100,000	$100,000
Carol's Roth IRA	Discount Brokerage	Self	$100,000		$100,000	$100,000
Carol's IRA	Big Brokerage House	Advisor	$500,000		$500,000	$500,000
Bank	Big Bank	Self	$20,000	$20,000		$20,000
Totals			$1,600,000	$20,000	$1,580,000	$1,600,000

Hypothetical Loss Similar To 2008 Financial Crisis				$0	($790,000)	($790,000)
Hypothetical Asset Value Loss				0.0%	-50.00%	-49.4%
					(1)	

Golden Rule Of 5% To 10%				Current Asset Values	$1,600,000
Maximum Loss Willing To Suffer	-10.0%			Potential Loss Illustrated	($790,000)
Preferred Risk Level	-5.0%			Asset Values After Loss	$810,000
				Gain To Fully Recover	97.5%

(1) Estimated based on 3rd party data. Hypothetical loss could be higher or lower.

Their new plan asset allocation includes placing $800,000 into Bucket #1, $100,000 into Bucket #2, $500,000 into Bucket #3, and $200,000 into a self-managed stock account as shown on the following page:

NEW PLAN ASSET ALLOCATION			Bob & Carol			
Account Name, Type, & Ownership	Bucket #2 - Liquidity & Safety - Cash	Self Managed Assets - Stocks	Carol's IRA Bucket #3 Growth Managed Portfolio With 10% StopLoss	Carol's IRA Bucket #1 Guaranteed Lifetime Income Fixed Index Annuity	Bob's IRA Bucket #1 Guaranteed Lifetime Income Fixed Index Annuity	Totals
Bob's IRA					$225,000	$225,000
Bob's IRA					$175,000	$175,000
Bob's IRA	$80,000					$80,000
Carol's IRA				$100,000		$100,000
Carol's IRA				$300,000		$300,000
Bob's Roth IRA		$100,000				$100,000
Carol's Roth IRA		$100,000				$100,000
Carol's IRA			$500,000			$500,000
Bank	$20,000					$20,000
Totals	$100,000	$200,000	$500,000	$400,000	$400,000	$1,600,000

2008 Fin. Crisis Sim. Loss	$0	($100,000)	($50,000)	$0	$0	($150,000)
Hypothetical Asset Value Loss	0.0%	-50.00%	-10.0%	0.0%	0.0%	-9.4%
		(1)	(2)	(3)	(3)	

New Portfolio Allocation	
Stocks - Self Managed	$200,000
Bucket #1 - Guar. Income	$800,000
Bucket #2 - Liquid/Safe	$100,000
Bucket #3 - Growth Stop Loss	$500,000

With Plan Asset Values	$1,600,000
Potential Loss Illustrated	($150,000)
Asset Values After Loss	$1,450,000

Gain To Fully Recover	10.3%

(1) & (2) Estimated based on 3rd party data. Hypothetical loss could be higher or lower.
(3) Fixed Index Annuity Guarantees are subject to the claims paying ability of each life insurance carrier.

If we have another 2008 Financial Crisis and the stock market drops -53.8%, the chart above shows:

- The gold box titled "Bucket #2 Liquidity & Safety Cash" holding $100,000 in the bank won't lose anything (-$0), as the bank funds are 100% protected against all stock market losses.
- The white box with red letters titled "Self-Managed Assets Stocks" holding $200,000 of stocks managed by Bob and Carol are projected to lose -50% which is a loss of -$100,000.
- The red box titled "Carol's IRA Bucket #3 Growth Managed Portfolio With 10% StopLoss" holding $500,000 of professionally-managed ETF's are projected to lose -10% which is a loss of -$50,000.
- The green box titled "Carol's IRA Bucket #1 Guaranteed Lifetime Income Fixed Index Annuity" holding $400,000 won't lose anything, as fixed index annuities with income riders are 100% protected against stock market losses.
- The green box titled "Bob's IRA Bucket #1 Guaranteed Lifetime Income Fixed Index Annuity" holding $400,000 won't lose anything, as fixed index annuities with income riders are 100% protected against stock market losses.

Bob and Carol's new portfolio has a total projected risk of loss of -$150,000, which is a -9.4% risk factor, an acceptable level of risk that fits within the *Golden Rule Of 5% To 10%*. If Bob and Carol suffer a -$150,000 loss that decreases their $1,600,000 to $1,450,000, their new portfolio will only require a recovery gain of +10.3% versus their original portfolio's +97.5% required recovery gain. Bob and Carol understand their actual losses could be higher or lower, but they are much more comfortable with the lower projected risk in their new asset allocation plan.

CHAPTER 28

COMPREHENSIVE WRITTEN RETIREMENT INCOME PLAN
SECTION #1C
FEE ANALYSIS

BY DAN AHMAD & JIM FILES

Bob and Carol's broker of 22 years had never provided them the total fees they were paying in writing. Bob and Carol thought they were paying 1% in total fees, because when they asked about fees, their broker would say something like they were "paying around 1% in fees." We completed a comprehensive fee analysis and found this wasn't true, not even close to the truth. The fee analysis (shown on the following page) revealed Bob and Carol were paying 3.08% per year in total fees:

CURRENT FEE ANALYSIS			
	Fees In Percentage	Value Of Asset Fees Are Assessed On	Fees In Dollars
Bank Funds	0.00%		
Total Costs Bank Funds	0.00%	$20,000	$0
Variable Annuity M & E Costs	1.50%	$380,000	$5,700
Sub-Account Fees	1.05%	$380,000	$3,990
Annuity Rider Fees	1.25%	$380,000	$4,750
Annuity Trading Costs - Hidden Estimated	0.81%	$380,000	$3,078
Total Costs	4.61%	$380,000	$17,518
Stock Portfolio Advisory Costs	1.20%	$200,000	$2,400
Trading Costs - Hidden Estimated	0.05%	$200,000	$100
Total Costs	1.25%	$200,000	$2,500
Mutual Fund Advisory Costs	1.50%	$1,000,000	$15,000
Mutal Fund Costs	0.61%	$1,000,000	$6,100
Trading Costs - Hidden Estimated	0.81%	$1,000,000	$8,100
Total Costs	2.92%	$1,000,000	$29,200
Total Average Weighted Costs		$1,600,000	$49,218	3.08%
		Portfolio Value	Total Annual Fees	Average Fees Paid On $1,600,000
Projected Total Fees Paid Through Age 85 (20 Years)			$984,360

The chart above shows the fees calculated for each part of their portfolio:

- The bank funds of $20,000 had a 0.00% annual fee so total annual cost is $0.

- Their variable annuity of $380,000 had the following fees:
  M&E (mortality and expenses) fees of 1.5% on
  $380,000, equaling annual costs of: $ 5,700
  + Sub-accounts fees of 1.05% on $380,000, equaling
  annual costs of: $ 3,990
  + Annuity rider fees of 1.25%, equaling annual
  costs of: $ 4,750
  + Estimated trading fees at the sub-account level
  of 0.81%, equaling annual costs of: $ 3,078
  = **Total annual variable annuity fees of 4.61%,
  equaling total annual costs of:**   **$ 17,518**

- Their stock portfolio of $200,000 had the following fees:
  Advisory fees of 1.2% on $200,000, equaling
  total annual costs of: $ 2,400
  + Estimated trading fees of 0.05% on $200,000,
  equaling total annual costs of: $ 100
  = **Total stock portfolio annual fees of 1.25%,**
  equaling total annual costs of: **$ 2,500**

- Their mutual fund portfolio of $1,000,000 had the
  following fees:
  Advisory fees of 1.5% on $1,000,000, equaling
  total annual costs of: $ 15,000
  + Mutual fund fees of 0.61% on $1,000,000,
  equaling total annual costs of: $ 6,100
  + Est. mutual fund trading fees of 0.81% on
  $1,000,000, equaling total annual costs of: $ 8,100
  = **Total mutual fund portfolio annual fees of 2.92%,**
  equaling total annual costs of: **$ 29,200**

They were paying 3.08% in fees on their $1,600,000
portfolio, equaling total annual costs of ....**$ 49,218**

Over the next 20 years to age 85, they were projected to
pay total fees of ………………..**$984,360**

New Portfolio Fee Reduction:

Bob and Carol's new plan allocated their $1,600,000 portfolio into the
following asset categories:

New Portfolio Allocation	
Stocks - Self Managed	$200,000
Bucket #1 - Guar. Income	$800,000
Bucket #2 - Liquid/Safe	$100,000
Bucket #3 - Growth Stop Loss	$500,000

- Their self-managed stocks had a 0.00% annual fee,
  so total annual cost was: $ 0

- Their Bucket #1 fixed index annuity annuities of
  $800,000 had 1.00% in total fees of: $ 8,000

- Their Bucket #2 bank funds of $100,000 had a 0.00% fee so total annual cost was: $ 0

- Their Bucket #3 growth with stop loss of $500,000 had 1.83% in total fees of: $ 9,150

Their total annual fees on their new $1,600,000 portfolio equaled…………………………..................... $ 17,150

Their total annual fee percentage on their new $1,600,000 portfolio equaled………………………........... 1.07%

Total annual fee savings were calculated as follows:
- **Current plan total annual fees** $ 49,218

- **Less new plan total annual fees**   -$ 17,150

- **Equals annual fee savings** $ 32,068

- **New plan projected fee savings over 20 years to age 85 …………………………………………........** **$640,360**

CHAPTER 29

COMPREHENSIVE WRITTEN RETIREMENT INCOME PLAN
SECTION #2
INCOME TAX ANALYSIS

BY DAN AHMAD & JIM FILES

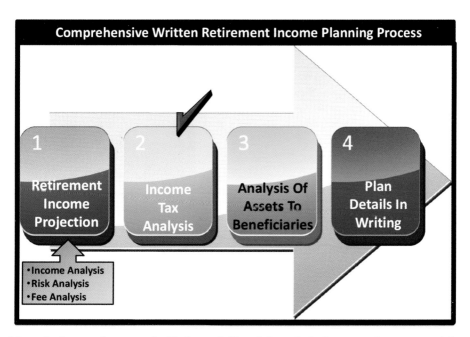

Now let's get down to it. Bob and Carol loved their new plan up to this point:

1. They increased their gross annual income from $78,000 up to $138,000.

2. They reduced their potential risk from a stock market crash similar to the 2008 crash from -49.4% to -9.4%.

3. They reduced their recovery gain needed from +97.5% to +10.3%.

4. They reduced their annual fee percentage from 3.08% to 1.07%.

5. They reduced their annual fees from $49,218 to $17,150.

6. They are projected to save $640,360 in fees over the next 20 years.

But, even with all these potential benefits, Bob and Carol were still freaked out about the potential income taxes they thought they would have to pay. An income tax analysis must be performed to eliminate their fears of paying too much income taxes. The first step of their income tax analysis is to determine how much of their total gross income is going to be reportable on their income tax return as a "taxable income source." In the chart below, 85% of their $54,000 social security benefits are taxable, the full $24,000 pension is taxable, and their worst fears looked like they came true as all $60,000 of their IRA distribution, highlighted in red, is considered taxable income. Their new plan brought in $138,000 of gross annual income with $129,900, highlighted in black, being potentially subjected to income taxes.

Bob & Carol		
Annual Income Tax Analysis - Married Filing Jointly Filing Status		
Income Type	Gross	Taxable
Social Security	$ 54,000	$ 45,900
Pension	$ 24,000	$ 24,000
Interest & Dividends	$ -	$ -
Wages	$ -	$ -
IRA Income	$ 60,000	$ 60,000
Misc Income	$ -	$ -
Total Income	$ 138,000	$ 129,900

The good news is that Bob and Carol do not have to pay income taxes on the $129,900 because they will get to reduce this number by the higher of their total itemized deductions or their standard deduction. Bob and Carol don't owe anything on their home so they don't itemize their deductions anymore. In the chart on the following page, Bob and Carol will claim their $24,000 standard deduction which will leave them with a $105,900 taxable income highlighted in black. The $105,900 of taxable income will create combined federal and California state income taxes of $20,267 highlighted in red.

By dividing the $20,267 of total federal and state income taxes into their $138,000 of gross income, you arrive at their combined federal and California state effective income tax rate of 15% highlighted in green. This means they will only pay a total of 15% combined federal and state income taxes on their $138,000 of total gross income:

- 11% in federal income taxes
- 4% in California state income taxes
- 15% in combined federal and California state income taxes

Bob and Carol were overjoyed to learn this is actually how the income tax rates work and that they won't be getting killed with income taxes simply because they want to use their assets to produce income. Would you be worried about paying 15% in combined federal and California state income taxes on $138,000 of gross income? Your individual state income taxes could be lower or higher if you live outside California.

Bob & Carol		
Annual Income Tax Analysis - Married Filing Jointly Filing Status		
Income Type	Gross	Taxable
Social Security	$ 54,000	$ 45,900
Pension	$ 24,000	$ 24,000
Interest & Dividends	$ -	$ -
Wages	$ -	$ -
IRA Income	$ 60,000	$ 60,000
Misc Income	$ -	$ -
Total Income	$ 138,000	$ 129,900
Total Income		$ 129,900
Less Standard Deduction/Itemized Deductions		$ (24,000)
Less Exemptions		$ -
Equals Taxable Income		$ 105,900
Federal & State Income Taxes		$ 20,267
Federal & State Income Taxes As A Percentage Of Gross Income		15%

The last two (2) steps in the income tax analysis are to determine what is Bob and Carol's net after income tax monthly income amount, and then to determine how much extra money they have on a monthly basis they can save after paying their anticipated monthly expenses. In the chart on the following page, the section highlighted in red shows their monthly gross income of $11,500 ($138,000 annual income divided by 12 months) reduced by $1,689 which is the amount of monthly income tax withholding they need to break even with taxes at the end of the year, resulting in their net after-tax monthly income of $9,811.

The section highlighted in black shows their $7,500 monthly budget which covers their current monthly living costs as well as $21,600 per year for travel. After subtracting the $7,500 of funds needed per month from the monthly net after-tax income of $9,811, they still have $2,311 extra they can save in the bank every month. What can Bob and Carol do with the extra $2,311 per month? Remember, they have already budgeted for $21,600 in travel, but they could spend more on travel if they liked, or they could save the money for future use.

If Bob and Carol want to buy a new car that will cost $50,000 in 24 months, can they save the $2,311 every month and then pay cash for the car? Yes, they can and then they won't have to worry about a car payment!

Bob & Carol		
Annual Income Tax Analysis - Married Filing Jointly Filing Status		
Income Type	**Gross**	**Taxable**
Social Security	$ 54,000	$ 45,900
Pension	$ 24,000	$ 24,000
Interest & Dividends	$ -	$ -
Wages	$ -	$ -
IRA Income	$ 60,000	$ 60,000
Misc Income	$ -	$ -
Total Income	$ 138,000	$ 129,900
Total Income		$ 129,900
Less Standard Deduction/Itemized Deductions		$ (24,000)
Less Exemptions		$ -
Equals Taxable Income		$ 105,900
Federal & State Income Taxes		$ 20,267
Federal & State Income Taxes As A Percentage Of Gross Income		15%
Monthly Net Income Analysis		
Gross Monthly Income		$ 11,500
Less Monthly Income Taxes		$ (1,689)
Equals Monthly Net After-Tax Income		$ 9,811
Less Anticipated Monthly Expenses		$ (7,500)
Equals Net Monthly Excess For Savings		$ 2,311

Should Bob and Carol increase their income by $60,000 per year if they are going to be in a 15% effective income tax bracket, if they can increase their travel budget by $21,600 per year, and still have $2,311 extra to save every month? Of course they should, and so should you. Remember, their plan is going to provide them income this month, income next month, income every month this year, income every month next year, and income every month for the rest of their lives, so they don't have to worry about running out of money. And if they don't have to worry about running out of money, Bob and Carol will be willing to use their assets to create income to improve their quality of life in retirement.

CHAPTER 30

COMPREHENSIVE WRITTEN RETIREMENT INCOME PLAN
SECTION #3
ANALYSIS OF ASSETS TO BENEFICIARIES

BY DAN AHMAD & JIM FILES

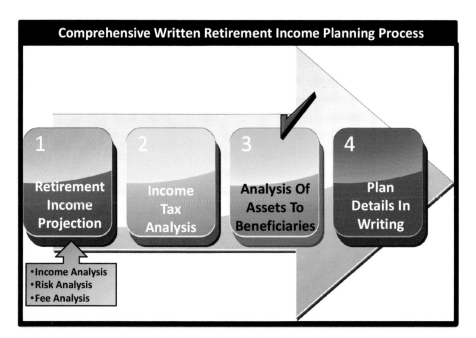

After we created Bob and Carol's income plan showing:

- How much income they would receive throughout retirement.

- That their income wouldn't run out for as long as they lived.
- They have decreased their risk by up to 90%.
- They reduced their fees by $32,000 per year and $640,000 over the next 20 years.
- They increased their annual income to $138,000 and kept their federal and state income taxes at 15%.

Like most retirees, after Bob and Carol were confident they would receive the amount of income they wanted, their income wouldn't run out for as long as they lived, and they wouldn't get killed with income taxes, they wanted to know how much money they can potentially leave to their beneficiaries. We have found that most retirees want to:

1. Use their assets to produce income for as long as they live to enhance their lifestyle.
2. Leave all remaining assets to their beneficiaries.

They have a son, Brian age 35, also an engineer like Bob, and a daughter, Susan, age 33, who is an attorney. Bob and Carol have two (2) grandsons from Susan and two (2) granddaughters from Brian.

The chart on the following page is divided into two (2) sections:

1. Left section: Year-by-year projected annual income from assets and cumulative income from assets.
2. Right section: Year-by-year projected assets that can be left to beneficiaries based on conservative annual growth assumptions, net of their income distributions from their assets.

The first section is dark green and titled **"Income From Assets."** Under this section there is a column headed with a bright green box titled **"Annual Income From Assets"** showing Bob and Carol what income they are projected to receive from their assets every year throughout their retirement. The chart shows in 2018 they are projected to receive $60,000 of income from their assets and in 2028 they are projected to receive $66,393 of income from their assets. Under the column headed with a turquoise box titled, **"Cumulative Income From Assets,"** in 2028 they are projected to have received $695,451 of cumulative income from their assets from 2018 through 2028.

In 2038, they are projected to receive $68,617 of income from their assets and their cumulative income through 2038 is projected to be $1,371,254. This means through age 85, Bob and Carol were projected to receive $1,371,254 income from their $1,600,000 portfolio. Well that's great but what's left for their beneficiaries?

			Income From Assets		Total Asset Value Analysis - Beneficiaries			
			Annual Income From	Cumulative Income From	Portfolio Values Net Of Income	Added Bank Values Net Of Income	Real Estate Values At	Projected Total Asset
Year	Bob	Carol	Assets	Assets	At 4.0%	At 1.0%	1.50%	Values
2018	65	65	$60,000	$60,000	$1,617,200	$27,732	$507,500	$2,152,432
2019	66	66	$60,000	$120,000	$1,619,488	$55,741	$515,113	$2,190,342
2020	67	67	$60,000	$180,000	$1,621,868	$84,031	$522,839	$2,228,737
2021	68	68	$60,000	$240,000	$1,624,342	$112,603	$530,682	$2,267,627
2022	69	69	$60,000	$300,000	$1,626,916	$141,461	$538,642	$2,307,019
2023	70	70	$65,436	$365,436	$1,623,939	$170,608	$546,722	$2,341,268
2024	71	71	$65,620	$431,056	$1,620,652	$200,046	$554,922	$2,375,620
2025	72	72	$65,808	$496,864	$1,617,038	$229,778	$563,246	$2,410,062
2026	73	73	$65,999	$562,863	$1,613,080	$259,808	$571,695	$2,444,583
2027	74	74	$66,194	$629,057	$1,608,761	$290,138	$580,270	$2,479,170
2028	75	75	$66,393	$695,451	$1,604,063	$320,771	$588,974	$2,513,809
2029	76	76	$66,597	$762,047	$1,598,965	$351,711	$597,809	$2,548,485
2030	77	77	$66,804	$828,851	$1,593,448	$382,960	$606,776	$2,583,184
2031	78	78	$67,015	$895,866	$1,587,490	$414,522	$615,878	$2,617,890
2032	79	79	$67,231	$963,096	$1,581,070	$446,399	$625,116	$2,652,585
2033	80	80	$67,450	$1,030,547	$1,574,164	$478,595	$634,493	$2,687,252
2034	81	81	$67,675	$1,098,222	$1,566,749	$511,113	$644,010	$2,721,872
2035	82	82	$67,903	$1,166,125	$1,558,799	$543,956	$653,670	$2,756,426
2036	83	83	$68,137	$1,234,262	$1,550,289	$577,128	$663,475	$2,790,892
2037	84	84	$68,375	$1,302,636	$1,541,191	$610,631	$673,428	$2,825,249
2038	85	85	$68,617	$1,371,254	$1,531,476	$644,469	$683,529	$2,859,475
2039	86	86	$68,865	$1,440,119	$1,521,116	$678,646	$693,782	$2,893,544
2040	87	87	$69,118	$1,509,236	$1,510,078	$713,164	$704,189	$2,927,431
2041	88	88	$69,375	$1,578,611	$1,498,331	$748,028	$714,751	$2,961,111
2042	89	89	$69,638	$1,648,249	$1,485,841	$783,240	$725,473	$2,994,554
2043	90	90	$69,906	$1,718,155	$1,472,573	$818,805	$736,355	$3,027,732
2044	91	91	$70,179	$1,788,334	$1,458,489	$854,725	$747,400	$3,060,614
2045	92	92	$70,458	$1,858,792	$1,443,552	$891,004	$758,611	$3,093,168
2046	93	93	$70,742	$1,929,535	$1,427,722	$927,646	$769,990	$3,125,359
2047	94	94	$71,033	$2,000,567	$1,410,957	$964,655	$781,540	$3,157,152

The second section is dark purple and titled **"Total Asset Value Analysis Beneficiaries."** This section provides an analysis of the asset values that can be potentially left to the beneficiaries, net of all income distributions, calculated on a year-by-year basis using what we feel are conservative asset return numbers. The analysis uses the following hypothetical assumptions:

- The column headed by the royal blue box titled **"Portfolio Values Net Of Income At 4.0%"** shows the amount of potential assets remaining in the portfolio, on a year-by-year basis, after Bob and

Carol have taken their income out every year and after the portfolio assets have averaged a 4.0% rate of return every year. In 2038, after Bob and Carol have taken out $1,371,254 of cumulative income, if their portfolio assets earn a 4.0% annual rate of return, there are still $1,531,476 of assets remaining in the portfolio. So how would you like to take out income totaling $1,371,254 from age 65 through 85, and just because you earned a 4.0% rate of return, you "accidentally" left $1,531,476 to your beneficiaries? Would that be OK? Did you have to give up anything to use your assets for income and still pass on a legacy?

- The column headed by the gold box titled **"Added Bank Values Net Of Income At 1.0%"** shows the amount of potential bank assets, on a year-by-year basis, in the portfolio after Bob and Carol have saved money each month and netted for any planned lump sum withdrawals. If the bank assets average a 1.0% annual interest rate, in 2038 Bob and Carol are projected to have $644,469 in the bank.

- The column headed by the white box with red letters titled **"Real Estate Values At 1.5%"** shows the value of all real estate, on a year-by-year basis, appreciated at an average annual rate of 1.5%. If the real estate assets average a 1.5% annual appreciation rate, in 2038 the real estate is projected to be worth $683,529.

- The column headed by the light purple box titled **"Projected Total Asset Values"** shows the total projected value of all assets on a year-by-year basis, decreased for all income distributions and increased for stated growth rates. In 2038, the total of all assets Bob and Carol own, net of the $1,371, 254 cumulative income distributions, is estimated at $2,859,475. This means in 2038 if Bob and Carol pass away, they have taken income from their assets totaling $1,371,254, and if their portfolio assets average a 4.0% return, their bank averages a 1.0% return, and their real estate averages a 1.5% return, they will potentially leave $2,859,475 to their beneficiaries.

The entire plan was created with the focus of meeting all of Bob and Carol's goals:

1. Increased their annual gross income from $78,000 to $138,000.
2. Increased their net after-tax monthly income from $5,800 to $9,811.

3. Provided enough income every month to pay for all their expenses plus save $2,311 per month.

4. Reduced their risk by up to 90%.

5. Saved them over $32,000 in fees per year.

6. Kept them in a 15% effective tax bracket on all their income for federal and state income taxes.

7. Potentially leave a large amount of assets to their beneficiaries when they pass away.

But it is even more important to understand they have all of these things without having to expose their assets to large losses by trying to earn a high rate of return. They don't have to earn 8%, 9%, 10%, 11%, or 12% to make their plan work perfectly. They will do just fine with 4.0% earnings on their portfolio assets, 1.0% earnings on their bank assets, and 1.5% appreciation on their real estate.

The key is that Bob and Carol no longer have to worry about their money, because for the first time in their life they are actually controlling their assets instead of letting their assets and their advisor control them. How would you feel if you didn't have to worry about your money any longer? How would you feel if you were in control of your financial security? How would you feel if you had a plan like Bob and Carol?

CHAPTER 31

COMPREHENSIVE WRITTEN RETIREMENT INCOME PLAN
SECTION #4
PLAN DETAILS IN WRITING

BY DAN AHMAD & JIM FILES

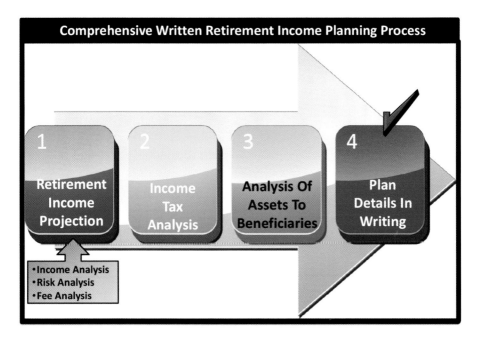

The fourth step in a comprehensive written retirement income plan is having all the details about your plan in writing. You have already received your retirement income projections, your income tax analysis, and your analysis of assets for your beneficiaries. Your plan details in writing ties everything about your plan together in a written document.

This is a complete record of the planning process and what is included in your plan, typically between 12 to 24 pages in length. The written details of your plan should include:

- Where you stood financially before your plan was implemented.
- Your retirement income sources such as pensions, Social Security benefits, wages, rents, and portfolio.
- Your worries, fears, concerns, and financial issues that need to be addressed.
- Current assets.
- Current risk level of how much you could lose in the next market crash, including recovery gain needed.
- The desired risk level of your new plan.
- Current direct and indirect (hidden) fees/costs.
- The specific goals you have for your new plan, meaning what you want to happen.
- The amount of income you and your spouse desire throughout retirement.
- Amount of assets that will be used to provide guaranteed lifetime income, either single or joint life.
- The amount of assets that will be kept liquid.
- The amount of assets that will be used for growth.
- What happens to the assets when you pass away.
- The reasons you are investing in each individual asset and how and when you plan to use each asset.
- How much income each asset will provide, how long the income will last, and how much can be taken out in a lump sum.
- A description of any principal protection and income rider for each asset.
- The advantages and disadvantages of each asset.
- The direct and indirect (hidden) costs, fees, and surrender charges for each new asset.
- One (1) to two (2) pages of advantages of your new plan.
- One (1) to two (2) pages of disadvantages of your new plan.
- Six (6) to twelve (12) pages of the detailed step-by-step process you will go through in your plan to have the highest probability of financial success during retirement.
- A place for you to sign and a place for your advisor to sign.

This document, whether 12 pages or 24 pages long, should be read out loud to you by your advisor, which can take an hour or longer. You should have the opportunity to ask questions and clarify anything that isn't 100% understandable because you have to remember, this is your money and you deserve to be treated this way. *We believe you deserve to finally understand your money.*

How would you feel if you were provided a comprehensive written retirement income plan, with the plan details read out loud to you, and making sure of your understanding? Wouldn't that feel awesome? This type of data and process is needed, even mandatory, in helping you create a stable and understandable plan on how you will receive income during your retirement that will never run out and keep you safe from all large stock market losses like what happened in 2008. *Nothing is more important to your financial security during retirement than to have a comprehensive written retirement income plan.*

If you do not have every detail about your money captured in writing:

- You do not have a plan at all.
- You have no way of knowing you won't run out of money.
- You have no way of knowing you won't suffer a big loss in the next stock market crash.
- You will not remember what you are doing and why you are doing it.
- You will not remember how to do it.
- You will have no way to measure your success or lack of success.
- You will have no way to grade your advisor.
- If you are married, your spouse will not understand why you are doing certain things or why you are not doing certain things.
- Your chances of attaining your goals are lower.
- You will not be able to stop worrying about your money.
- You are jeopardizing your entire financial security in retirement.

Having a written plan is a "roadmap" of how you are going to succeed financially in retirement. This will help you to understand your goals, objectives, and direction and will allow you to stay on course. If you had this written "roadmap," would you understand your plan for retirement income a little more? Do you think your plan would have a better chance of being successful? Do you think it would be easier to understand when it was time to make changes or when everything was looking good and shouldn't be disturbed? Do you think your spouse would understand it a little more? And do you believe if something happened to either of you, the other person would be in a protected and secure financial position? We think a comprehensive written retirement income plan will do all these things. Here is an image of the plan details section of your comprehensive written retirement income plan:

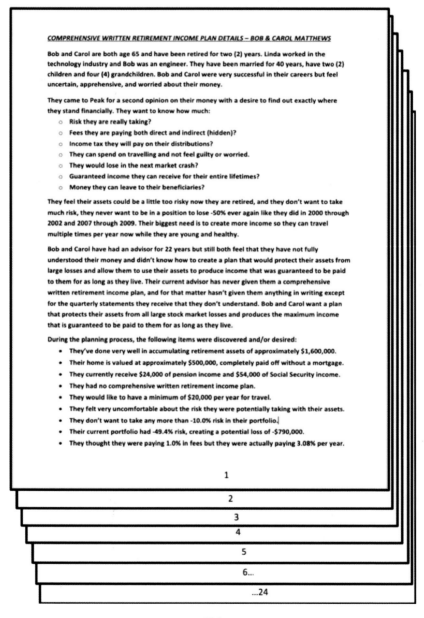

COMPREHENSIVE WRITTEN RETIREMENT INCOME PLAN DETAILS – BOB & CAROL MATTHEWS

Bob and Carol are both age 65 and have been retired for two (2) years. Linda worked in the technology industry and Bob was an engineer. They have been married for 40 years, have two (2) children and four (4) grandchildren. Bob and Carol were very successful in their careers but feel uncertain, apprehensive, and worried about their money.

They came to Peak for a second opinion on their money with a desire to find out exactly where they stand financially. They want to know how much:

- o Risk they are really taking?
- o Fees they are paying both direct and indirect (hidden)?
- o Income tax they will pay on their distributions?
- o They can spend on travelling and not feel guilty or worried.
- o They would lose in the next market crash?
- o Guaranteed income they can receive for their entire lifetimes?
- o Money they can leave to their beneficiaries?

They feel their assets could be a little too risky now they are retired, and they don't want to take much risk, they never want to be in a position to lose -50% ever again like they did in 2000 through 2002 and 2007 through 2009. Their biggest need is to create more income so they can travel multiple times per year now while they are young and healthy.

Bob and Carol have had an advisor for 22 years but still both feel that they have not fully understood their money and didn't know how to create a plan that would protect their assets from large losses and allow them to use their assets to produce income that was guaranteed to be paid to them for as long as they live. Their current advisor has never given them a comprehensive written retirement income plan, and for that matter hasn't given them anything in writing except for the quarterly statements they receive that they don't understand. Bob and Carol want a plan that protects their assets from all large stock market losses and produces the maximum income that is guaranteed to be paid to them for as long as they live.

During the planning process, the following items were discovered and/or desired:

- They've done very well in accumulating retirement assets of approximately $1,600,000.
- Their home is valued at approximately $500,000, completely paid off without a mortgage.
- They currently receive $24,000 of pension income and $54,000 of Social Security income.
- They had no comprehensive written retirement income plan.
- They would like to have a minimum of $20,000 per year for travel.
- They felt very uncomfortable about the risk they were potentially taking with their assets.
- They don't want to take any more than -10.0% risk in their portfolio.
- Their current portfolio had -49.4% risk, creating a potential loss of -$790,000.
- They thought they were paying 1.0% in fees but they were actually paying 3.08% per year.

1

2

3

4

5

6...

...24

CHAPTER 32

A SECOND OPINION
THE NEXT STEP TO ENHANCE YOUR FINANCIAL UNDERSTANDING AND SECURITY

BY DAN AHMAD & JIM FILES

By reading this book, you have taken the first step down the path of "financial enlightenment." Sit back and think about how much you have learned. Probably a great deal. Right now, we estimate you know more about retirement planning than 90% of the financial advisors in the United States! Imagine that! If this weren't true, you would have already heard all of the information in this book from other advisors, and you haven't. There is a high probability the way you view your money right now is vastly different than before you started reading this book. You have learned many facts and read our opinions on how to best plan for a secure retirement.

Many of the facts you learned are the complete opposite of what you have been told before. No matter what, right now in retirement, you are in a different position than you were at age 40, 45, or 50. You have to think differently, you have to plan differently, you have no other option than to succeed. So right now:

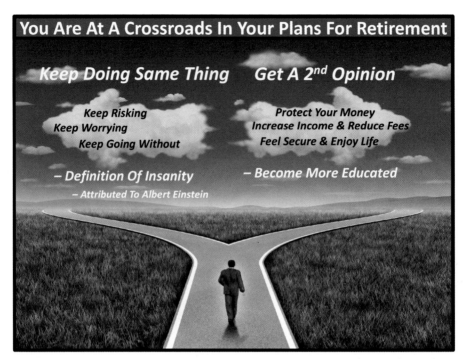

There are two (2) paths for you to choose from:

#1 – You can ***"Keep Doing The Same Thing,"*** because you really love your advisor or you really love to do the investing yourself. If you keep doing the same thing, you will keep risking your money, worrying about your money, and going without the things you saved the money for in the first place. If you take this path, we respectfully have to remind you that this is the classic definition of "insanity." You might have heard it said this way: "Insanity is continuing to do the same thing over and over again and expecting different results." Either way you heard it, please don't get mad at us, this phrase is thought to be attributable to Albert Einstein. If you do the same things with your money you've been doing for the last 20 years, you're going to get the same financial results, and you are going to continue to place your financial security, and your family's financial security, at risk.

#2 – You can ***"Get A 2nd Opinion"*** about your money from a top retirement planner. The planner you work with should educate you on how to protect your money by reducing your risk, increase your income, manage income taxes, reduce your fees, feel more secure, and allow you to enjoy your life at a higher level. And the ultimate goal is to make you far more educated about your money than you are now. The 2nd Opinion about your money will tell you exactly where you stand right now with your plans for retirement and whether everything is on track or if you need to make changes to increase your probability of success. Isn't that what you want right now? Either to know and verify you are doing everything you should be doing right now, everything is OK, and you are on track, or if you are currently not in the best position and you need to make changes to alter your course to increase your probability of success?

A *2nd Opinion* about your money is imperative simply because you already have your 1st Opinion; it's exactly what you are doing right now with your money at the advice of your current advisor or on your own. By definition, neither your current advisor, nor you, can give you a *2nd Opinion*. Right now, if you had a major medical issue, even if you had a long-time doctor of 30-years, wouldn't you seek a *2nd Opinion* about your health? Of course you would. You'd want to make sure you know exactly where your health stands right now and what options you have as the best treatment plan to get you as healthy as possible and as quickly as possible. It's the exact same thing with your money. Right now, your current assets are all you have, and you are not working and adding to your accounts any longer, so you can't afford to lose it or waste any of it.

A *2nd Opinion* about your money has no risk at all to you, and you should feel no guilt whatsoever in trying to find out about your money, because it's your money, not your advisor's money. When you meet with a new advisor, there are only two (2) possible outcomes from your *2nd Opinion* about your money:

1) They tell you that your current plan is on track and there is nothing you need to do that would increase your probability of success during retirement. How would you feel if you were told everything was great? How would you feel if your success was verified? I bet you'd feel pretty good.

-OR-

2) They will complete a comprehensive analysis and tell you things you should modify to increase your probability of having a successful retirement. Some people may only need to make minor changes

while others will need to make major changes. But whether you need a little work or a lot of work, wouldn't you rather find out right now that your plan for retirement has deficiencies or would you rather find out five (5) years from now when it could be too late?

Everyone needs a *2nd Opinion* about their money; it doesn't matter who you are, the amounts or types of assets you have, or how long you have worked with your current advisor. If you are willing to spend some time working on your finances, and you meet minimum asset requirements, many top retirement advisors across the United States will give you a free no-obligation *2nd Opinion* about your money. You can request they tell you how much risk you're taking and how you can reduce your potential for loss, the fees you're actually paying and how you can reduce your costs, how much income you can safely take out of your accounts and guarantee it for life, how much income tax you will pay by increasing your income, and how much money you can potentially leave to your beneficiaries.

In addition, simply by going through this type of process with a qualified professional who cares about your well-being, some advisors will actually be willing to give you a free financial plan at the end of the planning process that includes a retirement income projection, a tax projection, and a beneficiary projection. This type of service can be worth up to $5,000. We have seen some advisors provide this industry-leading level of service to retirees and pre-retirees whether you become their client or not. Wouldn't that be cool if it was free and there was no obligation? Have them put it in writing for you. You may ask why certain professionals would conduct their business this way – so up front, so transparent, so little pressure on the consumer? It's so they can get in front of more clients just like you who want help and information but don't want to feel any kind of pressure of any kind, at any time, during the process.

You have taken the first big step on your road to financial security by reading this book. Now it's time to take the next step, go get your *2nd Opinion* about your money as soon as possible. We promise, you'll feel a lot better about your money after you do!

SECTION 2

The Secret Ingredient For Your Retirement Recipe

Everything You Wanted To Know About
Fixed Index Annuities With Income Riders
But Were Afraid To Ask
Is Revealed
In The Chapters That Follow

CHAPTER 33

THE SECRET INGREDIENT

BY DAN AHMAD & JIM FILES

The best recipes are usually secret because the chef doesn't want to disclose the ingredients, the chef wants to keep the ingredients secret. If you don't have that secret ingredient, your dish will not come out as planned unless you get very lucky. The same thing can be said about your plans for retirement. If you don't have the proper plan, if you don't have that secret ingredient, the only way you will succeed is through hope and luck, because you will always be hoping that you will be lucky. This type of planning, or lack of planning, will create an endless amount of stress, anxiety, and worry, and will invariably lead to your lack of financial success.

During retirement, retirees want to reduce their overall portfolio risk, manage income taxes, minimize their total fees, increase their income, guarantee their income won't run out for as long as they live, have the opportunity to earn a competitive rate of return without taking excessive risks, never again suffer large losses like what happened to them in the 2008 Financial Crisis, and leave some money to their beneficiaries. *The vast majority of retirees have not been able to accomplish these goals for two (2) main reasons.*

1. We believe their lack of success is first due to not receiving the proper information to be able to make the correct financial decisions. They have never before been given all of the data included in *Momma's Secret Recipe For Retirement Success.* They never had a "roadmap." They based a large part of their retirement planning on "old-school" strategies, methodologies, or information that just doesn't work anymore (like "riding out all stock market losses"). It's like they are holding an 8-track tape and they are trying to make it play on their iPhone. It just isn't going to work.

2. The second reason for their lack of success in attaining these goals is they lack the one secret ingredient to tie their whole plan together. They may have money in the bank which we refer to as Bucket #2, and they may have money in the stock market which is Bucket #3, but they probably don't have money in Bucket #1. And Bucket #1 is the Secret Ingredient for retirement success. Bucket #1 is a fixed index annuity with an income rider.

A review of Bucket #1, a fixed index annuity with an income rider, the Secret Ingredient, provides:

- Guarantees you will never run out of income for as long as you live, even if you live past age 100, whether you are single or married.
- Guarantees your income for life even if your account value goes to $0.
- Guarantees you will never suffer a principal loss due to stock market losses, because even if the stock market loses -53.8% like it did in the 2008 Financial Crisis, you will lose 0%.
- The opportunity to earn a competitive rate of return based on a low-risk asset.
- Protection of current and future gains against stock market losses, you can't lose what you earned.
- Income tax-deferred growth of assets until distributions.
- The passing of all remaining asset to beneficiaries at your death.
- Low total fees typically averaging 1%.
- Income starting immediately or when needed.
- The opportunity for future income increases that are then guaranteed for life.

If you had a portion of your portfolio invested in an asset that really did provide all of these potential benefits, how would you feel? The remainder of this book exclusively discusses fixed indexed annuities with income riders: the most powerful secret ingredient for your own recipe for retirement success.

CHAPTER 34

FIRST THINGS FIRST
ANNUITIES 101

BY DAN AHMAD & JIM FILES

What would you guess is the number one reason why people decide not to purchase a fixed index annuity with an income rider as part of their overall retirement income plan? It's not because of surrender charges, fees, or lower returns. It's because the benefits of a fixed index annuity with an income rider simply sound too good to be true:

- How can your principal actually be protected against all stock market losses, when you have never had, or been offered, this benefit before?

- How can your income be guaranteed to be paid to you for as long as you live, even past age 100, and even if your account value reaches $0 when you have never had, or been offered, this benefit before?

- How can you earn a portion of index gains when the market goes up but never ever lose any of your current or previous gains from future losses, when you have never had, or been offered, this benefit before?

- How can you reduce the total fees you pay to an average of 1% when you have never had, or been offered, this benefit before?

- How can all these things be true when you have wanted all of these benefits for a long time, but no one has been able to provide them to you? If you don't have these benefits in your plan now, they surely can't exist, otherwise, you've made a big mistake. If you don't have these benefits in your plan, your advisor may not be looking after your best interests.

Here's the key: a fixed index annuity with an income rider is not too good to be true, you do get all these benefits. It's how they work. It's why they were designed. It's the *Secret Ingredient*. The goal of this special section of *Momma's Secret Recipe For Retirement Success* is to provide you a clear, factual, understandable explanation of fixed index annuities with income riders. Our definition of "understandable explanation" is a fair and balanced analysis which includes an accurate description of what a fixed index annuity with an income rider is, how it works, the advantages, the disadvantages, and multiple case studies showing different uses and applications for a fixed index annuity with an income rider based on different circumstances.

What really is a fixed index annuity with an income rider? An extremely summarized version of a definition for a fixed index annuity with an income rider is: *a contract with an insurance company that can be funded with cash (after-tax money) or IRA money, guarantees your principal against all stock market losses regardless of severity, protects all previous and current gains against all future stock market losses, guarantees your income for as long as you live even past age 100, provides you an opportunity for a portion of index gains, provides income tax-deferred growth of all earnings, is subject to surrender charges limiting your total liquidity, limits your overall returns providing lower returns than the stock market, taxes gains as ordinary income, and carries an annual fee (in most cases) to guarantee your income for life.*

An annuity is defined as follows by www.merriam-webster.com as: *a fixed amount of money that is paid to someone each year.* Isn't that what retirees and pre-retirees want from their money? What is the one constant desire retirees have for their money? It's to receive income for as long as they live, guaranteeing they will never be without income, thus eliminating their fear of running out of money.

An income rider is an additional benefit you can add to your fixed index annuity that carries an annual fee (in most cases). The main purpose of the income rider is to guarantee your income, and your spouse's income if married, for as long as you live, regardless of market performance, how long you live, or how much money remains in your account. Buying an income rider is simply buying insurance to guarantee your income will never run out for as long as you live.

Think about this, if you are like most retirees, your biggest fear is running out of money before you die, and even if you have had an advisor for many years, you probably didn't know you could buy insurance that guaranteed your income for life, for an extremely low overall total annual cost, typically averaging 1%. We have found the vast majority of retirees and pre-retirees can buy an income rider to guarantee their income for life, and pay lower overall fees than they are currently paying on their current assets with no income guarantees. An income rider will guarantee you will not run out of money, guaranteeing income will be paid to you for as long as you live.

The word "annuity" is very polarizing to consumers with some people seeming to love them and some people seeming to hate them. The authors respectfully believe that the majority of the negative opinions about annuities, whether it be from an advisor, consumer, or media source, are based on a minimum amount of facts and a maximum amount of conjecture. We have found that many people who aren't experts on annuities want to give you their opinions on annuities, and you may have heard the crude old saying about everyone having an opinion. To be more politically correct, we created our own saying:

Opinions are like armpits, everyone has two, and it is probably safer to stay away from both of them!
-Dan Ahmad and Jim Files

While our saying is not as famous as the comments below, we just believe they mean about the same thing:

Opinion is the medium between knowledge and ignorance.
~ Plato

Beware of false knowledge; it is more dangerous than ignorance.
~ George Bernard Shaw

Ignorance is the curse of God; knowledge is the wing wherewith we fly to heaven.
~ William Shakespeare

By giving us the opinions of the uneducated, journalism keeps us in touch with the ignorance of the community.
~ Oscar Wilde

While many people may want to give you "their opinion" on annuities, *Momma's Secret Recipe For Retirement Success* does not give you opinions, it gives you cold, hard, facts. Facts about the stock market, risk, returns, fees, taxes, asset allocation, having a written plan, and now a whole factual section on fixed index annuities with income riders.

On the website of the SEC – Securities and Exchange Commission, the SEC defines annuities as:

An annuity is a contract between you and an insurance company that is designed to meet retirement and other long-range goals, under which you make a lump-sum payment or series of payments. In return, the insurer agrees to make periodic payments to you beginning immediately or at some future date.

Annuities typically offer tax-deferred growth of earnings and may include a death benefit that will pay your beneficiary a specified minimum amount, such as your total purchase payments. While tax is deferred on earnings growth, when withdrawals are taken from the annuity, gains are taxed at ordinary income rates, and not capital gains rates. If you withdraw your money early from an annuity, you may pay substantial surrender charges to the insurance company, as well as tax penalties.

There are generally three types of annuities – fixed, indexed, and variable. In a fixed annuity, the insurance company agrees to pay you no less than a specified rate of interest during the time that your account is growing. The insurance company also agrees that the periodic payments will be a specified amount per dollar in your account. These periodic payments may last for a definite period, such as 20 years, or an indefinite period, such as your lifetime or the lifetime of you and your spouse.

In an indexed annuity, the insurance company credits you with a return that is based on changes in an index, such as the S&P 500 Composite Stock Price Index. Indexed annuity contracts also provide that the contract value will be no less than a specified minimum, regardless of index performance.

In a variable annuity, you can choose to invest your purchase payments from among a range of different investment options, typically mutual funds. The rate of return on your purchase payments, and the amount of the periodic payments you eventually receive, will vary depending on the performance of the investment options you have selected.

Variable annuities are securities regulated by the SEC. An indexed annuity may or may not be a security; however, most indexed annuities are not registered with the SEC. Fixed annuities are not securities and are not regulated by the SEC. You can learn more about variable annuities by reading our publication, Variable Annuities: What You Should Know.

We have provided this information as a service to investors. It is neither a legal interpretation nor a statement of SEC policy. If you have questions concerning the meaning or application of a particular law or rule, please consult with an attorney who specializes in securities law.

Sometimes consumers tell us they have heard that annuities are not good for them. We will then ask them:

- What kind of annuity are they referring to?
- Are they talking about an old-style single premium immediate annuity with life only payments?
- Are they talking about an old-style single premium immediate annuity with time specific payments?
- Are they talking about a fixed deferred annuity?
- Are they talking about an equity indexed annuity?
- Are they talking about a hybrid indexed annuity?
- Are they talking about a variable annuity without an income rider?
- Are they talking about a variable annuity with an income rider?
- Are they talking about a fixed index annuity without an income rider?
- Or are they talking about a fixed index annuity with an income rider?

Of course, they have no idea what type of annuity they are talking about. They typically respond they didn't know there was more than one (1) kind of annuity or that they just thought, or have been told, all annuities were bad. We will be focusing on educating you about fixed index annuities with income riders. We may mention life-only annuities, variable annuities, variable annuities with income riders, immediate annuities, fixed annuities, equity index annuities, hybrid annuities, single premium immediate annuities, or fixed indexed annuities without income riders, but we will be focused solely on educating you on exactly what a fixed index annuity with an income rider is, what it does, what it isn't, and how it works.

CHAPTER 35

IT'S TIME YOU LEARNED THE TRUTH ABOUT <u>FIXED INDEX ANNUITIES</u> <u>WITH INCOME RIDERS</u>

BY DAN AHMAD & JIM FILES

We have devoted this large section of *Momma's Secret Recipe For Retirement Success* to help you understand fixed index annuities with income riders because a fixed index annuity with an income rider is the only financial instrument that can provide you and your spouse income guaranteed for as long as you both live, protection from stock market volatility and losses, an opportunity to participate in a portion of index gains, potential for future income increases, a low fee structure, the opportunity to pass all funds remaining in your account at death to your named beneficiaries, access to your funds for income purposes either immediately or within 12 months, and a legally-binding and enforceable written contract regarding the promises made to you about your money.

TRANSLATION – a fixed index annuity with an income rider is the only financial instrument that:

- Eliminates 100% of stock market volatility from your account.
- Guarantees you won't lose principal even if the stock market goes down by -10%, -25%, or -50% or more.
- Credits you with a portion (not all) of the gains when the index your account is linked to goes up.
- Will pay you and your spouse income for as long as you both live, even to age 120+.

- Will pay you and your spouse income for life even if your account value goes to $0.
- Provides 100% tax-deferred growth while deferring income.
- Can provide guaranteed annual increases of 5% or more to your retirement income value.
- Will never decrease the amount of your monthly income.
- May actually provide the opportunity for future increases to your monthly income.
- Can potentially decrease the total fees you are paying each year by up to 75% or more.
- Will pay your beneficiaries 100% of all funds left in your account when you pass away.
- Can provide you the choice to receive income in as quick as 30 days or defer for many years.
- Provides absolute certainty to your funds and income.
- Puts all of your guarantees, promises, benefits, costs, and restrictions in writing.

Do you think these benefits could potentially enhance a retiree's probability for success? Do you think they could help you? If you like what a fixed index annuity with an income rider can do for you, focus on the benefits, not the name. The name "annuity" really should mean something that could provide you with some potentially significant benefits, but because of so much misinformation, it's almost a bad word.

If you like what an annuity can potentially do for you, but you just don't like the word "annuity," call it something else like a cupcake shop, because everyone likes cupcakes! Would you buy a cupcake shop if it guaranteed your assets against all principal losses due to stock market crashes, allowed you to participate in a portion of index gains and never lose the gains from future stock market crashes, and guaranteed your income for as long as you live even if your account value is $0? If you prefer, don't call it a fixed index annuity with an income rider, call it a cupcake shop if it makes you feel better!

There are many benefits to fixed index annuities with income riders, but like all financial instruments, there are also disadvantages including but not limited to:

- They are not liquid and shouldn't be used as a short-term asset alternative.
- You can't put all of your money in this type of plan, you need to keep some assets liquid and should use some assets for growth.
- The income rider can't be taken out in a lump sum, it can only be used to provide you income guaranteed for as long as you and your spouse live, regardless of stock market volatility and losses.
- They carry surrender charges if you try and withdraw all your money prior to a specific time period.
- Penalty-free withdrawals are usually limited to 10% per year, and in many cases can't be taken out until after 12 months.
- Some plans will allow you to receive guaranteed lifetime income to start within 30 days, and some will allow you to receive guaranteed lifetime income starting after one (1) year or more, depending on the specific plan. The key is to make sure you pick the plan that matches your income needs.
- Annual fees for the income rider typically range from 0% up to 2%, averaging about 1%.
- There are caps (maximum amounts), spreads (everything above a certain level), and participation rates (percentages of the index) that will limit your returns.
- You will not earn stock market rates of return, you will earn less.
- Your funds will not be invested directly in the stock market.
- Most plans pay a set guaranteed lifetime income amount once income starts while a few offer the potential for guaranteed lifetime increasing income options.
- While all gains are tax-deferred until you access your account, any gains distributed will be taxed as ordinary income.
- When the stock market goes down, you will not lose any money, but you will only receive a 0% return.
- Your account value can go to $0 but your guaranteed lifetime income would continue as such, and income would continue for life.
- Annuities are not exciting; you are not going to have an asset that screams to new highs with the stock market and then screams louder to new lows. They are built boring, protecting your principal and guaranteeing your income.
- You may be made fun of by friends, co-workers, family members,

and other advisors, because as the stock market has a +20% annual return every so often, you may have only received a hypothetical +10% annual return. It's true, you may be laughed at! At this time, it is important to remember why you bought the annuity in the first place, it's because when the stock market crashes -40% every seven (7) years on average since 1929, you won't lose anything, you'll receive a 0% annual return. (When this happens, no one will make fun of you, they may very well wish they had what you had.)

CHAPTER 36

HOW DOES ALL OF THIS WORK? HOW DO YOU SET UP A FIXED INDEX ANNUITY, AND WHAT DO YOU GET BACK?

BY DAN AHMAD & JIM FILES

You give a fixed index annuity company a lump sum of money by writing them a check or by transferring your IRA/457/403(b)/SEP/retirement plan on an income tax-free basis. In turn, the annuity company gives you an annuity contract which is a legally-binding written contract enforceable in a court of law.

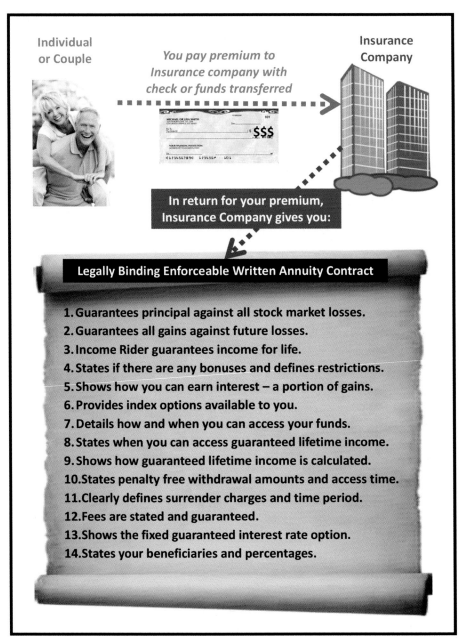

Individual or Couple

You pay premium to Insurance company with check or funds transferred

Insurance Company

$$$

In return for your premium, Insurance Company gives you:

Legally Binding Enforceable Written Annuity Contract

1. Guarantees principal against all stock market losses.
2. Guarantees all gains against future losses.
3. Income Rider guarantees income for life.
4. States if there are any bonuses and defines restrictions.
5. Shows how you can earn interest – a portion of gains.
6. Provides index options available to you.
7. Details how and when you can access your funds.
8. States when you can access guaranteed lifetime income.
9. Shows how guaranteed lifetime income is calculated.
10. States penalty free withdrawal amounts and access time.
11. Clearly defines surrender charges and time period.
12. Fees are stated and guaranteed.
13. Shows the fixed guaranteed interest rate option.
14. States your beneficiaries and percentages.

Every single thing the insurance company promises and guarantees you is in writing in your annuity contract including your principal being protected against all stock market losses, your income being guaranteed for as long as you live, all remaining assets passing on to your beneficiaries, how you access your money, the fees you pay, and how you earn interest in your account.

It's a shame that some advisors and news sources are completely uneducated about fixed index annuities with income riders, but are willing to "act and talk like an expert" by making negative comments about fixed index annuities without knowing enough about them to be rightfully able to do so. Many times, the negative comments center around how difficult fixed index annuities with income riders are to understand, or how they are so vague. There is nothing vague about a legally-binding written contract enforceable in a court of law that states everything in writing about where you have just placed your money.

- Your mutual fund doesn't give you a legally-binding written contract enforceable in a court of law.

- Your portfolio manager doesn't give you a legally-binding written contract enforceable in a court of law.

- Your advisor doesn't give you a legally-binding written contract enforceable in a court of law.

- Your brokerage account doesn't give you a legally-binding written contract enforceable in a court of law.

- But the insurance company providing your fixed index annuity with an income rider does. They give you a legally binding written contract enforceable in a court of law.

Think how you'd feel if you had all 14 things listed in the previous diagram, in a written contract given to you by the insurance company? Probably pretty good. How would you like to get all the promises made to you about your money in a legally-binding written contract? How would you like if all the promises made to you can be enforced in a court of law?

If the stock market crashes, you will not lose any money in a fixed index annuity with an income rider. If the index your contract is linked to goes up, you have the opportunity to earn a portion of the gain. Once you earn a gain, the gain and original principal are both protected against future stock market Losses. You can't take all your money out without penalty for a stated time period in your contract, but you can typically start taking out 10% of your account every year starting immediately after the first year, without any penalties.

You can set up a guaranteed lifetime income to start as quickly as within 30 days from when you fund your annuity contract. How would you like to deposit your funds today and know within 30 days you would start receiving monthly income that is guaranteed to be paid to you for as long as you live? Even if the stock market crashes the day after you start your contract, your account will not suffer any stock market losses and your income is guaranteed for as long as you live.

Fixed indexed annuity contracts with income riders will typically either give you the option to defer your income and receive a higher amount of income for every year you defer, or to take income immediately and have the opportunity to receive potential income increases in the future based on how your fixed index annuity performs each year.

CHAPTER 37

THIS MIGHT SOUND LIKE NEW STUFF, BUT ANNUITIES ARE SOME OF THE OLDEST FINANCIAL INSTRUMENTS IN HISTORY

BY DAN AHMAD & JIM FILES

We believe the main definition associated with the word "annuity" should be "income." Where did annuities come from, where did they originate? The word annuity is believed to be derived from the Latin word "annua" – translated as "annual stipends." The first annuity-like financial instrument in the world is believed to date back to 225 AD. If you can imagine back almost 2,000 years ago in Roman times, if you passed away and had assets, instead of leaving your beneficiaries lump sums of money, you might very well have left them income for as long as they lived. It seems like the Romans didn't trust their kids with a big chunk of money any more than we do! This lifetime gifting of income practice created the need for the taxing authorities to quantify the amount of money that would ultimately be paid to beneficiaries.

A really smart guy by the name of Domitius Ulpianus, a Roman judge, was credited with creating the first mortality tables in 225 AD. Old Domitius is kind of like the first actuary. Domitius figured out how long the average Roman would live and then calculated each individual's remaining life expectancy. Domitius then took this data and created what some say is the first annuity by calculating out how much income an individual would be paid per year based on age and amount of funds deposited.

The use of the *annua* continued on century after century, with individuals serving as "annua dealers" and even churches selling the lifetime payments to individuals. The first use of the *annua* concept by a government is thought to be the Dutch in the mid 16th century. The Dutch needed funds for war and other projects, and were paid lump sums of money by citizens, who in return received lifetime income from the Dutch government.

This fund-raising use by governments continued on into the 17th century, and the "tontine" was created. A government would collect money from a group of individuals, typically collecting the same amount from each individual, and would then pay each individual an annual income. As each individual owner of the tontine died, their share of the payments was distributed equally to the remaining living tontine owners. This continued on as each owner died, with survivors receiving larger and larger annual payments. The tontine was basically a combination of an annuity and the lottery.

Annuities first came to America in 1759 when Presbyterian ministers, as part of a group, were allowed to buy lifetime income from a fund established specifically for them. In 1812, over 200 years ago, the Pennsylvania Company for Insurance on Lives and Granting Annuities was formed as the first US company to offer annuities to individuals not part of a group.

In comparison, the first financial market type transactions in the world are thought to date back to the 1500's, but for the purchase and sale of bonds, debt instruments, not stocks. In 1792, twenty-four (24) brokers and merchants got together in New York and formed an alliance to trade securities. Their relationship was documented in what was called the Buttonwood Agreement. It wasn't until 1817 that the broker group from 1792 formed what was called the New York Stock & Exchange Board (NYS&EB).

In 1905, what is now known as TIAA-CREF was founded by Andrew Carnegie as the Teachers' Pension Fund.

Up until 1928, the growth of the annuity industry was very slow, but the stock market crash of 1929 and the Great Depression found many people looking for guarantees. People worried about the stock market dropping 90%, no jobs, no food, and no hope. After the big stock market crash, annuities offered through insurance companies grew in popularity because there were not many other safe and secure investment options available, same as today.

In the 1500's, some believe William Shakespeare was one of the first celebrity annuity-type buyers, reportedly investing significant funds into a transaction that would pay him income for his entire life.

In the 1700's, it is believed some of the most prominent individuals who bought annuities included:

- Benjamin Franklin
- George Washington
- Beethoven

In modern times, a few notable purchasers of annuities include:

- Winston Churchill
- Babe Ruth
- Charles Schulz
- Jane Austen
- Ben Stein
- Ben Bernanke
- Shaquille O'Neal

The most important finding, or rather non-finding, based on our extensive study, discussions, and research of the history of fixed annuities, and fixed index annuities, is that no one has ever lost one dollar of guaranteed principal, guaranteed lifetime income, or guaranteed death benefits from either investment losses in the stock market or insurance company failure, ever. Even if you had purchased a fixed annuity the day before the Great Depression, you would have been paid all the benefits guaranteed to you by the insurance company, throughout the Great Depression.

FIXED INDEX ANNUITIES WITH INCOME RIDERS WERE CREATED TO PROVIDE:

- Safety and security with principal protection against all stock market losses.
- An opportunity to earn a reasonable rate of return, without the chance of principal loss.

- Income for life for a single individual or a married couple.
- A low-fee (cost) alternative for retirement assets to provide long-term security.
- The passing of all remaining assets to beneficiaries.
- A legally-binding and enforceable written contract explaining all the details of the rights, benefits, costs, and restrictions of the plan.
- Peace of mind – the ability to stop worrying about losses or running out of money during retirement.

About Dan & Jim

Dan Ahmad and Jim Files are best-selling authors with Larry King, and have 50+ years of combined experience as lecturers, coaches, innovators, and financial professionals. Nationally recognized as two of the top Financial Advisors working exclusively with retirees, Dan and Jim create comprehensive written retirement income plans to help retirees avoid large losses and guarantee they won't run out of money for as long as they live.

Dan and Jim, Co-Founders of Peak Financial Freedom Group, have presented to over 20,000 attorneys, accountants, financial professionals, and consumers, recently received the 2019 Five Star Professional Wealth Manager Award, and are members of the National Ethics Association, received commendations from the California Attorney General's Office, California State Department of Education, Association of California School Administrators, California Teachers' Association, Faculty Association of California Community Colleges, 17 California State Universities, 66 California Community Colleges, National Network of Estate Planning Attorneys, and California Visiting Nurses Association.

Dan and Jim host the cutting edge "50 Shades of Money" radio show on the award-winning KFBK News Radio 1530 AM, and also on KSTE 650 AM and KHTK 1140 AM taking the "grey areas" out of money. They were promoted in 2015 in a powerful *Forbes Magazine* section titled "California's Financial Leaders," showcased in *USA Today*'s "Game Changers" in December 2018, seen multiple times on ABC, NBC, FOX 40 TV, and created over 150 financial education videos.

Dan and Jim have received over 50 industry awards and serve as one of four "Coaches and Mentors" for Financial Independence Group, one of the Nation's leading financial service firms with over 7000 financial professionals.

Dan has been a Certified Financial Planner™ since 1989, a former Enrolled Agent with the IRS from 1987-2016, an Accredited Tax Advisor, Fellow of the Estate and Wealth Strategies Institute at Michigan State University, Investment Advisor Representative, member of the National Society of Accountants, and is life insurance licensed. Jim has tremendous business experience including taking one of the companies he co-founded public, serving on Executive Management Teams for public companies, specializing in Mergers and Acquisitions, is an Investment Advisor Representative, and has his life insurance license.

Dan and Jim work daily with retirees to help them understand their money by creating comprehensive written retirement income plans to increase their income, create dependable income for life, reduce their risk by avoiding all large stock market losses like 2008, minimize their taxes, reduce fees, earn competitive returns, and efficiently pass assets to beneficiaries.

Dan and Jim have been business partners and best friends for 20 years, both raised locally, work in Roseville, CA and both live in Granite Bay, CA. Dan has been married to his wife Elaine for 25 years, they have two daughters Lexi and Tori. Jim has been married to his wife Tami for 35 years, they have a daughter Kyley, a son Cody, a daughter-in-law Martine, and granddaughters Colette and Elise.

Learn more at:

- www.peakuniv.com
- www.peakfin.com

CHAPTER 38

ANNUITY MYTHS – OR – LIES PEOPLE WILL TELL YOU ABOUT FIXED INDEX ANNUITIES WITH INCOME RIDERS

BY JOHN KIRKER

If your goals are to:

1. Protect your money against 100% of all stock market losses.

2. Guarantee you won't run out of income for as long as you live.

3. Receive the same or higher income for as long as you live regardless of stock market volatility or how long you live.

4. Pay a relatively low total annual fee of approximately 1%.

5. Have the opportunity to earn a competitive rate of return.

6. Defer 100% of the taxation on any growth until you take distributions.

7. Never subject current or previous gains to future stock market losses.

8. Pass 100% of all remaining funds at your death to your beneficiaries.

One of the only, if not the only, financial instruments you can use to do all of these things is a fixed index annuity with an income rider.

This description is 100% true. It can't be challenged based on conjecture or fact.

The Webster online dictionary provides the following definitions:

- *Myth: An unfounded or false notion*
- *Lie: To make an untrue statement with intent to deceive*

So, if something is unfounded or false, by definition you probably should not believe it. If someone tells you something untrue, trying to fool you, you probably shouldn't listen to them. People will tell you myths about fixed index annuities with income riders because they don't really understand how they work, or lies because they want to sell you something else. In this section we wish to debunk these myths and expose the lies. The myths most told and the lies most spread about fixed index annuities with income riders include:

(1). **Myth/Lie:** You will pay very high fees.

   Truth: This is not true with a fixed index annuity with an income rider as typical fees average right around 1.0%. A 1% fee is very low compared to the 3.0% or higher total fees we see the average consumer paying to have their portfolio managed, or to the 4.0% or even 5% fees we often see consumers paying for a variable annuity.

(2). **Myth/Lie:** There is a big commission that comes out of your money invested to pay the agent.

   Truth: There are no commissions deducted from your assets to pay the agent commissions. If you buy a fixed index annuity with an income rider for $1,000,000, you will get the full $1,000,000 deposited into your contract. The insurance company pays the agent, you don't.

(3). **Myth/Lie:** You can't access your money for a long time. It's completely and totally locked up.

   Truth: In the vast majority of plans, you can access funds after 12 months through either turning on your guaranteed lifetime income or taking up to 10% per year penalty free. Some plans even offer access to income as soon as 30 days from deposit. What you can't do is take out 100% of your money for a certain period of time without a surrender charge, just like a CD when you withdraw prematurely.

(4). **Myth/Lie:** If you take guaranteed lifetime income payments, and then pass away, the insurance company keeps your money and your beneficiaries get nothing.

Truth: In a fixed index annuity with an income rider, if you start taking guaranteed lifetime income using the income rider, and then pass away, 100% of the funds remaining in your account at death will be paid to your beneficiaries; the insurance company will not keep any of your money.

(5). **Myth/Lie:** You lose total control of your assets.

Truth: In a fixed index annuity with an income rider, you retain total control of your assets and do not relinquish them to the insurance company. You can turn income on when needed as the plan allows. You can take penalty-free withdrawals when needed as the plan allows. You can turn income on earlier or later as the plan allows. You can change beneficiaries at any time. You can take a lump sum of the net surrender value at any time. You can change your indexing options as time goes on. Finally, you can pass all remaining assets to your beneficiaries when you pass away.

(6). **Myth/Lie:** You will not get any growth.

Truth: In a fixed index annuity with an income rider, you have the opportunity for your assets to grow at a competitive rate based on a low-risk asset. You will not get full index returns, but you will have the opportunity to receive a portion of index gains without ever having to risk or expose any of your principal to a stock market loss. Your annual gain, called an index credit, will be calculated and limited by caps (maximum returns), spreads (a hurdle rate), or participation rates (percentage). The limits are necessary to provide you with 100% principal guarantees.

In 2017, when the S&P 500 Index was up 19.42%, it was fairly normal for fixed index annuities with income riders to provide 8% to 12% returns, but it is also important to understand returns are not guaranteed.

(7). Myth/Lie: The insurance company can change anything they want in your contract at any time.

Truth: In a fixed index annuity with an income rider, the insurance company can't change anything about your contract ever. Your annuity contract is a legally-binding enforceable written contract. All guarantees in your contract cannot be changed. This is one of the few assets that gives you guarantees in writing that can't be changed.

(8). Myth/Lie: Your income will always remain flat and never increase.

Truth: In a fixed index annuity with an income rider, you have the option of purchasing plans that provide you the opportunity for annual income increases. Some plans provide the option for a small fixed annual increase to your payments, similar to a pension. Some other plans allow you to receive annual income increases based on your annual earnings, and once you receive a "raise," your increased income becomes your new guaranteed lifetime income and cannot be reduced in the future.

(9). Myth/Lie: You can't access guaranteed lifetime income immediately or in a short time period.

Truth: In a fixed index annuity with an income rider, some plans will allow you to turn on your guaranteed lifetime income within 30 days of plan set up. For example, depending on your age, you may be able to buy a fixed index annuity with an income rider for $1,000,000 and start receiving $50,000 of annual guaranteed lifetime income within 30 days.

(10). Myth/Lie: You can still lose principal in a stock market crash.

Truth: In a fixed index annuity with an income rider, you will *never* lose principal due to any stock market crash. If you owned

320

a fixed index annuity with an income rider between 2000 through 2002 or 2007 through 2009, when the stock market lost -50% both times, you wouldn't have lost even one penny.

(11). **Myth/Lie:** The stock market will always beat annuity returns.

Truth: In a fixed index annuity with an income rider, in the years the stock market has positive returns, the stock market will almost always have higher returns. But when the stock market loses money, the fixed index annuity with an income rider will always have a higher return because you will never lose any money. If you look at the time period between 2000 through 2018, the S&P 500 Index increased by an annual compounded rate of 2.85% without considering fees. This rate is so low because of the huge losses the stock market suffered in 2000 through 2002, and 2007 through 2009.

(12). **Myth/Lie:** My income isn't really guaranteed for life, it will end if I live too long, if the stock market crashes, or if my account goes down to $0.

Truth: In a fixed index annuity with an income rider, your income is guaranteed for as long as you live, and, if you are married and choose a joint payout, for as long as your spouse lives. You receive a legally-binding enforceable written contract that guarantees you will continue to be paid income for as long as you live, similar to a pension, *even if you live past age 100,* even if the stock market crashes multiple times, and even if your account value goes to $0, your income will continue to be paid for as long as you live.

(13). **Myth/Lie:** You don't need an annuity: Other assets, like traditional Wall Street-type investments, "will protect my principal from stock market losses, guarantee my income for life, and provide an opportunity for a competitive return."

Truth: A fixed index annuity with an income rider, it is one of the only options that will guarantee your principal against all stock market losses, provide you guaranteed income for as long as you live, and offer the opportunity for an acceptable return.

Stocks won't do this. Mutual funds won't do this. Bonds won't do this. Real estate won't do this. Oil and natural gas won't do this. Gold won't do this. CD's won't do this.

(14). Myth/Lie: It's just simply too good to be true.

Truth: In a fixed index annuity with an income rider, you will have advantages and disadvantages. You will receive the benefits of protection against all stock market losses, income guaranteed for as long as you live, and the opportunity to make money when the market goes up without even having to put your gains at risk in the future. However, you will have to accept the negative aspects of surrender charges for a specific period of time (like a CD), not earning full stock market rates of return, and you will pay a fee, a relatively low fee, but still a fee. It's not too good to be true, it's a balanced and well thought out concept when explained and disclosed properly.

(15). Myth/Lie: Never buy an annuity in an IRA because an IRA already enjoys tax-deferral benefits.

Truth: Most retirees want to protect their IRA from stock market losses and guarantee they won't run out of income before they pass away, exactly what a fixed index annuity with an income rider is designed to do.

(16). Myth/Lie: Insurance companies aren't safe, they fail all the time and people lose money.

Truth: In a fixed index annuity with an income rider issued by a life insurance and annuity company, you have a very conservative plan that requires your funds to be backed up and secured by capital and surplus, and, even if the insurance company fails, no one has ever lost their guaranteed principal, guaranteed income, or guaranteed death benefit from a fixed type of annuity since they were first created in the 1700s.

(17). Myth/Lie: All annuities are bad and they are the worst thing you could ever buy.

> **Truth:** In a fixed index annuity with an income rider, you are protected against all stock market losses, receive income guaranteed for as long as you live, and have the opportunity for a competitive rate of return without ever having to put your gains at risk in the future. This is not bad, this is good. But a variable annuity has principal risk and typically extremely high fees, so we agree, you shouldn't buy a variable annuity. Also, a life only annuity will pay you income for life, but when you pass away, nothing is paid to your beneficiaries. So, if you have beneficiaries you want to leave money to, you should never consider a life-only annuity.

(18). Myth/Lie: Everything about a fixed index annuity with an income rider is awesome, it is perfect.

> **Truth:** There are many potential benefits to fixed index annuities with income riders, but like all financial instruments, there are also disadvantages including but not limited to:

- They are not liquid and shouldn't be used as a short-term asset alternative.
- You can't put all of your money in this type of plan, you need to keep some assets liquid and use some assets for growth.
- The income rider can't be taken out in a lump sum, it can only be used to provide you income guaranteed for as long as you live.
- There are surrender charges for early withdrawals.
- Typical penalty-free withdrawals are limited to 10% per year and, in many cases, can't be taken out until after 12 months.
- Some plans will allow you to receive guaranteed lifetime income to start within 30 days, but the majority will require you to wait for one (1) year, with some requiring deferral periods up to 10 years. Make sure to pick a plan that matches your income needs.
- Annual fees for the income rider range from 0% to 2%, with an average being approximately 1%.
- There are caps (maximum amounts), spreads (everything above a certain level), and participation rates (percentages of the index) that will limit your returns.

- You will not earn stock market rates of return, you will earn less.

- Your funds will not be invested directly in the stock market.

- Most plans pay a set guaranteed lifetime income amount once the income stream starts, while a few offer the potential for increasing income options.

- Gains are tax-deferred until distributed. Any gains distributed will be taxed as ordinary income.

- When the stock market goes down, you will not lose any money, but you will only receive a 0% return.

- With an income rider, during the guaranteed lifetime payout phase, your account value can go to $0, but your guaranteed lifetime income would continue for life.

Annuities are not exciting. You are not going to have an asset that screams to new highs with the stock market and then screams louder to new lows. They are built boring, protecting your principal and guaranteeing your income.

You may be made fun of by friends, co-workers, family members, and other Advisors, because as the stock market has a +20% annual return every so often, you may have only received a hypothetical +10% annual return. So, you may be laughed at. At this time it is important to remember why you bought the annuity in the first place: It's because when the stock market crashes -39.5% every seven (7) years on average, like it has since 1929, you won't lose anything, you'll receive a 0% annual return. When this happens, no one will make fun of you, they may very well wish they had what you had.

And when you are sleeping well at night, not worrying about ever running out of money, who is laughing now? You, all the way to the bank where you will deposit the monthly income check from your fixed index annuity with an income rider month after month after month… for as long as you live.

About John

John Kirker brings a wealth of honesty, common sense, and wisdom to his clients and the financial industry as a whole. Throughout his career, he has always been involved in the financial industry in one form or another, and has enjoyed every minute of it; it's where he feels most at home.

John began as a writer when he was just six years old. He wrote many a fine work of fiction while preparing himself for what his family thought was a career in the field of the written word. But John hit college right at the birth of the information age, and he found he had a passion for the beautiful science called technology. At this same time, the business classes he took sparked his interest in finances.

After graduating with a degree in Information Systems with a minor in Journalism, John by chance found that he had a knack for financial advising. John was introduced by a mutual friend to Dan Ahmad, who became his longtime friend and mentor, and who got John started in the financial field, training him as a financial advisor.

John and his wife Colleen have two boys, Justin 23 and Liam 21. Both boys are pursuing their own careers in the financial services industry. After college, John focused his efforts on literally trying to change the financial industry, developing what he saw years ago as a major deficiency: lack of proper financial planning software. His desire was to formulate new concepts that would inspire people to think about the benefit of planning as they were heading toward retirement.

John wrote several financial planning software packages and eventually co-founded a web-based financial technology startup that aided advisors and consumers with dealing with the uncertainties of retirement. It was a what-if scenario based on actual historical return rates for the stock, bond and treasury markets. The software was truly ahead of its time and helped financial advisors serve tens of thousands of clients.

John consulted for a large investment company creating and programming on-site commercials via the company's in-house advertising agency. These commercials entertained and educated thousands of consumers. During that time, he also was involved in the television commercial industry producing and directing several spots for local insurance agencies while also contributing 3D animation and filming customer testimonials.

John's life has finally come full-circle, and once again, he finds himself immersed in the financial services industry. John sees the next 20 years of his life as a time to give back for everything he has received in life. He provides comprehensive retirement income and planning services in his role as a fiduciary, helping retirees and pre-retirees make the best financial decisions to meet their financial goals and retire as worry-free as possible. This book is part of John's written contribution to all who want to take the risk out of their retirement, and it also lays to rest many untrue investment myths common in the industry.

CHAPTER 39

MYTH: "ALL ANNUITIES ARE THE SAME – AND THEY ARE ALL BAD."

BY LESLIE DAVIS

It may sound silly, but I feel bad for the word "Annuity" because the poor little fella gets criticized on a daily basis! It seems like 50% of the individuals I've met think they hate annuities, while 50% think they love them. To me, an annuity is not just a type of financial vehicle *per se*, but also a collection of valuable benefits.

For example, let's say you're having a B-B-Q with your closest neighbors one evening. The neighbor to the right of you owns a beautiful new Tesla, it's red and shiny, sitting on display in his driveway. You overhear the owner of this beauty telling the neighbor on your left how much he loves cars and wants four more. It just so happens that this neighbor to the left owns a Yugo from the 1980's. The Yugo's owner responds by saying "I hate cars, they are the worst, I never want another car!" The word car brings to mind four wheels that get you from point "A" to point "B", but you can't put a Tesla and Yugo in the same "car" category, just like you can't put all annuities into one "annuity" category.

When you talk about or hear about an annuity, the first thing you must discern is what type of annuity is being discussed, because you don't want to make the mistake of calling a Tesla and a Yugo the same thing, right?

At the beginning of this section, in the two (2) chapters titled *"The Secret Ingredient"* and *"Annuities 101"* you learned about the basics of a fixed index annuity with an income rider. You learned that Fixed Index Annuities with an Income Rider provide principal protection against market losses, potential for growth through interest credits based on an external index, guaranteed income for life that does not take away the owners control of the asset, the ability to pass the remainder of your account value at death to your beneficiaries, and typically, a low total annual fee structure between 1.00% and 1.25%.

The late great John Wooden is often quoted as saying, "It's what you learn after you know it all, that really counts." So now let's breakdown the other three (3) main types of annuities and give each their own credit or lack thereof:

- **Single Premium Immediate Annuity**
- **Fixed Deferred Annuity**
- **Variable Annuity**

Single Premium Immediate Annuity – The oldest, and probably most recognizable, type of annuity is called a "Single Premium Immediate Annuity" or SPIA for short. Here, you pay a lump sum to an insurance company and the insurance company guarantees to pay you income monthly, quarterly, semi-annually, or annually for a specific time period or for as long as you live, even if you live to be 200 years old! This payout can be established for a single life or joint life, single or joint life with remainder of premium guaranteed to be refunded, or a guaranteed period of payments such as five (5) years or longer. These annuities will typically pay an overall interest rate that is higher than CD rates. Most of these annuities do not have annual fee or front-end loads. The guaranteed income payments are not affected by stock market volatility or losses.

www.Investopedia.com defines an immediate annuity as:

"An immediate payment annuity is an annuity contract that is purchased with a single payment and pays a guaranteed income that starts almost immediately. Also called a "single-premium immediate annuity (SPIA)," "income annuity" or simply an "immediate annuity," an immediate payment annuity generally starts payment one month after a premium is paid and continues for as long as the annuitant (buyer) is alive or for

a specific period of time. The longer an annuitant lives the better their return will be. Such annuities are especially suitable for retirees who are concerned about outliving their savings."

Similar to social security, you cannot request an advance paycheck or a lump sum payout. There is no opportunity for growth as this type of annuity is meant for one thing and one thing only: <u>income</u>. Once the insurer has your funds, you almost always lose control of your asset moving forward, save for the guaranteed payments you receive. Depending on how long you receive income payments, you could easily "use up" all your principal over time, which reduces or eliminates the monies that could be passed on as a legacy to your heirs. In this case, your family is essentially "disinherited" because the insurer typically keeps any funds left at the time of death. This last point is where the phrase, "the insurance company keeps your money if you die" comes from.

Fixed Deferred Annuity – The second type of annuity is called a "Fixed Deferred Annuity", in which you pay a lump sum to an insurance company; some contracts will also allow for additional periodic premiums, and your annuity is guaranteed to earn a stated minimum interest rate and could receive an even higher interest rate. The insurance company then pays you a guaranteed interest rate each year and also pays you guaranteed income or your principal plus interest at some time in the future, meaning your income benefit is deferred. Your principal and income are not affected by stock market volatility or losses.

www.Investopedia.com defines a fixed deferred annuity as:

"A type of annuity contract that allows for the accumulation of capital on a tax-deferred basis. In exchange for a lump sum of capital, a life insurance company credits the annuity account with a guaranteed fixed interest rate while guaranteeing the principal investment. A fixed annuity can be annuitized to provide the annuitant with a guaranteed income payout for a specified term or for life."

There are special types of Fixed Deferred Annuities called "Multi-Year Guaranteed Annuities" or "MYGA" for short. MYGA's are very similar to a CD, but have additional benefits. MYGA's provide a fixed interest rate guaranteed for a set number of years, for example, "4% guaranteed for 5 years." Most fixed deferred annuities do not have a front-end load and do not assess annual fees, but almost all of them will assess a surrender charge for a specific time frame for premature withdrawals. Almost all fixed deferred annuities will offer access to 10% of your funds per year without penalties starting after 12 months. All growth is tax-deferred until withdrawn. All growth withdrawn is taxed as ordinary income when withdrawn, unless qualified as a Roth IRA and may be subject to an additional 10% tax penalty before age 59½.

Variable Annuity – The third type of annuity is called a Variable Annuity, also known as a "VA". A Variable Annuity is considered a "Security" in the same way stocks and mutual funds are, because the entire Variable Annuity value can decrease, meaning you can lose principal, from market volatility and fees. With a Variable Annity, you pay the insurance company a lump sum of money and the insurance company allows you to allocate your money into one or more subaccounts, which invest in underlying mutual funds, but they are managed by the insurance company. Your subaccounts will increase or decrease each year providing you a gain or loss for the year. All interest is tax-deferred until withdrawn, at which time it is taxed as ordinary income and may be subject to an additional 10% tax penalty before age 59½.

www.Investopedia.com defines a variable annuity as:

"A variable annuity is a type of annuity contract that allows for the accumulation of capital on a tax-deferred basis. As opposed to a fixed annuity that offers a guaranteed interest rate and a minimum payment at annuitization, variable annuities offer investors the opportunity to generate higher rates of returns by investing in equity and bond subaccounts. If a variable annuity is annuitized for income, the income payments can vary based on the performance of the subaccounts."

You have potentially higher upside with potentially higher risk. Unfortunately, if you are lucky enough to benefit from higher potential upside, the typical fees inside a Variable Annuity can be fairly high and can eat away at your gains. There can be a death benefit, typically at an added fee, that affords some level of protection for the beneficiaries. You can also buy a rider to provide guaranteed lifetime income in many variable annuities. Most Variable Annuities do not have a front-end load, but total annual fees can reach as high as 6.5% per year, every year.

Variable Annuities seem to be responsible for the majority of the controversy and bad press on annuities. Ken Fisher's infamous "I Hate Annuities" campaign was originally targeted and focused on the negative aspects of Variable Annuities. I can state without reservation that the only thing Ken Fisher and I have in common about annuities is we both dislike Variable Annuities. The problem is that many people, even respected financial professionals, lump ALL annuities into one category, and try to make all annuities sound bad, so that they can promote whatever asset they are selling. I've seen it time and time again.

MEET CINDY – AN EXTREMELY ENERGETIC AND AUTHENTIC SINGLE 65-YEAR-OLD RETIRED FEMALE

Long hours, late nights, unmeasurable sacrifice, and years of dedication. This is how Cindy planned for retirement. She worked hard to get here, probably just like you. Cindy's goal: peace of mind that comes with knowing where you stand, probably just like you.

Cindy grew up with her mom raising her as a single parent. Her mom always remembered and worried about the Great Depression, probably like your parents did. Cindy worked on a farm from age nine (9) on and also helped care for her younger siblings. Needless to say, Cindy learned how to work hard, very hard. She also discovered how much she loved to care for people, and she found herself raising her own children as well as focusing her life's work on helping non-profit organizations.

Like many of us, Cindy wondered if retirement would ever come, and if it did, would it just be OK or would it be fantastic? The idea of slowing down and resting on a little bit of land outside the city limits with a few horses sounded really nice. She could almost see herself sitting on her porch swing, sipping a tall glass of iced tea, with a good book and no place she needed to be.

But now this powerful woman found herself distraught. Cindy had been saving like crazy for over 20 years, working hard for her horse farm and afternoon iced tea. She took the advice of the same advisor she really liked for 20 years, who invested her assets for growth into what he called a "diversified portfolio of high-quality mutual funds" and assured her every year she could live out her dream retirement. Cindy recalls the current advisor never really talked about risk reduction or guaranteed lifetime income, and he always "poo-pooed" annuities. Now at age 65, ready to retire, her advisor told Cindy the plan he created for her didn't work as planned, so she would need to cut her spending by over 20% or she would need to work for five (5) more years until age 70. Literally, in a split second, all her dreams went up in smoke. This information hit Cindy like a ton of bricks. No more horse farm or afternoons spent reading books and sipping tea, just five (5) more years of working and saving and hoping it turned out better next time.

I have seen situations like this over and over, but in a lot of situations, this isn't the end. People like Cindy still have options to get their retirement plans back on track. For example, here is one way Cindy could approach it:

- It looks like Cindy was probably taking too much risk with too much of her retirement savings. If we go through another 2008-type stock market decline, she could lose a significant portion of her portfolio, perhaps as much as 40%. At her age, I would probably suggest that she reduce her exposure to market risk and allocate a portion of her portfolio to more conservative or guaranteed investments and strategies.
- We would also look at how much she was paying in fees. For example, if she was earning 4% each year in her investments, but paying 2-3% in fees, she's barely keeping up with inflation. We would evaluate other investment choices to help reduce her fees and keep more of what she earned in her own pocket.
- We would then look at how much income her portfolio is able to produce. If her fees are higher, that can dramatically reduce the amount she is able to withdraw for income.

Many studies have been done on "safe withdrawal rates" from a diversified portfolio. Michael Finke, Ph.D., CFP®, a professor and coordinator in the Department of Personal Financial Planning at Texas Tech University concluded that because of the current financial environment and low interest rates, the failure potential of the 4% rule was much higher than ever imagined. Finke recommends a safer 2.6% drawdown instead.

In Cindy's case, if her advisor worked for a large brokerage firm, the advisor was probably limited in what products he could offer Cindy, so he sold her what he was paid to sell her – oftentimes, it's that simple.

The problem is the traditional mix of mutual funds, and/or stocks and bonds didn't work for Cindy. There are powerful options for guaranteed lifetime income that fall outside the traditional mutual fund and/or stock and bond options that most advisors focus on.

Instead of using solely a volatile portfolio of mutual funds to try and draw the majority of her income from, Cindy could instead use a fixed index annuity with an income rider to provide her monthly income that was guaranteed to be paid to her for as long as she lives, and it would not be reduced by stock market volatility or losses. The simple change could allow Cindy the assurance that she had the income she needs for the rest of her life. Her dreams of her horse ranch, porch, iced teas and books, could come true after all.

Let us continue to educate ourselves. Although there are many opinions on what we should invest in, continued advancement changes those options so quickly that we must keep our eyes and ears open.

As Robert E. Lee said, "The education of a man is never completed until he dies."

About Leslie

Born and raised in the Midwest, Leslie Davis was blessed to complete both high school and college early, receiving her degree from Missouri State University in Springfield, MO. As a young professional, Leslie started her journey in the financial planning world by joining an independent brokerage firm in downtown Kansas City. Her entry into the financial field was not what she had expected after leaving college. She realized very quickly that there was not much actual planning and strategy taking place around her when it came to building proper retirement plans. Thinking back to watching her own parents build their retirement over the years through their blood, sweat and tears, she understood that this was no way to approach helping individuals prepare for the final one-third of their lives.

Roughly two years into her career, Leslie decided that there had to be a better way to help build truly dependable plans that involved all the important pieces of the planning process, not just the "newest, coolest funds." This led her in the direction of a new career option she had never dreamed possible, becoming an advisor for financial advisors.

As one of the youngest on staff, Leslie was asked to join a consulting firm in Leawood, Kansas that specialized in educating and helping independent advisors around the country build and expand their businesses. After a year of in-depth industry education and traveling the country, and meeting with the engineers that create the financial products, Leslie was welcomed as a senior consultant.

In that position, Leslie educated and built plans for over 500 financial professionals from coast to coast. This intense learning curve of planning and teaching difficult case design day-in and day-out to other advisors helped hyper-expose her to the trials and pitfalls of planning for retirement.

Just a few years into her consulting career, Leslie decided to take her knowledge and background to the next level by leaving consulting and starting her own planning company. This was the birth of True Peace Financial Solutions LLC located in Overland Park, Kansas. Leslie dreamed of creating an educational environment for clients to truly be able to understand their financial planning options in a comfortable atmosphere, helping pre-retirees and retirees alike build financial independence for the retirement of their dreams.

Over a decade into her career, Leslie has built a thriving family-centered practice, with a wonderful support staff. Leslie is the radio show host of multiple different radio shows in the Kansas City area, including KMBZ. She also teaches financial literacy workshops at many local Kansas City companies such as Black and Veatch, City of Olathe, South Law, and more. As an author and radio talent, Leslie loves to give back to the community through education. When Leslie is not working, she enjoys boating and taking in the beautiful Midwest sun with her family!

CHAPTER 40

MYTH: A TAX DEFERRED ANNUITY DOES NOT BELONG IN AN IRA

BY ENYI KANU

When you were young and began saving, one of your goals was to save money to create future financial security in retirement. People have an IRA or 401(k) primarily to provide them income in retirement, yet studies reveal that the top financial concerns retirees have are:

- Running out of money.
- Stock market volatility and losses.
- Healthcare costs that can increase beyond their control and wipe out their savings.
- Not having a retirement plan.

With these concerns in mind, the optimal investments for your retirement would be assets that protect your principal against stock market losses and provide lifetime income This is due to the fact that the real objective of creating a retirement strategy is not only to provide income but to provide dependable income that would be paid to you for as long as you live.

CD's, stocks, bonds, mutual funds, real estate, REITs, gold, limited partnerships, oil and gas, etc., do not necessarily pay you lifetime income, and none of them would pay you income after your account value drops to $0.

337

The proper annuity can do that. **Imagine never running out of income, no matter how long you live and no matter what happens in the Stock Market. How would that make you feel?** An annuity, such as a fixed index annuity with an income rider is a retirement vehicle that can:

(1) Protect your principal against stock market losses.
(2) Provide you the opportunity to earn a competitive rate of return.
(3) Provide you an income for as long as you live, and if married, for as long as your spouse lives.

So, what exactly is a fixed index annuity with an income rider?

A fixed index annuity with an income rider is a legally-binding contract that is issued by an insurance company. The proper annuity contract can protect your principal against stock market losses, and income will be paid to you for your lifetime based on the contractual promises made by the insurance company. These provisions are dependent on the financial strength of the insurance company.

Please note, it is essential to do your homework before trusting your life savings to any company, because one of the few times that provision can be changed is in the event that the company goes out of business. If you are working with a financial professional, they should do the due diligence to mitigate this risk.

The myth that a tax-deferred annuity does not belong in an IRA stems from the argument that annuities offer the same tax-deferral benefits as IRAs. This myth does not take into account that some annuities offer additional protective features to your retirement savings that most other financial vehicles cannot provide. Many recent studies state that the most significant financial fear retirees and pre-retirees have is that they will run out of money, because they didn't save enough. They also fear they could lose their money in the stock market. Imagine, everything you worked for vanishing due to a stock market crash, or other unforeseen economic or political turmoil. The stock market is risky and volatile, which could result in you losing as much as 50% or more of your money. The big question in retirement is, **"How much can you afford to lose?"** When you lose money, it may take several years to recover, and you may never recover if you are also taking income withdrawals from the account. **You don't want to be on a financial roller coaster with your life savings when you need it for income.** This is the financial risk that you can help mitigate with a Fixed Index Annuity.

A Fixed Index Annuity with an Income Rider is an ideal foundation and investment for a portion of your retirement funds. Examples of annuities that most people don't realize are Social Security and pensions. A major advantage for those who receive these benefits is that they don't have to worry about the stock market negatively affecting these two (2) income flows. Almost all retirees love receiving Social Security and/or pension benefits month after month for as long as they live, because they provide a lifetime stream of income.

Over the last decade several reports, including data from Towers Watson, have been completed and confirm that the happiest and healthiest retirees are those with the highest levels of monthly fixed incomes from sources such as pensions, social security, and annuities. When income is high and dependable, anxiety wains. People tend to live longer because they don't have the fear and worries associated with financial stress as a result of uncertainty. *Ultimately, having financial peace of mind is what all retirees strive for, so this is WHY annuities belong in your retirement planning.*

CASE STUDY #1

Let's look at a hypothetical example of a gentleman we will call Bob who is turning age 70, and retired three (3) years ago. Bob and his wife Tina, also age 70, had been working with an advisor, Dave, for 20 years, while Bob was accumulating assets for retirement. Bob thinks Dave did a pretty good job in helping him grow the assets, but at this point, Bob doesn't want to take the risk he has been taking with most of his assets being in the stock market. He wants to create a dependable income stream that will last for as long as he and his wife Tina survive. He wants a written plan that covers all the details about what he and Tina will be doing with their money. Bob has asked Dave for significantly lower risk, lifetime income, and an actual plan, but Dave always says to keep a high percentage of the assets in the stock market, doesn't believe in annuities, and Dave has never provided Tina and Bob with any kind of written plan.

So, Bob and Tina went searching for a second opinion about their money, to try and find a firm who would provide them with all the things they desperately wanted, but were not getting from Dave. Bob and Tina had done quite well in amassing a little over $2,000,000 of taxable and tax-deferred assets. Bob and Tina met with Louis, their new potential advisor. Louis asked many questions, Bob and Tina told Louis what they wanted from their money:

   a. Protection of some of their asset principal from stock market losses.
   b. Reasonable investment returns.
   c. A portfolio designed to provide them stable lifetime income to supplement their social security, pension and dividends.

Louis was able to provide Bob and Tina the following six (6) point summary of their current portfolio and where they stood with their current approach:

1. There was no planning to minimize taxes, including provisional income taxes.
2. There was no planning to receive lifetime income.
3. They had an extremely low and unacceptable income-stability score. This means they were depending on volatile assets with inconsistent, income streams to cover more than 50% of their basic living expenses. They had a high probability of running out of money during their lifetime.
4. They had an extremely high and unacceptable risk score, exposing them to too much downside risk for retirees who need a consistent flow of income. If the stock market suffered through another crash like what happened in 2008, it was estimated Bob and Tina could lose up to 45%, or $900,000, of their $2,000,000 portfolio.
5. Bob and Tina were measured at an acceptable risk level of 5%, meaning the maximum they were comfortable losing in a stock market crash was 5% or a maximum loss of $100,000. This simply means if the stock market crashes and goes down 50%, they don't want to go down more than 5%
6. Dave had always told them their asset advisory fees were 1.0%, but their total fees including mutual funds fees and trading costs were over 3%.

With Bob and Tina's approval, Louis created a plan to address the issues Bob and Tina faced. The plan recommendations included:
1. Increasing their liquid bank savings from $20,000 to $200,000. They are planning to buy a car and do a major kitchen remodel next year. This would also cover six (6) months of living expenses,

including providing for the identified two non-recurring major expenses, so funds are needed to be earmarked and set aside.

2. Invest $800,000 into a diversified portfolio with risk reduction strategies. They won't have the opportunity to earn the highest returns, but they will have a significant amount of principal protected against large stock market losses. Distribute $30,000 per year as income from this account.

3. Invest $1,000,000 into a fixed index annuity with an income rider and immediately turn on income of $50,000 per year expected to be paid to them for as long as at least one of them is living. The $1,000,000 has no risk of stock market losses.

4. Create a total annual gross income of $190,000, made up of $60,000 pension income, $50,000 of joint Social Security income, $50,000.00 from their annuity and $30,000.00 in dividends and income from their stock and bond portfolio. This created approximately $13,000 per month of net after-tax income.

5. Reduce the total annual fees they are paying by more than $31,000.

6. Provide them with a Comprehensive Written Retirement and Income Plan that is continuously reviewed and modified as their life evolves.

For the first time in their financial lives, Bob and Tina had clarity and peace of mind about their financial future. They stopped feeling anxious about their money as they now understood what they were doing and where their lifetime income was coming from with complete certainty because they had a plan. They were able to think about and establish the legacy they desired for their family for generations. Louis's discipline and process earned him and his firm some new satisfied clients!

CASE STUDY #2

Let's look at a second hypothetical example of Fred and Martha Kendrick, both age 72. Fred retired twelve (12) years ago from Procter and Gamble "P&G". They had a portfolio consisting primarily of P&G stock. When Mr. Kendrick retired from P&G at age 60, the value of his retirement rollover was $5,000,000. Despite understanding the risks of his concentrated position in one stock, he insisted on holding onto his P&G stock, believing the dividends and their Social Security income would always take care of their needs.

For the next twelve years, their expenses increasingly exceeded their Social Security, plus dividends from the stock, forcing them to continuously sell shares of stock to meet their expenses.

As they sold stock, their dividends declined, forcing them to sell even more shares of stock in a downward spiral. Now in their seventies, they realized that their risk of running out of money was very real, as their portfolio was now worth only $4,000,000, 20% less than the original rollover.

They needed $150,000 of annual income from their portfolio, but the dividends were now only $120,000 per year. They knew they had to do something and do something quick. One factor was that they both had longevity in their families with all four (4) parents still alive in their mid-90's!

An allocation was created to leave $2,000,000 in the P&G stock, providing dividends of approximately $60,000 per year and $2,000,000 was used to buy a fixed index annuity with an income rider. This was now expected to provide them $100,000 of joint lifetime income. Their total new plan annual income was now projected at $160,000 per year from their assets. The proper fixed index annuity with an income rider should provide them a minimum annual income of $100,000 for as long as at least one of them was living. It also provided them the opportunity for their income to increase each and every year they receive a positive return on their plan. Once their income increases, it will never decrease even if the stock market declines. The proper fixed index annuity with an income rider also provided them principal protection that the $2,000,000 will never suffer a loss from a stock market decline.

Fred and Martha felt extremely comfortable that their new plan should help them accomplish their goals of:

1. Never running out of money for as long as they live.
2. Having a high probability of leaving a large amount of money to their children.
3. Reducing the exposure they have in the stock market.
4. Having a comprehensive written retirement income plan.

[The aforementioned Case Studies are for illustration purposes only.]

About Enyi

Enyi Kanu is a speaker, thought leader, author and entrepreneur with over 30 years of experience in the financial services industry. He helps people preserve and transfer wealth, build wealth, manage taxes and receive lifetime income using traditional and Alternative Strategies. He has been featured by numerous professional organizations and the media, including *Fortune*[1], *Forbes*[2], *Bloomberg Businessweek*[3] and *Money*[4] magazines. As an author and speaker, he has delivered numerous presentations on sound income, investment, tax planning and risk management strategies. He received an Oppenheimer award for "Achieving the highest level of professional excellence in an ever-changing economic environment."

He is the Founder and Chief Investment Officer of kANU Asset Management, LLC., a Cincinnati-based Registered Investment Advisory (RIA) firm. He was Senior Vice President and Certified Portfolio Manager at Wachovia Securities. Before Wachovia, he was Vice President, Investments at Dean Witter Reynolds (now Morgan Stanley), which he joined in 1988. Enyi has extensive work experience in business, finance, planning, and management. He received an MBA in Finance from Xavier University in Cincinnati, Ohio and a Bachelor of Science degree in Business Administration from the University of Benin, Nigeria. He has FINRA Series 3, 7, 9, 10, 63 and 65 licenses, Amex Put and Call Securities Professional and licenses. Enyi is an investment professional with certifications in "Investment Policy & Asset Allocation," "Manager Search & Selection" and "Performance Measurement & Evaluation." He was also a member of Wachovia Securities "Chairman's Circle of Excellence."

Enyi's investment consulting discipline derives from Modern Portfolio Theory that he has developed into "The kANU Modern Portfolio Theory Plus", which incorporates traditional and non-traditional asset classes, proper diversification, asset allocation, asset location, and risk balancers in the client's investment policy. Enyi believes this complement is critical to optimal investment portfolio performance, risk management, and the accomplishment of the client's objectives. He has also worked with various institutions advising on financial matters. He is a member of the Cincinnati USA Regional Chamber CEO Round Table and has served on numerous boards, including The Ohio Parents for Drug Free Youth, the American Red Cross, 4C for Children and the International Association of The Greater Cincinnati Area.

Enyi founded kANU Asset Management in 2004 to deliver world-class advice and

---

1. Author: Sean Huncherick, Fortune Magazine December 2018, page 61.
2. Forbes Magazine December 31, 2018 page 82.
3. Bloomberg BusinessWeek December 10, 2018 page 49.
4. Money December, 2018, page 26.

resources to a distinct, discerning high net-worth clientele, through a Family Office Structure – a virtual family office with a holistic approach to wealth management, where the successful and wealthy can establish their financial haven. Their team approach changes the way clients think about their money.

In partnership with financial specialists all over the world, Enyi and his team work tirelessly on behalf of their clients. By aligning with like-minded boutique firms worldwide, kANU Asset Management provides their clients with access to a rigorously-assembled multi-disciplinary team of professionals and subject matter experts, with substantial credentials including JD, CPA, FA®, CFP®, ChFC®, LLM, CLU®, CIMA® LUTCF®, MBA and more.

---- 000 ---- 000 ---- 000 ----

CHAPTER 41

MYTH: "I DON'T HAVE ACCESS TO ANY OF MY MONEY IN AN ANNUITY DURING THE SURRENDER PERIOD."

~ Suzie Uninformed

BY JOSEPH (JOE) Di PAOLO

JOHN AND JOYCE

It's Monday evening at 6:00PM, Joyce and her husband John are sitting in the lobby of a reputable financial planner in their hometown of Chicago. John's a little miffed he's spending his night off at an advisor's office and wonders if he'll make it home in time for Monday Night Football. Joyce tries to be of a positive mindset and explains to John the importance of the meeting as they will both be retiring next year, and they really don't have a plan.

John doesn't believe he needs an advisor and has told Joyce that he'll "handle it" when the time comes. The thought of John "handling it" is a bit unnerving to Joyce as the last thing he handled by himself without professional help was a multi-country trip in Europe spanning three weeks where itinerary coordination apparently wasn't a priority on John's list. Most nights were spent canceling and rescheduling hotels and flights, talk about anxiety!

To Joyce, her retirement is very important, and she believes thorough planning is needed to be successful. The receptionist asks them to fill out an information sheet for the advisor, so she may get a better idea of their goals and objectives. Some of the questions made John and Joyce really think about what is important to each of them individually, and jointly as a couple. Questions regarding investment and income priorities revealed a disunion in personal preferences that would need to be addressed. John could tell at this point he was not going to make kickoff, and he was bummed because the Bears were favored!

The biggest differences with the couple's objectives were potential return, access to their money, and safety. To John, the most important element to his portfolio was access. His coworker, Terry, had just purchased a 10-year annuity as part of his retirement strategy and had mentioned it to John. Unfamiliar with the investment vehicle, John did some research online and saw an article entitled, "I hate annuities and you should too." After the read, John vowed to never buy an annuity because the article said the money is locked up during the surrender period and wasn't accessible. He thought Terry was an idiot for buying one but would never tell him that to his face. John's second priority was growth. The last few years in the market were pretty good and he wants to continue the 12% return per year he's receiving in his 401(k).

Joyce's priorities are a little different. First and foremost, to Joyce, her retirement nest egg was her security blanket and she didn't want to lose it. She also wanted to make sure it provided enough income that would last for as long as John and herself were alive.

PRIORITIES

I have found retirees typically want their assets to be protected against large losses, provide dependable income for life, have the opportunity for moderate growth, and provide access to some of their funds to meet their needs. Everyone likes the idea of having access to their money, because it gives us all "a sense of control." The ability to access your money is called liquidity. According to Investopedia, liquidity refers to how easily assets can be converted to cash.[1] Checking accounts are liquid, already in cash, but real estate is illiquid, potentially taking months to covert to cash.

1. Source: https://www.investopedia.com/terms/l/liquidity.asp

NOTHING IN LIFE IS FREE

Your money needs to be somewhere at all times. Whether it is in a banking account, brokerage account or under the mattress, a destination must be chosen. And regardless of its location there is a cost. Whenever I evaluate a portfolio, four questions always surface. They are:

- How safe is the portfolio?
- How much income can be generated and how long will it last?
- What is the potential rate of return of the portfolio?
- How liquid is the portfolio?

These are the questions everyone should ask in order to make a prudent investment. Although I'm always looking, I've yet to find one investment that provides 100% safety, a high level of dependable lifetime income, opportunity for acceptable growth, and 100% liquidity simultaneously. So "something" has got to give. That "something" always has a cost. A cost can be something you give up or something you don't receive.

For instance, if all of a portfolio is in cash in the bank, your "cost" is you are going to earn a very low return. If $100,000 is in the bank earning 1% the annual growth is $1,000, but when the same $100,000 earns 10% in a more risky asset the annual growth would be $10,000; so, the opportunity cost for carrying immediate liquidity in the bank would be $9,000, very high.

Over the last eight years, CD rates have plummeted and paid significantly less than 2% according to www.BankRate.com, but during the same 8-year period, the S&P 500 Index was up over 150%! That is a serious cost for safety. But there also is a cost for the opportunity to earn the 150% return, the cost is risk of principal loss, the S&P 500 Index crashed and plummeted -53% from October 2007 to March of 2009.

An important part of any retiree's journey is to create the optimum portfolio that strikes the perfect balance between safety, income, growth, and liquidity.

LIQUIDITY IN DISGUISE

The financial markets aren't as liquid as they appear. Most people think that stocks and bonds are always fully liquid. And although we have very efficient and liquid markets, thanks to the market makers of Wall Street, the market doesn't guarantee 100% liquidity. There was illiquidity in the days following 9-11 and the New York Stock Exchange closed down for 4 months starting 7/31/1914 at the advent of World War I.[2] Outside of such extreme examples, more common instances would be the illiquidity of an individual stock or bond under financial duress. Take General Motors bondholders illiquidity when the auto giant filed bankruptcy or Lehman Brothers' shareholders illiquidity as they collapsed September 15, 2008.

One often overlooked point investors fail to contemplate when considering the liquidity of their stock and bond portfolios, is the liquidity cost during adverse market conditions, meaning at what price will their asset be sold at when they need the funds liquidated. A huge cost of liquidity in the stock market can be caused by short-term price fluctuations of the asset being sold. If the assets price, say a stock, stays level and it is liquidated, everything is fine, you have 100% liquidity. But what if a stock was at $100 and then when you sold it the stock was at $70? If you sold 1,000 shares, your liquidity cost would be $30,000 because you lost $30 per share when liquidated. So, even though the stock and bond account is liquid, the liquidity cost could be excessive. This example could be notably higher when considering brokerage fees.

Part of the market makers/brokers role is to provide liquidity to the market. They do this by setting prices by which they are obligated to buy and sell. According to the U.S. Bureau of Statistics, during economic crises, securities dealers inflate their spreads to account for higher risk which increases costs while prices are simultaneously falling.[3]

A prudent way to evaluate liquidity in a personal portfolio is to also account for the cost of liquidity. Is it accurate to call an account fully liquid if one must pay a considerable amount of the account, in certain instances, to access it? For example, if one needed 100% of their money and it costs 10% in losses and costs, wouldn't it be only 90% liquid?

---

2. Source: https://www.advisorperspectives.com/articles/2014/07/29/the-great-war-the-nyse-and-a-legacy-of-strength
3. Source: https://www.bls.gov/opub/btn/volume-6/pdf/cost-of-crisis.pdf

ALL PARTIES HAPPY…EVENTUALLY

John and Joyce are back for their second meeting with their advisor and anticipating their plan. The advisor assured them that he would prepare a strategy that would provide adequate liquidity, safety, income, and rate of return opportunity for the myriad of curve balls that life may throw at them. They had saved roughly $1 million dollars for retirement and were concerned it wouldn't be enough.

They had both heard from their 401(k) providers that a reasonable amount to withdraw from their portfolio was 3% per year to ensure they would not run out of money during their retirement. They are expecting to live into their 90's as they are both healthy and have great genes. With the amount they both would like to travel, Joyce figures they would certainly need more than the 3% recommended withdrawal amount even though they both had social security benefits and John's pension. She is hoping the advisor shares a plan with at least 45K per year from the portfolio and a high probability of success. As they were waiting for the advisor to come into the conference room with their plan, John and Joyce clinched each other's hands in anticipation of the results of their plan.

The advisor walked into the room with a pep in his step and a warm smile. This immediately put the couple at ease. John thought, there is no way bad news is coming with the smile the advisor was giving back at him. After a few pleasantries, the advisor started to review the couple's goals and objectives as indicated in the previous meeting. Joyce, impatient but apologetically, interrupted and asked to get right to their results. "Will we have enough?" she asked.

She finally exhaled a sigh of relief when her advisor showed her a strategy to withdraw over $50,000 per year with a probability of success ratio of over 94%. Joyce was beaming but John's inner cynic started to doubt and thought it sounded too good to be true. He wanted more details. When the advisor told him approximately 50% of the strategy would be in fixed indexed annuities, John became unhinged. Remembering his coworker Terry, he said to the advisor, do you think I'm an idiot!? What makes you think I would tie my money up in annuities? The advisor understood the misinformation John received and started to explain the strategy and liquidity in greater details.

The advisor explained all of the annuities in their plan had plenty of access for their situation as they all offered a 10% per year penalty-free withdraw. John and Joyce only needed 5% for their plan to work. He pointed to the fact that even if all their retirement were in annuities, in their case, they could access 100K per year with no penalty. Joyce chimed in and said if they took 10% per year, then in ten years they would be out of money. "Why would we ever want to do that?" she chided John.

The advisor proceeded to explain to the couple he felt more comfortable advising families to mitigate liquidity cost by not having most of their money in the markets. Markets are unpredictable and if stocks, bonds, or similar instruments need to be sold in order to provide income, an unknown liquidity cost may be assessed if the investments are sold in a down market. With the type of annuities recommended, even if more than the 10% penalty-free withdraw was taken, the surrender charge is predetermined and annually decreases until the surrender schedule is complete.

In other words, the liquidity cost is set and known in all years if needed, unlike the markets, and if planned and used properly (up to 10% per year) the cost can be avoided. Continuing on, the advisor showed John and Joyce a Monte Carlo simulation, which is a simulation of a given portfolio, stress-tested against 1000's of various market conditions. With their current portfolio, the rate of probable success was only 79%. This meant that John and Joyce had a 21% chance of running out of money considering the same $50,000 annual income withdrawal. Joyce couldn't imagine going into retirement knowing they would have a 21% chance of running out of money and ending up "poor" after how hard they had saved. The advisor then explained that layering in fixed indexed annuities removes the downside risk of erratic markets and the probability of success increased to 94%. John said, "Well that's a lot more manageable." and Joyce concurred.

The advisor provided John and Joyce additional education on how the fixed index annuity would not lose money when the stock market crashes again, will allow them to participate in a portion of their index gains, would not place any of their previous or current gains at risk of stock market loss, will provide income that is guaranteed by the insurance company for as long as they live, provide any funds left in their account when they die to their beneficiaries, and on average carries a low, overall annual fee. In some cases, with proper planning, the annual fee can actually be eliminated. The advisor then reiterated all these benefits were available to John and Joyce because they were placing approximately 50% of their retirement assets into fixed indexed annuities, while keeping the other 50% liquid.

The advisor told John to think of their money as two (2) buckets of water. The first (1st) bucket (stocks, bonds, mutual funds, cash) could be used for anything they wanted and could be completed drained without any restrictions as it was "liquid". The second (2nd) bucket (fixed index annuity) was meant to provide them water (income) for as long as they lived, even if they lived past age 100. The advisor asked John, "Do you think you would ever need to take out more than $500,000 in a lump sum during your retirement years?" John replied it was highly unlikely, almost a 0% chance. John then stated "OK, I get it. We will have part of our money liquid and available and part of our money providing income guaranteed for as long as we live, so we won't be locking up all our money, only the portion we want dependable income from!" Joyce asked John how he felt about this type of plan and John replied, "Now that I understand it, I love it!"

Joyce and John agreed to the plan put forth by the advisor, and for the first time in their lives they both felt confident about their retirement and their future.

Summary of Footnote Sources:
1) https://www.investopedia.com/terms/l/liquidity.asp
2) https://www.advisorperspectives.com/articles/2014/07/29/the-great-war-the-nyse-and-a-legacy-of-strength
3) https://www.bls.gov/opub/btn/volume-6/pdf/cost-of-crisis.pdf

About Joe

Joseph (Joe) Dipaolo, CFP®,ChFC®, CLU® is the founder of Dipaolo Financial Group and has been in the financial industry since 1998. Early in his career, he was on the corporate side of finance but moved to private wealth management in 2007. He is a graduate of Franklin University with a Bachelor of Science degree in Financial Planning and is dedicated to the constant pursuit of educating himself and the public on financial matters.

Joe DiPaolo is a CERTIFIED FINANCIAL PLANNER™, a Chartered Financial Consultant, ChFC® and a Chartered Life Underwriter, CLU®, which are some of the most comprehensive planning designations in the financial planning industry.

Joe is a chapter president for the Society For Financial Awareness (S.O.F.A), which is a national non-profit 501(c)(3) organization, committed to curing the financial illiteracy problem in America through educational workshops to the public, local colleges, and to corporate employees.

Joseph is happily married to his wife and business partner Karen, and has two wonderful boys currently studying financial planning and accounting at the University of South Florida.

CHAPTER 42

MYTH: YOU CAN'T MAKE MONEY AND PROTECT YOUR PRINCIPAL FROM MARKET LOSSES

BY KEITH BARRON

When it comes to investments, most retirees and pre-retirees want two main things from their money:

1. Make money when the stock market goes up.
2. Not lose any money when the stock market goes down.

It really comes down to those two very simple sentences. The problem is most people realize they can't make money without taking the risk of losing money. They have been schooled on this fact their entire investing lives. Risk equals reward. The bigger the risk, the bigger the return. Nothing ventured nothing gained.

The good news is that everything you have been told about having to risk your principal in order to earn an acceptable return is false and misleading. You can make a gain when the stock market goes up and not lose one penny of your principal or any previous gains when the stock market goes down. Even if the stock market crashes -50% like it did twice in the last 20 years, you don't have to lose anything. I know, it sounds too good to be true. Here are the main catches:

(a) When the stock market crashes you don't lose anything, but when

353

the stock market goes up you don't get all of the gain, you only get a percentage of the gain.

(b) You can't take all of your money out in a lump sum for a specific time period without incurring a surrender charge. However, most plans offer you the ability to take out 10% a year without any penalty starting after the first 12 months.

(c) You will not earn the full stock market return; you will get a portion.

The secret ingredient in Momma's recipe for a successful retirement is the power of indexing within a fixed index annuity. The indexing concept is simple; it allows you to:

(i). Make money when the stock market goes up.
(ii). Not lose any money when the stock market goes down.

You keep your life savings safe. All the principal and gains you previously earned are guaranteed by the insurance company. It means you have the ability to participate in a portion of good markets without any of the downside risk to your savings. It's like putting your money into a safety deposit box that stays locked during the entire year when the stock market crashes and then opens for you to make new deposits every year the stock market has a gain. It is a contractually-guaranteed, legally-enforceable promise from the insurance company that you will never lose principal due to stock market losses; so the only uncertainty is how much you will make when the market goes up. I believe that kind of uncertainty is acceptable.

Think about this for a moment. If you have your money in the stock market, and you make a 50% gain, let's say you had $1,000,000 and then after the 50% gain you had $1,500,000. That would be an awesome gain. You made $500,000! You would be so happy that the $500,000 was your money! But, is it really? Nope, it's not. Because what happens to your $500,000 gain the next time the stock market declines? Yep, you got it; you lose part or all of your $500,000 previous gain. Not good at all.

So how about we turn the table on those stock market losses. The power of indexing in a fixed index annuity protects all your previous gains from all current and future stock market losses. If you make $500,000 of gain in a fixed index annuity, you will never give back ANY of the $500,000 due to a loss in the stock market. How would you like to make $500,000 and then not have to worry about losing it?

Our retirees tell us that one of their greatest fears, if not their greatest fear, is running out of money before they leave this world. Since Social Security provides only 40% of the average American retiree's income, our clients know that their savings must make up the difference, especially if they don't have a pension. They remember that their parents had a pension that was the second leg of a three-legged stool and that their savings provided the third leg for needed income not covered by the first two. Over the last few decades, pensions, or defined benefit plans, are quickly vanishing from corporate retirement systems and are being replaced by defined contribution plans, such as 401(k)s.

This change in retirement strategies has shifted much of the risk from the corporate plan to the individual to provide the necessary income to last a lifetime. This risk is difficult to determine for any one individual since the sequence of returns in stocks, bonds and other investments is highly unpredictable. Unpredictable returns in the years just before or in the early years of retirement can spell financial success or devastation when depending upon a good market for a successful outcome. When you add on an income rider to the fixed index annuity, you now have principal protection, the opportunity to earn an acceptable rate of return, and income guaranteed for as long as you live!

Why do we discuss the possibility of large losses in depth in this book? It's because bear markets—stock market losses of -20% or more—more often than not catch most investors by surprise. The stock market doesn't tell you in advance that it's going to crash, if it did, no one would ever lose any money. The typical reaction seems to be disbelief that bear markets can happen, as though bear markets are some kind of accident that might well have been prevented. The reality is that bear markets come and go. Between 1929 and 2009 there were fifteen bear markets. On average, that happened about every 5.33 years, with each one lasting about a year and a half and an average 38% decline (47% in 2001 to 2002; 57% in 2008-2009). Taking income from investments in a bear market can make it difficult to ever fully recover. Can there be a better way?

THE STORY OF JOE AND ANN

Joe and Ann are a couple we know who chose separate paths with their retirement savings in 2007. They suffered a severe setback in the Technology Bubble between 2000 through 2002, when the stock market crashed, and they lost nearly half of their retirement savings. But by 2007, with continued contributions and a good bull market, Joe and Ann were almost back to even, regaining a good bit of their "investment confidence." Joe felt he was finally getting ahead. Ann, being risk-averse, and not as confident in the stock market as Joe, decided to put her retirement savings into a fixed index annuity. She was convinced this was the wiser choice and challenged her husband Joe to put at least part of his savings there as well. Joe was amused but convinced he could do better in the market. Then between 2007 through 2009, the Financial Crisis and ensuing stock market crash hit, causing Joe's portfolio to lose more than -50%. Joe would need a 100% return just to get back even. Invested in the stock market from 2000 to the end of 2016, Joe's return was less than the market because of investment fees and expenses. (The S&P 500 compounded return in that 17-year period was 2.51%.) Ann never lost a penny in her annuity and to this day continues to be ahead of her husband's long-term investment performance despite the recent bull market for Joe.

Now the story does not end here for Ann and Joe. Both are nearing retirement, and they were afraid of what the next inevitable bear market might do to Joe's life savings. Worrying that he may never be able to retire, Joe has sought the safety of the fixed index annuity for part of his portfolio. He tells us they both now have "peace of mind" and, despite any future market volatility, he and Ann can sleep at night.

Many, many retirees have told us that they want to mitigate or eliminate several of the major risks they face in retirement–the financial risks that come with living a long life, the risk of outliving income, the risk of volatile markets and the risk of drawing income from diminished savings, especially in down markets. Our clients, like Joe and Ann, are using fixed index annuities as a way to preserve their life savings and enjoy a comfortable retirement.

ELIMINATING MARKET RISK: THE POWER OF INDEXING

A fixed index annuity is a type of fixed annuity that has additional options for earning a better than an average rate of interest than you might get in a CD, money market or other fixed account. In a fixed annuity, the owner transfers the investment risk to the insurance company and in return receives a guarantee of the principal deposited if held to term (usually between 3 and 10 years).

Fixed index annuities, also known as equity indexed annuities, were created in 1995 to provide risk-averse savers the ability to follow a market index without exposing their hard-earned savings to market risk. The typical fixed index annuity has no fee associated with it, unless a rider, such as a guaranteed lifetime income rider, is attached, and even then the average fee is typically very small, around 1%. In a fixed index annuity, the principal is guaranteed against all stock market losses, and the interest is linked to an external market index.

On the anniversary date, policyholders can pick a fixed interest rate (in most annuities), or they can choose one or more indexing strategies linked to a market index, for instance the S&P 500 or the NASDAQ. The indexing strategy will be subject to, or limited by, what is called a CAP which is a maximum rate of return that can be earned, a SPREAD which is an earnings "hurdle" that must first be met before you earn money, or a PARTICIPATION RATE that gives you a percentage of the index gain. In many annuities, a combination of these can be used. A common indexing strategy is the annual "point-to-point" between the anniversary dates. For example, if the index strategy had a gain of 10% in a given year, the insurance company may credit you 8%. The other 2% will go to pay the company's expenses and the cost for participating in the index. What happens if there is no gain in the market or if the index is down 38%? In this case, you will not earn any interest, but you will not lose any of your principal – "zero becomes your hero." It is one thing to risk losing a "golden egg." It is another matter to risk the life of the goose that keeps laying the golden eggs!

How can investing only the interest in the index achieve a better than average rate of return? The insurance company takes the interest on your savings in their general fund and buys an option to purchase shares on the market index at some point in the future. If the index is up at the end of the term, the company buys the shares, sells them for a profit, subtracts the cost for doing this and credits the remaining interest to your annuity. You are able to "mirror" the upward movement of the index without being subjected to a loss if it goes down. If the index crashes, it would be like looking into the frigid water of a calm lake in winter, you see your reflection on the water's surface, but you are not in the lake; instead you are safe, warm and dry–protected from the elements. Indexing works in a similar way. Your principal is safe as you "look" into the index. What is "invested" in the index is only the interest earned from the insurance company's holding of your insured principal.

Since your principal is not invested in the market, participation in the index has three critical features. First and most important, only the interest on your principal is at risk, that is, you might earn if the index is up or you may earn nothing if it is down. Second, when interest is credited, it is locked in as part of your insured principal and not subject to further market risk. Third, the index "resets" on the anniversary date with a new starting point for participation in the index. This becomes the new "floor" for participation. Any increase in the index will now be measured from this point forward. What is impressive is that a volatile index can actually have a positive effect on earnings over time.

YOUR PRIVATE PENSION: INCOME FOR LIFE

Fixed index annuities can also provide a guaranteed income for life. You can have your own version of a "private pension-like lifetime income stream" by adding a guaranteed lifetime income rider to the annuity at the time of purchase. The insurance company guarantees the payments for the rest of your life, but also for the life of your spouse if a joint life income is selected. Income riders provide lifetime income while preserving a death benefit to heirs of whatever money remains in the annuity at the time of death.

Several companies now offer the option for increasing this income each year by the gains credited in the index even in the years after the underlying account value has been drawn down to zero. The ability to have rising income can be an important hedge against inflation, especially since Social Security has never kept up with inflation and most pensions provide only a level income for life.

Compelling new research by economist Roger Ibbotson, professor emeritus at Yale School of Management and a ten-time recipient of the Graham and Dodd Award for Excellence in financial research, demonstrates that fixed index annuities have the potential to outperform bonds over both short and long periods of time. A stock/index annuity portfolio compares favorably with a stock/bond blend in its performance.

Index annuities, however, can both grow and protect your assets without the risk inherent in bonds that comes from rising interest rates that will cause bond values to fall. The research by Ibbotson and others (Blanchett, Pfau and Fink) shows that index annuities make a suitable alternative to bonds in a portfolio, but unlike bond income ladders, they can guarantee an income for life.

Indexing can work in all market cycles because your principal is never actually in the market. Our clients, like Joe and Ann in the story above, can have their cake and eat it too. By using these index strategies, our clients don't have to worry, dread or fear that they will lose that part of their portfolio that they want to keep protected. They have put the power of indexing to work for their retirement—an all-important "secret" ingredient in Momma's recipe for retirement success!

About Keith

Keith Barron, Ph.D., Ed.S., LUTCF, FSCP, CLTC is co-founder and CEO of Barron Financial Group, LLC in Columbia, SC. He's an author, public speaker, educator, and a retirement planning specialist. Keith and his wife, Laura, were married in 1979 and have three sons and four grandchildren.

Throughout his career, Keith has helped thousands of South Carolinians prepare for retirement. He also teaches retirement planning courses at the University of South Carolina and Midlands Technical College. As a board-certified National Certified Counselor (NCC), Keith approaches retirement planning in a comprehensive way that serves his clients and their families with a compassionate dedication to act in their best interest.

When his father passed away in 2007, Keith discovered that Wall Street brokers and real estate speculators had lost a small fortune, adding another story to the devastating consequences of poor financial planning. Motivated by this, Keith decided to make a change in his career and joined Laura as a business partner in retirement planning. Together, they founded Barron Financial Group in 2009. He's now passionate about helping clients develop strategies that'll help them protect, grow, and eventually transfer their wealth to those they love and the causes they care about.

Over the years, Keith has been very active in his church, Boy Scouts, and the greater community. He's been a Red Cross volunteer since 1999 and is the lead for Red Cross Disaster Mental Health in Central South Carolina. He's responded to eight disasters, including working with the families and victims of September 11. Keith loves reading, traveling, and the outdoors—especially hiking, backpacking, canoeing, and biking. Most at home in the wilderness, Keith roams the North Carolina mountains or paddles his canoe on the black water rivers of South Carolina. His faith in God finds its most profound fulfillment when serving others and enjoying nature.

Keith is a good-standing member with the National Association of Insurance and Financial Advisors (NAIFA), the Better Business Bureau (BBB), the National Ethics Association (NEA), and the American Counseling Association (ACA).

CHAPTER 43

SAFETY – SHOULD I HIDE MY MONEY UNDER THE MATTRESS OR TRUST AN INSURANCE COMPANY?

BY LAURA BARRON

Twenty years ago, Sarah and Mark were 55 years old as they reviewed their plans for retirement. They both had done an excellent job accumulating assets of well over a million dollars. Mark felt confident they could trust the expert advice of their broker at a large firm to continue making money for them in mostly stock market investments during retirement. Sarah and Mark were very confident the income from their stock market investments, Social Security, and a small pension would allow them to self-insure for long-term care, stay fully invested in the market, and live a very comfortable retirement in a nice neighborhood. They were totally confident they would never run out of money.

Now at age 75, Sarah needed a lot of financial help. So many things had changed over the years. Mark had just passed away after requiring two (2) years of nursing home care, and they went through two (2) major stock market crashes during the Technology Bubble from 2000 through 2002 and the Financial Crisis from 2007 through 2009. Sarah's portfolio had been cut in half, to $500,000, due to two (2) major retirement risks--the stock market crashes and long-term care needs.

Sarah vaguely remembered hearing about a financial tool that could put a safety net around her savings, reaping rewards from the upside of the market without the downside. After reviewing everything she had left, and what she needed, it was determined that Sarah could not afford to take any principal risk and needed as much dependable income as possible. She again remembered about that "safe" financial tool, and she tried to remember the name.

She remembered it protected her assets against 100% of stock market risks, paid her guaranteed income for as long as she lives, even past age 100, continued the exact same income with no decreases or interruptions even if the stock market crashes, and passes all remaining assets in the account when she dies to her son. What was it called? What was it called? Oh yeah, it was a fixed index annuity with an income rider! Sarah loved how the fixed index annuity with an income rider worked and the benefits it provided, but she wondered about the safety of insurance companies. This sad case study with a happy ending motivated me to write this chapter about the safety of insurance companies. What was missing in their original plan? Protection of their assets!

WHY SHOULD I TRUST AN INSURANCE COMPANY?

People often ask, "How safe is my money in a fixed or fixed indexed annuity?" and "How safe are the life insurance companies that provide them?" Many people remember terrible market losses when 401(k)s became "201(k)s" and the many years of hard work it took to just get back to even. If they are still working, they are worried about Social Security solvency and whether their pensions will be protected. Retirees feel they cannot withstand another market loss such as the ones in 2001 and 2008 – "I've just retired and cannot go back to work." So what is it about insurance companies and the fixed annuities they offer that make them so safe, and what would happen if an insurance company were to fail?

To start, we should discuss how secure life insurance companies have been over time, unlike more volatile investment vehicles. The life insurance industry has provided financial protection to millions of people throughout history, unlike any other financial services sector. This financial protection has continued through almost any crisis you can think of: horrific wars, depressions and recessions, deadly worldwide epidemics, stock market crashes and through the unpredictable cycles of inflation and deflation. No other institution can match the protection provided by life insurance companies.

During the Great Depression, life insurance companies provided the financial bedrock for Americans when more than 10,000 banks failed. Many people are surprised to know that the insurance companies of the United States bailed out the banking industry during this time, not the federal government.

Many wealthy people lost their fortunes during the Great Depression. Babe Ruth, the baseball legend, must have looked like a financial genius during that time as he was able to live very comfortably when people all around him were penniless and stood in bread lines after the 1929 crash. You see, early in his career, Babe Ruth talked to an insurance agent who convinced him to put a portion of his annual salary into an annuity. When Babe's health declined, and he was forced to retire in 1934, he was able to take $17,500 annually (which would equate to about $300,000 per year in today's dollars). His wife, Claire, was able to continue living a comfortable lifestyle on a guaranteed income provided by another annuity he had set up to protect her.

HOW SAFE IS MY MONEY?

Many people ask what happens if an insurance company fails? Should the insurance company that issues an annuity become insolvent, it is backed by the state guaranty association (up to a specified maximum in each state typically somewhere between $250,000 to 300,000 for each person depending on the state). Each insurance company operating in a state must join the guaranty association in order to conduct business there. In the event that a company fails, the assets of the other member insurance companies provide a safety net for the insolvent company's policyholders because, should that happen, the other companies must assume the liabilities and protect the guarantees of the failed company.

I learned firsthand how safe life insurance companies are. In 1989, a few years before I got into the insurance business, my husband and I purchased a $150,000 life insurance policy from Executive Life, one of the largest life and annuity companies in California. Little did we know at the time, but Executive Life would become insolvent in 1991. At the time, Executive Life was the largest insurance company in America to have ever failed, a great surprise to us and the whole financial world.

Although this failure continues to be one of the most written about and most cited failures of a life and annuity company, we never lost a single penny or a minute's sleep. Life insurance companies remain one of the most stable industries in America. We still have the policy today through what is now Aurora National Life Assurance.

No one has ever lost $1 of guaranteed principal, income, or death benefit in a fixed annuity or fixed index annuity with an income rider due to the stock market crashing, the economy collapsing, or insurance companies failing. Even if the annuity was purchased the day before the Great Depression, and before the stock market crashed -90%, no guaranteed annuity principal was lost, no guaranteed income payments were missed, and no guaranteed death benefits were lost.

Instead of federal regulation, the laws of each state mandate that insurance companies keep a legal reserve to protect the assets of every policyholder and also join the state's legal reserve pool. One of the strictest and most important requirements, is the "dollar-for-dollar reserve" that requires that for each $1 collected in premium, the insurance company must have on hand at all times, that same $1. The legal reserve of an insurance company must be equal to the surrender value of every life and annuity policy, including any interest that has been earned. So, that means that ALL the money set aside in premium is there at the insurance company at ALL times plus the interest it has earned. Additionally, there is surplus capital for added safety equaling about 5 cents per dollar surplus. Each state insurance department conducts periodic audits to verify that the legal reserves are sufficient to protect each policyholder.

Doesn't it give you peace of mind knowing that if this nation were to experience a total financial collapse, the insurance companies would be the last to fail? Did you know that the insurance companies of North America hold more assets than all of the banks worldwide? Many insurance companies were "stress tested" during the last financial crisis. This confirmed that life insurance companies, because of the amount of reserves that they are required to hold, would be able to pay all of their policyholders and operate for some time (several years in some cases) without running out of money. Policyholders can rest assured knowing that their hard-earned dollars are protected so well.

WHO ELSE USES INSURANCE AS A SAFE MONEY VEHICLE?

Insurance companies are so safe that banks use them to protect their underlying assets. Here's how it works: banks are required to have what are called "Tier One" assets which form the financial foundation upon which the bank is built. Tier One Capital is composed of very safe and liquid assets that includes cash, short-term notes, demand deposits, loans from the government and even gold bullion (they are not allowed to hold equities, i.e., stock, in Tier One Capital). Since the 1980s, almost 25% of Tier One Capital is held within life insurance policies bought by banks on their executives and key employees. What is astounding is that these banks have placed more money into "Bank-Owned Life Insurance" (BOLI) than what they have on reserve with the FDIC!

Banks, as well as many large corporations, often fund their top executives' retirement by using insurance companies. A great example is Ken Lewis, CEO of Bank of America, who is guaranteed to receive approximately $3.6 million each year for life in retirement starting at the age of 60. Think about this: the CEO of Bank of America/ Merrill Lynch is "banking" on an insurance company to provide him guaranteed lifetime income. Lewis is not using Bank of America deposits or Merrill Lynch investments to fund his retirement! Instead, he depends on a high cash-value life insurance policy issued by an insurance company. These plans are becoming increasingly popular for retirement and cover many CEO's, highly paid executives and university coaches, including, for example, Dabo Sweeney, Clemson's football coach, and Dawn Staley, University of South Carolina Women's basketball coach.

A recent trend with major corporations is to transfer the risk of their pension plans to annuities with insurance companies. By doing so, this reduces their liability and exposure to volatility in the markets. A few examples of pensions now protected by insurance companies are: CBS transferred $100 million of its pension liabilities into a group annuity; FedEx "shipped" $6 billion of its pension obligations to MetLife; Molson Coors transferred approximately $1 billion to Athene; Conoco Phillips transferred $130 million in pension obligations to Prudential; Raytheon transferred about $1 billion to Prudential; and the list goes on and on. LIMRA (Life Insurance and Market Research Association) reports that pension transfers to insurance companies exceeded $26 billion in 2018.

Many of my clients have no pension and even if they do, they will purchase an annuity with lifetime income so that they can create their own "private pension" and enjoy their "golden years" of retirement without worry, knowing they can receive a steady paycheck for the rest of their lives, no matter how long they live.

ANNUITIES, A STABLE, SAFE ASSET TO PROTECT YOUR RETIREMENT

Just like other forms of insurance that you may already have, like life, health and car insurance, annuities are offered by safe, large life insurance companies as a way to protect your retirement. More specifically, fixed annuities and fixed indexed annuities are financial products offered by these companies to provide a dependable strategy to preserve and grow retirement savings in a tax-deferred manner with certain guarantees, providing protection from some of the more threatening financial risks you might face in retirement. One way you could think about an annuity is as an insurance policy for your life savings and retirement income.

Overall, because insurance companies are so safe, retirees and pre-retirees who put their retirement savings into fixed and fixed indexed annuities can have peace of mind knowing that they will not lose any of their savings and they will not run out of money.

About Laura

In 2009, Laura Barron co-founded Barron Financial Group, LLC with her husband and business partner, Keith Barron. Their firm's mission is to guide clients to and through retirement, utilizing income and investment planning, legacy and estate planning, and tax-efficient strategies. They're also skilled in navigating the complexities of Medicare and help clients plan for long-term care (LTC).

Barron Financial Group's mission is to make a positive, life-giving difference in the lives of their clients and their loved ones by helping them envision their dreams and create a comprehensive plan to grow, protect, and transfer their wealth; delivered with the highest level of personal service and professional integrity.

Laura graduated from the University of North Carolina at Greensboro. Upon graduation, she was employed at an insurance company in Greensboro, NC. Years later, Laura and Keith moved to Washington, DC., where she worked for one of the largest broker-dealers in the country at that time. There, she worked closely with traders in her office and Wall Street brokers on a daily basis.

After taking a few years off to be with her young children, Laura and her husband moved to Columbia, SC in 1994, where she became the manager of senior services for a local insurance agency. During this time, she helped clients at or near retirement solve the many problems they face, including the challenges of healthcare and the risk of outliving their retirement savings.

Three years later, Laura formed her own company to help retirees navigate those same complex retirement issues, and set out to show her clients what she's always done—offer proven ways to protect their assets and provide a lifetime of economic security.

Thanks to her honesty, integrity, and commitment to client satisfaction, Laura has been recognized as a top producer for several insurance companies, but believes she better serves her clients by being an independent producer.

Laura has been a member of the National Association of Insurance and Financial Advisors (NAIFA) for many years and has served on the board of her local association in various roles. She's also a member of the National Ethics Association (NEA), and the Better Business Bureau (BBB). Laura has also earned several designations, including the Certification for Long-Term Care (CLTC), National Social Security Association (NSSA) and the Life and Annuity Certified Professional (LACP).

Laura and Keith have been married since 1979, and have three children and four grandchildren who all live in Columbia. In her free time, she enjoys exercising, exploring the outdoors, hiking, canoeing, reading, traveling, and spending time with family.

CHAPTER 44

MYTH: ALL ANNUITIES ARE BAD, AND THEY ARE THE WORST THING YOU COULD EVER BUY

BY ALLAN COLLIER

Jack had a big grin on his face as he and Jenny, his wife of 35 years, drove through downtown San Antonio on the way to their favorite restaurant. It was a beautiful evening in late spring. Jenny looked over at Jack and asked him, "What are you smiling about?" Jack replied, "For the first time in a long time, I'm not worried or feeling anxious about our finances." They'd both been retired for three (3) years, and until now, Jack worried a lot about the stock market being too volatile, not earning a good rate of return, paying too much in fees, and most of all…their money running out during their lifetimes. Jack basically worried about everything, and he found as time passed, he seemed to worry even more.

Jack told Jenny, "I'm really smiling because finally, at age 65 we both can finally relax, have more fun, and live a stress-free retirement." At this very moment, Jack was very proud of Jenny and himself. Just yesterday, Jack and Jenny had set up a new retirement income plan with a new advisor, Steve, with the goals of significantly reducing their risk, having the opportunity to earn a competitive rate of return, decreasing their fees, and creating dependable income that was guaranteed for as long as they both lived. Jack felt so good because before making this change, they never really understood their money and they always felt too risky.

Now they felt calm and at peace. They felt like they'd achieved Financial Freedom.

Steve had years of experience in the retirement income planning field and helped Jack and Jenny place $1,000,000 of their portfolio, approximately 50%, into a fixed index annuity with an income rider which would protect their principal from all stock market losses and would give them income for as long as they both lived, even past age 100! Their plan would give them $50,000 per year of annual income guaranteed for as long as they lived, regardless of stock market crashes, and would pay any remaining funds in the account to their beneficiaries after Jack and Jenny both passed away.

Previously they had worked with a broker at a big national firm for 25 years and thought of their broker, Bob, as a friend, but Jack and Jenny weren't 40 years old any longer, and didn't want to invest like they were 40 years old. They had told Bob many times in the last few years since retiring they tried to be conservative with their money, didn't really want to lose anything at all, and wanted a dependable income stream they could rely on.

Jack and Jenny had asked Bob about safe assets like annuities, but Bob always told Jack and Jenny the same thing over and over again, "that the stock market is where you need to keep your money, you're in it for the long-term, you'll get big rates of return, and you'll ride out any market dips." Jenny was amazed Bob called a big stock market loss a dip, Jenny always silently thought to herself Bob was a "dip" for saying something like that, because he was talking about their money, their future, their security.

Jack and Jenny had worked with Bob for so long, like so many retirees and pre-retirees, they made the mistake, the critical mistake of thinking that if Bob, whom they thought of as a friend, whom they've known for 25 years, was not able to give them what they asked for, then surely it just didn't exist, and no one else out there could give it to them. Like so many people, Jack and Jenny were complacent and put themselves in a terribly risky position simply because they thought Bob was their friend looking after their best interests, and there was nothing better out there.

Then Jack and Jenny got a huge wake-up call! The stock market dropped -10% in a month, and they lost -$200,000 of their $2,000,000 portfolio.

This happened a month after Jack and Jenny had met with Bob—who had again dismissed their requests for a far more conservative portfolio. Losing $250,000 of their hard-earned assets put Jack and Jenny over the edge. Jack's heart raced, feeling like what he imagined a heart attack would feel like. Jenny's fear and anxiety were even higher than Jack's because she worried about the money and also that Jack might actually have a heart attack. Jack called Bob and Bob told Jack that they "…just needed to ride it out, they were in it for the long term, and don't worry about the short-term loss."

After Jack got off the phone, he looked grey and stone-faced at Jenny. Jack told Jenny they couldn't keep doing this; he wasn't willing to live through another 2000-2002 or 2007-2009 when they lost -50% during each stock market crash. They were still working then and recovered by the time they retired, but with far less saved than they had planned because most of the gains were needed just to recoup their losses. "If we suffer another big loss again, and we're taking large income distributions which we need to live on, it is virtually guaranteed we'll run out of money."

This is why Jack and Jenny got wise and turned to Steve for help. Steve met with Jack and Jenny on five (5) separate occasions to educate them and create an actual written plan for their money.

Now, back to Jack and Jenny driving in their car with Jack smiling big. Jack's cell phone rang, it was Bob calling. Jack answered on speakerphone saying a pleasant "Hello!" Bob skipped the pleasantries yelling into the phone that he just saw that Jack and Jenny had transferred their money out of the funds he was managing and place them with a new advisor. Jack replied that he had sent Bob an email two (2) days ago informing him that they were transferring their funds. Bob said, "I haven't checked my email because I'm down in the Bahamas for vacation." Jenny went on to say that, "The email thanked you for all the work you had done for us over the years, but now we needed to go in a different direction."

Bob demanded to know where they transferred the money to. Jack calmly replied that, "Where it went wasn't important, why it went somewhere is important." Jack went on to say, "We made changes because we felt our needs weren't able to be addressed by your firm as we wanted less risk, we wanted a guaranteed stream of income, we wanted to pay less in fees, and we wanted an opportunity to earn a decent rate of return without taking excessive risks."

In a disgusted tone, Bob told Jack and Jenny that it sounded like you put your money into an annuity. Jack told Bob that, "We did put the money into an annuity." Bob told Jack and Jenny they'd talked about annuities before and that he'd told them annuities weren't right for them and were terrible vehicles in general for their funds. Jenny spoke up and said, "You're right Bob, you told us that, but you never educated us on why."

Bob replied, "It's because it's the worst thing you could have done with your money, your money is locked up and you'll never get it back. In an annuity you can still lose principal from stock market losses, your income isn't really guaranteed for as long as you both live, you will pay huge fees every year, you won't earn anything on the account, it's locked up for 10 years and you can't use it until then for income, and worse, when you die the insurance company keeps the rest of your money."

Jack told Bob, "Jenny and I met with our new advisor five (5) times, and we can say with absolute certainty everything you just said isn't true. We bought a fixed index annuity with an income rider that provides 100% safety of principal against all stock market losses, even if the stock market loses -50% we won't lose a penny. It provides us joint guaranteed lifetime income even if we live past age 100. It costs us total annual fees of 1.1% with no hidden fees, which is far lower than the 3.1% of total fees we were paying you. It provides us the opportunity for a moderate rate of return based on not taking risks with our principal. The plan allows us to take out income immediately from the plan, and we don't have to wait. And when we die, our beneficiaries get paid 100% of whatever is left in our account!"

Bob's countered with, "You won't earn full stock market returns!" Jenny told Bob, "That's the only current thing you've said, but we also aren't going to suffer any stock market losses at all either."

Jack and Jenny told Bob, "Thanks again for everything you have done for us, we wish you nothing but the best." Jack looked at Jenny and told her, "This call just reaffirms we made the right decision, especially now knowing Bob was trying to feed us all kinds of incorrect information just to keep our money with him, not looking after our best interests, but looking after his own."

Unfortunately, this type of dialogue happens every day between retirees and the advisors they have had for many years, who no longer are able to provide what they need for a safe, secure retirement. Bob, and advisors like Bob, will tell their soon to be ex-clients wrong information merely to try and keep them as a client. These advisors use incorrect facts (lies) to try and scare away retirees who could potentially benefit from owning a fixed index annuity with an income rider.

When an advisor makes a blanket statement like, "All annuities are bad, and they are the worst thing for you," it's just pointing out several possible things about the advisor making these statements:

1. The advisor either can't sell annuities, not being licensed, or his/her company does not offer them.
2. The advisor simply prefers to sell other things, either it's more comfortable, or they are making more money.
3. The advisor is ignorant about annuities; he/she hasn't been educated.
4. The advisor is not looking after the true best interests of his/her clients.

If a retired couple like Jack and Jenny state they want:

1. 100% safety of principal against all stock market losses, even if the stock market loses -50%.
2. Guaranteed lifetime income even if one or both live past age 100.
3. Low overall fully-disclosed fees.
4. An opportunity for a moderate rate of return based on not taking any principal risks.
5. Income available immediately, or if preferable, in the future.
6. To pass on all remaining assets in the account to their beneficiaries when they die.

There is only one single financial instrument that can provide all of these benefits in one (1) package: **a fixed index annuity with an income rider.** If a retiree wants these things, and their advisor says all annuities are bad, and the only thing that can provide all of these things is a fixed index annuity with an income rider, is the annuity terrible or is the advisor bad? We are going with the latter!

Some of the negatives of a fixed index annuity with an income rider are:

1. You can't take all your principal out in a lump sum for a specified time period, or you will incur a surrender charge. You can always take out your money at any time, but with the same type of withdrawal restrictions as a CD. You also should never put all of your money into an annuity, only put the portion you want to generate guaranteed lifetime income and be protected against stock market losses.

2. You will pay a fee that typically averages 1% per year. This will typically be less than the average total fees we see retirees charged in their old accounts.

3. You will not earn full Stock Market rates of return. If you want full stock market returns, you have to be willing to accept full Stock Market losses, and I'm betting you are not.

Why are there numerous myths about fixed index annuities with income riders out there on the internet or propagated by advisors? It's because some of the things they say used to be true or are true about a different type of annuity, here are two (2) examples:

1. One of the oldest forms of an annuity is called a life-only annuity. You give the insurance company a lump sum of money, giving up control of your principal forever, and they pay you income for as long as you live. When you die, the plan ends. If you die early the insurance keeps the rest of your money, and if you live a long time you beat the insurance company.

   I call this an "old school" annuity and while they still exist they are only recommended in very rare circumstances. I call buying one of these types of annuities "committing annuicide."

   A fixed index annuity with an income rider does not work this way, it provides you guaranteed income for as long as you live and then pays your beneficiaries any money left in your account when you die.

2. Another type of annuity that has caused many people heartburn is called a variable annuity, which is classified as a security, like a stock or mutual fund. Variable annuities have variable account values, meaning they can go up and down, meaning you can lose

not only principal, but after you make a gain, if the market crashes, you can then not only lose principal but also lose some or all of your previous gains. Variable annuities also have very high fees, we've seen some costing clients as much as 6.5% per year.

A fixed index annuity with an income rider doesn't work this way; it guarantees you will never lose any principal from stock market losses and it also guarantees once you earn money, you will never lose any of your past earnings from future stock market losses. And we see most fixed index annuities with fees that are 50%-80% less than a variable annuity.

If your goals are to protect your principal against all Stock Market losses, receive an income guaranteed to be paid to you for as long as you live, have an opportunity to earn a reasonable rate of return, pay a low overall annual fee, have the power to turn income on now or later, and leave all remaining funds to your beneficiaries, then I can unequivocally state that a fixed index annuity with an income rider is not the worst thing you could ever do with your money.

Just ask Jack and Jenny!

About Allan

Fred Allan Collier, best known as Allan, has been assisting retirees and pre-retirees in Huntsville, Houston, Sugar Land…and now, all over Texas since 1988. He has a passion for educating those in or nearing retirement about the strategies they must consider when it comes to their money. This has led Allan to host countless educational seminars like, "Money, a conversation about safety."

Allan's goal is helping his clients protect and preserve their assets, increase their retirement income and eliminate or reduce their fees. These goals, amongst many others, are what help Allan prepare his clients for the phase of life in which accumulation is no longer a top priority. He focuses on asset distribution which requires a very different set of rules than those that may have helped you grow your assets. Allan believes that no client should have to worry about the safety of their money during retirement. After all, retirement is about spending time with family, playing golf, going on cruises and simply enjoying the pleasures of not having to go to work every day. In short, enjoying one's money.

Allan's understanding of retirees and their needs has been enhanced through his fiscal conservative beliefs and the personal and fiscal care he was able to provide his own parents until their deaths in 2004 and 2014. He knows the importance of family and strives to treat his clients as if they are part of his, each day.

— Will Rogers said, "I am more interested in the return OF my money, than ON my money."
— And Zig Ziglar said, "You will get all you want in life, if you help other people get what they want."

"These two quotes come up often in my daily thoughts which I think further affirms what I do for my clients." ~ Allan Collier

Allan is a United States Navy veteran having proudly served on the USS Harry E. Hubbard in Vietnam from 1967-1969. He is also a graduate from Sam Houston University with a degree in Education.

Allan has four lovely daughters, four granddaughters and finally, one grandson! His children are his legacy, and his hope is that they inherit his desire to help others so as to make the world a better place, one family at a time. Allan also met the love of his life, Linda, and together they travel and enjoy playing golf on the Golf Channel Amateur Tour as much as possible.

CHAPTER 45

MYTH: THE STOCK MARKET WILL ALWAYS OUTPERFORM A FIXED INDEX ANNUITY

BY MIKE KOJONEN

The Full Truth: You will not earn stock market returns with a fixed index annuity, but you will never ever suffer any stock market losses either.

If you are smart, and retired or soon to retire, this alone should motivate you to read this chapter.

Walter and Shirley

It was a chilly March night in 2009 as Walter and Shirley parked their car in silence on a quiet street in a very nice suburb in Madison, Wisconsin. They both felt cold, lost, guilty and hurt, but mostly an overwhelming amount of fear and anxiety. The news they had just received at the hospital was devastating, changing their lives forever.

It was ironic because, until tonight, Walter was always the one handing out the bad news to people, seeing the fear in their eyes because of the bad news he delivered about their failed health. Walter was a cardiac surgeon and had been an excellent one for many years. He was very successful and had always made enough money so Shirley could focus all her efforts on raising their four (4) children, who all received graduate degrees and called their parents every week.

Walter was turning 66 in two (2) months, his planned retirement age for the last 30 years. He was a man who set and met his goals. Shirley was 65 and always trusted Walter to take care of the money, and up until tonight, her unconditional trust was warranted.

Back in June 2007, Walter met with John, his advisor he had for 20 years and learned he had achieved his goal of accumulating assets of $3,000,000 to retire at age 66. John stated the assets plus Social Security would allow Walter to retire at 66, live their desired lifestyle, and they could travel the world for years to come as they planned.

Fast forward to March 2009, three hours before they were parked in their driveway. Walter and Shirley met John at the hospital after Walter's shift. Walter knows medicine is a young man's game. His energy, focus, and motivation were not the same anymore. He'd been planning for this day, to retire at age 66, so 99% of him was already out the door. Shirley was looking forward to having him home.

Walter and Shirley expected a celebratory meeting with John ushering Walter into retirement. However, the grave look on John's face as he entered Walter's office reminded Walter of the look on his own face when he had to tell a family one of their loved ones was going to die. But in this case, John didn't say to Walter and Shirley that they were going to die, but instead, he told them their plans for retirement and Walter retiring at age 66 were dead.

In a shaky, dry, raspy voice, Walter demanded an explanation. John stated the Financial Crisis between October 2007 through March 2009, with its -53% stock market loss, caused their retirement plan failure.

John stated the portfolio value now in March 2009 was only $1,500,000 which included the $100,000 of new investments Walter made since June 2007. Walter remembered John saying over and over again during the last 1½ years to "not worry about the short-term losses" and just "ride out the volatility" and just "stay the course" and "everything will be OK." Well, it was not OK.

Walter was sweating profusely, heart racing, thinking he was having a heart attack, that he could actually die right there. Shirley took Walter's hand and he calmed down, she was always a calming influence. Moreover, now that their finances were totally screwed up, she couldn't afford to have Walter die and leave her alone now. She needed him to keep working!

Then Walter was given the most incredible gift in his life...he woke up. It was actually March 2019. He was having the same nightmare he had been having for the last year. He would be turning 66 and planned to retire in two (2) months, and the recurring dream always left him lying there shaking, in a pool of his own sweat.

Shirley woke and asked if the dream was the same. Walter said, "Yes." Shirley told Walter "You can't keep going like this...we can't keep going like this...I am worried you actually will have a heart attack before you retire. You're worried the market is going to crash and we'll suffer a huge loss like we did in 2008, you're worried we'll run out of money during retirement, and you're worried we won't earn a decent rate of return unless we continue to take high risk." Walter blurted "You nailed it, everything that I'm worried about in my nightmare, everything, and I only told you about the details in my dream once, how'd you do that?" Shirley smiled and said, "Honey, we've been married for 42 years, by now you should've realized I'm a good listener."

Shirley didn't think John, Walter's advisor, was a good listener. Shirley had heard Walter tell John many times that Walter worried about losses, their income lasting, and searching for some growth without taking excessive risks. John always responded, "The Market's doing great, you've made money, you're in it for the long-term, you need maximum growth for retirement success, and we'll make up any losses." Shirley tried to voice her opinion that she agreed with Walter. John's responses made her sick to her stomach, so she stopped attending the review meetings with Walter.

With Walter a little calmed down after his nightmare, Shirley then told Walter it was time for a change. They had been given the solution but didn't act on it. About a year ago Walter and Shirley had met with another advisor, named Jim, who specialized in retirement income planning and conservative asset allocation strategies, for a second opinion about their money. Shirley was very excited about the meeting, but she was amazed at how guilty Walter felt about "going behind John's back." Shirley told Walter their money was their money, their money was not John's, and they needed to make sure their retirement was going to be secure. Walter told Jim he wanted a plan that would give them three (3) things:

1. Reduce their risk from a big stock market loss.
2. Give them an income they could both depend on for as long as they both lived.
3. A chance for moderate growth without taking too much risk.

Jim met with Walter and Shirley five (5) times to develop a plan. Jim told Walter and Shirley his analysis showed their current financial position:

1. If we have another 2008 Financial Crisis type stock market loss, they were projected to lose 51% of their $3,000,000 portfolio, a potential loss of -$1,530,000, leaving them $1,470,000 in their portfolio to draw income off of and last their entire lives.
2. Based on current financial metrics, they shouldn't take more than 3% in distributions per year, $90,000, to have a 95% probability their money won't run out.
3. Their current portfolio would have made 18% in 2017, but to get this return, they would have to be willing to lose the -51% that was projected. The only way to get stock market returns is to take stock market losses as well.
4. They had no plan, just statements for their portfolio, that they didn't understand.

One of Jim's recommendations was to place $1,500,000 into a fixed index annuity with an income rider. This plan would guarantee they would never suffer a loss from stock market volatility, receive $90,000 of income guaranteed for as long as they lived, and the opportunity to earn a moderate rate of return. The remaining $1,500,000 would be invested in the stock market using risk mitigation strategies and the bank. The new plan was projected to reduce their risk in a significant stock market loss from -51% down to -8%, and it also decreased their fees by over $20,000 per year.

Walter and Shirley really like the plan Jim created, but Walter was stuck on the fact that when the stock market went up the fixed index annuity wouldn't get 100% of the stock market gain. Jim told them as a hypothetical example, if the stock market earned 19% in 2017, their fixed index annuity might have earned between 8%-12%, but when the stock market crashed more than -50% as it did during the 2008 Financial Crisis, their fixed index annuity wouldn't have lost anything, it would have returned a 0% return for the year.

Walter and Shirley talked about the plan Jim created, Shirley was 100% for it, she told Walter it met all their requirements. But Walter was stuck on earning maximum returns and told Jim they wouldn't be going with his plan. Shortly after making this decision, Walter's nightmares began. And now, he wanted them to end. Shirley told Walter she was calling Jim today and setting up a time to implement the plan he had recommended a year ago. To her surprise, Walter simply said, "Thank you."

If you are like most retirees and pre-retirees, you are probably like Walter and Shirley in that you want three (3) main things from your assets:

1. To protect the assets that have been accumulated from large stock market losses. You don't want to lose what you have worked so hard to accumulate.
2. "Peace of Mind" of receiving dependable lifetime income—so you don't have to worry about running out of money and being a financial burden on your children.
3. Earn a reasonable rate of return without taking excessive risks. Most retirees have told me if they can earn 4%-6% returns without having to face 2008-like losses ever again they will be happy.

In my years working with retirees and pre-retirees, I have found these to be universal truths. However, at the same time, when I meet with a new client, they typically don't have any of these three (3) components in their current plan for retirement.

Many financial professionals and organizations tell retirees and pre-retirees to stay away from fixed index annuities because they will never earn stock market returns. First of all, you don't buy a fixed index annuity to match stock market growth, you buy it for the same reason Walter and Shirley did: risk reduction, secure income, and moderate growth without excessive risk. Stock market growth can be both "positive" in the form of gains and "negative" in the form of losses.

Losses hurt you far more than gains help you. I have found people tell you incorrect and negative data about fixed index annuities for three (3) main reasons:

I. They don't understand fixed index annuities, have never been adequately trained on fixed index annuities, and literally don't know how they work.

II. They aren't allowed to sell fixed index annuities to their client(s) because of the firm they work with. This is just like a Ford dealership never recommending that you consider, purchase, or even test-drive a Lexus. Even though the Lexus is a better car, the Ford guy is going to keep saying that a Lexus isn't for you.

III. They get paid to sell you something else.

These are not your "grandma's" annuities! When looking for the right FIA, typically there are several ways that these accounts can grow. These are called the allocation/index options. Some of the most common options include annual point-to-point, monthly point-to-point, spread option, and participation rate option. As you plan your retirement income strategy, make sure to review these options with your advisor. Let's talk about one of my favorite "uncapped" strategy options: the participation rate strategy. A fixed index annuity with a participation rate of 50% means you will receive 50% of the total index gain for the year, but will never suffer a loss. For example, if the index used is the S&P 500 Index, and it increases by a hypothetical 20% in a given year, if your participation rate is 50%, you would receive a hypothetical 10% return for the year from the fixed index annuity, less than the stock market but still pretty good. If the S&P 500 Index drops -50%, you don't lose anything.

Think back to why you started to save your money in the first place? It was to create dependable income throughout retirement. What would happen if you suffer a -50% loss and you are taking income distributions? Nothing good! You would need to either reduce your income, stop your income, or face the almost certainty of running out of income before you die. You don't have to take as much risk as you have been told to have a successful retirement. For example, if you need $90,000 per year of income on a $3,000,000 portfolio, you don't have to take a lot of risk to do so, and you don't have to earn a huge rate of return to do so.

If you are invested in the market and it is down, then you are forced to sell your investments at a loss. You wouldn't want to sell your house at a loss, would you? And even worse, you would have to make up the loss with an even bigger gain. Why would you want to sell your investments at a loss? By having a distribution plan, you don't have to sell your investments at a loss. For all the money you worked so hard to save, it will be equally important to know how to distribute those dollars for income in retirement. Most people have never even heard of "a distribution plan."

The following chart shows a hypothetical $3,000,000 mutual fund and/or stock portfolio that suffers a -50% loss in year one (1), then earns +12% per year in years two (2) through ten (10), while taking out $120,000 of income per year, disregarding potential fees and income taxes. At the end of the tenth year, the projected portfolio value is $2,053,770. Your loss could be larger or smaller, and positive returns are not guaranteed.

Year	Hypothetical Annual Return	Start Of Year Asset Value	Annual Income	Gain/(Loss)	End Of Year Asset Value
1	-50%	$3,000,000	($120,000)	($1,500,000)	$1,380,000
2	12%	$1,380,000	($120,000)	$165,600	$1,425,600
3	12%	$1,425,600	($120,000)	$171,072	$1,476,672
4	12%	$1,476,672	($120,000)	$177,201	$1,533,873
5	12%	$1,533,873	($120,000)	$184,065	$1,597,937
6	12%	$1,597,937	($120,000)	$191,752	$1,669,690
7	12%	$1,669,690	($120,000)	$200,363	$1,750,053
8	12%	$1,750,053	($120,000)	$210,006	$1,840,059
9	12%	$1,840,059	($120,000)	$220,807	$1,940,866
10	12%	$1,940,866	($120,000)	$232,904	$2,053,770
Total Of Returns	58%				

This next chart shows a hypothetical $3,000,000 fixed index annuity that earns 4% per year in years one (1) through ten (10), never suffers a loss, while taking out $120,000 of income per year, disregarding potential fees and income taxes. At the end of the tenth (10th) year the projected portfolio value is $3,000,000. Positive returns are not guaranteed.

Year	Hypothetical Annual Return	Start Of Year Asset Value	Annual Income	Gain/(Loss)	End Of Year Asset Value
1	4%	$3,000,000	($120,000)	$120,000	$3,000,000
2	4%	$3,000,000	($120,000)	$120,000	$3,000,000
3	4%	$3,000,000	($120,000)	$120,000	$3,000,000
4	4%	$3,000,000	($120,000)	$120,000	$3,000,000
5	4%	$3,000,000	($120,000)	$120,000	$3,000,000
6	4%	$3,000,000	($120,000)	$120,000	$3,000,000
7	4%	$3,000,000	($120,000)	$120,000	$3,000,000
8	4%	$3,000,000	($120,000)	$120,000	$3,000,000
9	4%	$3,000,000	($120,000)	$120,000	$3,000,000
10	4%	$3,000,000	($120,000)	$120,000	$3,000,000
Total Of Returns	40%				

In Conclusion

It seems that the mutual fund and stock portfolio did far better, because adding up the losses and gains showed a total of returns of +58%, while the fixed index annuity only showed total returns of +40%. And yet, the mutual fund and stock portfolio only ended with $2,053,770 after ten (10) years of $120,000 annual income, while the fixed index annuity ended up with the same $3,000,000 with which they started. Based on these simple examples, which portfolio do you think performed better? Walter and Shirley agree with you, the fixed index annuity. Now all of you can sleep through the night—with sweet dreams.

About Mike

Mike Kojonen is the founder/owner of Principal Preservation Services LLC, with offices in Woodbury, MN and Hudson, WI. He has been in the financial services industry since 2002, helping clients with budgeting and finance. He now solely focuses on helping pre-retirees and retirees with necessary retirement planning.

Too many people are overconfident yet underprepared for retirement. Every week, clients come into Mike's office with retirement accounts, but no retirement plan. They have no idea if or when they can retire, or even what retirement would look like. His goal is to inform, educate, and direct them to put them on the path to succeed in retirement – without the stress.

Mike Kojonen's mission is for his clients to be able to achieve their goals by having a solvent retirement plan and to live retirement the way they dreamed of. He is able to do this by implementing strategies that are simple to understand, but hardly talked about or utilized in the industry. However, the relationship Mike holds with his clients isn't just about the strategies or the plan he implements with them, he has a true desire to earn the trust of all his clients. Building a foundation based on integrity, honesty and consistency is extremely important to him. This helps ensure an open communication environment for his clients, so that they are educated and understand what their retirement will really look like.

He states: "When my clients tell me that they now have 'peace of mind' knowing that they don't have doubt or feelings of anxiety about their retirement – to me, that is the greatest feeling of accomplishment!"

Mike, a Minnesota native, currently resides in Somerset, WI. He and his wife, Angie, have nine children (six girls and three boys) along with three dogs and three cats. He loves to play golf, travel, and spend time with his family and friends, and is a strong advocate of giving back to the community and an active member and supporter of his church. He has a strong faith in God which guides and leads him, his family, and his business.

CHAPTER 46

THE RETIREMENT INCOME MYTH

INCOME RIDERS AND SEQUENCE OF RETURN RISK

BY DAVE LOPEZ

Myth:
You shouldn't buy an annuity because the stock market is the best place for you to invest for dependable retirement income that will last for as long as you live.

You are retired and want a high level of dependable income from your savings that is guaranteed to last for as long as you live. You research on your own. You talk to your Advisor. You even ask friends and family what to do, because you desperately want to know the truth about how to protect your principal, and guarantee you won't run out of income late in life.

You were probably told that the best way to succeed with your investments in retirement is to try and get the highest rate of return, because this will allow you to draw the highest level of income during retirement, keep pace with inflation, and provide you the highest probability your money will not run out. While this sounds good, historical data does not support this in any way shape or form.

The more volatile an asset is, the less you can confidently withdraw if your goal is to make sure it lasts for as long as you live. And as you have read in this book, the stock market can be very volatile and you should assume it may continue to be so. Since 1929, every seven (7) years on average the stock market crashes approximately -40%. If you are withdrawing money from retirement accounts that lose -40% on average every seven (7) years, how do you expect your funds to last? You are right, you can't![1]

THEN IN YOUR RESEARCH SOMEONE TELLS YOU ABOUT AN ANNUITY.

And you immediately recoil at the thought of buying an annuity, because you remember things you have read or been told in the past. You may have heard from an Advisor, the internet, or a family member that annuities are bad tools in all circumstances for all people. Following this advice could end up putting your retirement security in jeopardy. Common sense dictates that if annuities were bad in all circumstances for all people, the State Insurance Regulators that oversee annuities would not allow them to be sold. If this was true, your State Department of Insurance would simply shut the sales of annuities down, immediately. This hasn't happened and it won't happen. In fact the opposite is true, new recommendations have been made for the Federal Government to allow annuities to be available in all your retirement accounts, including 401(k)'s.[2]

I have found that the vast majority of Advisors that push the agenda that, "All annuities are bad in all circumstances," are often Advisors that have set up their practice to sell only market-based products like Stocks, Bonds, and Mutual Funds. As such, they do not, or cannot, offer annuity products. That's a lot like a car salesman who only sells cars telling you that pickup trucks are a waste of money. The truth is both cars and trucks are useful but for different needs. The same is true for investment tools, and the same is true for annuities.

So, why is it that using Stocks and Mutual Funds to guarantee your income in retirement may not be the best tools for the job?

1. Strategas Research Partners, LLC
2. US Department of Treasury Press Center 10/24/2014, Treasury Issues Guidance to Encourage Annuities in 401(k) Plans (https://www.treasury.gov/press-center/press-releases/Pages/jl2673.aspx) (https://docs.house.gov/meetings/WM/WM00/20190402/109255/BILLS-116HR___ih.pdf)

Let's examine the time period from 1979 – 2008, a period of 30 years. Assume we receive these returns in retirement. Let's keep it simple:

- You invest $1,000,000 in a portfolio—a combination of stocks and mutual funds.
- You receive an average return of 7.23% per year after fees.
- You draw out 5% per year, ($50,000) for income in retirement.

That sounds like a perfect scenario. You grow your money at 7.23% yearly. You only take out 5% ($50,000) yearly. You are confident you will:

- Protect your principal.
- Guarantee you never run out of money.
- And even grow your nest egg by 2.23% yearly. (7.23% growth less 5% withdrawals).

BUT THAT IS NOT WHAT WOULD HAVE HAPPENED.

Not only would you not have protected your principal, you would have run out of money.

That's right, you would have gone broke! Now how is that possible? How could you average 7.23% yearly over a 30 year period, take out only 5%, and go broke?

The answer? Because of an investment risk most of us have never been told about and never discussed with our Advisors. It's called, _Sequence of Return Risk_, and if not planned for, it could cripple your retirement plans and leave you broke late in life—with no income stream and no remaining savings.

When withdrawing money every month from your retirement accounts, the "average rate of return" on your investments no longer matters. See the two (2) scenarios in our Graph below. If your annual returns had happened in the same order they did from 1979-2008, (scenario #1), you would have been able to withdraw your 5% each year and still end up with over $2.6 million dollars! The average rate of return over the 30-year period: 7.23% after fees.

389

That's great. You took out the money you needed and still grew your account to over $2.6 million dollars for your heirs. That, you think to yourself, is how I was told it would work.

But, what if the returns are different? If the order of those returns to your retirement accounts had simply been reversed, (scenario #2), you would have gone broke by year 15! That's right, by receiving the exact same returns but simply reversing the order of those returns you would have run out of money in 15 years and your account would be depleted. The average rate of return over this 30 year period? **The same 7.23%!**

		Scenario #1 - Actual Annual Returns		Scenario #2 - Returns Reversed	
		S&P 500 Index Annual Change Plus/Minus	Net Value After $50,000 Income & 2% Annual Fees	Reverse S&P 500 Index Annual Change Plus/Minus	Net Value After $50,000 Income & 2% Annual Fees
Year	Age				
1979	70	9.34%	$1,023,400	-35.61%	$573,900
1980	71	28.91%	$1,248,797	2.16%	$524,818
1981	72	-9.98%	$1,049,191	11.65%	$525,463
1982	73	12.71%	$1,111,559	5.55%	$494,117
1983	74	18.58%	$1,245,856	8.44%	$475,938
1984	75	0.81%	$1,181,030	21.94%	$520,840
1985	76	26.74%	$1,423,217	-21.27%	$349,641
1986	77	17.59%	$1,595,097	-10.02%	$257,614
1987	78	3.85%	$1,574,606	-11.82%	$172,012
1988	79	7.57%	$1,612,312	18.49%	$150,376
1989	80	30.65%	$2,024,239	25.95%	$136,392
1990	81	-9.24%	$1,746,714	32.30%	$127,718
1991	82	27.82%	$2,147,716	18.73%	$99,086
1992	83	4.34%	$2,147,973	35.20%	$81,982
1993	84	6.90%	$2,203,223	-1.36%	$29,227
1994	85	-1.36%	$2,079,195	6.90%	$0
1995	86	35.20%	$2,719,488	4.34%	$0
1996	87	18.73%	$3,124,458	27.82%	$0
1997	88	32.30%	$4,021,169	-9.24%	$0
1998	89	25.95%	$4,934,239	30.65%	$0
1999	90	18.49%	$5,697,895	7.57%	$0
2000	91	-11.82%	$4,860,446	3.85%	$0
2001	92	-10.02%	$4,226,220	17.59%	$0
2002	93	-21.27%	$3,192,779	26.74%	$0
2003	94	21.94%	$3,779,419	0.81%	$0
2004	95	8.44%	$3,972,813	18.58%	$0
2005	96	5.55%	$4,063,848	12.71%	$0
2006	97	11.65%	$4,406,010	-9.98%	$0
2007	98	2.16%	$4,363,059	28.91%	$0
2008	99	-35.61%	$2,672,113	9.34%	$0
		7.23%		7.23%	

THE POTENTIAL DANGEROUS IMPACT OF "SEQUENCE OF RETURNS RISK"

The following chart includes two (2) hypothetical illustrations for Jim and Hope:

Scenario #1 - showing they earned S&P 500 Index annual increases on their $1,000,000 from 1979 through 2008, paid 2% in annual fees, and withdrew $50,000 (5%) of income per year.

Scenario #2 - showing they earned S&P 500 Index annual increases on their $1,000,000 from 1979 through 2008 with returns in reverse order, paid 2% in annual fees, and withdrew $50,000 (5%) of income per year.

Scenario #1 & Scenario #2 Average Annual S&P 500 Index Increase

Truth:

The stock market carries principal risk, a high level of sequence of return risk, and with these, a tremendous amount of dependable income risk.

The stock market cannot provide dependable income as evidenced by the lowering of the "Safe Withdrawal Rate" from 6% back in the 1980's down to 3% currently.[3]

Fixed index annuities with income riders provide principal protection, an opportunity to participate in stock market appreciation, and consistent, dependable income guaranteed for as long as you live.[4]

Hypothetical Case Study

Let's take a look at a hypothetical case study of a working couple. We will call them Jim and Hope.

Jim and Hope have been working for 40 years. Jim and Hope are both age 65. They have scrimped and saved over the years, skipping vacations, hand-me downs for the kids, passing on new cars and putting in extra hours at work. They were willing to make these sacrifices over the years in order to set aside enough money to retire someday to live comfortably in retirement and not run out of money, no matter how long they lived. Through all the years of savings, tightening the budget and working overtime, they have managed to save $750K for retirement. They want to use the $750,000 to create income.

Their Plan...

After carefully looking at their spending and itemizing the bills, Jim and Hope believe they will need $50K/year from the $750,000 in savings in order to supplement their other income, (Social Security and one Pension). Hope's Mom is 102 and still doing well. Jim and Hope want

---

3. The *4% Rule is Not Safe in a Low-Yield World* by Michael Finke, Ph.D., CFP®, Wade D. Pfau, Ph.D., CFA & David M. Blanchett, CFA, CFP®

4. Fixed insurance and annuity product guarantees are subject to the claims paying ability of the issuing company and are not offered or guaranteed by Alphastar. Investing involves risk including the potential loss of principal. No investment strategy can guarantee a profit or protect against loss in periods of declining values. Past performance does not guarantee future results.

to be sure they would have enough money to withdraw their $50K/year even if they live as long as Hope's Mom.

Jim and Hope believe they have done the math and feel confident with their plan. $50K per year in withdrawals was just 6.6% of their $750K. As they have five years until they retire, they are hoping that by age 70 their next egg will grow from $750K to $1 Million dollars. If that happens their withdrawals of $50K/year will only be 5% of their next egg. They have heard that the Stock Market averages over 7% yearly over time so that will give them enough, even if the return is a bit lower over their retirement. They feel pretty good. They plan to leave their money invested exactly as it has been over the last 20 years. As long as they don't panic if the market drops, they believe they will be okay.

So, their plan is to:

1. **Work five more years until they turn 70.**
2. **Set aside $750K from their current savings for income in retirement.**
3. **Keep funds invested in Stocks and Mutual Funds and hope it grows to $1 Million by age 70.**
4. **Plan on a 7% average yearly return in retirement.**
5. **Start taking $50K withdrawals each year for living expenses at age 70.**
6. **Plan on their money lasting until age 102 or more.**

Jim and Hope have never heard of "Sequence of Return Risk" or how it could impact their retirement plan.

When they first started saving, Jim remembers the "safe withdrawal rate" being between 5% to 6%. And this was true...way back then. So Jim thought he was being very conservative using 5% as the withdrawal rate they could safely take out of their savings. But as we discussed, the new current "safe withdrawal rate" is just 3%.

This means Jim and Hope should not take out any more than $30,000 per year from the $1 Million in savings they hope to have at age 70. This would leave them $20,000 short every year!

An analysis was run for Jim and Hope that showed them taking $50,000 *per year of income distributions, and even if they earned a 7.23% average rate of return, they could go broke as soon as age 85. (See graph on page 390.)*

Jim and Hope are stunned. The numbers and projected income distribution they have based their plans for retirement on are completely different now, they are 40% lower! This means their plan won't work.

For the first time, they start to investigate other options for generating the income they need. They agree they have two (2) main goals for a new asset allocation strategy: eliminate stock market losses and receive income guaranteed for as long as they live. In their minds it is simple, they should be able to find multiple assets that can do this. So they search and search, but they don't find anything that will work the way they want... until they come across a weird sounding plan called a fixed index annuity with an income rider.

They discover a fixed indexed annuity with an income rider could protect their money against all stock market losses, regardless of how big, and would guarantee them income every month for the rest of their lives, no matter how long they lived. Jim and Hope investigate a little more and find that it is a good possibility for their plan. They find a fixed index annuity with an income rider that, at age 70, will generate $54,124 per year in income for the rest of their lives. The income is guaranteed, even if they live past age 100 like Hope's Mother. In fact, if one of them lives to age 100, they would have received over $1.6 Million dollars! ($54,124/year x 30 years).[5]

They are amazed to find out that not only is their dream of $50K/year realized, but that they can take out over 80% more than their original plan allowed. ($54K is 80% more than the $30K recommended from the market-based plan). Furthermore this income is guaranteed. They will never worry about running out of money.

CONCLUSION

When you create your retirement income plan, I believe it is prudent to

---

5. Generic Fixed Indexed Annuity with 10% simple interest IAV accumulation, 5-year deferral, 5% joint life w/d rate at age 70.

take "Sequence of Return Risk" into consideration. Stocks and Mutual Funds have never given the same rate of return year after year. As a result, "Sequence of Return Risk" could cause your plan to fail, and you run out of money.

A second lesson here is that you need to be clear about your goals. Once you have identified your goals, you can begin to look for the investment strategy that best accomplishes them. In our example, if your goals were principal protection against stock market losses and guaranteed income for life, you would look for an investment strategy that is specifically designed for that purpose, such as a fixed indexed annuity with an income rider. Regardless of stock market performance or losses, your income is guaranteed, reducing your risk.

Building out your retirement plan is like building a house. Before you begin, you want the right tools for the job, knowing each tool has a purpose. Using the wrong tool can cost you time, money, and a big headache. Investments, like any tools, are all different. Each investment tool is designed for a specific job, with each having its own advantages and disadvantages. And just like building a house, you will want the right tool for the job.

By limiting yourself to just a few financial tools, namely Stocks, Bonds and Mutual Funds, you drastically limit your options to guarantee your principal against stock market loss and get a high level of income guaranteed for as long as you live.

Your takeaway.

A fixed indexed annuity with an Income Rider is only a tool, it's neither good nor bad. And like any financial tool, it has advantages and disadvantages. But, it is a tool designed for two (2) main purposes:

1) To protect your principal against stock market losses
2) To generate guaranteed income for life

Don't risk your retirement or limit the income you can take because you have limited yourself to only a few investment tools.

Biographical References (Footnote #3 Authors):

— Michael Finke, Ph.D., CFP®, is a professor and Ph.D. coordinator in the Department of Personal Financial Planning at Texas Tech University (Michael. Finke@ttu.edu).

— Wade D. Pfau, Ph.D., CFA, is a professor of retirement income at the American College (wadepfau@gmail.com).

— David M. Blanchett, CFA, CFP®, is head of retirement research at Morningstar Investment Management (david.blanchett@morningstar.com). Electronic http: //ssrn.com/abstract=2201323

About Dave

Dave Lopez has been featured as a contributor in many publications including *Yahoo! Finance, Market Watch,* and *The Star Tribune.* He is a recognized speaker on the topic of Retirement Planning. Through workshops and adult education classes, Dave has presented on over 200 occasions to over 4,000 attendees over the last 9 years. Through his classes and workshops, Dave walks attendees through a step-by-step process to build out a plan for their retirement, using strategies designed to protect and preserve assets, manage market risk, increase retirement income and reduce taxes.

Dave is an Investment Advisor Representative with AlphaStar Capital Management and the Founder and Managing Member of ILG Financial, located in Stafford, Virginia. ILG Financial is a member of the Better Business Bureau and the Fredericksburg Chamber of Commerce. Dave is also proud to be a member of the National Ethics Association.

Dave graduated from James Madison University with a double major in Mathematics and Computer Science. After graduation, he spent 18 years in the Insurance Industry helping clients protect assets from loss. In 2008/2009 Dave watched several family and friends struggle with the loss of their life savings when the Stock Market crashed. He was amazed to see that most had no real plan for managing their savings. This drove Dave to look into a system based on fact and data that families could utilize to build out a plan for retirement. Each plan is unique, and factors-in negative events that could affect their retirement.

Dave and ILG Financial currently have over 70 Million dollars under management for their Clients in a combination of Investments and Insurance-based tools.

Dave is happily married to Cheryl, his wife of 28 years, and is the proud father of Megan, Christian and Madison. As the founder of ILG Financial, he has been working with families and individuals building unique individual retirement plans for the last 10 years.

You can connect with Dave at:
- DaveLopez@theilg.com
- www.ILGFinancial.com

CHAPTER 47

MYTH: A FIXED INDEX ANNUITY WITH AN INCOME RIDER PROVIDES NO LIQUIDITY

AND YOU DON'T HAVE ACCESS TO YOUR MONEY FOR A LONG TIME

BY JAIME N. COWPER, CLTC, NSSA®

One of the primary objections I hear about fixed index annuities with income riders is that you don't have access to your money for a long period of time, called the "surrender period." The "surrender period" simply means you cannot take out all of your money in a lump sum before a specified time period without paying a premature withdrawal penalty, like a CD. So generally, the statement that you have "no access to your money" is not the case. The truth is that you won't have access to ALL your money for a certain period of time, but in almost all cases you will have some access, in some cases even immediate access, to a portion of your assets. Unfortunately, some people, even financial advisors, are unable to put aside the incorrect information they have heard about fixed index annuities with income riders, and really listen to the facts about how fixed index annuities with income riders, and access to them, actually work. Because of this, many people may miss out on something that could be a perfect fit for their retirement strategy.

Think about it, there is this mysterious financial product out there called a fixed index annuity with an income rider that provides you:

1. Protection of your principal against all stock market losses.
2. An opportunity to earn a competitive rate of return based on a low-risk asset.
3. Income guaranteed to be paid to you for as long as you live, even past age 100.
4. The ability to pass on 100% of the funds remaining in your annuity when you die to your beneficiaries.
5. A low overall total annual fee of typically right around 1%.

And to receive all these benefits, one of the disadvantages is that you can't take all your money out in a lump sum without incurring a premature withdrawal penalty. Were you really going to take all of your money out in a lump sum anyway? Probably not!

Now I am going to explain the ways in which a person does have access to fixed index annuities with income riders and the reasons why having limited access is not necessarily a bad thing. Later, I will give you an example of how a hypothetical couple, who were pre-retirees, used fixed indexed annuities with income riders along with traditional investments to help them achieve peace of mind, by constructing a comprehensive financial plan that works for them in retirement. I will outline a sample client income plan that includes fixed indexed annuities with income riders and allows for adequate access to their money.

1) Free withdrawals

Most annuities have what is called a surrender period. A surrender period is the time a person must wait until they can withdraw all of their money without a penalty. Notice how I said all. Most fixed index annuities with income riders have a free withdrawal provision that allows a person access to their money during this period. The typical free withdrawal amount is 5-10% of the contract value per year, starting in year 1 or year 2. This means that a person could take out some of their money every year until the end of the surrender period, without a penalty. If they take more than the 5-10% that is allowed each year they would incur a penalty. This penalty is referred to as a surrender penalty. Fixed index annuities with income riders have a surrender schedule that states what the penalty is if the person withdraws more than they are allowed. After the end of the surrender period, the contract is considered fully liquid. This means that a person could withdraw as much as they want without a penalty, or close the whole account, penalty free. There are many different kinds of fixed index annuities with income riders with various surrender schedules and free withdrawal options. All contracts are unique, and it is essential to know the facts about the fixed index annuity with an income rider that you are considering and how it fits into your overall strategy.

2) Income Riders

Income riders have become another popular way to access money from fixed indexed annuities. Income riders are an additional benefit that can be added to certain fixed indexed annuities creating a fixed indexed annuity with an income rider. The typical income riders grow at a guaranteed rate, usually a different and maybe even higher rate than the account value, and can be used for one fundamental purpose: to create guaranteed lifetime income at some point in the future. Typically, the riders offer a guaranteed growth rate or an enhanced rate compared to the growth of the contract value. Then at some point in the future, the contract owner can trigger income payments based on the income value and age of the owner or annuitant. When the rider is triggered, it generally amounts to about 4-6% of the income value amount. These riders provide a way for clients to grow their money safely and at a higher rate than the contract. Some income riders have options with an increasing income payout and others stay flat for life.

These riders typically do not allow for flexible withdrawal options. Once triggered the amount may not increase, unless an income rider with an increasing option was chosen, but it is guaranteed for the life of the client. This could be a good fit for someone who is looking for additional guaranteed income in the future. It is probably not a good fit for someone who wants to make various random withdrawals of different amounts over time. Unlike annuitization (which I will cover later) if a person triggers income using the rider, there may still be money left over for beneficiaries when they pass away. These types of contracts work well as part of an overall strategy.

3) Annuitization

Annuitization is an interesting topic. In my opinion, this is one of the terms that leads to misconceptions about annuities as a whole. Some believe that if you have an annuity, you are forced to annuitize. This is never true with a fixed index annuity with an income rider. All annuities provide for the option to annuitize, but in most annuities, you are typically not forced to exercise this option. In a fixed index annuity with an income rider, you are never forced to annuitize your contract to receive guaranteed lifetime income. So, what is annuitization? Annuitization is the process of converting an annuity into a series of periodic income payments. Annuities may be annuitized for a specific period or for the life of the annuitant and/or joint annuitant. If you annuitize, it means that you essentially trade your full account value for a guaranteed income for life.

The amount that the insurance company will pay you is based on your life expectancy and interest rates. The insurance company will determine the amount based on several factors. When interest rates are high, this can be an attractive feature, but not so much when they are low. Some people don't want to give up their full principal value for this guarantee. One of the primary advantages to annuitization is an income stream that you can never outlive. One of the disadvantages is that if you pass away even a day after you annuitized the contract if you have chosen a life only annuity, which we very rarely ever recommend, the insurance company keeps your money. In other words, no money goes to your beneficiaries. So, if you have beneficiaries, a "life-only annuitization" is usually not recommended. So, in an "annuitization" you give up the use of your money, but if you live to 110, you still receive the income. It is a contract. There are cases where it makes sense for a person to annuitize, but there are many factors to consider before making this choice.

Hypothetical Case Study

Josh is age 61 and works making $80,000 per year, and his wife Andrea is age 59 and works and also earns $80,000 per year.

Josh and Andrea would like to retire in 5 years if they can meet their annual gross income goal of $100,000. They have $2,000,000 saved in total assets between their 401(k)s and a couple of IRAs. All of their money is currently invested in mutual funds, over 90% in stock (equity) mutual funds. They also have about $20,000 in the bank. They don't have a lot of debt, but their house will not be paid off for about ten more years. Living comfortably in retirement is most important to them. Their primary concerns are not running out of money for as long as they live and not losing a lot of money in the stock market. They lost a lot, almost -50%, during the market crash in 2008 and didn't want to go through that again. Although it would be nice to leave some money for their kids when they pass, they want to enjoy their money in retirement first and foremost. Their kids just finished college, so Josh and Andrea plan to ramp up their savings over the next five years.

Josh and Andrea need an income plan, a real income plan. They should try to position their assets in a way that provides for some principal protection, income guarantees, and long-term growth. This type of plan allows for plenty of guaranteed income to meet their daily expenses, potential growth, and liquidity access for additional fun money and for emergencies. They should try and maximize their social security and use their other assets to meet their income goals and fill the gaps until they trigger their monthly benefits. Let's say that after reviewing a properly prepared social security analysis, Andrea decides to take her benefit at 64 and Josh is waiting to trigger his at 70. They could then put half of their money into three different fixed index annuities with income riders and half of their money into three different investment strategies intended for potential growth using professional money management.

Two (2) of the fixed index annuities with income riders could start to provide income in their 60s and 70s. They could also put a smaller amount into another fixed index annuity with an income rider that they could plan to let grow and access in their late 70s or early 80s if they need additional income due to inflation or increased health care costs. It could very well be beneficial to utilize a combination of penalty-free income withdrawals and income riders to provide for the needed income.

They can place the other half of their money, about $1,000,000, in a money management platform invested in the Stock Market that would be fully liquid and available to them with no penalties for withdrawal at any time other than market fluctuations. A smart strategy might be to use three (3) different buckets with different investment strategies.

1. The first one could be a short-term bucket. They could plan to access this one to supplement income in the first five (5) years of retirement, to allow some of the fixed index annuities with income rider monies to grow. This bucket has lower volatility than the other two.

2. The second bucket could be a total diversification strategy with medium risk and higher long-term growth potential than the first.

3. The third bucket could be an aggressive bucket that is earmarked for long-term growth. This one has the highest potential volatility, but the highest long-term growth potential of the three. In the years where the growth bucket does well, Josh and Andrea can shave off the earnings and replace some of the money coming out of the short-term bucket. The invested dollars could help to fill the income gaps in the early years, but then also provide access for the fun money.

When Josh and Andrea need a little extra for a vacation or to replenish their savings, they could take it out of the short-term bucket.

SUMMARY

Fixed index annuities with income riders can be a good fit for many retirees and pre-retirees for part of an overall plan, and the strategy can provide for adequate access to your money. The fixed index annuities with income riders provide the principal protection and some income guarantees. The money invested in the Stock Market provides for potentially higher growth and full liquidity. Would it really matter if Josh and Andrea couldn't access all of their $2,000,000 each year? Probably not. If they had $1,000,000 in liquidity would this more than likely meet every emergency or need they could encounter? Probably. How about you, would it really matter that you couldn't access all of your money each year? Probably not. But if you could access half of it in a lump sum, would you be OK? Probably.

Most people only take out income distributions of what they need so that their money will last and they want to minimize the tax burden. With the strategy that I have laid out, you can have principal protection against all stock market losses with the fixed index annuities with income riders, and can take advantage of the potential upside of the stock market over time with the stock market investment strategies, understanding you do have principal risk. If you knew that some of your money and income was protected with the fixed index annuities with income riders, wouldn't you feel more comfortable staying the course with the stock market investments during a market correction? Without some protection, some folks may be tempted to pull their money out of the market at inopportune times. With both strategies working well together, you would be able to potentially take advantage of different market cycles to maximize your financial success and security.

About Jaime

Jaime N. Cowper, CLTC, NSSA® is the Founder and President of Unity Financial Advisors and is passionate about helping people retire with peace of mind and provide protection for their families. She specializes in comprehensive retirement planning, which includes providing financial guidance and services for those nearing or in retirement. She is committed to helping clients to preserve their assets for retirement, develop a reliable income plan, discuss and implement a plan for long-term care, and leverage money to the next generation or charity. Jaime is an Investment Advisor Representative under Planners Alliance, LLC, an SEC Registered Investment Advisory Firm. She currently holds a Series 65 license and life and health insurance license in multiple states. She is also certified in long-term care planning. Additionally, she obtained extensive training in the area of social security and holds the certificate of National Social Security Advisor.

Jaime has been quoted or featured in *Kiplinger's Personal Finance, Advisors Magazine, U.S. News and World, Yahoo Finance, The NY Daily News* and *MSN Money.*

Jaime is a former basketball player at St. Clair County Community College where she earned a full athletic scholarship and credits her many years of playing the sport to developing a great work ethic, discipline, and leadership skills.

After graduating from Oakland University in 2004 with a B.A., she developed a passion for helping people achieve their financial goals while working at Fifth Third Bank as a personal banker. Working at the bank made her realize that she wanted to be able to help people achieve a broader range of financial planning goals. She then pursued a new agent training program at MassMutual Financial Group in 2005 where she remained a career agent for three years. During that time she met her mentor and had the benefit of his knowledge and mentorship in years that followed. In 2014, Jaime formed Unity Financial Advisors. She prides herself on her personal service, independence, and objectivity to provide the best solutions to her clients.

Connect with Jaime at:
- www.unityfinancialadvisors.net
- jcowper@unityfinancialadvisors.net
- www.facebook.com/unityfinancial
- (248) 885-8176

CHAPTER 48

MYTH: A FIXED INDEX ANNUITY WITH AN INCOME RIDER DOESN'T REALLY PAY GUARANTEED INCOME FOR LIFE, IT CAN STOP AT ANY TIME

BY DOUG RAY

Truth: A fixed index annuity with an income rider is a legally-binding written contractual guarantee that you will get paid income for as long as you live, even if you live past 100 years old. If you are married and you choose a joint payout, it guarantees to pay the exact same amount for as long as at least one of you is living.

Your lifetime income is contractually guaranteed not to decrease because of:

1. Stock market losses.
2. Stock market volatility.
3. Using up all assets in the account.

In addition, when you die, a fixed index annuity with an income rider guarantees all funds remaining in your account are paid out to your named beneficiaries, the insurance company does not keep the remaining funds. Someone gets your money, either you or your beneficiaries.

In a fixed index annuity with an income rider, your principal is 100% protected against stock market losses and volatility, your income is guaranteed for life and is 100% protected against stock market losses and volatility, and the insurance carrier is legally bound and obligated to continue to pay you income for as long as you are living. Aren't these the exact things you, as a retiree or pre-retiree, want from your money?

Some of the downsides of a fixed index annuity with an income rider include the facts that you can't take all your money out in a lump sum for a specific time period without incurring a surrender charge, you won't earn full stock market returns, and you will pay a fee. To me, when I look at these negatives, and I compare them to all the positives, I can only think of one thing: the positives far outweigh the negatives. You can't suffer any loss at all, your total fees will be approximately 1%, and your income is guaranteed for as long as you live.

So why does Ken Fisher talk trash about annuities? The simple answer is that when you buy an annuity, Ken Fisher doesn't make any money. Ken Fisher would rather you invest with his firm, and they will primarily place your funds into stocks and bonds which have principal risk and do not provide a guaranteed lifetime income. So, if two (2) of the main goals retirees and pre-retirees want from their money are:

1. Principal protection against market losses.
2. Dependable income guaranteed for as long as they live.

How is Ken Fisher and Fisher Investments providing these two (2) things retirees and pre-retirees want so desperately? Simple answer: Ken Fisher is not and Fisher Investments are not.

So let me ask you this, if you have money at Fisher Investments, and the market goes through another crash like what happened during the 2008 Financial Crisis – when the S&P 500 Index was down -53.8% – and you are taking out income during and after the crash, and then you run out of money – is Ken Fisher, and Fisher Investments, going to continue to pay you income for as long as you live if your account value is $0?

I will answer this for you. If you have money with Ken Fisher at Fisher Investments, and the stock market crashes, and you run out of money while you are taking distributions, ***KEN FISHER*** *and* ***FISHER***

INVESTMENTS WILL NOT CONTINUE TO SEND YOU INCOME PAYMENTS.

But Ken Fisher and Fisher Investments will continue to bad-mouth annuities. Makes you kind of think a little bit, huh?

WE'D LIKE YOU TO MEET MARK AND MARY

Mark has worked for his company, which sells automotive parts nationally, since graduating college 40 years ago. When he started at the company, like many people in his generation, his company offered a pension that would pay him a guaranteed monthly income for life. The older employees at his company, some of his mentors, told him that the pension was very rich and he would have a great retirement combining the guaranteed monthly pension benefits with his Social Security. They told him all he had to do was keep working at the company, keep doing an excellent job, and keep moving up the ladder. And as hard work and luck would have it, by the time Mark retired at age 62, he was second in command, rising to the position of CFO. Mark was the finance expert at his company, the Chief Financial Officer.

In the late 1990s when Mark held the position of national sales Manager, the company went through several business and financial problems and the company was forced to terminate the pension plan, and Mark was given a lump sum of money to roll over to an IRA. Mark was in his early 40's, had been handed a $1,000,000 check to roll over to his IRA, so he really didn't think too much, or worry about, those lost guaranteed monthly pension income benefits.

At age 62, when Mark retired, he and his wife Mary had accumulated $3,000,000 of total retirement assets. In their minds, in one way it seemed like a large amount of money, and in another way, they worried that it might not be enough. At age 62, Mark decided Mary and he would defer taking their Social Security benefits because they would get 35% more benefits by waiting until age 66. For Mark and Mary, this was the best decision, even though it would take them living into their early 80's to break even from giving up the lost Social Security income had they filed at age 62.

Mark started taking out $90,000 per year from his $3,000,000 rollover IRA at age 62. After income taxes, Mark and Mary netted $6,700 per month which covered their standard monthly budget but didn't leave a lot of money for the extensive traveling they planned to do during retirement. It also didn't allow them to save money in the bank every month like they did when Mark was working. Mary had worked hard herself raising their four (4) children who had now blessed them with eight (8) grandchildren.

Mark had spent 80 hours per week managing the finances for his $500,000,000 company, and he was very good at it. Before he retired, he was making $250,000 per year and bringing home $14,000 per month after income taxes and his 401(k) contributions. Mark had always hoped they would have the same net take-home income during retirement, but right now they were getting less than ½ of that amount, receiving just $6,700.

Mark didn't think he could, or should, take out more than $90,000 of income per year from his assets because he was afraid of two main things:

1. Suffering another large loss to the portfolio like what happened to him during the 2000 Technology Bubble between 2000 through 2002 when he lost -52%. He fully recovered by 2007 when you include all his added contributions between 2003 through 2007 only to lose -54% during the Financial Crisis between 2007 through 2009. He knew another loss of this magnitude, during retirement, while they were taking large income distributions and not adding any more money to the pot, would be catastrophic.

2. Running out of income during their lifetimes and having to somehow survive just on their joint Social Security benefits.

Mark knew if either of these things happened, his worst financial fear would come true; they would be poor, their lifestyles having to change and be significantly reduced forever. No more Barrington's every Friday night...but wait, we will get back to that!

IT'S DATE NIGHT

Mary ordered the Hudson Valley Foie Gras to start and the pan seared halibut for her entrée. Mark ordered the rope-grown P.E.I. mussels for his appetizer and the pan-roasted veal cutlet for dinner, adding sides of spinach with caramelized garlic and truffle mash potatoes for Mary and himself to share.

Paul, the head waiter at Barrington's in Charlotte, North Carolina, who had been serving Mark and Mary every Friday night since the restaurant opened in 2000, asked if they would like a bottle of wine that night? Mark squinted and reviewed the familiar wine listings and after a few minutes asked for the 2006 Axios Cabernet Sauvignon. Paul was impressed and asked subtly if this was a special occasion.

Mary smiled and told Paul that Mark turned 65 today and just as importantly it was his three (3) year anniversary since retiring at 62! Paul, the epitome of understatement, simply nodded his head and headed toward the wine cellar. Mark and Mary loved the small number of tables and the family feel, but mostly they loved the food, the wine, and Paul, at Barrington's.

Mary looked into Mark's eyes and wished her high school sweetheart a Happy Birthday. She thought he looked sad and asked if he was OK? Mark said that nothing was better than sitting at their favorite restaurant, at their favorite table, looking across the table at the most beautiful lady in the whole restaurant. She asked Mark then why he looked so sad. Mark thought for a little while and then replied because he was worried, and he was worried a lot. Mary got nervous and wondered if Mark wasn't happy with their marriage any longer and asked him. Mark actually coughed up a bunch of water at Mary's question and then stammered that everything was perfect with their marriage and he loved her very much, but he was worried about their money.

Mark's statement caught Mary even more off-guard than if Mark had just admitted to having an affair! Mark had always taken care of the money for the family, Mary thought he must have done a good job, they were retired, and still eating dinner every Friday at Barrington's, and he'd been the CFO at his huge company. How could he feel afraid about their money now?

Mark told Mary he worried constantly that the stock market would crash again like it does every seven (7) years on average since 1929 and they would lose -50% or more of their assets, virtually guaranteeing they would run out of money. He also said he was almost paralyzingly afraid they would run out of money during their lifetime, and because Mary would almost certainly live longer than him, he felt guilty he would leave her on this planet with no money left.

Mary was stunned. She felt a little light-headed and she hadn't even had one little sip of wine yet. At that moment she needed a drink, and wondered where in the heck was Paul with their bottle and glasses? Mark told Mary he had been looking for a solution since retirement that could reduce their risk and give them a high level of dependable income that was guaranteed for both of their lives, but to date, he had been unsuccessful. Mark told Mary he had received a ton of advertisements from Ken Fisher and Fisher Investments, but when he spoke with their representative on a few different occasions, he was advised to go with one of their stock and bond portfolios. Mark wasn't comfortable with the risk they recommended. Mark said when he asked them about an annuity he had heard about that would provide him 100% safety of principal against all stock market losses and would give Mary and him income guaranteed for as long as they both lived, he was told to "stay away from annuities."

Mary asked Mark if he had spoken to Steve about this. Steve was married to Barb, and they had been Mark and Mary's best friends for over 30 years. Mark said he hadn't spoken to Steve about it because he was embarrassed to have to admit to Steve that he didn't have total control of their finances. Steve had been a banker and Mark thought Steve probably knew a lot more about money than he did.

Mary told Mark that Barb had recently told her that she and Steve had recently moved their portfolio away from the broker they (Steve and Barb) had been using for over 20 years. Mark was stunned as this was the same broker Mark used for their money. Mark used the same broker only because Steve did and he trusted Steve. Mary told Mark that Steve and Barb wanted more income that was guaranteed for life and wanted significantly less risk than they were previously taking. Mary said Steve and Barb worked with a new advisor who put together an actual plan for them. The written plan showed Steve and Barb how they could reduce their risk of principal loss by over 75% and receive $100,000 of income guaranteed for as long as they lived off of their $2,000,000 of assets.

Mary added that Barb said they were going to use what was called a fixed index annuity with an income rider and that they, Steve and Barb, couldn't lose any money in a stock market crash, would get the $100,000 of income paid to them for as long as they both lived, and any assets remaining when they passed away would be paid to their children. Barb said she almost forgot that their new plan had total annual fees of 1.1% with the fixed index annuity with the income rider as compared to the 2.6% fees they were paying to their previous broker, saving them $30,000 in fees every year!

Now it was Mark's turn to be stunned. Mark trusted his best friend Steve implicitly. Based on what Mary had told him, their $3,000,000 would generate $150,000 per year of guaranteed annual income. Adding in $60,000 of joint Social Security income they could turn on now would give them $210,000 of annual gross income. Mark did a quick calculation in his head and was shocked to find that Mary and he would be able to bring home net after-tax monthly income of $14,000! They could make the same exact amount of net income as when he was working, increasing their net monthly income by $7,300.

Mark's eyes were watering when he looked into Mary's eyes and told her he wasn't worried any longer, they could take the trips they had always planned, maybe even three (3) big trips per year now when they were young and healthy. They could help pay for their eight (8) grandchildren's college educations, save money every month for as long as they lived, wouldn't have to worry about big losses, and they wouldn't have to worry about their income ever running out...

And just as importantly, they could keep coming to Barrington's every Friday night for the rest of their lives. Perfect timing as Paul just pulled the cork on their wine.

Bon Appetit Mark and Mary!

About Doug

Doug Ray has been a financial advisor for 30 years and realized very early in his career the critical difference in the financial needs of those 5 to 10 years on either side of retirement as compared with those still building careers and retirement portfolios. Transitioning from asset building to asset protection and creating protected retirement income became the focus of his practice and professional education. Doug has guided hundreds of families to transition successfully into retirement, confident in knowing they've secured protected income that supports their lifestyle.

Born in Winston Salem, Doug graduated from East Carolina with a B.S. in Business Administration, then served eight years of active duty in the U.S. Navy as a combat aviator and instructor. During his instructor tour in Pensacola, he completed his MBA with a concentration in finance. He and his family returned to N.C. in 1988 where he worked for Merrill Lynch. In 1998, Doug opened his own practice as an independent financial advisor better able to offer his clients the best financial products for their goals without the captive product mentality of corporate financial firms. He has offices in South Charlotte and Clemmons with clients throughout North and South Carolina.

Doug Ray has been a Top of the Table member for the last nine years, representing the top 1% of all insurance and financial advisors in the world. He holds an MBA as well as designations as a Retirement Income Certified Planner® (RICP®), Chartered Financial Consultant® (ChFC®) and is a licensed insurance professional for life and long-term care products in North and South Carolina. He hosts 'The Wealth Guardians' Radio Show heard on WPTI 94.5FM, the Piedmont's Talk Radio Saturday mornings and holds frequent public workshops on financial topics that can affect retirement income that include social security optimization, taxes in retirement, and long-term health care planning.

Doug and his wife Sherrie have been married 38 years and are blessed with two sons, a beautiful daughter-in-law and two cherished grandchildren. Doug is a member of Harrison United Methodist Church and has completed the Dave Ramsey Financial Peace University Course. In the past, he's served as a facilitator of Crown Financial Ministries, a faith-based financial program. He's raised funds for the Make-A-Wish Foundation through his radio show and continues to give back to his community through church and community organizations, including providing educational seminars. His hobbies include golf, collecting coins and cheering his beloved Green Bay Packers, East Carolina Pirates and of course, the Carolina Panthers.

CHAPTER 49

MYTH: "THE INSURANCE COMPANY WILL KEEP ALL YOUR MONEY WHEN YOU DIE."

BY PAUL SEAL

Annuity Truth: If you choose what is called a "Life Only Annuity" the insurance company will pay you income for as long as you live, but there are no funds left for your beneficiaries when you die. This is the "old-fashioned" style of annuity most people think of.

Annuity Solution: If you don't want the insurance company to keep your money when you die, then simply don't buy or select a "Life Only Annuity." You can buy a fixed index annuity with an income rider that will provide you income guaranteed for as long as you live and will pay 100% of all funds remaining in your annuity to your beneficiaries when you die.

Running out of money is one of the biggest fears retirees and pre-retirees have to battle. One of the only ways to eliminate your fear of running out of money is to create an income stream that is guaranteed to be paid to you for as long as you live, like a pension. One of the only financial instruments you can purchase that will provide you guaranteed lifetime income, is an annuity. So, you just have to make sure you buy the right type of annuity.

413

Dave and Betty are typical retirees who are both age 65 and want income from their assets that will never run out for as long as they live. They were so happy when they found an annuity that would pay them income for as long as they both lived. But then they discovered after they both passed away there was no money that would be left for their kids, so now they were depressed and against the idea of an annuity. This is because they had contemplated buying a "Life Only Annuity."

Just like Dave and Betty, you probably don't want to buy a "Life Only Annuity." You also probably don't want to buy a variable annuity that has principal risk and typically, extremely high fees (some as high as 6.5%). But just like Dave and Betty, you still want and need guaranteed lifetime income. So, what the heck is a retiree or pre-retiree supposed to do?

What if Dave and Betty found a special type of annuity that has no principal risk from stock market losses, provides the opportunity for index gains based on a percentage of total index growth, has a very low fee structure, provides you income for as long as you live and for as long as your spouse lives (if you choose a joint payout), and passes 100% of all remaining funds in the annuity when you die to your named beneficiaries? Dave and Betty would probably say "Heck Yes!" to this type of annuity. This is called a fixed index annuity with an income rider. What do you think of this kind of special annuity? Pretty fancy huh?

Annuity Myth Totally Debunked: If Dave and Betty, or you, buy a fixed index annuity with an income rider, you will receive income guaranteed for as long as you live, and it is guaranteed that 100% of the funds in your annuity at your death will be paid to your named beneficiaries, none of the assets in your annuity will be kept by the insurance company.

What is it that most of us want? What is it that Dave and Betty want? What is it that you want? Probably to protect our assets against losses, have the opportunity to receive an acceptable rate of return, receive a high amount of income that is guaranteed to last for as long as we live even if past age 100, and then pass any remaining assets to our loved ones and/or our charities. Again, one of the only, if not the only, financial instrument that can do these things is a fixed index annuity with an income rider.

LIFETIME PAYOUT – INCOME FOR LIFE

Let's take a look at the Income payout using an income rider in action. Mike is at age 65 and Leslie is 62. Mike is retiring after working as an engineer for 32 years, and Leslie retired from her job as an office manager two years ago. They have a daughter and two wonderful grandchildren they love to visit and spoil as much as they can. Both worry about making sure they have enough of an income to pay the bills and still be able to travel to see David and Elizabeth, their grandchildren. Mike also worries about Leslie and how to make sure Leslie will continue to live the same lifestyle if he passes away before her. He is determined to make sure she is always taken care of.

They have saved a little over a million dollars between their 401(k)'s and with playing in the stock market a little, when they had some excess money over the years. They know that leaving all their money in the market could be a recipe for disaster if there is a big correction in the market. After talking to a financial advisor, they decide to buy a fixed index annuity with an income rider using $500,000 of their assets. They like the idea of guaranteeing their principle by moving half of their money out of the crazy ups and downs of the market. They also like the idea of creating a guaranteed source of income for life, no matter how long they live.

After using the money they've invested in the market to fund their retirement for nine years, they decide to start taking income from the annuity using the joint payout option. The advantage of the joint payout option vs. the single payout is the income will be paid out over both lifetimes, not just Mikes. When Mike turns 75, he and Leslie will receive $63,927 each year regardless of how long they live. The big thing that Mike wants is making sure Leslie will continue to receive the same income every year, if she outlives him, even if she lives until she's 115. His main goal of taking care of Leslie, his princess, is no longer a source of worry for him. This strategy is especially important when Leslie is younger than Mike and is expected to live many years after he passes.

STRETCH IRA STRATEGY – GREAT FOR BENEFICIARIES

By using a stretch IRA strategy or sometimes called a legacy strategy you can potentially stretch the value of your assets and continue to allow the tax deferral benefit to continue to your children and/or grandchildren. If this strategy is implemented properly, you can allow several generations to benefit, not just a single beneficiary.

This strategy is implemented by a beneficiary who receives a traditional IRA as an inheritance. The Stretch IRA Strategy allows a beneficiary to minimize income taxes and maximize total income benefits from the inherited IRA by "stretching" the income distributions from the inherited IRA over the entire life of the beneficiary who inherits the IRA. So instead of taking a lump sum distribution of the inherited IRA, and getting killed with a huge income tax bill on the lump sum, the beneficiary can spread the income taxes out over many, many years.

There are multiple benefits this strategy accomplishes. The first is transferring monies from one generation to another in a more efficient manner. Another big benefit is the continuation of tax-deferral. This will allow the monies in the inherited IRA to continue to grow over time but only have to pay taxes on the monies as they are withdrawn. This allows beneficiaries to control their tax liability somewhat – based on that year's total income. The third benefit is that the beneficiary can treat the inherited IRA in a way that places the inherited IRA as a retirement vehicle for the beneficiary.

Each year the beneficiary will be required to take out a minimum distribution of the inherited IRA. However, if for some reason the individual needs to take a larger distribution for income or an emergency, they can take out as much as they want in any given year. By giving the individual the control and flexibility within the strategy, it helps to remove the worry associated with the "what ifs" of life and retirement.

MULTI-GENERATIONAL STRETCH OR LEGACY IRA STRATEGY CASE STUDY.

This case study is based on an assumed hypothetical 4%, non-guaranteed, illustrated rate of return.

Jean is 62 years old, and retiring from teaching after 40 years. She has a nice pension and a small inheritance from her husband Ben, who passed away three years ago. She also has $500,000 that she has saved in her 401(k). After crunching the numbers with her accountant, she's comfortable that she'll be able to afford the retirement lifestyle she wants and still let her travel from time to time using her pension, the inheritance, and her Social Security benefit. Since she feels she doesn't need to rely on the $500,000 she has in her 401(k), she decides to purchase a fixed index annuity with an income rider. Everything is working out as she plans and since she has not needed to withdraw any money from the fixed index annuity, so at age 70 ½ she begins taking RMD's (required minimum distributions) and continues to receive them until she is 79 when she passes away. During her lifetime, assuming a conservative 4% annual earnings rate, based on the RMD table used by the IRS, she has received a total payout of $ 278,392.

When Jean passes, her son inherits the IRA which has been growing and has a balance of $684,569. Her son Jackson, age 55, continues to receive the RMD payments of the inherited IRA until he passes at age 83. Jackson will receive a $1,046,648 during his lifetime, and upon his death, the remaining monies in the IRA will be passed on to his son Parker.

When his son Parker receives the monies left in the policy as the sole beneficiary, he receives $348,620 that he can use to create a lifetime payout for him, or he can continue the strategy of only taking the RMD payouts and still be able to pass monies on to his heirs.

So, we can see that by using the stretch IRA strategy, the $500,000 that Jean opened the annuity with has created payouts for herself and her son Jackson of $ 1,325,040 and given her grandson Parker $348,620 before he starts earning any interest on the monies. Three generations are able to enjoy the benefits of Jean's decision.

ACCUMULATION STRATEGY – NO INCOME NEEDED.

As we've seen from the previous examples a fixed index annuity with an income rider allows us to create an income to protect ourselves and also our families. But, what if we just have money in the bank or in the market? We don't need to create an income, yet we want to get money out of the bank or our money market account to avoid falling behind due to inflation or market risk. There is a strategy we can use to help in legacy planning in this case, as well using an accumulation product without the income rider as we've seen earlier.

Let's look at Gary, a supervisor for a local utility company, and Martha, an administrative assistant. Gary has a great pension that will take care of them during retirement and allow them to continue to travel across the country in their RV. After settling into retirement for five years, they've found that they have plenty of money each month and are not worried about running out of money in the future. They are having a great time traveling, spending time with friends and family, and feel they will enjoy the retirement they've worked so hard for – just using Gary's pension.

However, they do have $150,000 in the in the market with a money management firm. Over the years they've watched the account value rise and fall with the market. The last time the market dropped they lost over $46,000, and it took years for them to get even. They want to leave as much as they can to their children and grandchildren, and they have concerns. What if the markets drop between now and when they pass? How long will it take for them to get even again? They've decided they're no longer comfortable with this and want to protect these monies.

But, they do have a small nagging question that concerns them. What if? What if something big happens and they do need to access this account. Can they protect the monies and have access to them if they have an emergency? After voicing this concern to their advisor, they learn that with most accounts, they can access the account by withdrawing a set percentage each year if they need additional monies to help them out in a jam.

They know they'll never need to create an income since Gary already has a pension. So, after some research, they select a fixed index annuity without an income rider to make sure that future generations will inherit at least the amount of money they placed in the account from the first day. An accumulation product has a number of advantages and gives Gary and Martha something they want the most, flexibility.

Just like you, they want the flexibility to control their monies. This gives them the ability to specify how their hard-earned monies are passed on upon their death. They decide who the beneficiaries are and what percentage each beneficiary is entitled to. They can also adjust the beneficiaries as the family grows and changes in the future. Most importantly, they guarantee the beneficiaries will receive at least what is in the account today, even if the stock market crashes.

In the examples we just looked at, Mike and Leslie used the fixed indexed annuity with an income rider to create a lifetime payout. Jean used the income rider to stretch the length of time tax-deferred monies can last to provide for future generations. Gary and Martha selected a product without the income rider to their principle and hedge against inflation and market risk.

In each case, just like you, they have different needs, wants and dreams for their future. They were all able to accomplish the goals of protecting their assets against loss, have the ability to receive an acceptable rate of return, and a high amount of income that is guaranteed to last for as long as they live, even if past age 100. The one thing they all have in common with one another is making sure they can pass any remaining assets to their loved ones.

Are you looking for something to protect yourself, your spouse, and your family? Do you want to make sure that you can help future generations take advantage of any money left after you pass?

Again, one of the only, if not the only, financial instrument that can do these things is a fixed index annuity.

About Paul

As the President and Owner of Ascendant Wealth Strategies, Inc., Paul Seal knows a thing or two about helping his clients meet their financial needs. His 15-year career in the financial services industry began as a passion for helping people pursue their goals, and he takes pride in delivering personalized attention that is often lost in larger firms.

Ultimately, Paul's goal is to ensure that each one of his clients achieves the peace of mind that only comes with financial preparedness, and he is grateful for the opportunity to guide his clients and their families towards that stability.

Paul spends time traveling with his wife and two sons. He is also involved with his local church, his son's Little League teams, and their Cub Scout Pack. He's a big supporter of the Boy Scouts of America, having obtained his Eagle Scout Award in 1983. He firmly believes that the values of these organizations are instrumental to financial planning: One should always be prepared, be a great team mate, and ready to serve the community!!

CHAPTER 50

AN INCOME STREAM YOU CAN'T OUTLIVE

THE HOLY GRAIL OF RETIREMENT PLANNING

BY ROBERT M. RYERSON, CFP™, CLTC™

A tale of three very different investors, with the very same problem…and the safe and sound solution for all of them.

Every retiree and pre-retiree worries that they could run out of money during retirement. Most people literally fear there could be a day in their future when their income stops, and they end up poor. During my 35 years as a financial planner, the most common and pressing questions clients ask me are:

- How can I retire and stay retired?
- How can I guarantee I will avoid running out of money during retirement?

People know there are many factors that can cause their assets to run out and their income to stop before they die, such as large stock market losses or a chronic illness—they just don't know how to protect themselves against such catastrophic events. The good news is that there are safe and solid solutions available today for all of these risks and potential problems.

Do you have these same types of fears and worries? Probably so. Do you ask the same Big Retirement Questions? Probably so. To help you understand how you can possibly be helped in terms of eliminating your fears and worries about running out of money, we will discuss three different hypothetical situations in which powerful solutions were formulated to help people who did not have success using traditional investments and income planning. The solutions in these case studies are based on using 'the secret ingredient' of Momma's Secret Recipe For Retirement Success: Fixed Index Annuities with income riders.

AGNES AND HOWARD – THEY HAVE THE CD BLUES.

The first story is about Agnes and Howard, who are in their mid-seventies, and who have been very conservative "certificate of deposit and bank accounts only" investors for the past 35 years. They had managed to accumulate about $600,000 in various bank accounts and had a CD portfolio of around $550,000 that had served them well, in terms of income, for many years. That is until the Federal Reserved instituted their "Zero Interest Rate Policy" (ZIRP) in 2009, after the crisis of 2008.

By 2011, they realized they were in trouble. They had previously counted on the interest on their CDs or other bank account holdings for income, and when interest rates were in the 5-7% range for these types of holdings, they could count on perhaps $2,500-3,500 per month of reliable income coming in. They assumed that they could count on this income from the bank, with these guaranteed principal vehicles, for as long as they lived.

However, when interest rates collapsed to near zero after the 2008 crisis and stayed there, they began to realize that not only were they losing the long-term battle against rising costs of living if their CD rates didn't keep increasing, they were experiencing a huge drop in their ongoing interest income streams. Their $550,000 "safe money" CD portfolio with an average yield of 5% had been producing a much needed $27,500 of interest for them every year, or about $2,292 per month. But now that same portfolio of CD's, with the average yield now around 1%, produced only $5,500 per year of interest, which was $458 per month. Where were they going to get the missing $22,000 per year, or $1,834 per month, of income that they needed? Savings accounts and checking accounts were even worse choices, by the way, with yields closer to 0.10%.

Agnes and Howard wanted three (3) main things:

1. A higher level of monthly income—at least the $2,292 to which they were accustomed.
2. Safety of principal against all stock or bond market losses.
3. A guarantee that the $2,292 of monthly income would be paid for as long as they both lived.

Agnes and Howard realized that the bank, where "their money is safe in that brick building on the corner," no longer provided them with the income they needed to survive—interest rates were just too low. The simple solution for Agnes and Howard was to purchase fixed index annuities with income riders for $550,000. With this plan, their $550,000 was guaranteed against all stock market losses, and they would receive the needed $2,292 per month, guaranteed for as long as they both lived.

DOLORES – DIVIDENDS GOING, GOING, GONE!

The second case study is about Dolores, a single 65-year-old middle management professional who recently retired from IBM. Dolores had concerns about the great longevity in her family, and her desire to not become a burden to family members if she developed a chronic illness or cognitive impairment in her old age. She had managed to accumulate just over $1,000,000 in IBM stock over her long career there, and was pleased to consider the roughly $48,000 per year in cash dividends a safe and reliable supplement to her other retirement income.

The problem was that stock dividends are never guaranteed, and that IBM itself was a prime example of what could happen to dividend income. She had almost forgotten about the long rough-patch IBM had years ago, because she was busy at work, and not paying too much attention to the dividend aspect of the shares at that time.

In March of 1993, IBM made a huge 55% cut to their dividend, and it took 13 years for that dividend to get back to the 1993 level! But IBM was not alone in cutting dividends. There was a 43% cut that Eastman Kodak made in 2003, and a full elimination of the dividend that Citigroup shareholders suffered in the '08 crisis, and more recently a 50% cut that GE made on 11/13/17. The dividend cuts that Citigroup, GM, Wachovia Bank, Kodak, and a host of others made were never restored, and often were a precursor to further trouble.

With the aging of the population, and with the current bull market now over ten years old without experiencing any serious corrections, it is likely that more people with very concentrated risk in one stock will come to be reminded that dividends do not provide income that you can depend on for as long as you live. In Dolores's case, she was able to create $48,000 of guaranteed lifetime income using fixed index annuities with income riders. She also received chronic illness benefit riders within those contracts.

JOE AND SUSIE – REAL ESTATE BARONS?

The third case study is about Joe and Susie, in their late 50s, who were big believers in, and far more comfortable with, rental real estate than they were with stocks, bonds, and mutual funds. While real estate investing is certainly another logical way to build wealth and future income for retirement, it is also not without risks. In addition to the risk of the tenants doing damage to the property, there is also the risk of the tenants not paying the rent, and defaulting on the lease, as well as decreasing property values, and higher than expected taxes and maintenance costs.

Evicting people can be difficult, expensive, time-consuming and frustrating. Joe and Susie had been through damaged apartments and eviction battles previously, but more recently, they even had a tenant go to jail for a couple of years, and they had to fight the court to regain access to their own property while receiving no rental income during the whole process.

So, needless to say, they realized they needed to make some changes and do some different planning as they headed toward retirement. After doing some soul-searching, they realized they were tired of being landlords, admitted that their total returns were not what they had expected, and wanted a steady income that they didn't have to work so hard to earn.

Joe and Susie sold one of their real estate properties, from which they were receiving $40,000 in net-after-expenses annual income, and netted

$1,000,000 from the sale. They used these funds to purchase fixed index annuities which, at age 62, would provide them with over $75,000 in annual income, guaranteed for as long as they both lived. So think about that – they nearly doubled their income, and never had to deal with tenant issues again!

IN SUMMARY

As retirement income planners, we very often need to point out to our clients that none of the traditional investment vehicles or portfolios that we used in our three (3) hypothetical case studies can actually create income streams that can be counted on for as long as they live—not stocks… not bonds… not CDs… not real estate… not options and not trading systems either.

In all these circumstances, one of the most powerful solutions to guarantee principal against all stock and bond market losses, and just as importantly provide lifetime income guarantees, is a fixed index annuity with an income rider. If the right contracts are chosen, they may even have the opportunity for increased income on an annual basis.

We tell our clients that there are at least ten compelling reasons to put some of their more serious money—money needed to produce guaranteed retirement income for life—into a fixed income annuity with an income rider.

Ten Great Reasons to Use a FIXED INDEX ANNUITY (FIA) to Create an **Income for Life** in Retirement

1. No other financial product or vehicle can do it—give you a guaranteed income stream as long as you live—as a fixed index annuity with an income rider does. As many Americans are already aware, we have a pension crisis in the country, and the Trustees of the Social Security system warn us every spring about the shortfalls and cuts that are coming to that program. We think it is smart, therefore, for all Americans (especially those without a traditional pension coming to them in retirement), to build a solid guaranteed income stream for themselves, which they can layer on top of any Social Security that they receive.

2. Longevity risk (the risk of living too long and running out of money)—This is the major concern for retirees in most of the retirement surveys taken, and is successfully eliminated with the use of one or more fixed index annuities with an income rider. In fact, if multiple contracts are used, the retirees can "turn on the tap" every few years on another contract, to give themselves an income boost or inflation adjustment.

3. Low or no annual costs—Unlike their very expensive cousins, the variable annuities, fixed index annuities with an income rider typically have an average 1% annual total cost, meaning they are cheaper than most mutual funds and virtually all managed money programs—with no market risk to boot! By contrast, I have seen the typical variable annuity contract carry total fees in the 3% to 5% per year range. Every fixed index annuity with an income rider does have a surrender schedule which addresses early withdrawals, as do the variable annuities.[*]

4. Interest rate risk—Bond portfolios carry default and reinvestment risk; that is, the risk that interest rates, and hence, income streams, will be lower when a bond matures, and the funds need to be reinvested in a new bond. Fixed index annuities with income riders, however, guarantee that the income will never decline, regardless of the interest rate environment. There is also no default risk borne by the owner of a fixed index annuity with an income rider.

5. The risk of inflation can be successfully addressed, at least partially, by a fixed index annuity with an income rider that includes the opportunity for an increasing income stream for a period of years, or for as long as the fixed index annuity with an income rider owner lives. Over time, these increases may be substantial, and can, therefore, help retirees address cost of living increases.

6. In certain states, some newer fixed index annuities with an income rider offer a "Chronic Illness" benefit rider, under which income payments are increased significantly, if you cannot perform two

---

[*] Please note that if you surrender or withdraw more than the "free withdrawal amount" from an FIA in the early years of the contract, you may be subject to an early withdrawal penalty, which may result in your receiving less than your full principal balance.

of the six Activities of Daily Living, and other conditions are met. There is usually little to no cost for these riders, so it may be worth seeking them out if you have not planned to address long-term healthcare risks yet. While these riders are not a substitute for a long-term care insurance policy, they can provide extra funds for chronic illness expenses, with no underwriting involved.

7. Virtually all fixed index annuities with an income rider come with a guaranteed death benefit feature. Unlike the circumstance in which a mutual fund or stock owner dies in the midst of a stock market crash or prolonged bad stock market cycle, the fixed index annuity with an income rider owner is assured of always leaving their original invested capital and any accrued growth (reduced by withdrawals) to their loved ones in any and every type of market or economic environment.

8. If structured properly, fixed index annuities with an income rider can help retirees control or even reduce tax liabilities in retirement. In particular, the conversion of the fixed index annuity with an income rider to ROTH IRA status, if purchased in an IRA account, will make the pension-like stream of income from the fixed index annuity tax-free for as long as the owner lives, and will insulate that income stream from any tax increases that may come down the road.

9. Unlike traditional stock, bond, and mutual fund portfolios, which are subject to market risk every day, fixed index annuities with an income rider offer a guarantee of principal at all times* and in all types of economic or market environments. Additionally, in general, any earnings or growth that has been experienced in the fixed index annuity with an income rider contract is also guaranteed never to go backward. As a result, the contract owner can have peace of mind that his or her retirement nest egg held in the fixed index annuity with an income rider will always be there, and can only increase in value.

10. Unlike traditional pensions that are received from employers, a fixed index annuity with an income rider offers the same monthly income, like a pension, which is guaranteed for life, but allows the contract owner to maintain control over the underlying capital base,

even after beginning the income stream, and as long as there is money left in the contract. While fixed index annuities with income riders are intended to be long-term vehicles, they do not have to be a permanent decision. While the primary objective is lifetime income, it is a great benefit to have the flexibility of being able to move your capital elsewhere at all times, if the situation warrants.

About Robert

Robert M. Ryerson, CFP™, CITRMS™, CLTC™ is the chief economist and lead planner at New Century Planning in New Jersey.

Robert (Bob) Ryerson entered the financial industry in 1984 as a broker and earned his Certified Financial Planner designation (CFP) in 1991. This prestigious designation allows Robert to assist in a variety of areas such as financial, estate, insurance and retirement income planning, to name a few. Over time, as he witnessed the growth of the nationwide identity theft epidemic, he was encouraged to do more research into the subject and became a Certified Identity heft Risk Management Specialist (CITRMS) in 2014. This designation and knowledge help him implement Identity Theft protection strategies in his clients' overall financial plans. His ongoing research in this field led him to write the book, *What's The Deal With Identity Theft? A Plain English Look at our Fastest Growing Crime* in 2016.

Robert also began to see the devastating effects that unplanned healthcare costs can have on retirees. His concern grew about the possibility of his clients accidentally disinheriting their loved ones as a result of the costs of chronic illness and long-term care needs. In view of his lifelong mission of educating others, he co-authored the 2013 book, *What You Don't Know About Retirement Will Hurt You*, which focuses specifically on addressing healthcare in retirement.

Bob is passionate about helping guide people to a secure and tax-efficient retirement. His study of the baby boomer demographic trends, in concert with the nation's poor fiscal condition, has led him to concentrate on the issue of longevity risks and the need for reliable and sustainable income streams for retirees. He is enthusiastic about walking people through the various concepts, strategies and steps that will improve their overall position in terms of safety, tax-efficient lifetime income and meeting legacy desires.

Bob is an experienced estate administrator and advises clients on various aspects of estate and legacy planning, with a focus on asset preservation and distribution planning. He most recently earned his "Certified in Long-Term Care" (CLTC) designation in January of 2019.

In his free time, Bob enjoys traveling, reading, teaching, and spending time with his wife, Lisa, and four daughters, Christine, Maggie, Nicole, and Genevieve.

CHAPTER 51

INFLATION
MAY COME BACK
WITH A VENGEANCE

BY DAVID REYES

*Inflation is as violent as a mugger, as frightening as an armed robber
and as deadly as a hit man.*
~ Ronald Reagan

Myth: INCOME ALWAYS STAYS FLAT IN AN ANNUITY, IT NEVER INCREASES.

In 1980 when Ronald Regan became president, he inherited an economy with an inflation rate of over 13%. From 1971 to 1981 the average inflation rate per year was nearly 7.5%. Imagine living in those times today. This would mean the cost of your goods and services would double in a decade. Even assuming an inflation rate of just 3.5% per year if you retired at age 60, you would need to double your income by age 80.

Inflation erodes your purchasing power. A cost-of-living adjustment must be included in your retirement budget just to maintain your current standard of living. The question is, what can you do to help ensure that your income has a chance to keep up with inflation?

You have been told that investing in the stock market is a way to hedge against inflation. As your investments go up, they are worth more and should help with inflation. Well, that is until your portfolio gets cut in half, just like during the Technology Bubble from 2000 through 2002 and during the Financial Crisis from 2007 through 2009, when the market was down over -50% each time.

It doesn't mean that you should not own equities, it means you can't be "naked in the market" because do you really want your retirement income invested in anything that could crash? The safest way to protect your retirement income from inflation and increase your income during retirement is what I call "The Perfect Annuity."

First, you have to create a plan that provides you dependable income, and one that is guaranteed to be paid to you for as long as you live. Then secondly, you need to build-in opportunities for your income to increase.

How do you like the sound of receiving income guaranteed for as long as you live? Even if you live past age 100, even if the stock market crashes multiple times, you also have an opportunity to receive increases to your guaranteed lifetime income in the future! Moreover, as soon as you receive an income increase, it becomes your new guaranteed lifetime income for the rest of your life? Wouldn't that be nice? It's important to understand your income can be established for a single life or for a joint life if you are married.

There are different options available for potential income increases we use in planning cases:

I. Build in a guaranteed income increase that would happen at a specific time in the future. This is straight-forward and moderately easy to do with a little planning. The goal is to establish an income amount that currently meets the needs of the retiree or pre-retiree, and also establish a separate part of the plan that will provide you with additional income at a specific point in the future, and that will last for a specific time period or for your life.

II. Build an automatic income increase that would start immediately. This also is straight-forward and will require establishing a lower amount of initial income so that income is guaranteed to increase every year by a certain percentage.

III. Build in the opportunity for income increases in the future based on positive Index Credits and market performance from a fixed index annuity with an income rider. This requires no more work and can provide the opportunity for potential significant income increases in the future. We will explain this option in more detail in this chapter.

Let's use a hypothetical example to help explain this powerful combination:

- Rick and Kristen are retired and are both age 60.
- They want to put $500,000 of their $1,000,000 IRA into a Fixed Indexed Annuity plan that will provide Joint Guaranteed Lifetime Income.
- Their joint payments are $20,000 per year.
- They want the option for income increases based on Index Credit performance.
- ***They have an opportunity for their payments to increase by as much as 3% per year or more over time.***

The plan is set up to guarantee Rick and Kristen will receive $20,000 per year for as long as they live. If Rick passes away, Kristen will continue to receive the $20,000 of income until she passes away. If Kristen passes away first, Rick will continue to receive the $20,000 of income until he passes away. Any money left in their fixed index annuity with the income rider after they both pass away will be paid to their named beneficiaries.

Now here's the fun part, in the years they receive positive index crediting on their fixed index annuity with the income rider, they will also receive an increase to the guaranteed lifetime income payments. So once they receive an income increase, the increased income amount can never go below that new higher income amount, even if the stock market crashes in the future!

So, they start at a minimum of $20,000 of annual Guaranteed Lifetime Income, and the $20,000 is the lowest amount of income they will ever receive for as long as they both live. However, if for example, their income increased to $21,000, the $21,000 becomes the new annual Guaranteed Lifetime Income, and the $21,000 is now the lowest amount of income they will ever receive for as long as they both live.

Now let's expand our hypothetical example and analyze what would have happened with their plan and the annual payments they would have received based on the Index Credits from 1999 through 2013. It's important to understand that this is hypothetical data, there is no guarantee the stock market will increase, and no guarantee you would receive any raises at all.

In this specific illustration, we have limited the index crediting and their income payment increase to 3% per year (note that in other cases, the increase could have been higher or lower). This means when the S & P 500 Index increases, their payment will increase by up to a maximum of .3% a year. When the S & P 500 Index goes down, their annual payment will stay at the most recent and highest income level until there is another payment increase.

Through 2013 we have constructed the following table to show the data we will use in our summary graph. The table includes data from 1999 for the S & P 500 Index returns as well as the Guaranteed Lifetime Payments with increases as they occurred:

Year	Annual S&P 500 Index Increase	Annual Lifetime Payment Increase: Max = 3% Per Year	Annual Guaranteed Lifetime Income With Increases
1999	19.53%	3.00%	$20,000
2000	-10.14%	0.00%	$20,600
2001	-13.04%	0.00%	$20,600
2002	-23.37%	0.00%	$20,600
2003	26.38%	3.00%	$20,600
2004	8.99%	3.00%	$21,218
2005	3.00%	3.00%	$21,855
2006	13.62%	3.00%	$22,510
2007	3.53%	3.00%	$23,185
2008	-38.49%	3.00%	$23,881
2009	23.45%	3.00%	$24,597
2010	12.78%	3.00%	$25,335
2011	0.00%	0.00%	$26,095
2012	13.41%	3.00%	$26,095
2013	29.60%	3.00%	$26,878

This hypothetical analysis shows in 1999 that the annual Guaranteed Lifetime Income started at $20,000. The S & P 500 Index had a great year in 1999 and went up by +19.53%. But the annual payment increase was limited to just 3%. So, for the year 2000, the new increased Guaranteed Lifetime Income went up to $20,600. This $20,600 is the new Guaranteed Lifetime Income and can never go down.

In 2000 the S&P 500 Index lost -10.14% so there was no payment increase received. For the year 2001, the $20,600 Guaranteed Lifetime Income payment is locked-in, even though the S&P 500 Index lost -10.14%.

In 2001, the S&P 500 Index had a second (2nd) consecutive loss, this time of -13.04% so there was no payment increase received. For the year 2002, the $20,600 Guaranteed Lifetime Income payment is locked-in, even though the S&P 500 Index lost -13.04%.

In 2002, the S&P 500 Index had a third (3rd) consecutive loss, this time of -23.37%, so there was no payment increase received. For the year 2003, the $20,600 Guaranteed Lifetime Income payment is locked-in, even though the S&P 500 Index lost -23.37%.

In 2003, the S&P 500 Index had a great year and went up by +26.38%. However, the annual payment increase was limited to just 3%. So, for the year 2004, the new increased Guaranteed Lifetime Income went up to $21,218. This $21,218 is the new Guaranteed Lifetime Income and can never go down.

In 2004, the S & P 500 went up by +8.99%. But the annual payment increase was limited to just 3%. So, for the year 2005, the new increased Guaranteed Lifetime Income went up to $21,855. This $21,855 is the new Guaranteed Lifetime Income and can never go down.

In 2005, the S&P 500 went up by +3.00%. The annual payment increase was also 3%. So, for the year 2006, the new increased Guaranteed Lifetime Income went up to $22,510. This $22,510 is the new Guaranteed Lifetime Income and can never go down.

In 2006, the S&P 500 went up by +13.62%. But the annual payment increase was limited to just 3%. So, for the year 2007, the new increased

Guaranteed Lifetime Income went up to $23,185. This $23,185 is the new Guaranteed Lifetime Income and can never go down.

In 2007, the S&P 500 went up by +3.53%. But the annual payment increase was limited to just 3%. So, for the year 2008, the new increased Guaranteed Lifetime Income went up to $23,881. This $23,881 is the new Guaranteed Lifetime Income and can never go down.

In 2008, the S & P 500 Index suffered a loss of -38.49% so there was no payment increase received. For the year 2009, the $23,881 Guaranteed Lifetime Income payment was locked-in even though the S&P 500Index lost -38.49%.

In 2009, the S&P 500 went up by +23.45%. But the annual payment increase was limited to just 3%. So, for the year 2010, the new increased Guaranteed Lifetime Income went up to $24,597. This $24,597 is the new Guaranteed Lifetime Income and can never go down.

In 2010, the S&P 500 went up by +12.78%. But the annual payment increase was limited to just 3%. So, for the year 2011, the new increased Guaranteed Lifetime Income went up to $25,335. This $25,335 is the new Guaranteed Lifetime Income and can never go down.

In 2011, the S&P 500 was flat at 0.00%. The annual payment increase was also 0%. So, for the year 2012, the Guaranteed Lifetime Income stayed flat at $25,335. This $25,335 is the Guaranteed Lifetime Income and can never go down.

In 2012, the S&P 500 went up by +13.41%. But the annual payment increase was limited to just 3%. So, for the year 2013, the new increased Guaranteed Lifetime Income went up to $26,095. This $26,095 is the new Guaranteed Lifetime Income and can never go down.

In 2013, the S&P 500 went up by +29.60%. But the annual payment increase was limited to just 3%. So, for the year 2014, the new increased Guaranteed Lifetime Income went up to $26,878. This $26,878 is the new Guaranteed Lifetime Income and can never go down.

In 1999, the Guaranteed Lifetime Income payments started at $20,000 and by 2014, and after 15 years of S&P 500 Index volatility, the

Guaranteed Lifetime Income payments increased to $26,878.

We then took this data and created a graph line of the Annual Guaranteed Lifetime Income that we superimposed on top of what the S&P 500 Index graph would have looked like. The following graph is not to scale but does teach the concept of increasing payments when the market is up, and guaranteed level payments when the market is down or flat.

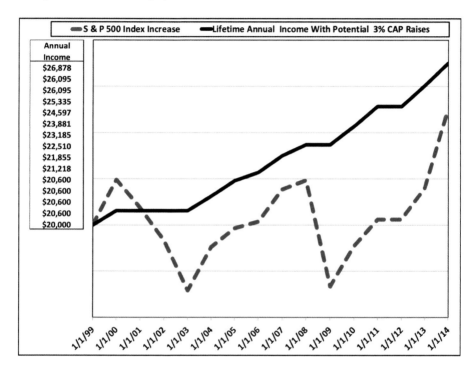

The goal you should have as a retiree is to establish Guaranteed Lifetime Income, a plan that works like a Private Pension. In this chapter, we showed how you might not only be able to establish Guaranteed Lifetime Income, but also create the opportunity for you to have increasing income in the future.

About David

During his first year as an advisor, David's grandfather Kermit passed away after fighting dementia for over five years. The cost of his long-term care completely bankrupted his estate, teaching David a valuable lesson on the importance of proper planning and the protection of assets. He promised that anyone who he was able to help, clients, family or friends, would never have to go through this devastating financial and emotional experience.

David Reyes has been an advisor for over 20 years and is the founder of Reyes Financial Architecture, a Registered Investment Advisory Firm whose primary goal is to support, assist and advise clients in the planning of their retirement. Reyes Financial Architecture specializes in retirement planning, retirement income planning, social security and portfolio risk management strategies. Working in collaboration with CPA's, attorneys and other advisors, David ensures that all planning is not only implemented but also integrated. This collaborative team approach seeks to ensure the highest probability of success.

David Reyes is a distinguished graduate from UCLA's Personal Financial Planning program and a graduate of Wharton Business School's Retirement Income Planning Certification program. David also holds multiple licenses in the financial, real estate and insurance fields and has proudly been named 2015 Advisor of the Year by the National Social Security Advisor Association (NSSA) for his advocacy to educate retirees on maximizing their retirement income.

David is featured in many magazines and publications such as *Kiplinger Personal Finance Magazine* and *Boomer Market Advisor* and is co-author of five books on retirement, retirement income planning and estate planning. His latest book written with bestselling author Jack Canfield is titled, *Momma's Secret Recipe for Retirement Success.*

David also advises and conducts educational workshops for corporations, professional and public groups including CPA's and attorneys on retirement, tax, estate planning and asset protection. He is also the host of "The Retirement Architect Radio" heard every Saturday on AM 1210 KPRZ and AM 1170 KCBQ.

David and Julie have been blessed with three wonderful children. David's hobbies include tennis, church fellowship and spending time with his family.

CHAPTER 52

STOCK MARKET RETURNS SOUND SEXY, BUT ARE THEY REALLY??

BY JOSH GENTRY

Let's talk about the Stock Market. Ask yourself, would you like to have stock market returns for the rest of your life? Since 1900 the Stock Market has averaged a 10% return. That is a strong return! That is also why financial advisors encourage people to start investing early so that they can capitalize on these great stock market returns and receive compound interest over time. We are currently enjoying another bull market, and most people are pleased with the returns they are getting in their 401(k)'s. In a perfect world, we would be getting these types of returns leading right up to retirement, through retirement, and up to the day we take our last breath. One problem with this idea is we do not live in a perfect world. The other problem is that times have changed, dramatically. Since 1999, assuming the S&P 500 Index closes on December 31, 2018, exactly where it ended today October 11, 2018, which was at 2,728 points, for the last 20 years the S&P 500 Index would have increased by only 3.15% per year. Quite a difference from 10%!

There is nothing that guarantees that you will only receive 100% of the upside of the market. There is another side to this story. The stock market also goes down. Not only does the stock market go down, but it goes down faster than it goes up. You should remember reading earlier in the book that if you lose -50% in a stock market crash like what happened during the Technology Bubble between 2000 through 2002, and the

Financial Crisis between 2007 through 2009, you needed a +100% gain just to recover your losses. A financial advisor once told me that the stock market takes the stairs up and the elevator down. This is not as concerning for young adults since they have time to recover from market crashes. For older folks on the other hand, this creates a problem. . . a major problem. The average person works 90,000 hours before retiring. Do you think it is wise for someone who has worked 90,000 hours to have all his or her money in the stock market? Don't forget, the market takes the elevator down, and it takes the stairs back up. No one has a crystal ball giving us a heads up when the elevator is going to go to the basement.

It's unfortunate that there are people who are approaching retirement and are still 100% invested in the market. They are literally sitting on a ticking time bomb. There are no take-backs, no do-overs and no "mulligans" for you golfers, after the market crashes. I remember seeing a CNN article that explained the effects of the 2008 crash. In 2009 there was a dramatic increase in suicide cases that were directly tied to the stress of the market meltdown. Do not leave yourself exposed when there are other options available to help mitigate the risk that the market carries. In my opinion, there just isn't enough awareness in the public about the risk of the Stock Market and that there are other solutions available to mitigate that risk and create a smooth landing into retirement.

A general rule of thumb in the financial industry is the "Rule of 100". The Rule of 100 means that if you take the number 100 and subtract your age, the number you get represents the percentage of your investments that should be invested in the stock market. So, if you are 65 years old and you have $100,000, then you should have $35,000 in the stock market while $65,000 should be invested in instruments that provide safety and downside protection. Keep in mind that the rule of 100 is not a perfect science, but it will give you an idea of where you should be and if you are too heavily invested in risky or safe investments.

The most important advice that I can give anyone about their finances is to find a holistic advisor that is a fiduciary and offers full financial planning. A "fiduciary" by law has to provide you advice that is in your best interests. The financial world is confusing, and there are a lot of advisors who do not have your best interest in mind. And there are many advisors that may have your best interest in mind but cannot possibly act in your best interest because they're not licensed to do so. A lot of advisors will tell you to "ride it out" in the stock market when in reality, you should be working with a holistic advisor on creating a well-thought-out plan that protects you and your family from the many pitfalls that exist.

I mentioned the Rule of 100, but if you are working with the right financial professional you will have a much more in depth discussion about what your risk tolerance is, and your investments will be perfectly customized to your specific needs. I hope that I am not coming off as someone who does not like the market, because if I am, that is just not accurate. I love the market and the long-term gains that can be captured from investing in it. It is important though to keep everything in perspective and see the market as it is, a world that has large upside potential…and also large downside potential. There are several tools that you'll need to use when it comes to your finances. It may be helpful to look at your advisor as a financial architect who will use several tools to help put together a strong financial house for you and your family.

Think of your financial life as a hike up Mount Everest. Every serious climber wants to make it to the summit of Mount Everest as it is the world's highest mountain, and it's the ultimate challenge for a mountaineer. Think of climbing up the mountain as Stage One of Retirement Planning which you learned previously is what is called "Asset Accumulation." In our financial life, retirement is the summit which can also be difficult to climb and requires a lot of effort and wisdom. Most of the time, hikers will train more for the journey up the mountain than they do for the journey back down. Most people will focus on the rate of return that they can get from investing in the stock market to grow or accumulate their assets, but lack a plan for when they reach the summit of retirement and have no idea how to protect their assets against large losses and create income that is guaranteed to last for as long as they live.

Around 290 hikers have died climbing Everest, and most of those deaths occurred while descending the mountain. Going down the mountain is much different to going up the mountain. Going down the mountain requires using different muscle groups, different strategies, and a whole new perspective. Think of the journey down the mountain as Stage Two of Retirement Planning which you learned previously is what is called "Asset Preservation and Income Distribution." Stock market returns are a great way to get up the mountain in your financial life, but when nearing retirement, it is important to start making the pivot to a new perspective and a new strategy for the descent down. It is critical that you care as much, if not more, about planning for the climb down than you did for the climb up or you'll find yourself in a regrettable situation. If you fail to plan, you are planning to fail. The part of your life that is leading up to retirement is called Stage One of Retirement Planning – *Asset Accumulation.*

You are accumulating as many assets as you can so that you can build a retirement nest egg. It's not as scary to take on the risk of the stock market because time is on your side, and you will be able to ride out the market so that hopefully you can capture high rates of return over the long-term. The part of your life that starts at retirement is called Stage Two of Retirement Planning – *Asset Preservation and Income Distribution.* It is entirely different from the accumulation phase. Stage Two is no longer about getting the highest rate of return. It is about using what you have accumulated and efficiently orchestrating those funds in a way that'll ensure that you never run out of money. By the way, outliving their money during retirement is the #1 concern of retirees today. If you have a good financial advisor, the stock market can drop 40% and your retirement plan and your income will remain intact. Simply put, the distribution phase is no longer about the return on your money as it is about the return of your money for as long as you live.

I mentioned earlier that there are several tools in the toolbox that are needed to put together a strong financial plan. I would like to focus on an effective tool that is primarily used during the distribution phase. It is the fixed index annuity with an income rider. This is a product created by insurance companies, many of which have been around since before the Great Depression, weathering several bull and bear markets. Fixed index annuities with income riders provide you the opportunity to enjoy the benefits of partial stock market returns, but you will also have complete downside protection. Of course, there needs to be a trade-off if you are receiving a benefit as great as downside protection.

The trade-off is that you will not get the full returns of the stock market and there is a time commitment. I'll give you an example. There is an A+ rated mutual company that offers a fixed index annuity that will currently give you a 50% participation rate on the S&P 500, meaning that you get half of the gains from the S&P 500 but none of the downside. If the S&P 500 returns 10% during the year, this specific index annuity would give you a rate of return of 5%. If the next year, the S&P 500 drops 10%, the fixed index annuity would give you a rate of return of 0%. This is just one example of how a fixed index annuity can help you hedge against the risk of the stock market. There is no free lunch in this world. If you want stock market returns, you must be willing to bear the risk that comes with the stock market. Not many people have the stomach for that nor is it responsible if you are currently in or near retirement.

Maybe it will be helpful to think of retirement as a game. The game is to remain retired and not to go back to work. Better yet, the game is to remain retired and to leave a legacy. I like to compare retirement to baseball, specifically the Kansas City Royals. The Royals won the world series in 2015, and they did it by being disciplined and not making mistakes. Other teams were flashier that year and had more home runs, a better overall batting average, and certainly better starting pitchers. But the Royals were the better team. Sometimes the Royals would hit home runs, but most of the time they were hitting singles and doubles with the occasional sacrifice bunt. A fixed index annuity with an income rider is like hitting mostly singles and doubles but every now and then you can expect a home run. If the market goes negative, just think of that as a walk, or base-on-balls, not exciting but you didn't lose anything, you got a 0% rate of return, and there's a good chance you'll bounce back in the following year.

If you haven't figured it out yet, a fixed index annuity with an income rider is sleep insurance. It's hard to put a price tag on peace of mind. I'll provide one more example of a fixed index annuity with an income rider that helps with leaving a legacy. Some plans will actually provide you a bonus to use for either your future income purposes or for your beneficiaries if you don't use your money. Using a hypothetical, non-guaranteed 3% annual earnings example, a premium deposit of $1,000,000 would be worth almost $2,000,000 for guaranteed lifetime income for you after ten years or for your beneficiaries to take out over a period of five (5) years or longer at any time after you pass away. And this type of plan can be obtained with no annual fee. The biggest negative is that you can't take your lump sum out for ten years, but you can take out up to 10% per year every year from year two (2) moving forward. Don't get caught in thinking that you must have stock market returns to be successful, especially during the distribution phase. It doesn't make any sense to fall in love with your investments. True financial wisdom is falling in love with results.

What it really boils down to is what your vision for retirement is. I don't know about you, but I don't want to be a retiree that is constantly checking the stock market and my accounts hoping that there hasn't been a correction resulting in a dip in my retirement funds. I don't want to have the thought lingering in the back of my mind that I could run out of money and I would be forced to go back to work someday. Every presidential election brings uncertainty to the markets and I don't want to be nervous about a potential stock market crash while I'm nearing or am in retirement. What I do envision is spending a lot of time with my wife, kids, and grandkids. I want to travel and gain new experiences. I want to be able to relax at family barbeques knowing that I have downside protection from the market and that no matter what happens, I have a plan that is using several tools ensuring that my financial house will stay intact. I hope that you too will find this peace of mind in retirement.

It's a good exercise to think through what you want your retirement to be. Don't leave your retirement exposed to the dangers of the stock market because you are being greedy in trying to chase down stock market returns. Ask your financial advisor about fixed index annuities with income riders and how they may very well fit into your overall retirement plan.

About Josh

Josh Gentry is recognized as one of the most successful annuity marketers in the country. He is deeply involved in the practices of his advisors daily; serving as a virtual extension of their office. While Josh is a product specialist, he spends the bulk of his time working with his advisors to create the most effective marketing platform possible based on their resources and needs. He is consistently taking complex sales and marketing ideas and turning them into easy-to-implement strategies for the best in the business.

Josh grew up in a small Kansas town with a population of 1,200. He graduated from Kansas State University in 2007. He jumped right into the IMO world, spending nine years with a local firm before joining FIG in 2017.

When he isn't helping some of the best in the business get even better, you can find Josh spending time with his wife, Whitney, and their identical twin daughters, Anniston and Reese. As a family, they are often walking around, swimming, or just relaxing in the comfort of their home with friends. Josh's other hobbies include golfing, hiking, playing softball, going to Kansas City Chiefs and Kansas State Wildcats football games, and traveling to new and exciting places.

CHAPTER 53

REDUCE YOUR STRESS BY STRESSING VOLATILITY

BY CHRISTOPHER KICHURCHAK

What are your greatest concerns when thinking about retirement? Will you have enough money to hit your lifetime goals? Will you be able to fund and transfer an estate to your beneficiaries or charity of choice? Will you have enough to survive all the financial ups and downs through the road of life?

If you think about the past year, have you taken a vacation? Before you left, I am sure you spent quite of bit of time planning your trip. What are your travel arrangements? Where are you staying? What is your budget for food and entertainment?

Think about how much time you spent planning that vacation. In fact, each year, do you spend more time planning your vacations or your retirement? Most people I have spoken with spend more time planning a vacation than planning their retirement. The reason: "It's more fun!"

In truth, the answer may not lie in the idea that planning a vacation is more fun than planning a retirement. The actual answer is more probable that planning a vacation is more easily quantified. Planning your expenses on a trip that lasts a week or two is fairly easy to calculate. By comparison, planning out your expenses for the next twenty to thirty years is a much greater challenge.

The first step in working toward a successful retirement is to develop a plan. Just like going on a vacation, you are going to need to know how much this very long retirement "vacation" will cost. You need to make sure you consider how much your lifestyle actually costs. That's right – you will need to do the "B" word as in "Budget." But creating a "Retirement Budget" is different from the type of budget you created when you were working. When you were working and saving for retirement you had to make a "tight budget,"…a "reduce the costs budget,"…a "cut the waistline budget." We call these kinds of budgets "Bad Budgets" simply because no one likes them! Your "Retirement Budget" is what we call a "Good Budget." It needs to include all the costs for you to live an extraordinary life throughout retirement.

You will need to add in the unexpected surprises that life throws your way as well; things like home repairs, increased medical expenses, changes to taxes, changes to social security, and even the possibility that those charity cases we finally got to move out (the kids) all of a sudden need a donation to bail them out of financial turmoil.

If we think about who we learned the strategies of how to plan for retirement from, many of us have taken notes from those closest to us, our parents. The problem, arguably, is that the techniques they used are not necessarily the most sophisticated methods available, and quite possibly are now outdated—what might have worked in their day does not necessarily work today. Your parents probably used the same sophisticated tool as every other person in their generation – none other than the yellow legal pad! To determine if they were able to retire, they grabbed that yellow pad and a pen. They used the pen to draw a line down the middle of the page. On the left side of that line, they wrote down all of their monthly expenses and on the right side all of their monthly income. If the right-hand side was higher than the left, they were set to retire.

The problem is that there are future calculation and cashflow issues. Those issues include inflation, market swings, and those other unexpected surprises I spoke of earlier. One of the biggest and easiest issues we can begin to plan for is inflation. Though it is not steady, the average rate of inflation for the last twenty years is around 2.7%. (**See link at end of chapter.*) To make things easier, we can use a constant inflation rate of 3% to factor in the amount of money we will need monthly to keep pace with increasing lifestyle costs.

A very basic goal-based financial plan can be used to see if you are on the right path. The illustration below will give you an idea if you have enough money saved for retirement. This is a cash flow graph that assumes a 6% rate of return and a 3% rate of inflation.

Years to live	$30,000	$40,000	$50,000	$75,000	$100,000
	Savings needed to retire, given a number of years to live and annual income desired (in today's dollars)				
30	$612,032	$816,043	$1,020,054	$1,530,081	$2,040,108
25	$542,882	$723,842	$904,803	$1,357,204	$1,809,606
20	$463,057	$617,409	$771,761	$1,157,642	$1,543,522
15	$370,910	$494,546	$618,183	$927,274	$1,236,365
10	$264,538	$352,717	$440,897	$661,345	$881,793
5	$141,746	$188,995	$236,244	$354,366	$472,488

[This illustration is not intended to serve as a prediction or guarantee of future values or results.]

Let's assume you spend $80,000 per year throughout retirement funding your lifestyle needs and taxes. To figure how much you will need to have saved, subtract out all of your guaranteed income such as Social Security and pensions. For example, if Social Security is paying you $30,000 per year, then you will only need $50,000 per year from your savings to fund your retirement. Next, assume the time you will live during your retirement. If you assume you will live twenty years in retirement while needing $50,000 per year from your savings, then you will need to have $771,761 saved the first day of retirement. Based on a 6% return and 3% inflation, you will survive and keep pace with all twenty years. Just don't live any longer!

But, what if you do live longer? What if the road of life throws some twists and turns your way? We need to plan for these what-if scenarios. The easiest scenario we can plan for is reality. In looking at the graph above, we are assuming a constant 6% rate of return. In reality, does the market actually provide constant returns? Of course not!

Let's run another scenario. Starting with $100,000, what would happen if we actually factored in market ups and downs.

Year	Scenario A (Average 6%)	Total	Scenario B (Average 6%)	Total
0	Start	$100,000	Start	$100,000
1	+6%	$106,000	+10%	$110,000
2	+6%	$112,360	+10%	$121,000
3	+6%	$119,101	+10%	$133,100
4	+6%	$126,247	-10%	$119,790
5	+6%	$133,822	+10%	$131,769

[This illustration is not intended to serve as a prediction or guarantee of future values or results.]

In the above example, both Scenario A and Scenario B have the same average rate of return. But by changing from a constant rate of return to a more realistic return pattern, we now have reduced our potential for retirement funding success. By adding one abnormality, a market correction in year 4, our total portfolio value was reduced by nearly 2%, and that was only after five years. Imagine what would happen if we have the same volatility over 20 or 30 years. The impact would be profound!

This illustration shows our second major issue we need to plan for during retirement: volatility. Because we live in a world where our investment returns vary greatly year over year, volatility is unpredictable. Goal-based financial plans overstate our ability to retire successfully because returns vary. The higher the volatility, the farther we stray from our financial goal.

Let's take this problem with volatility and expand on the potential issues. When is the worst year to have a bear market? The answer could be during the first year of retirement. Here is that example:

Year	Scenario A (Average 6%)	Total	Scenario C (Average 6%)	Total
0	Start	$100,000	Start	$100,000
1	+6%	$106,000	-20%	$80,000
2	+6%	$112,360	+20%	$96,000
3	+6%	$119,101	+10%	$105,600
4	+6%	$126,247	+10%	$116,160
5	+6%	$133,822	+10%	$127,776

[This illustration is not intended to serve as a prediction or guarantee of future values or results.]

REDUCE YOUR STRESS BY STRESSING VOLATILITY

Again, both scenarios have an average of 6% rate of return. Even though we maintained the same average rate of return, our ending value has now been reduced by over 4.5%! The impact of the bear market is astonishing.

Because volatility is not fundamentally predictable, we cannot assume success with a constant rate of return on our portfolio. We need to use statistical analysis to determine the probability of success. By using the law of large numbers, we can gauge the probability of success and failure.

A test that measures the probability of success with randomized volatility is called a *Monte Carlo* analysis. Using thousands of simulated returns over one's life expectancy, the *Monte Carlo* analysis can predict whether you will make it through life while hitting your intended goal. This process also uses a cash flow analysis to make sure your life expenses are funded appropriately. Statistically speaking, a *Monte Carlo* analysis result of 70% or greater is considered a successful outcome.

CASE STUDY

Bob and Linda Smith are concerned about their financial ability to retire and stay retired financially. They have amassed a retirement nest egg of around $1,200,000. They have a guaranteed income of $43,000 per year. They have calculated their cost of living during retirement to be $106,000 per year, taxes included. Their risk tolerance profile showed that Bob and Linda are moderate investors. Based on a goal-based financial plan assuming a 6% constant return and 3% annual inflation, the Smiths should have $1,131,000 to fund their retirement need.

To correctly analyze their possibility for success, we ran a *Monte Carlo* simulation based on their cash flow income need. During the base case calculation, we found that Bob and Linda Smith have an 80% chance for retirement success with normal volatility calculations. This means that normal market volatility alone causes a 20% failure in their plan, meaning they have a 1-in-5 probability their plans for retirement will fail—not good. Though this is a statistically viable plan, it is a bit disconcerting knowing that the plan has a 20% chance of failure.

The next test was to see how a bear market, typically defined as a -20% or larger loss, in the first year of retirement followed by normal market volatility, would impact the plan. The *Monte Carlo* simulation found that

Bob and Linda only have a 49% chance of success through retirement. This means that 51% of the simulations ended with the Smiths running out of money during their joint lifetime. This is a huge and unacceptable failure and needs to be fixed.

In situations such as this, volatility is the main culprit for failure in retirement. We need to make sure the portfolio is set up in a way that we have a high probability of attaining the 6% average rate of return, but also minimize the impact of volatility. Based on the Smiths having a moderate level of risk in their portfolio, we needed to make sure their investments are allocated appropriately to maximize potential return while minimizing the effects of volatility.

We need to address the fixed income portion of the portfolio to make sure the foundation is strong. We also need to make sure the fixed income portion of the portfolio has enough strength so the Smiths could draw income when the market is down, thus reducing high draw ratios due to market losses. We also need to make sure there is substantial dependable and guaranteed income to support their need for income throughout the rest of their lives.

The Smiths can achieve their goals by using a fixed indexed annuity with an income rider. This type of annuity has exactly the benefits the Smiths need to solve their volatility issues at retirement. First, the basic features of the annuity allow Bob and Linda Smith to use indexing strategies that participate only in the upside performance of the market. In a down market, this annuity puts a shield around the money protecting it from any loss. This limits some of the concerns with negative returns in a volatile market.

The second feature of the annuity proves to be the key to making this plan successful. The guaranteed lifetime withdrawal benefit adds a guaranteed interest rate and minimum guaranteed income to be paid to them on a joint basis for as long as they both lived.

We decided to run *Monte Carlo* tests to determine the impact of using this strategy. Our first test found that if we allocated $350,000 to this fixed indexed annuity with an income rider, the base case simulation had a 92% success ratio. However, when testing the effects of a bear market we still only had a 69% success. We were heading in the right direction but not there yet.

Our final test resulted in an even better recommendation. We simulated the effects of allocating $400,000 into the fixed indexed annuity with an income rider. The *Monte Carlo* showed that in the base case, we were able to raise their success ratio from 80% to 94%. To fully confirm our recommendation, the bear market test was next. When stressing the plan and testing the effect of a bear market in the first year of retirement, the *Monte Carlo* went from 49% success to 74%. This is clearly a far better result for the Smiths.

When planning your retirement, it is important that you complete your plan with eyes wide open. There is an old joke that goes, "How do you make God smile? Tell him you've got a plan." Though we may not fully know what lies in wait for us on the road ahead, we can make prudent decisions with realistic expectations and an alternate route for any detours or potholes we may encounter. If you are going on the retirement "vacation," plan accordingly, but most important, follow through.

About Chris

Christopher Kichurchak is President of Independence Wealth Advisors. As a Chartered Retirement Planning Counselor®, Chris specializes in the wealth management and financial planning needs that his clients face in retirement. As an Investment Advisor Representative, Chris works with individuals to develop custom wealth management strategies, focusing on concise financial solutions and relationships built on trust. He has experience developing and implementing financial strategies that encompass each step of his clients' financial life cycle, and offers personalized solutions for asset optimization, retirement planning, risk management, and wealth preservation.

Since beginning his career in financial services in 2001, Chris has gone on to become a Million Dollar Round Table Top-of-the-Table qualifier, an honor that distinguishes him among the top professionals in the financial services industry. Chris believes that client education is the foundation of client service. He teaches financial planning strategy classes and has been featured on CNBC and 19 Action News. Also, Chris has been featured in numerous publications including *TheStreet.com, US News and World Report, Kiplinger's*, and *Forbes*.

Chris holds a BSBA in Financial Economics from Bowling Green State University. He proudly serves both the Cornerstone of Hope and Ronald McDonald House of Cleveland as a member of their boards' finance committee.

Chris lives in Hinckley, Ohio with his wife Anne, daughters Lilly and Sammy, and their two dogs. In his free time, he enjoys swimming, hiking, golf, baseball, and movies.

CHAPTER 54

MYTH: IF YOU BUY AN ANNUITY TO INCREASE YOUR INCOME YOU WILL GET KILLED WITH INCOME TAXES

BY RANDY KROGH

THE BIG BAD WOLF – INCOME TAXES

Reality: In 15 minutes after reading this chapter, you will understand income taxes better than you have in your entire life, you will not be afraid to use your assets for income, and you will feel absolutely confident you won't be getting killed with income taxes in retirement—all by teaching you the BASICS of income taxes:

1. What is gross income?
2. What is taxable income?
3. How do the income tax brackets and rates work?
4. Case studies: How much tax do I have to pay?

1. Gross Income – Gross income is the total income you receive, such as pension income, IRA income, Social Security income, interest, and dividends. All gross income is not necessarily taxable income. For example, at least 15% of your Social Security will be tax-free.

2. Taxable Income – Taxable income is the amount of your income that you will pay income taxes on. This will almost ALWAYS be substantially less than the total gross income you receive. The simple formula to calculate out taxable income is to add up all the income you receive that is taxable, subtract out the higher of your standard deduction or itemized deductions, leaving you with your taxable income, which you will be taxed on.

3. Income Tax Brackets and Rates – For 2018, there are seven (7) federal income tax brackets and rates. The rates range from 10% to 37%. In this chapter, we will only discuss federal income tax rates and federal income tax brackets to help you understand this complex subject! Depending on where you live you may pay state income taxes also. Please consult with your income tax advisor.

2018 Federal Tax Brackets And Rates For All Filers:

	Married Filing Jointly	Single
10% Bracket	$ 0 - $ 19,050	$ 0 - $ 9,525
12% Bracket	$ 19,050 - $ 77,400	$ 9,525 - $ 38,700
22% Bracket	$ 77,400 - $ 165,000	$ 38,700 - $ 82,500
24% Bracket	$ 165,000 - $ 315,000	$ 82,500 - $ 157,500
32% Bracket	$ 315,000 - $ 400,000	$ 157,500 - $200,000
35% Bracket	$ 400,000 - $ 600,000	$200,000 - $500,000
37% Bracket	$ 600,000+	$500,000+

	Head Of Household	Married Filing Sep
10% Bracket	$ 0 - $ 13,600	$ 0 - $ 9,525
12% Bracket	$ 13,600 - $ 51,800	$ 9,525 - $ 38,700
22% Bracket	$ 51,800 - $ 82,500	$ 38,700 - $ 82,500
24% Bracket	$ 82,500 - $ 157,500	$ 82,500 - $ 157,500
32% Bracket	$ 157,500 - $ 200,000	$ 157,500 - $200,000
35% Bracket	$ 200,000 - $ 500,000	$200,000 - $500,000
37% Bracket	$ 500,000+	$500,000+

The majority of retirees incorrectly believe all of their income is taxed at their single highest rate. For example, if a single retiree makes $160,000 of annual income, he/she will typically think they will pay 32% federal income taxes on the $160,000. This is not true for two (2) reasons:

1. 100% of gross income is not taxable.
2. The federal income tax rates are graduated and pertain to certain ranges of income. We call this a "Stair-Step" income tax rate system.

Many retirees have told us their CPA and/or Financial Advisor warned them that any additional income would **"push them into the next tax bracket."** This statement puts a tremendous fear in every red-blooded, IRS-fearing, American. The advisors should have told the retirees any additional income they earned would be taxed at their highest rate, but all their original income would continue to be taxed at the lower rates.

The following 2018 married-filing-jointly Federal Income Tax graph helps explain our **"Stair Step Tax Rate Charts"** showing that you only pay higher tax rates on increased income, the higher steps, and still pay the lower tax rates on the lower steps:

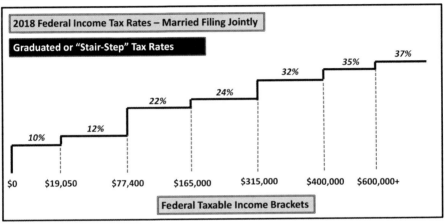

The first part of your taxable income, between $0 and $19,050, $19,050, is taxed at 10%:

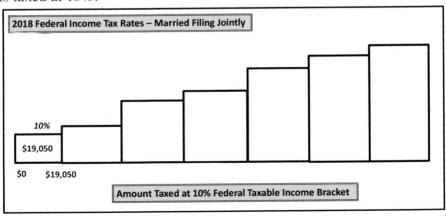

The second part of your taxable income, between $19,050 and $77,400, $58,350, is taxed at 12%. The first part of your taxable income up to $19,050 is still taxed at 10%. Only the taxable income amount above $19,050 up to $77,400 is taxed at 12%. We call this a "Stair Step Tax". Once you "Step Up" to the next bracket or step, only the taxable income *"above the previous step"* is taxed at the higher rate. The taxable income on the *"lower step"* is still taxed at the lower 10% rate:

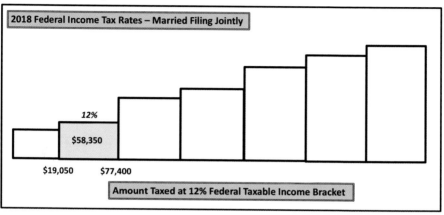

The third part of your taxable income, between $77,400 and $165,000, $87,600, is taxed at 22%. The first part of your taxable income up to $19,050 is still taxed at 10%, and the second part of your taxable income between $19,050 and $77,400 is still taxed at 12%. Only the taxable income amount above $77,400 up to $165,000 is taxed at 22%:

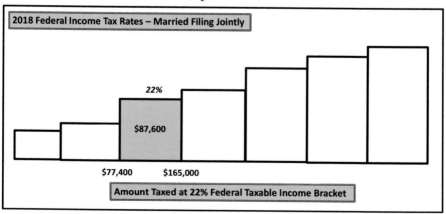

The fourth part of your taxable income, between $165,000 and $315,000, $150,000, is taxed at 24%. The first part of your taxable income up to $19,050 is still taxed at 10%, the second part of your taxable income between $19,050 and $77,400 is still taxed at 12%, and the third part of your taxable income between $77,400 and $165,000 is taxed at 22%. Only taxable income above $165,000 and up to $315,000 is taxed at 24%:

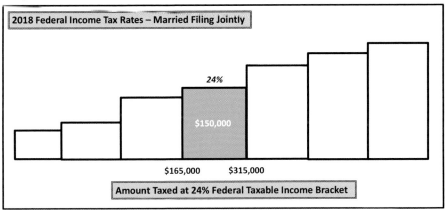

The fifth part of your taxable income, between $315,000 and $400,000, which is $85,000, is taxed at 32%. The first part of your taxable income up to $19,050 is still taxed at 10%, the second part of your taxable income between $19,050 and $77,400 is still taxed at 12%, the third part of your taxable income between $77,400 and $165,000 is taxed at 22%, and the fourth part of your taxable income between $165,000 and up to $315,000 is taxed at 24%. Only the taxable income amount above $315,000 and up to $400,000 is taxed at 32%:

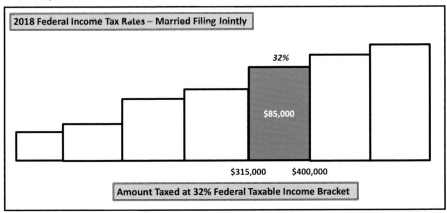

The sixth part of your taxable income, between $400,000 and $600,000, which is $200,000, is taxed at 35%. The first part of your taxable income up to $19,050 is still taxed at 10%, the second part of your taxable income between $19,050 and $77,400 is still taxed at 12%, the third part of your taxable income between $77,400 and $165,000 is taxed at 22%, the fourth part of your taxable income between $165,000 and up to $315,000 is taxed at 24%, and the fifth part of your taxable income between $165,000 and up to $315,000 is taxed at 32%. Only the taxable income amount above $400,000 and up to $600,000 is taxed at 35%:

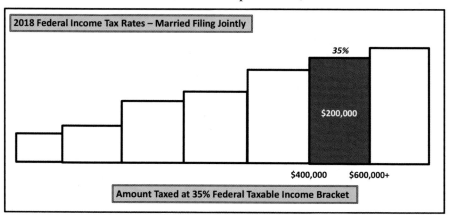

The seventh part of your taxable income, all taxable income above $600,000, is taxed at 37%. The first part of your taxable income up to $19,050 is still taxed at 10%, the second part of your taxable income between $19,050 and $77,400 is still taxed at 12%, the third part of your taxable income between $77,400 and $165,000 is taxed at 22%, the fourth part of your taxable income between $165,000 and up to $315,000 is taxed at 24%, the fifth part of your taxable income between $165,000 and up to $315,000 is taxed at 32%, and the sixth part of your taxable income between $400,000 and $600,000 is taxed at 35%. Only the taxable income amount above $600,000 is taxed at 37%:

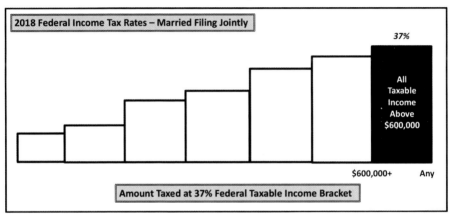

The entire seven (7) tax brackets for the Married Filing Jointly category can be expressed as follows:

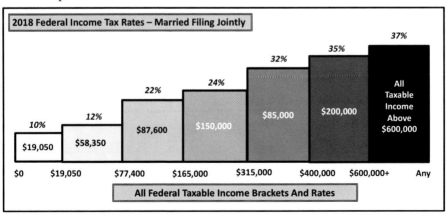

We have just discussed the federal income tax brackets and rates for the Married Filing Jointly category. Below we have outlined the seven (7) federal income tax brackets for federal income tax returns filed as Single, Head Of Household, and Married Filing Separately.

The 2018 seven (7) Federal Income Tax brackets and rates for an individual filing a Single return:

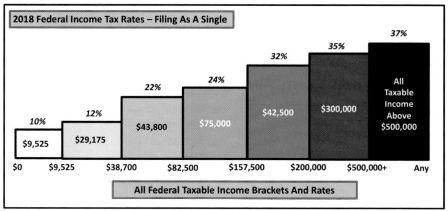

The 2018 seven (7) Federal Income Tax brackets for an individual filing a Head Of Household return:

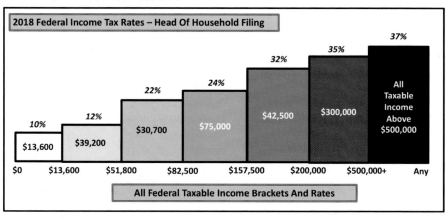

The entire 2018 seven (7) Federal Income Tax brackets for an individual filing a Married Separate return:

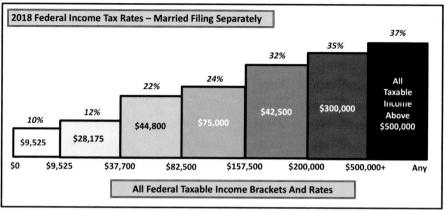

So by now, you should "get" that you will not pay one (1) high income tax rate on all your income. This will most likely help you to understand you will pay a lower overall income tax rate than you thought before you read this chapter. The following two (2) case studies will complete the explanation.

CASE STUDY #1

- Bill and Mary: retired and both at age 65.
- Receive $60,000 of pensions and $40,000 of Social Security.
- The $100,000 covers their monthly costs but does not leave them extra money for taking two (2) big trips per year they always planned.
- They have $2,000,000 of assets they are not using for income, because their CPA and broker stated if they receive any more income, they will get killed with taxes. They were advised to defer income until age 70 ½.
- This means they would have to wait until age 70 to travel. What if their health is not as good then? What if one of them has passed away?
- We advised Bill and Mary to immediately start taking out $100,000 per year of income distributions from their IRA's, increasing their gross income from $100,000 per year to $200,000 per year. They loved the idea but were freaked out about paying too much in income taxes.

- We allocated a portion of their assets into a fixed index annuity with an income rider that allowed us to guarantee their $100,000 of annual income from their assets for as long as they live. They don't have to worry about running out of money.
- And their income tax projection shows they don't have to worry about getting killed with income taxes:

```
    $ 60,000  Pension income
 +  $ 40,000  Social Security income
 +  $100,000  IRA income
 =  $200,000  Total income
 - ($  6,000) Less non-taxable Social Security Benefits
 =  $194,000  Gross reportable income
 - ($ 24,000) Less standard deduction
 =  $170,000  Taxable income
 =  $ 29,379  Federal income taxes
```

They will pay 14.69% tax on their $200,000 of gross income. $29,379 of federal income taxes divided by $200,000 of gross income equals 14.69% of federal income taxes. Right now, at age 65, they can use their assets to create income to do all the traveling they dreamed of. Bill and Mary's tax calculation:

```
10%   on first   $ 19,050 of taxable income   = $  1,905 taxes at 10% bracket
12%   on next    $ 58,350 of taxable income   = $  7,002 taxes at 12% bracket
22%   on next    $ 87,600 of taxable income   = $ 19,272 taxes at 22% bracket
24%   on last    $  5,000 of taxable income   = $  1,200 taxes at 24% bracket
                 $170,000 of taxable income   = $ 29,379 total federal taxes
```

$29,379 taxes / $200,000 gross income = 15% Effective federal income tax rate

Their net monthly income after income taxes would look like this:

```
    $ 5,000  Monthly pension gross income
 +  $ 3,334  Monthly Social Security income
 +  $ 8,333  IRA monthly income
 = $16,667  Total gross monthly income
 - ($ 2,448) Monthly income tax withholding
 = $14,219  Net monthly income after income taxes (How much they
            can spend every month)
```

Bill and Mary will only pay 14.69% in federal income taxes on their $200,000 of annual gross income and will have $14,219 per month of net after-tax income to spend!

CASE STUDY #2

- Nancy is 60 and is a retired school teacher. She receives a teacher's annual pension of $50,000. She does not receive any Social Security benefits.
- She has an IRA worth $1,400,000 that she is taking $10,000 from each year.
- The $70,000 of annual pension and IRA income covers all her monthly costs and allows for a little traveling, but she wants to take her entire family on a big trip every year.
- She has always been afraid that if she increased her IRA income distributions, her income taxes would be so high she wouldn't have anything left after the taxes!
- We advised her to increase her income distributions from her IRA from $10,000 per year up to $70,000 per year. This would give her enough extra money to take the entire family on a big trip every year and would allow her to save about $2,000 per month every month into her bank account.
- So we increased her annual gross income from $60,000 per year to $120,000. She loved the idea but was very afraid of the income taxes.
- We allocated a portion of her assets into a fixed index annuity with an income rider that allowed us to guarantee her $60,000 of annual income from her assets for as long as she lives. She doesn't have to worry about running out of money.
- And her income tax projection shows she doesn't have to worry about getting killed with income taxes:

```
  $ 50,000  Nancy's teacher's pension income
+ $ 70,000  IRA income
= $120,000  Total income
- ($ 12,000) Less standard deduction
= $108,000  Taxable Income
= $ 20,210  Federal income taxes
```

467

She will pay 16.84% in taxes on her $120,000 of gross income. 16.84% of federal taxes divided by $120,000 of gross income equals 16.84% of federal income taxes. Right now, at age 60, Nancy can receive $60,000 more in income per year to make wonderful memories every year with her family. Nancy's tax calculation:

10%	First	$ 9,525 of taxable income	=	$ 953 taxes at 10% bracket
12%	Next	$ 29,175 of taxable income	=	$ 3,501 taxes at 12% bracket
22%	Next	$ 43,800 of taxable income	=	$ 9,636 taxes at 22% bracket
24%	Last	$ 25,500 of taxable income	=	$ 6,120 taxes at 24% bracket
		$108,000 of taxable income	=	$20,210 total federal taxes

$20,210 taxes / $120,000 gross income = 16.84% Effective federal income tax rate

Nancy's net monthly income after income taxes would look like this:

$ 4,167 Nancy's teacher's pension gross income
+ $ 5,833 IRA monthly income
= $10,000 Total gross monthly income
- ($ 1,684) Monthly income tax withholding
= $ 8,316 Net monthly income after income taxes

Nancy will only pay 16.84% in federal income taxes on her $120,000 of annual gross income and will have $8,316 per month of net after-tax income to spend!

SUMMARY

We spent a considerable amount of time in this chapter because we believe retirees cannot and will not maximize their incomes without truly understanding the tax ramifications of increasing their incomes. The *"Fear Of Taxes"* has kept so many retirees from living their retirement dreams. We hope this chapter has opened your eyes to the FACT that income taxes should not stop you from increasing your income and doing EVERYTHING you wanted to do in retirement!

About Randy

Randy Krogh is in constant pursuit of success through his life passions, and in doing everything he possibly can to help people in any way. Randy credits his achievements in life, his can-do attitude and his always-do-the-right-thing motto to his parents. They instilled in him the value of hard work, the importance of each individual, and that a life of service to others through honesty and integrity is paramount to success and happiness.

Randy's first big success came from his life passion for music and performing. At age 9, he started singing and performing with three siblings. As a teenager, music became a full-time career. He toured the country performing in Las Vegas, Disney World, Sea World, conventions, fairs, and universities. By 16, after moving to Atlanta from Utah, many called their family the Osmond's of the South.

At the peak of his musical career in 1991, Randy, his two brothers, and sister signed a recording and production contract with EMI Records. The group loved singing together and was successful, but as time went on each member started their own family which didn't fit too well with each member having to be gone from home for weeks at a time.

Randy transitioned his musical career to a 25-year (and counting) successful career in the financial industry, which began in mortgage lending. After six years of growing other companies, Randy embraced the entrepreneur within and co-founded his own holding company in 1999. The new company had three subsidiary businesses: mortgage lending, real estate sales/franchising, and financial planning services.

The mortgage operation was a huge success operating in 28 states with 900+ employees. The real estate enterprise grew to 28 franchises with over 1,200 realtors. Eventually, both companies were sold. The third-leg, financial planning, was planned but not operating initially.

After the 2008-2009 Financial Crisis, Randy saw many friends and family members' portfolios drop by 50%. This crisis revived Randy's passion for building a financial planning company to do the right things by the client. In 2011, Randy met Dan Ahmad, who was a top financial advisor, and at that time had 30 years of experience in the industry.

Randy discovered Dan shared his same passion and mission – to help others make good decisions with their money. Randy was fully convinced of Dan's process after Dan created plans for Randy's family members. Randy saw up close that the plans, the process, literally changed his family members' lives. After working with Dan and his partner, Jim Files, for several years, Randy moved his family across the country to Sacramento to use his skills as Director of Business Development in growing Peak Financial Freedom Group.

Randy's greatest joys and accomplishments have been getting his wife, Carrie, to fall in love with him at BYU, being married to her for 29 years (and counting), and raising their four children – Spencer, Gabrielle, Christiana, and Eliza. Even after all these kids, Randy still "busts a move" and performs whenever he can.

CHAPTER 55

MYTH: YOU DON'T NEED A FIXED INDEX ANNUITY WITH AN INCOME RIDER
BECAUSE MANY OTHER WALL STREET-TYPE TRADITIONAL INVESTMENTS PROVIDE THE EXACT SAME BENEFITS

BY CODY FILES

Truth: A fixed index annuity with an income rider is the only asset that provides all of the following benefits:

- *100% principal protection against stock market losses.*
- *100% protection of current and previous gains against all future stock market losses.*
- *Opportunity for competitive growth.*
- *Lifetime income guarantees for a single or joint life.*
- *Income not reduced by stock market volatility.*
- *Fees averaging approximately 1%.*
- *Potential for increased income.*
- *100% of remaining assets at death passed to beneficiaries.*
- *A legally enforceable written contract outlining and protecting your rights.*

No other asset, other than a fixed index annuity with an income rider, provides ALL of these benefits in one single package.

I have found 99% of the retirees and pre-retirees have five (5) main objectives for their money; I call them the ***"BIG 5"*** :

1. To protect what you have worked so hard to accumulate and never suffer a large principal loss.
2. Earn an acceptable rate of return based on a low-risk asset.
3. Receive income guaranteed for as long as you live, even past age 100.
4. Not get gouged with hidden fees.
5. Leave all remaining assets when you pass away to your named beneficiaries.

It's common for a normal run-of-the-mill advisor to recommend using Wall Street-type traditional investments like stocks, bonds, mutual funds, exchange-traded funds (ETF's), commodities, CD's, precious metals, and other similar instruments to accomplish the "BIG 5". Here's the rub: *Wall Street-type traditional investments* do not, and cannot, provide all "BIG 5" benefits you desire for your long-term financial security. It doesn't matter what your broker, advisor, friend, colleague, brother, wife, or even what Ken Fisher says over and over and over again – none of the *Wall Street-type traditional investments* can meet all "BIG 5" objectives.

I have composed the chart on the following page based on data I have researched during my time in the financial industry, based on what I have seen happen to the following assets retirees and pre-retirees have owned. This concept, called "Asset Behavior", was originally published in *Don't Bet The Farm* written by Dan Ahmad and Jim Files, with inclusion granted by authors. The whole key is learning how assets "behave," because if you know how assets are expected to "behave" you will not have any "false expectations" and be surprised by their behavior.

Why is this so important? Because if you expect an asset never to lose principal and then the stock market crashes and you lose -50%, how badly off would you be? Pretty bad. Or how about if you expect an asset to pay you $50,000 per year of income for as long as you live, and then at age 80, when you are still in good health, your income terminates. . . how badly off would you be?

Asset Client Owned	Sometimes Made Money	Never Lost Money	Principal Was Guaranteed	Earnings Protected Against Loss	Never Had Principal Volatility	Stable Income Potential	Income Was Guaranteed	Income Was Always Paid	Never Had Income Volatility	Income Guaranteed For Life
1st & 2nd Deeds of Trusts	X					X				
Alternative Investments	X									
Businesses	X									
CDs - Certificate of Deposits	X	X	X	X	X	X	X	X		
Coins	X									
Commodities & Futures	X									
Corporate Bonds	X					X				
Corporate Bond Mutual Funds	X					X				
Day Trading Assets	X									
Fixed Indexed Annuities + Income Rider	X	X	X	X	X	X	X	X	X	X
Government Bonds	X	X	X	X		X	X	X		
Government Bond Mutual Funds	X					X		X		
Leasing Programs	X					X				
Loans to Business Partners	X									
Loans to Clients, Co-Workers, Friends	X									
Loans to Family Members	X									
Money Market Accounts	X	X	X	X	X	X	X	X		
Municipal Bonds	X					X				
Municipal Bond Mutual Funds	X					X				
Mutual Funds	X									
Natural Gas & Oil Investments	X									
Precious Metals/Precious Metal Funds	X									
Program Trading Assets	X									
Real Estate Investment Trusts - Private	X					X				
Real Estate Investment Trusts - Public	X					X				
Real Estate Limited Partnerships	X					X				
Real Estate Office Buildings	X									
Real Estate Options	X									
Real Estate Personal Residences	X									
Real Estate Raw Land Investments	X					X				
Real Estate Rental Homes	X					X				
Real Estate Shopping Centers	X					X				
Real Estate Warehouses	X					X				
Savings Accounts	X	X	X	X	X		X	X		
Stock Aggressive & Growth Mutual Funds	X									
Stock Balanced & Conservative Mutual Funds	X									
Stock International Mutual Funds	X									
Stock Options	X									
Stocks	X									
Third-Party Asset Management	X									
Variable Annuities	X									
Variable Annuities with Withdrawal Rider	X					X	X	X	X	
Variable Annuities with Income Rider	X					X	X	X	X	X

The categories at the top of the chart include:

- Sometimes Made Money
- Never Lost Money
- Principal Was Guaranteed
- Earnings Protected Against Loss
- Never Had Principal Volatility

- Stable Income Potential
- Income Was Guaranteed
- Income Was Always Paid
- Never Had Income Volatility
- Income Guaranteed For Life

The chart on the preceding page is not inclusive of all assets, and your assets in these categories could have performed better or worse. The last line in the chart shows the only asset, out of all of these assets, that I have always seen "behave" and meet all the chart criteria, was a fixed index annuity with an income rider. A fixed index annuity with an income rider as part of your overall asset allocation can potentially help reduce your overall risk and increase your overall retirement success.

In addition to assets not "behaving", let's look at some of the risks you could possibly face during retirement:

I. <u>Market Volatility Risk:</u>

Most of us have felt the fear of losing money in falling markets. The Technology Bubble from 2000 through 2002 and the Financial Crisis between 2007 through 2009 left many retirees and pre-retirees examining statements that had decreased by -50% or more! A -50% loss requires a +100% gain just to break even. In your lifetime you have seen the stock market crash, bond prices crash, real estate prices crash, gold crash, oil crash, commodities crash, in all cases leaving you with less money in your portfolio.

Can Wall Street-type traditional investments reduce market volatility risk?
Usually not, as market volatility comes from Wall Street-type traditional investments. Funds are invested in a market or markets and other than CDs, government bonds, money market accounts, and savings accounts, these types of assets are subject to principal loss from their specific market volatility.

Can a fixed index annuity with an income rider reduce market volatility risk?
100% of the time. A fixed index annuity with an income rider provides a guarantee that an investor's principal and returns are protected from market volatility by shifting the risk to an insurance

company. If the stock market crashes -50%, the fixed index annuity with an income rider is contractually guaranteed not to lose anything.

II. <u>Retirement Income Plan Risk:</u>

Recently, when discussing retirement planning, a gentleman summed up his concerns perfectly by saying:

> *"I don't know where I am, I have no idea where I am going, and I am absolutely confused on how to get there!"*

This type of frustration is what keeps most people from feeling confident about retirement. It's because their advisor has not created an actual written retirement income plan for them. A comprehensive written retirement income plan can help mitigate retirement risks while providing a plan on how to succeed.

Can Wall Street-type traditional investments reduce retirement income plan risk?

Usually not, simply because these types of assets are typically volatile and can lose a significant amount of principal during a market decline and none of them provide a guaranteed lifetime income. So how can an actual plan be created that is accurate and can be believed and relied on by a retiree if big principal losses can occur or the income could run out? The answer is that it can't be. How much confidence would a retiree have with this type of plan? Not much.

Can a fixed index annuity with an income rider reduce retirement income plan risk?

Definitely, a fixed index annuity provides the most important ingredient for a successful retirement income plan: income guaranteed to be paid to you for as long as you live. A whole plan can be created and built around income that can't run out even if you live past age 100.

III. <u>Income Tax Risks:</u>

One of the biggest income tax issues I see is when retirees are paying income taxes on money they are not using for income currently. I have seen so many people who receive taxable dividends and capital gain distributions from their portfolio, and they are not using these taxable distributions for income, they simply reinvest the funds and pay the income tax every year like an additional fee on their portfolio. I have seen retirees with a $3,000,000 portfolio pay income taxes on $150,000 of portfolio taxable income they are not using. These same people wonder why they have to pay $10,000 in additional estimated income taxes every quarter.

Can Wall Street-type traditional investments reduce retirement income tax risk?

Usually not, simply because many of these types of assets create taxable income, dividends, and/or capital gains for them to be successful for you. Think about it, the only way you would consider a Wall Street-type traditional investment to be successful is if it makes you money, and in many cases the gains in the form of interest, dividends, and or/capital gains are taxed currently. There is a benefit in that long-term capital gains and certain dividends can receive preferential income tax treatment.

Can a fixed index annuity with an income rider reduce retirement income tax risk?

Yes. A fixed index annuity provides a tremendous income tax benefit to retirees and pre-retirees. 100% of all gains on an annual basis are income tax-deferred until those gains are distributed. When distributed, the gain will be taxed at your ordinary income tax rate, as any principal (cost basis) is distributed income tax-free. So, if you had $3,000,000 in a non-IRA portfolio that was creating $150,000 of taxable income every year that you weren't using, that was forcing you to pay an additional $40,000 of income taxes each year on the $150,000 of income you weren't using, how would you feel? Not good!

You could reposition your $3,000,000 of assets into a fixed index annuity with an income rider, and you could defer 100% of all growth until you took income distributions. If you earned $150,000 on your fixed index annuity with an income rider, and didn't need the income, you wouldn't have to report the $150,000 gain on your income tax return, thus saving you $40,000 in income taxes that year. You won't be able to take a lump sum distribution of 100% of your funds for a specific time period, but in most plans, you could take out up to 10%, or $300,000 per year starting in the 13th month without any penalties or fees. When you pass away, your beneficiaries can spread out the taxation of all the gain you have deferred over many years, minimizing the income taxes they will pay.

IV. <u>Longevity Risk:</u>

Most retirees' biggest fear is running out of money during retirement. Advances in medicine, diet, and health are resulting in longer and longer life expectancies for us all. Now, with many people living into their 90's and beyond, longevity risk, the risk of running out of money, has become even greater. In a recent study, the National Center for Health Sciences stated that in upper-middle-class couples age 65 today, there is a 43% chance that one or both will survive to age 95.

Can the Wall Street-type traditional investments eliminate longevity risk?

Usually not, simply because the Wall Street-type traditional investments do not provide guaranteed lifetime income and carry principal volatility and potential principal losses. Assume you have $1,000,000 of retirement assets invested in Wall Street-type traditional investments and you need to take out $50,000 per year, which is 5%, from these assets. What if you lose -50%, bringing your $1,000,000 down to $500,000. You still need the $50,000 per year of income, but the $50,000 now becomes a 10% income distribution rate which carries a high failure probability.

Can a fixed index annuity with an income rider eliminate longevity risk?

100% of the time. A fixed index annuity with an income rider is built for conquering longevity risk. The principal is never at risk of loss from any market declines and the income is guaranteed to be paid to you for as long as you live, regardless of market volatility and losses, and your living past age 100. If you live so long, and you use up all the account value in your fixed index annuity with an income rider, you will still be paid your guaranteed lifetime income for as long as you live. Your stocks won't do that. Your mutual funds won't do that. Your managed portfolio won't do that. Only a fixed index annuity with an income rider will do that.

Meet Jay and Judy Our Hypothetical Case Study:

Jay and Judy are both age 57 and working, hoping to retire in five (5) years, working through age 62. Right now they are concerned about retirement as they are not clear about their current investments, if they are the right investments, and what they need to do to retire properly.

They decide to reach out to a financial advisor who specializes in retirement income planning. During an initial meeting they reviewed all their investments with the advisor. Their investment portfolio included the following:

- $400,000 between 6 different taxable investments accounts
- IRA accounts totaling $400,000
- Bank assets of $150,000
- $250,000 in 401(k)'s and making additional annual contributions
- Both have Roth IRA's totaling $150,000
- Their home is paid off with a current value of $375,000
- Jay has a $20,000 annual pension he will take at 63
- Jay's Social Security at age 63 is $1,541
- Judy's Social Security at age 63 is $1,380
- Desired net after-tax monthly retirement income of $7,000 per month
- Jay and Judy are both contributing $10,000 each year to their 401(k) plans at work
- They can save an additional $30,000 a year

They expressed their concern about losing money due to recent market volatility. They explained that they lost over -40% of their money during the corrections in 2000-2002 and 2008-2009. They do not feel they are in a position to lose money again, especially so close to retirement.

They also indicated they have been watching the news about the escalating debt of the U.S. government and are convinced that taxes will be higher in the future. They are interested in Roth Conversions and wanted to know more.

After reviewing Jay and Judy's resources, discussing their hopes and goals, and considering their options, their financial planner presented the following financial plan:

- Jay and Judy max out their contributions with their employer retirement plan by contributing $24,500 each, $49,000 jointly, to the Roth 401(k) accounts instead of a tax-deferred account.
- Move both Roth IRA's into a Roth IRA funded with a fixed index annuity with an income rider that will protect these assets against all stock market losses and provide joint guaranteed lifetime income that can increase each year their investment generates a return.
- Move the IRA's totaling $400,000 into the same type of fixed index annuity funded in their IRAs.
- Keep $100,000 in savings and move the $50,000 balance and the $400,000 of taxable investments into a managed account with a low fee structure focused on risk management.
- They both will take their Social Security benefits at age 63 and Jay will take his pension at age 63 also.

Projected annual gross income of $120,000 provides estimated net after-tax monthly income of $9,000 per month, giving Jay and Judy $2,000 to save each month. Their estimated effective combined federal and state income tax rate is estimated at 9%.

Jay and Judy's certain income, those income sources guaranteed for life, from pension, Social Security, and the fixed index annuities with the income riders, total more than $80,000 per year. Joint lifetime income from the fixed index annuities with the income riders provide the opportunity for increased income any year they receive a positive return on their plans. When they pass away, Roth assets will transfer tax-free to their beneficiaries. Jay and Judy now have a plan they can count on and feel secure with. They no longer have to wonder or worry, they know exactly where they are heading and how to get there.

About Cody

Cody Files is an exceptional individual, both personally and professionally. He is honest and loyal, the kind of guy you want as a best friend. He is strong and reliable, the kind of guy you want in your family. And he is trustworthy and dedicated, the kind of guy you want as your financial advisor. Cody is committed and focused on helping his clients achieve total financial freedom. Financial freedom is what Peak Financial Freedom Group's entire business model has been created to achieve for their clients. These two words, Financial Freedom, are the impetus that drives Cody in his relentless pursuit to achieve all wants, needs and desires that are set forth by clients seeking advice.

Cody was brought up in an entrepreneurial family. His father is the current CEO and co-founder of one of the fastest growing Financial Planning firms in the nation, and it makes sense that he naturally gravitated to the financial services industry. It pleases him immensely to be able to carry on the family spirit of doing the very best to help people succeed and accomplish their dreams in retirement.

Cody started his career at the Summit Companies in July of 2008 and was part of a small and select team that grew the company to over $750M of assets under management. Beyond Cody's extensive knowledge in retirement planning, he has significant knowledge in conservative asset allocation planning, helping retirees and pre-retirees protect what they've worked so hard to accumulate. Cody focuses on protecting his clients from large stock market losses like what happened during the Technology Bubble from 2000 through 2002 and the 2008 Financial Crisis, and helps to guarantee they will never run out of money for as long as they live.

Cody's thirst for education puts him among a select group of advisors whereby he holds the designation of Certified Financial Planner™. He achieved this status young in life in order to apply his academic knowledge to his investment recommendations, and ultimately making sure his clients have the very best direction in retirement planning.

He received a degree in Financial Services from San Diego State University and at the time there were less than five Universities around the world offering such a degree. He continued his education by attending Cornell University-Johnson Graduate School of Management, with a focus in Business Strategy.

Cody feels fortunate to work and learn from two very accomplished professionals, Jim Files and Dan Ahmad, founders of Peak Financial Freedom Group. They have been remarkable mentors and have accelerated Cody's career. Their unique methodology of working with retirees is mirrored in Cody's passionate appetite for providing the most comprehensive retirement planning to soon-to-be retired people and retirees. When Cody is not advising clients, he spends time with his wife Martine and two daughters, Colette and Elise.

CHAPTER 56

GUARANTEED TAX-FREE INCOME FOR LIFE THROUGH ROTH CONVERSIONS

(and WHY the NEW TAX LAW is a GIFT to PRE-RETIREES)

BY LOUIS R. TERRERO, CPA
– Registered Investment Advisor

This book has addressed many of the worries retirees and pre-retirees face. Let's face it, if you are a retiree or pre-retiree, the worries you have about your money are numerous, perhaps endless! One concern that is a big part of life is about your income taxes. On the federal and state level, income taxes must be factored into the retirement income plan. When you talk about retirement income, it's not what you get that's the most important - it's how much you get to keep after paying your income taxes!

Many retirees don't know how to plan for income taxes or simply ignore the impact income taxes may have on their retirement income. Making the problem worse is that many advisors and other financial professionals don't provide guidance in this area. Retirees and pre-retirees will usually go to their tax preparer once per year to have their income taxes prepared and accept the result on the bottom line of the returns. Planning, if any, is limited to projecting the current year's income, determining whether there might be a refund, and perhaps calculating estimated tax payments.

When you really think about it, the biggest items in your monthly budget are:

(a)...travel? No!
(b)...eating out? No!
(c)...entertainment? No!
(d)...shopping? No!

It's income taxes, as they consume a significant proportion of your monthly retirement budget. Because of this, tax planning for retirement is essential.

The key question that retirees and their financial professionals must address is....how can retirement income after taxes, the amount you actually get to keep, be maximized?

BRAD AND NANCY

Brad is 65 years old, and Nancy is 60. Brad has arrived at work early every day for over 40 years at the auto parts manufacturing business he joined after graduating from college. Nancy works part-time for their church. They have worked with a broker for over 20 years, and have asked for an actual written financial plan many times, but they have yet to receive one. As a result, they have been trying to educate themselves by going to educational seminars, reading books, and conducting research on the internet. After a lot of time and a great deal of effort, they have not really found anything that would allow them to:

1. Protect their principal against all stock and bond market losses.
2. Earn a reasonable rate of return when the markets go up.
3. Receive income guaranteed for as long as they live.
4. Minimize income taxes on their guaranteed lifetime income distributions for as long as they live.

They want to work five more years until Brad is 70 and Nancy is 65. They have done an outstanding job accumulating assets of over $1,000,000 in Brad's 401(k) plan at work. The concept of tax-free income appeals to them. However, they want all their assets and income sources to be part of a written comprehensive retirement income plan that addresses the various financial risks retirees face. By their basic calculations, it looked like they would be able to retire comfortably at age 70 and be financially secure.

Then the other shoe dropped.

Brad was let go by his employer two (2) weeks after his 65th birthday. His employer declared bankruptcy and was cutting every cost he could. Up until now, Brad was weighted heavily in equity (stock market) funds in his 401(k) plan. He understood he was taking a significant amount of risk as he was working and trying to maximize his accumulation of assets.

The strangest thing happened when he learned of the company bankruptcy and his termination. His first thought was about how much money he had previously lost in his 401(k) when the stock market crashed. During the Technology Bubble from 2000 through 2002, he also remembered losing -45% and then during the 2008 Financial Crisis he remembered losing almost -50%.

When these losses happened and Brad and Nancy discussed their options, they both said they never wanted to go through that again. However, here they were, ten years after the most recent big losses in 2008, and they were still invested the same way, with the same risk levels. Brad recognized this, and it scared him now that he no longer had a job and probably wasn't going to find a new one at his age and might be forced into retirement five (5) years earlier than planned.

Also, Brad knew he would be required to start receiving required minimum distributions (or RMD's) from his 401(k) account at age 70½ regardless of whether he wanted or needed such distributions. Finally, Brad realized that tax rates were low in 2018 due to the recently passed tax law, but he feared that rates would increase after the law's provisions are scheduled to expire in the year 2025.

The following explains how Brad and Nancy addressed the tax rate risk on Brad's retirement savings – all part of a larger comprehensive written retirement income plan.

Brad rolled over the funds from his former employer's 401(k) plan to an IRA. This rollover is income tax-free, as it essentially is the movement of tax-deferred funds directly from one custodian – his former employer's 401(k) – to another custodian (his new IRA account). The significance of this rollover is that Brad now was in control of his retirement funds.

Rather than investing his rolled over IRA funds in the stock or bond markets, Brad rolled his 401(k) money into a money market fund. This protected their capital from the volatility of the financial markets while he and Nancy investigated the most appropriate investment vehicles for them. Remember, they wanted to:

1. Protect their principal against all stock market losses.
2. Make a reasonable rate of return when the stock market goes up.
3. Receive income guaranteed for as long as they live.
4. Minimize income taxes on their guaranteed lifetime income distributions for as long as they live.

After talking to multiple advisors, they had narrowed the search down to only one asset being able to offer all these things in one package; low cost, fixed index annuities with income riders from stable, well-known, and highly-rated insurance carriers.

For maximum flexibility to accomplish their long-term goals, Brad purchased five (5) fixed indexed annuities with income riders, each for $200,000 in his name as the IRA owner and joint guaranteed lifetime income owner and with Nancy as the primary beneficiary and joint guaranteed lifetime income owner (their four children were named as equal contingent beneficiaries). Now that his new IRA portfolio consisted of $1,000,000 of fixed index annuity contracts with income riders, Brad and Nancy's hard-earned retirement savings could not lose even $1 from the stock or bond market downturns. Even a -50% stock market loss would mean a 0%, or $0 loss in their five (5) fixed index annuity with income rider contracts. In addition, when the indexes within their annuities increase, they would receive a portion of the gain each year. In short, Brad and Nancy had transferred all of their market risk to a large highly-rated insurance carrier in exchange for a guaranteed income for life in the future.

Brad and Nancy did not stop here. In 2018 they then began the process of converting one of the five (5) $200,000 contracts from his IRA to a Roth IRA. By simply filling out a form and submitting it to the annuity company Brad now had $200,000 in a Roth IRA account. Roth conversions involve a simple bookkeeping entry on the part of the financial institution, which gets reported to the IRS. Importantly, when monies are converted from a traditional IRA to a Roth IRA, the IRS treats this as a taxable event.

Usually, Brad did not like to pay taxes, but in this instance, he and Nancy were willing to pay taxes (at their current top rate of 22%) because they were concerned that taxes would increase in the future. Brad and Nancy also recognized that tax rates are currently near historic lows. Specifically, every year for the next four (4) years, they plan to convert the four (4) remaining $200,000 fixed index annuities with income riders from Brad's traditional IRAs to Roth IRAs, from 2019 to 2022 and pay the resulting taxes. After the last contract is converted and all his annuities are in a Roth account, he will have guaranteed tax-free income streams for life, whenever he decides to "turn on the taps" so to speak.

THE BACKGROUND

There is a strong possibility that the recent "lower income tax rates" signed into law in December 2017 by President Trump will have to increase at some point in the future.

Our nation is already struggling to honor its ever-rising financial commitments – including our growing national debt. These financial promises and challenges create pressure on our representatives in Washington to raise revenue and increase taxes. So far our elected representatives have avoided increasing taxes and instead have met our nation's financial commitments by borrowing increasing amounts of money. For example, in the year 2000 our national debt was $5.7 trillion, but by the spring of 2018, the deficit had grown to $21 trillion.

This seemingly endless ability of our elected officials to "kick the can down the road" will of course come to an end at some point, as eventually other nations will not want to lend to us anymore (i.e., buy our treasury bonds) when they become too concerned about our ability to pay them back. Many nations are already moving toward reducing their use of, and dependence on, the U.S. dollar to conduct international trade.

As of 2018, our country's biggest expenses are Social Security, Medicare, Medicaid, and interest on the national debt. They represent approximately 82% of every tax dollar. It is projected that these four expenses could eventually balloon to 92 cents for every tax dollar. That will leave eight cents to pay for everything else! In his book *Comeback America*, fiscal expert and former Comptroller General of the United States, David

Walker, CPA, warned us that taxes need to double if the country is to meet its ever-mounting promises and obligations. *Forbes* and other respected publications have proclaimed similar messages. Additionally, the Congressional Budget Office recommended that tax rates double in order for Social Security, Medicare and Medicaid to remain unchanged. Currently, many other industrialized countries have top marginal tax rates that are at or around the 50% level; America's top bracket is currently 37%. As recently as the 1970s our top marginal tax rate was 70%! Thus, from a historical perspective, the eight years from 2018 to 2025 of low tax rates can serve as a great help for pre-retirees to shift large amounts of money from their tax-deferred retirement accounts to tax-free Roth accounts.

To summarize, on a national level there are signs everywhere that indicate tax rates need to increase in the future. Also, as individuals, regardless of whether or not tax rates increase, retirees will probably pay more in taxes than they anticipated because they lose the deductions that they enjoyed during their working years.

CONCLUSION

One of my co-authors, Robert M. Ryerson, in Chapter 50 in this book, lists ten great reasons to use a fixed index annuity with an income rider to create an income for life in retirement:

1. Guaranteed income as long as you live
2. Addresses longevity risk
3. Low annual costs
4. Protection from interest rate risk
5. Protection from inflation risk
6. Potential protection from financial risks associated with chronic illnesses
7. Guaranteed death benefits to heirs and other loved ones
8. Potential tax benefits
9. Protection from loss of principal
10. Maintain control of the underlying capital base

This chapter has expanded on and explained the eighth reason, potential tax benefits with proper planning. With Roth conversions, you can create tax-free income for as long as you live (or as long as you and your spouse live – if you are married)! Owning fixed income annuities with an income rider in your Roth IRA can potentially provide you with these benefits:

i. Exclude income from your Roth IRA from federal and state tax returns, legally. No 1099 forms, reduced recordkeeping for you, less stress, more time available to truly enjoy the things that really matter such as your children and grandchildren, hobbies, traveling, etc.

ii. Free yourself from the burdensome and quirky IRA RMD rules. Roth IRAs are not subject to required minimum distribution rules. You do not have to take out any money from your Roth IRA accounts…ever (unless you'd like to, or feel you need to).

iii. Enjoy more of your Social Security benefits. Income from Roth accounts is not included as taxable income on your income tax returns, which can then potentially reduce the amount of your Social Security income on which you will have to pay taxes. In brief, up to 85% of your Social Security benefits will be subject to taxes at your highest marginal brackets if your provisional income exceeds the IRS thresholds.

iv. Leave money to your beneficiaries income tax-free. When you pass, if there is still money remaining in your Roth fixed income annuities with income riders, your descendants and other loved ones will inherit those balances income tax-free. Traditional IRAs and other qualified retirement accounts create taxable income for your beneficiaries, while Roth IRAs are passed income tax-free.

In summary, the combination of Roth conversions and fixed index annuities with an income rider could quite possibly be the best of both worlds. Fixed Index annuities with an income rider will provide guaranteed income for life and, when simultaneously held in a Roth IRA, this income is never taxed. The six steps to take are:

1. Roll over retirement funds from your employer's custodian to a traditional IRA account which you control.

2. Use the IRA funds to purchase one or more guaranteed fixed income annuities with income riders.

3. Convert those IRA annuities to Roth IRA annuities over time. The eight (8) year period of historically low-tax rates, starting in 2018 and ending in 2025 is an ideal period of time in which to shift money over to the tax-free world of Roth IRAs.

4. Pay the taxes on the Roth conversions. As mentioned above, Roth conversions can be spread out over several years to ease the tax burden. If this conversion process can be completed before reaching 70½, then the retiree will have successfully avoided all of the rules, regulations, time frames, and potentially harsh penalties associated with required minimum distributions.

5. Allow the annuities to "bake" or compound as long as possible, and then …

6. When desired or needed, turn the annuities into tax-free income streams for life.

The above steps, of course, are part of a comprehensive, long-term retirement income/financial plan that should be carefully drafted by and implemented with the guidance of a team of experienced retirement income planning professionals.

About Louis

Louis R. Terrero, CPA, Registered Investment Advisor, has been in the financial services industry since 1978, starting his career as an auditor for one of the "Big 8" CPA firms. He has experience in many areas ranging from compliance and auditing to annuities and investments, and most recently has obtained the Certification in Long-Term Care credential. This extensive knowledge has led Louis to teach accounting, economics and taxation courses as an adjunct professor at various colleges and universities in the New York City metropolitan area since 1991. Louis's diverse background and passion for educating others help him serve his clients in ways that he takes much pride in.

Financial and investment planning are two areas in which Louis feels he can provide significant value to his clients. He has been working with individuals and businesses in New Jersey and New York for several years on various financial planning topics and strategies, including retirement planning, college funding, insurance planning and estate planning (in concert with elder care attorneys). He has always taken a "team of professionals" approach to serving his clients' needs and will regularly include in his portfolio planning and management, agents and advisors whom he believes can add value to the process. Mr. Terrero believes that having access to a team of professionals who work in concert for the client's needs and goals results in more solid and comprehensive long-term plans.

Clients are of the utmost importance to Louis and his team, all of whom are dedicated to developing lasting relationships. This is why they spend so much time getting to know and understand the clients' needs before any recommendations are made. They strive to provide clear, easy to understand explanations of suggested financial strategies and services for a more secure financial future, so that their clients are comfortable and in agreement before implementation steps are taken.

In his free time, you can find Louis spending quality time with his family and friends, following New York's professional sports teams, reading historical novels, and traveling.